LAND OF LIVING ROCK

Also by C. Gregory Crampton: *Standing Up Country* (1964).

This is a Borzoi Book, published by Alfred A. Knopf, Inc.

LAND OF LIVING ROCK

The Grand Canyon and the High Plateaus:
Arizona, Utah, Nevada

C. Gregory Crampton

ALFRED A. KNOPF: NEW YORK, 1972

This is a Borzoi Book,
published by
Alfred A. Knopf, Inc.

Published in the United States by Alfred A. Knopf, Inc.,
New York, and simultaneously in Canada
by Random House of Canada Limited, Toronto.
Distributed by Random House, Inc., New York.
Library of Congress Catalog Card Number 73-136312
Manufactured in the United States of America
ISBN: 0-394-42695-9

gift 2003 $17 95

FIRST EDITION

*To Patricia and Juanita
and your generation,
seekers after beauty in the
American Land*

Preface

This book is a historical portrait of one of the most beautiful places in the world. It extends from the Pink Cliffs of Utah south across and beyond the Grand Canyon to the San Francisco Peaks of Arizona, and from Lee's Ferry and Lake Powell west to Lake Mead and Las Vegas in Nevada. It is the southwestern extremity of the Colorado Plateau and it is the masterpiece of the Colorado River.

Many millions of people have seen it in part, but only a few have seen it all. The popular image of the Grand Canyon country has been provincial and local. The entrepreneurs in the region have followed established trails and stayed to the rails and highways and airways. Students have written of geology or botany or archaeology. State and county histories have followed state and county lines. Travel literature has guided the sightseer only to the parks and monuments. Few indeed are aware of the natural entity of the region which sweeps back from both rims of the Grand Canyon to cover parts of three states.

In this book I have attempted to describe this land, to unify its long history, and to show what those who created the history felt about their experience. I have attempted a complete biography of an entire region. My own acquaintance with the canyon country of the Colorado River dates back thirty years. This blossomed into an enduring love affair, one issue of which was the book Standing Up Country, the Canyon Lands of Utah and Arizona, a historical description of the great slick-rock wilderness adjoining the Land of Living Rock upstream from Lee's Ferry. That book was my first regional biography.

The research on this book has been a splendid adventure. I've traveled the jeep roads, hiked the canyons, floated the rivers, and hedgehopped the mesas and the plateaus. Many acquaintances and friends have interpreted and taught me about the canyon country and I have brought their ideas and information into this book. And I have distilled from the mass of literature touching the region what I thought to be the significant facts and explanations. To those who have preceded me in print I am indeed grateful; most of their names will appear in the appended bibliography.

A number of individuals in the Grand Canyon country have shared their experience and knowledge: Juanita Brooks, Maurine Whipple, Omer Bundy, C. M. Bundy, Tone Foremaster, A. Karl Larson, Reed Mathis, W. R. Mathis, Vilate Hardy, Joseph C. Bolander, Melvin Schoppman, William and Julia Leithead, Elizabeth Mather, and Fay R. Hamblin taught me much about southern Utah and the Arizona Strip. W. G. Bass, Emery C. Kolb, Lemuel Paya, and Don C. Talayesva gave me important information about the South Rim country and the Indian life of Grand Canyon region.

From more distant places, Howard C. Price, Jr., and Virginia Nutter Price, Ruby N. Tippets, Louis

Marble Canyon. The Colorado and the cliffs at the mouth of Nankoweap Creek. Arizona.

Schellbach, Rosalia Tenney Payne, Edna Hope Gregory, William C. Weeks, E. D. Weeks, Harold E. Anthony, Mildred Johnson, G. M. Farley, B. Sachs, David F. Myrick, Natt N. Dodge, Dudley C. Gordon, and the late Weldon F. Heald have given me valued assistance and loaned important materials. I have learned much from those who have long studied the river and the canyons: P. T. Reilly, Otis R. Marston, Harry Aleson, and Larry Sanderson.

A number of photographers whose works appear in this book have given me diverse and valuable information as well as some of their greatest pictures. In Arizona: Parker Hamilton, Hildegard Hamilton, William L. Werrell, Flagstaff; Arthur A. Twomey, Tad Nichols, Dan Jones, Tucson; Allen T. Malmquist, Moccasin; Barry M. Goldwater, Phoenix and Washington, D.C. In Utah: Frank Jensen, Holladay; Ron Smith, Salt Lake City. In Nevada: Bill Belknap, Boulder City. In California: Philip Hyde, Taylorsville; John M. Kitchen, Fresno; David Muench, Josef Muench, Santa Barbara; William C. Miller, Pasadena; John S. Shelton, Claremont; Joseph L. Dudziak, Vallejo; Ralph W. Dietz, Ridgecrest. In Pennsylvania: George L. Beck, Finleyville. Some photographers whose pictures appear herein are acknowledged elsewhere in this preface.

I have relied heavily on many public servants for help only they could supply: W. L. Rusho and William J. Williams, U.S. Bureau of Reclamation of Salt Lake City and Boulder City, Nevada, respectively. U.S. Geological Survey: Maurice E. Cooley at Tucson; W. L. Heckler at Santa Fe: Francis M. Bell at Denver; John Blee at Lee's Ferry. Edward L. Pittman, U.S. Bureau of Land Management, St. George, Utah; J. O. Kilmartin, Board on Geographic Names, Washington; Aleita A. Hogenson, National Collection of Fine Arts, Smithsonian Institution, Washington; Mary D. Wright, Utah Travel Council, Salt Lake City; Adrian F. Atwater, Department of Highways, State of Nevada, Carson City; William D. Johnston, Arizona State Highway Department, Navajo Springs.

I owe a big debt to the dedicated people in the National Park Service: Robert M. Utley, Frederick R. Bell, Washington; William E. Brown, H. V. Reeves, Santa Fe; Merrill D. Beal, Warren H. Hill, Jay Pogue, Louise M. Hinchliffe, J. Donald Hughes, Grand Canyon National Park; John H. Riffey, Grand Canyon National Monument; Carl E. Jepson, Roland H. Wauer, Zion National Park; Louis W. Hallock, John Barnett, Bryce Canyon National Park; Robert W. Olsen, Jr., Raymond J. Geerdes, Pipe Spring National Monument; William J. Briggle, Wayne B. Alcorn, Glen Canyon National Recreation Area; Vernon D. Dame, Lake Mead National Recreation Area.

Edna Mae Thornton, Peggy Smith, Norma R. Marquart, county recorders, respectively, of the Arizona counties of Coconino, Mohave, and Yavapai, and Helen Barker, county recorder of Washington County, Utah, made available the primary documents in their custody.

Officials of business firms graciously provided information about their operations in the Grand Canyon region: Union Pacific Railroad Company; Atchison, Topeka & Santa Fe Railway Company; American Airlines; Fred Harvey Company; Southern California Edison Company; White Motor Corporation.

Years ago my first extensive reading about the Grand Canyon country was done in the American Library in Paris and since then I have put myself in debt to the New York, Los Angeles, Phoenix public libraries; the Bancroft Library, University of California, Berkeley; Huntington Library, San Marino, California; Engineering Societies Library, New York City; and the Library of Congress and National Archives, Washington.

I am especially grateful to the following individuals and their staffs who made collections under their charge available to me: Everett L. Cooley, Curator, Western Americana Department, Marriott Library, University of Utah; Bert M. Fireman, Director, Arizona Historical Foundation and Curator, Arizona Collection, Hayden Library, Arizona State College, Tempe; James H. Fraser, and his successor, Delbert C. Dobyns, Special Collections Librarian, The Library, Northern Arizona University, Flagstaff; Phyllis Ball, Special Collections Librarian, University of Arizona Library, Tucson; Harold H. J. Erickson, Director of Libraries, and Celeste Lowe, Curator, Nevada Collection, Dickerson Library, University of Nevada at Las Vegas; David Heron, Librarian, University of Nevada, Reno; Elizabeth Beckstrom, Librarian, Dixie College, Utah; Inez S. Cooper, Special Collections Librarian, College of Southern Utah, Cedar City.

Marguerite B. Cooley, Director, Library and Archives, State of Arizona, Phoenix; Earl Olsen, Assistant Church Historian, Church Historian's Office Library, Church of Jesus Christ of Latter-day Saints, Salt Lake City; Dorothea Hering, American Geographical Society, New York City; Sylvia Henry, Librarian, Long Island Collection, East Hampton Free Library, East Hampton, New York; Dorothy V. Dalton, Reference Librarian, Las Vegas, Nevada, Public Library; Walter A. Wood, The Arctic Institute of North America, Washington; Michael Harrison, Fair Oaks, California.

The directors and staffs of a number of museums across the country have been uniformly helpful: Edward B. Danson, Director, Alexander J. Lindsay, Jr., Curator of Anthropology, Katherine Bartlett, Librarian, Museum of Northern Arizona, Flagstaff; Edwin N. Ferdon, Associate Director, Arizona State Museum, The University of Arizona, Tucson; Elva Breckenridge, Assistant Custodian, Sharlot Hall Museum, Prescott, Arizona; Roy Purcell, Director, Mohave Museum of History and Art, Kingman, Arizona; Dorothy E. Martin, Librarian, Los Angeles County Museum; Delmar Kolb, Director, Museum of New Mexico, Santa Fe; Paul A. Rossi, Director, Thomas Gilcrease Institute of American History and Art, Tulsa, Oklahoma; Carl Schaefer Dentzel, Director, Southwest Museum, Los Angeles; Gilbert F. Stucker, Department of Vertebrate Paleontology, American Museum of Natural History, New York City.

I cheerfully acknowledge the splendid contributions in time and materials made by the historical societies: Charles S. Peterson, Director, Margaret Lester, Curator of Photographs, Utah State Historical Society, Salt Lake City; Sidney B. Brinckerhoff, Director, Margaret J. Sparks, Research Librarian, Arizona Historical Society, Tucson; Marion Welliver, Director, Nevada Historical Society, Reno; Maryellen Vallier Sadovich and Elbert B. Edwards, Southern Nevada Historical Society, Henderson and Boulder City, Nevada; Harry Kelsey, State Historian, State Historical Society of Colorado, Denver; Joyce E. Harman, Ohio Historical Society, Columbus.

On my own campus at the University of Utah, Salt Lake City, I am pleased to acknowledge the assistance of David E. Miller, Professor of History and Director, Center for Studies of the American West; Alvin L. Gittins, Professor of Art; Walter P. Cottam,

Professor Emeritus of Botany; Guy E. Smith, Professor of Modern Languages; John D. Sylvester, graduate student in history. Financial assistance in support of certain aspects of the research was granted by the University of Utah Research Fund.

Professional colleagues in other institutions have given freely of help and advice: Robert C. Euler, Professor of Anthropology, and Jay Dusard, Instructor in Light Graphics, Prescott College, Prescott, Arizona; John Harvey Butchart, Professor of Mathematics, and Ronald L. Ives, Geographer, Department of Geography, Northern Arizona State University, Flagstaff; Dwight L. Smith, Professor of History, Miami University, Oxford, Ohio; William C. Darrah, Professor of Biology, Gettysburg College, Gettysburg, Pennsylvania; Joseph G. Hall, Professor of Biology, San Francisco State College; Douglas W. Schwartz, Professor of Anthropology, University of Kentucky, Lexington; David H. Miller, Assistant Professor of History, Cameron College, Lawton, Oklahoma; Gustive O. Larson, Professor of Church History, Brigham Young University, Provo, Utah.

I appreciate the generosity and cooperation of all these and other people and institutions. I have tried to put to good use the material given me. If I have not done so, the fault is mine and not theirs.

To Alfred A. Knopf, Angus Cameron, and R. D. Scudellari of the Knopf organization, my appreciation for their personal interest in the production of this beautiful book.

Merrill K. Ridd, Associate Professor of Geography, University of Utah, prepared preliminary maps and diagrams used as a basis for final illustrations. Virginia W. Anderson and Mary Jane Anderson assisted in the selection and preparation of photographs. Darlene Walker, Helen R. Hadley, and Margaret Hermansen typed the manuscript. I acknowledge the improvement brought to the text by the close editorial scrutiny of Rebecca H. Latimer and Sandra Caruthers Thomson. My wife, Helen M. Crampton, has shown a constant patience with the requirements of research and authorship. I have dedicated the book to my daughters, good traveling companions in the canyon country of the Colorado.

C. Gregory Crampton, January 1972

XI

THE LAND

THE ROAD

THE WATER

THE BEAUTY

Illustrations

THE LAND

1
Grand Canyon Country

2
Living Rock

WATER POWER · SOUTH RIM · THE NORTHWARD TILT

3
Five Faces of Grand Canyon

MARBLE · KAIBAB · KANAB · UINKARET · SHIVWITS

---

*The Grand Canyon is a sublime spectacle
throughout its entire length—279 miles.
Here at Mile 277 the canyon walls tower over
3,000 feet above the water. Arizona.*

1
Grand Canyon Country

The view of Grand Canyon from the South Rim must be one of the most familiar landscapes in the world. From various points along a thirty-mile drive between Hermit's Rest and Desert View most of the many millions of visitors have enjoyed their first and often only look at the awesome spectacle. Indeed, nearly everyone thinks of the Grand Canyon in terms of the view from this limited section of the South Rim, as fewer people have seen the canyon from the even more limited viewpoints along the opposite North Rim. But while millions have visited the South and North rims, only a comparative handful are acquainted with the great and open expanses that make up the rest of the Grand Canyon country.

Of course, if you've been to Grand Canyon you'll recognize a number of landmarks in the area even though you may not associate them with the canyon: the San Francisco Peaks, for instance, standing high on the horizon, visible for a hundred miles from the east, west, and north, marking the southern gateways to Grand Canyon National Park; the jagged, towering line of Echo Cliffs, ranging eighty miles south from Lee's Ferry to the old Indian town of Moenave; the sinuous Vermilion Cliffs winding back and forth across the Utah–Arizona boundary for a hundred and fifty miles; the lofty towers of Zion Canyon; the bright pink pinnacles at Bryce Canyon; the warm, shimmering waters of Lake Mead; Havasu and Toroweap.

But how many know Tincanebits and Meriwitica? Or Manakacha and Watahomigi? Or Granite Park and Grand Wash, Uinkaret and Shinarump? Or House Rock Valley and Blue Moon Bench? These, and a thousand other landmarks spread throughout the Grand Canyon country, belong to a rare land where the air is clear, and the people are few, where the earth is nearly naked and the desert is painted.

This, the southwestern part of the Colorado Plateau, is the most colorful land in the world. Profound canyons and massive, elevated plateaus, primary features of the plateau, find classic expression. The Colorado River dominates the section. It not only largely created the entire magnificent landscape but it has dramatically divided the country in two by carving out the Grand Canyon, that masterpiece of land sculpture 279 miles long.

The boundaries of the Grand Canyon country are precise and easy to follow. On a map of the states of Arizona, Utah, and Nevada locate Flagstaff and then move clockwise, touching Kingman, Las Vegas, St. George, Cedar City, Bryce Canyon National Park, Page, Tuba City, and back to Flagstaff. These places around the periphery provide orientation. Now, with more eye to detail, go around again. From the San Francisco Peaks and Flagstaff, as a point of beginning, draw on your map a line west to Bill Williams Mountain. Stay on a west course and keep north of the

Kanab Canyon five miles above the Colorado. Arizona.

Cavern at the water's edge, Mile 33, Marble Canyon. Arizona.

Santa Fe Railway and U.S. Highway 66—Interstate 40—until you come to the Grand Wash Cliffs east of Kingman. Your line is close to the head of the southern tributaries of the Colorado where it flows through Grand Canyon. Loop northward now for over a hundred miles following the Grand Wash Cliffs which are bisected dramatically by the Colorado River as it emerges from them to form the mouth of Grand Canyon. Near the Arizona–Utah border these cliffs give way to a jumble of flat-topped mesas and mountains which seem to merge with the contrastingly sharp, hog-backed ridge of the Virgin Mountains immediately to the west.

Now carry your line north a little way into Utah to the Virgin River and follow it up past St. George to the Hurricane Cliffs and thence north to Cedar City which stands very near the divide separating the drainage of the Colorado River from that of the Great Basin. Now follow the divide eastward along the southern escarpments of the elevated Markagunt and Paunsaugunt plateaus from Cedar Breaks National Monument to Bryce Canyon National Park. Then follow down the Paria River to Lee's Ferry on the Colorado. Thence a line drawn roughly southward to Tuba City and on to Flagstaff will parallel the Echo Cliffs, cross the Little Colorado River and bring you back to where you began. You have described a great circle enclosing the Grand Canyon section of the Colorado Plateau.[1]

The area encircled on your map seems to be largely blank. There are a few small towns and a trading post or two. Although blacktop roads reach the North and South rims of Grand Canyon National Park, and they will carry you to Zion and Bryce national parks and Cedar Breaks, Pipe Spring, Wupatki and Sunset Crater national monuments, the only major highway to cross the region is U.S. 89—the historic road between Utah and Arizona. All other major routes only skirt the edges. No railroad enters the area except a branch of the Santa Fe which reaches the South Rim at Grand Canyon Village. Dirt roads, probably not shown on your map, are much more common. Far more interesting than blacktop, these may take you to the seldom-visited rim viewpoints at many places along either side of the Grand Canyon, or to remote stock-watering ponds, or to a lumbering camp on the Kaibab Plateau, to a ranch—or to nowhere. There is no vehicular crossing of the Colorado River between the Navajo Bridge across the Marble Canyon and Hoover Dam, a distance of over 350 miles by river and by lake.

The river and its great canyon hold together this section of the Colorado Plateau. The river has created two halves which form the whole. Within it there is much diversity, but its geographical unity is evident nearly everywhere, often with dramatic impact.

The unity and oneness, the wholeness of the Grand Canyon country is not apparent to the casual observer; it is fragmented by a profusion of man-made boundaries: state, county, national park, national monument, national forest, national game preserve, national recreation area, Indian reservation, to say nothing of section, township, and range. Look at your map again and you will see that the Colorado River from the upper end of Grand Canyon National Park to Lake Mead is plastered over with a number of jurisdictions often done in bright and commanding colors, a different color for each unit. The political boundaries that cut up the Grand Canyon country tend to cause people to consider it politically rather than in terms of its history or its natural regions. Thus to many the Grand Canyon and Grand Canyon National Park are synonymous. Man-made boundaries serve the purpose for which they were intended, but in the Grand Canyon country they never define or entirely encompass the natural geographical or physiographical unities, and they have little to do with the larger chapters of history.

The Grand Canyon National Park encloses a generous segment of Grand Canyon but only a segment; the canyon does not begin and end at the park boundaries. At Bright Angel Creek, inside the park, the canyon is about ten miles wide and over one mile in depth. At Granite Park, 132 miles below Bright Angel and far outside the boundaries of the park, the canyon is still over a mile deep and ten miles wide. Upstream fifty miles from Bright Angel Creek, above the park, the canyon at Tatahotso Point is deeper proportionally than at either Bright Angel or Granite Park. The distance there from rim to rim is only a mile and a half, but the canyon is over half a mile deep. There, at the bottom of the canyon, the river runs through a narrow slot where the walls rise sheer almost from the water's edge. Throughout the Grand Canyon country the river flows unimpeded, and the boundaries mean little except as they jar the harmony of the natural ensemble.

Apart from the boundaries, which after all do not touch the land, man over the centuries has altered the Grand Canyon country very little. It remains much as it was when the first Europeans approached well over four hundred years ago, a quiet wilderness, a land of sweeping open space and magnificent vistas. The reasons for this are found in the chapters of history. For about three hundred years men thought of the Colorado River as a route, a road, that from the interior of the continent would lead them westward to the sea. The next approaches were made by scientists and surveyors, and by exploiters and developers. The latter two found a few arable acres, some grass, timber, and minerals, but there was precious little water except in the canyon depths. Settlements had to be limited to those stretches along the banks of the few living and accessible streams. The canyon country of the Colorado offered a frontier limited in resources, lacking in promise, and repelling all but the hardiest of pioneers.

But the scientists and the surveyors discovered a land not only of high interest to science but one which they described as beautiful and sublime. Their reports were illustrated by expedition photographers and artists, and these works prompted a flow of visitors who came to see at first hand the natural wonders of the Grand Canyon country. Then in the twentieth century the creation of national parks and monuments enclosing parts of the landscape attracted a flood of tourists whose way was eased by the building of a railroad, paved roads, and comfortable hotels. And now all the world is familiar with the Grand Canyon district, at least with parts of it—the parts easiest to reach. Yet back from the roads the open spaces remain open; they are largely unvisited, and to many they are as bewildering and mystifying as the great canyon itself.

Indeed, throughout the literature the word "mystery" is the one most commonly used to describe the Grand Canyon country. It's a good, honest word. By using it men have admitted their incapacity to comprehend the meaning and reality of so vast a thing or to understand or solve the problem of its origin and creation.

Pick up your map again and study the place names. Throughout the long history of this region men have laid over the land a mosaic of names which often will tell you something about their attitudes and feelings and even their approaches to understanding. To know the names that men have given is to know something of the history of the land.

Spain gave us the Rio Colorado, the perfect name. And Spain's men of God—the Franciscans—who were the first Europeans to explore the region intensively, remembered the saints when they came to name places—Santa Barbara, San Jose, San Francisco, San Antonio. Mundane were the Sulphurous River of the Pyramids, Puerto de Bucareli, and Sierra Blanca. Las Vegas, Santa Clara, and Rio Virgen were named during the Mexican period, and later arrivals remembered the discoverers of the Grand Canyon country with Coronado Butte, Cardenas Butte, Escalante Butte, and Garces Terrace. Nevada (from Sierra Nevada) is of Spanish origin, of course, and Arizona and Utah are adaptations of Hispanicized Indian names.

Once the Grand Canyon country fell to the United States after the war with Mexico, government explorers were sent to look for routes and roads. If you let your eye follow along the Santa Fe Railway and U.S. Highway 66—Interstate 40—across northern Arizona, you will see some of their names: Humphreys Peak, Ives Mesa, Sitgreaves Pass, and Beale Springs. Those who came later—after the Civil War—were more concerned with science and survey. By 1900, Powell, Thompson, Dellenbaugh, Gilbert, Dutton, Walcott, Howell, Ward, and Wheeler had quite thoroughly studied the region and, for the most part, their choice of place names was sensitive and refreshing.

In a land where color is everywhere to be seen, the government scientists named the great lines of cliffs for their predominant colors—Pink, White, and Vermilion—and the most predominant strata in Grand Canyon was called the Redwall Limestone. They chose Indian names for the massive plateaus—Markagunt, Paunsaugunt, Shivwits, Uinkaret, Kanab, Kaibab, and Coconino. For variety they gave names like these to lesser features: Bright Angel Creek, Witches' Water Pocket, Sockdolager Rapids, Marble Canyon, Smithsonian Butte, House Rock Spring, Wild Band Pocket, Thousand Wells, Iceberg Canyon, Vulcan's Throne, and Vishnu Temple.

The men of the Powell Survey were zealous in the use of Indian names. In addition to the names of the great plateaus we are indebted to them for Unkar, Chuar, Kwagunt, and Nankoweap, all creeks in the Grand Canyon heading on the Kaibab Plateau. But there are also Mukuntuweap and Parunuweap, the two main gorges in Zion National Park, and Toroweap Valley in Grand Canyon National Monument.[2] All the living tribes within the region—Havasupai, Hualapai, Mohave, Paiute, Hopi, and Navajo—have buttes, creeks, points, and other features named for them.

Indeed, Indian names are spread all over the map of the Grand Canyon region. Here are a few: Shinumo Altar, Moenkopi, Parissawampitts Spring, Sowats Canyon, Kanabownits Spring, Topocoba Spring, Mokiac Wash, Kanarra Mountain, Pocum Cove, Pakoon Spring, Chickapangi Mesa, Tuba City, Wickytywiz. A number of the rocks of the region—the sedimentary strata—bear designations commemorating the Indian names of the Colorado Plateau: Wasatch, Kaiparowits, Wahweap, Navajo, Kayenta, Chinle, Shinarump, Moenkopi, Kaibab, Toroweap, Coconino, Supai, Muav, Tapeats, Chuar, Shinumo, Hakatai.

The Indians themselves put names on very few features of the landscape; when they did, they let nature speak for itself; the name usually described the actual feature. Thus Kanab, a Paiute word meaning "Place of the Willows," was given to Kanab Creek where the banks were green with willows. To the Paiutes Kaibab means "Mountain-lying-down," which is just the way the Kaibab Plateau appears from a distance. Indian personal names are likely to be descriptive of the physical features or peculiarities

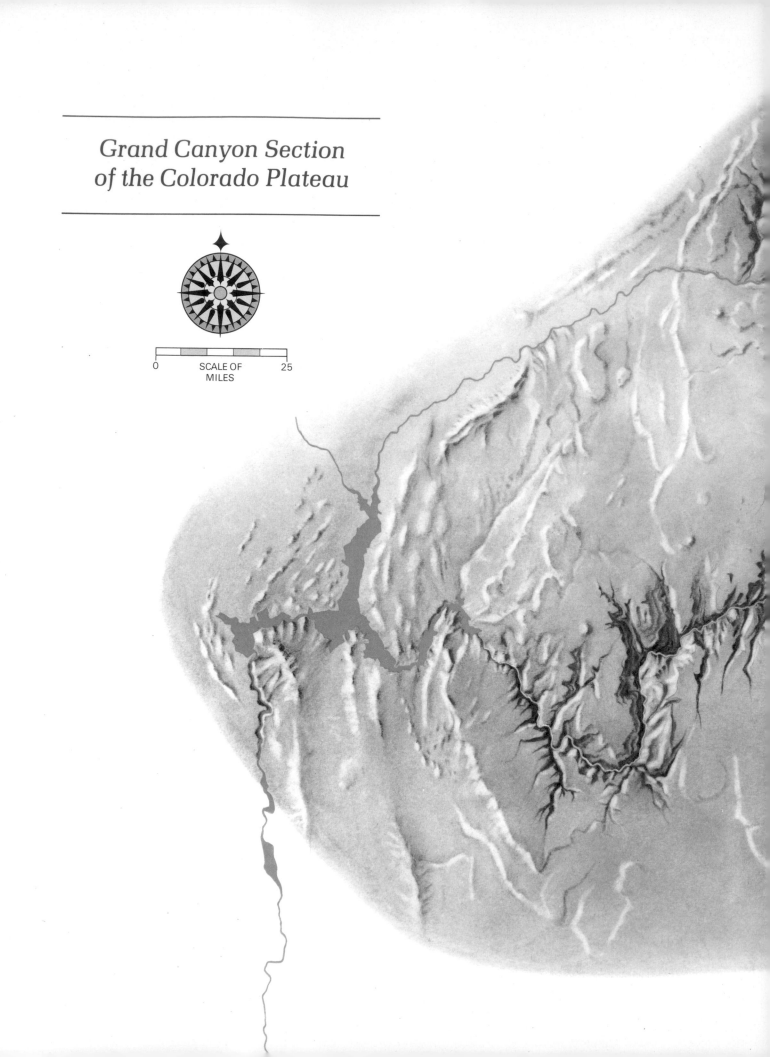

Grand Canyon Section
of the Colorado Plateau

SCALE OF
MILES

0   25

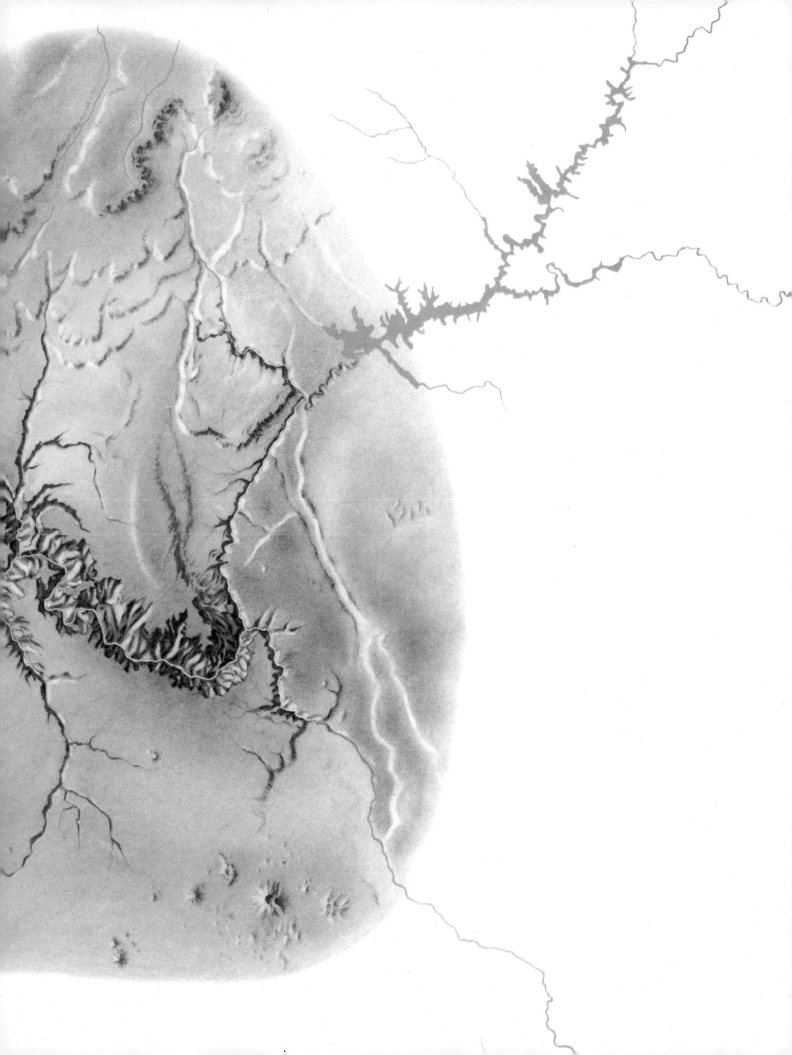

of the individual; even tribal names may relate to a natural feature. The name Havasupai means the "Blue-Green Water People," for their canyon home is on the banks of a beautiful stream of blue-green color. To name a feature of the landscape, or even a person or a tribe, after something other than that descriptive of its essential character would be to the Indian artificial and unnatural.[3]

After the scientists came the exploiters and developers—the railroad builders, farmers, miners, ranchers, and homesteaders, and they were followed by the reclaimers, the engineers, the seekers after beauty, and the tourists. Now the family names of the new pioneers began to appear on the map: Kingman, Lee, Rowe, Hamblin, Crozier, Spencer, Whitmore, Bass, Babbitt, Mooney, Young, Stewart, Hance, Tanner, Bryce, and Bonelli.

When they didn't honor themselves these pioneers and the later-comers let loose their imaginations, producing Swallow Park, Music Mountain, Eminence Break, Petal Hills, Soap Creek, Maiden's Breast, Tater Canyon, Pillow Mountain, Painted Desert, Shadow Mountain, Prismatic Plains, Roaring Springs, Crazy Jug Point, Additional Hill, Mule Shoe Bend, Valley of Fire, Singing Cliffs, and Petticoat Hills. Mormon settlers added Coop Knoll, Fredonia, Hurricane, Kolob Terrace, Orderville, Pipe Spring, Temple Bar, and Zion. Miners and stockmen came in with El Dorado, Asbestos, Copper, and Carbonate canyons, Silver Reef, Hermit Creek, Sourdough Well, Grama Canyon, Robbers' Roost Spring, Burnt Corral Rim, Horsethief Tank, Bean Hole Ranch, and Prospect Valley.

And these: Jumpup Point, Toothpick Ridge, Sunshine Point, Sciatic Gut; Fracas Canyon, SB Point, Petrified Hollow, Poverty Flat; Catstair Canyon, Pastry Hills, Snap Point, Flagstaff; there was also Hellhole Bend, Canyon Diablo, Hades Knoll, and Purgatory Flat. But there was also Guardian Angel, Canaan Ranch, Tabernacle Dome, and God's Pocket.[4]

By the names they leave, you shall know them. After the Indians, few were content to live in a natural world without trying to change it. As waves of men or whole moving frontiers approached the Grand Canyon country they gave us the chapter heads of history as they named the land. For most of them the canyon and the plateaus were a backdrop, a stage where each player acted out his part.

It was tough country, hard to get through or across. It offered its limited resources with a grudge. Up to the twentieth century, few found any enjoyment in it. There was scarcely any water—just bare rock, high desert, sharp, steep mesas, cliffs, and canyons. The river itself personified the entire region; it was rough, savage, inaccessible, and inhuman.

As elsewhere on the American frontier, the pioneer in the Grand Canyon country battled nature. He calculated the odds of winning; he scarcely thought about its aesthetic qualities. Fired by the spirit of progress, busy building his home, his fortune, and sometimes the Kingdom of God in the virgin wilderness, the pioneer found the struggle at times exhilarating, though not always rewarding. When it came to place names, those who did battle honored themselves, win or lose. But the names showed humor, too, and loneliness, adventure, homeliness, frivolousness, and even burlesque.

But there is little in the literature of the pioneer period suggesting appreciation of the natural landscape; not many good things were said about the hills, the cliffs, and the canyons. The fur trapper, James Ohio Pattie, in 1826 described the Grand Canyon as "these horrid mountains." Fifty-five years later in St. George, John Taylor, president of the Mormon Church, said, "Our mountains have very large feet," and by that he meant that the mountains occupied large areas, leaving only small tracts—"little, forbidding, barren places"—to the farmers. The mountains existed as a measure of the man; otherwise they had little value.

By the 1880s, however, the scientific studies of the Powell and Wheeler surveys had brought the Grand Canyon country to the eyes of the world. Before the end of the decade, visitors from home and abroad were coming to see, enjoy, and worship at the rim of the canyon painted by Thomas Moran, drawn by W. H. Holmes, photographed by Jack Hillers and T. H. O'Sullivan, and written about by John W. Powell, Clarence E. Dutton, and Grove K. Gilbert. The completion of the Sante Fe Railway in the same decade put the South Rim within easy reach, and in 1901 the Santa Fe extended a branch line to the rim itself.

Once started, the flood of tourists never stopped, except for short intervals. To accommodate visitors and the continuing interest of scientists the Geological Survey began the preparation of special maps of the Grand Canyon in the vicinity of South Rim. By 1908 the Bright Angel, Vishnu, and Shinumo sheets had appeared. Done by François E. Matthes and Richard T. Evans, they were masterpieces of topographic art. They were drawn on large scale (1 : 48,000), the contour interval was set at fifty feet, and heavy lines coincided with prominent strata like the Coconino Sandstone and the Redwall Limestone.

Valley of fire. Nevada.

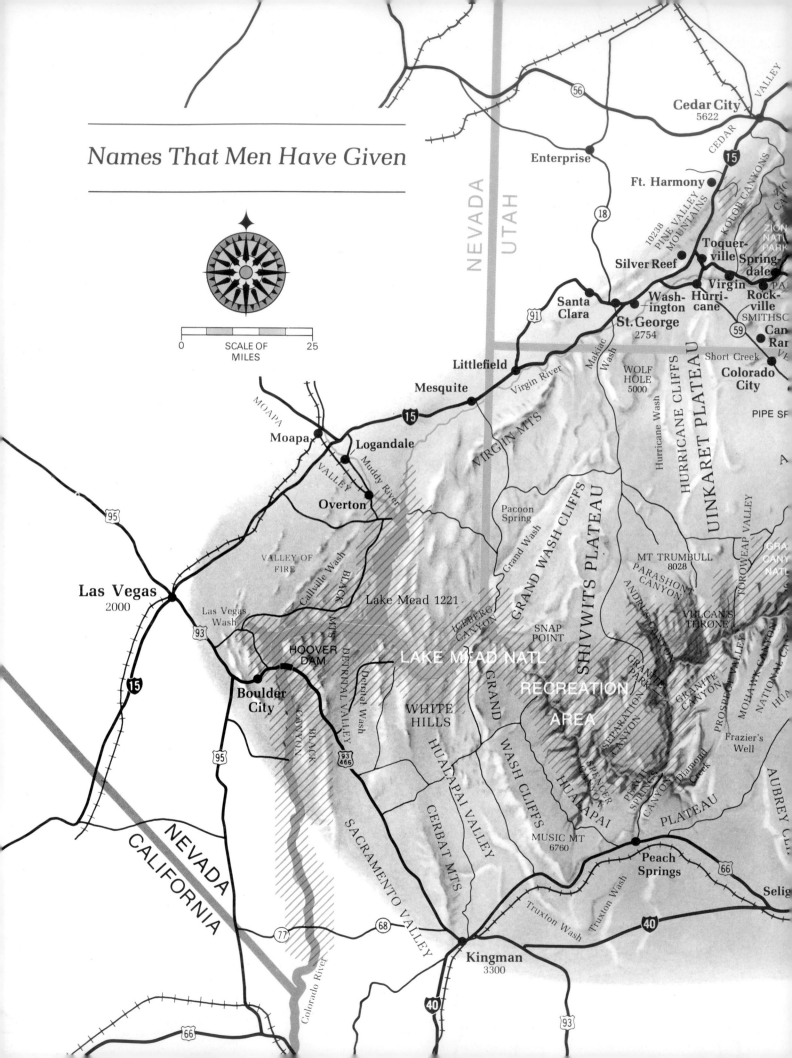

Names That Men Have Given

SCALE OF
MILES
0   25

NEVADA   UTAH

Cedar City
5622

Enterprise

Ft. Harmony

Toquer-
ville

Silver Reef   Spring-
dale

Santa
Clara   Wash-
ington   Virgin   Rock-
ville

Hurri-
cane

St. George
2754   SMITHSC

Can
Rar

Littlefield   Short Creek

Colorado
City

Mesquite   Virgin River

WOLF
HOLE
5000

PIPE SF

MOAPA

Moapa   Logandale

Muddy River

Overton

VALLEY

Pacoon
Spring

VALLEY OF
FIRE

Grand Wash

Lake Mead 1221

MT TRUMBULL
8028

Las Vegas
2000

Las Vegas
Wash

Iceberg
Canyon

SNAP
POINT

VULCAN'S
THRONE

HOOVER
DAM

LAKE MEAD NATL

RECREATION

AREA

Boulder
City

WHITE
HILLS

GRANITE
CANYON

Frazier's
Well

SACRAMENTO VALLEY

HUALAPAI VALLEY

CERBAT MTS

HUALAPAI

PLATEAU

AUBREY

Colorado River

MUSIC MT
6760

Peach
Springs

Selig

NEVADA
CALIFORNIA

Truxton Wash

Kingman
3300

They were a joy to behold and to study. The scale permitted the river to have width, the depth of the canyon at any point could be read easily, and the intricacies of the canyon's architecture were clear and apparent. And the prominent features all bore arresting names.

Matthes and Evans had found as they labored on the survey that only a few of the more massive and prominent geographical features had been named. So as they surveyed they named. And what names! Dutton of the Powell Survey before them had led off with names like "Hindoo" and Ottoman, Shiva and Vishnu, and Vulcan's Throne. Now on the new maps (with additions on later editions by those who liked the trend) the world, like it or not, found the canyon suddenly sprinkled over with dozens of mythological, classical, and religious names, including many of the heroes and heroines of the Arthurian romances.

The great buttes, pinnacles, monuments, towers, and promontories became "temples," "shrines," "thrones," and "castles." A partial sampling finds Apollo, Diana, Jupiter, and Venus in the company of Galahad, Excalibur, Lancelot, Merlin, and Queen Guinevere, as well as Brahma, Krishna, Ra, Set, Osiris, and Zoroaster. Add to these Castor, Freya, Isis, Pollux, Thor, Wotan, and the Holy Grail for a mythological gallery that circles the globe. These and a good many other romanticisms, interspersed with the names of Indians, prospectors, prominent geologists and explorers, and fanciful and descriptive names, make for a whimsical mélange pervasive enough to take most anyone's mind off the land forms which the maps so beautifully portrayed.

The world at large probably liked it. By giving it an outlandish name, you may rob a landscape of its character and even dwarf it, but you have at least reduced it to human terms. Yonder butte towers over three thousand feet. Call it Vishnu Temple and you can cope with it. Over there is a lesser butte standing maybe seventeen hundred feet tall. It takes on manageable meaning if you call it Cheops Pyramid. "What a lugging in by the ears of questionable characters!" said John C. Van Dyke. "A series of numbers would have been less agonizing and quite as poetic." Said W. M. Davis about names like Shiva and Vishnu,

Cattle range on the Arizona Strip.

"they are unnaturalized foreigners."[5]

But what's in a name? It was to the canyon area covered by the Bright Angel, Vishnu, and Shinumo quadrangles that the traveling public came to see and to enjoy on whatever terms it liked. It was this area that formed the heart of Grand Canyon National Monument established in 1908 and made into a national park in 1919. Even the most unemotional and unimaginative tourist was likely to be shaken by the first sight of the Grand Canyon, and the weird names lent meaning to a landscape otherwise difficult to absorb. Indeed the alien and exotic nomenclature to many must have been far more attractive than it was repulsive. And now the rest of the canyon, beyond the boundaries of the park, faded from the public ken.

Not long after 1919, a few more segments of the Grand Canyon country were brought into the system of national parks—Zion and Bryce national parks, Cedar Breaks and Grand Canyon national monuments, Lake Mead National Recreation Area, and the small and specialized Pipe Spring, Sunset Crater, and Wupatki national monuments. The establishment of so many parks and monuments even more tended to contract the public view from the regional to the local. A clutter of boundaries resulting from these and other reservations helped the matter along. Forgotten was the whole, passed by in favor of the parts. The famous visitors, the artists, photographers, and the writers visited the best-known places and by their appearance and works made them even better known.

But throughout time nearly everyone had been satisfied with the partial view. The route seekers sought roads (as in a later day the engineers have sought dam sites), farmers and stockmen looked for soil and water and grass, miners sought the placers and the outcrop. The visitors and the tourists found more than they could absorb in the parks. Only a few have been able to take the measure of the whole incomparable Grand Canyon country like Powell and Dutton.

Instead, the disjointed view prevails. Some of the parts are well known, of course, but as far as the public is concerned the rest of it is unknown land, as much of a mystery as it ever was. Generally, when people think of the Grand Canyon district they are likely to think only of Grand Canyon National Park, not a grand circle of country two hundred miles across, a land of massive, classic plateaus divided but held together by a sublime canyon masterpiece nearly three hundred miles long.

Living Rock

WATER POWER

Sweeping back from the rimlands of Grand Canyon are seven great plateaus—high and arid, sparse in population and vegetation—each separated from the other by long lines of cliffs or plunging monoclinal slopes and often capped with volcanos, cinder cones, and lava flows. Water has dissected the plateaus and created many canyons, their walls aflame with color. Off to the north in Utah, two more plateaus—the lofty Markagunt and Paunsaugunt—face southward and dominate the skyline in three magnificent escarpments—the Pink, the White, and the Vermilion cliffs. Here and there and subordinate to the great plateaus are mesas, isolated buttes, minor terraces, and rock platforms.

Indeed, topographic features typical of the Colorado Plateau are all found in the Grand Canyon country, but everything is done on a larger, more lavish scale. The plateaus are higher, the cliffs are grander, the terraces longer, the canyons deeper, the volcanic features greater. As elsewhere on the plateau the skyline is long, level, and unbroken save for the isolated volcanic mountains and cinder cones which here and there rear up as your eye sweeps around the horizon. Even the long lines of cliffs. dis-

sected and cut up as they may be, almost always break away from a horizontal plane.

Approach the Grand Canyon from either side and you travel for miles across level country. You are on a plateau top, and although it may tilt a little you probably won't notice it. Then suddenly you find yourself at the rim of the canyon. The impact of the first view is probably intensified by the absence of any preparation for the experience. All at once, without notice or warning, the canyon bursts upon you. Few minds can absorb so full a view fast enough to avoid a breathless state of shock.

Such a sudden and breathtaking view is common in the Grand Canyon country where the skylines are nearly horizontal and the topography angular. When you are on the rim of the canyon notice the parallel bands of rocks, dyed various colors, and the horizontal lines, many of which indicate steps, which may extend all the way from the rim of the canyon down to the water's edge.

The steps, forming a giant staircase, are characteristic of the tabular relief found throughout the Grand Canyon section and the rest of the Colorado Plateau. This profile is the result of differential erosion of the many layers of consolidated sedimentary rocks that comprise the plateau. The height of the individual steps is dependent on the thickness and hardness of the rock strata of which they are com-

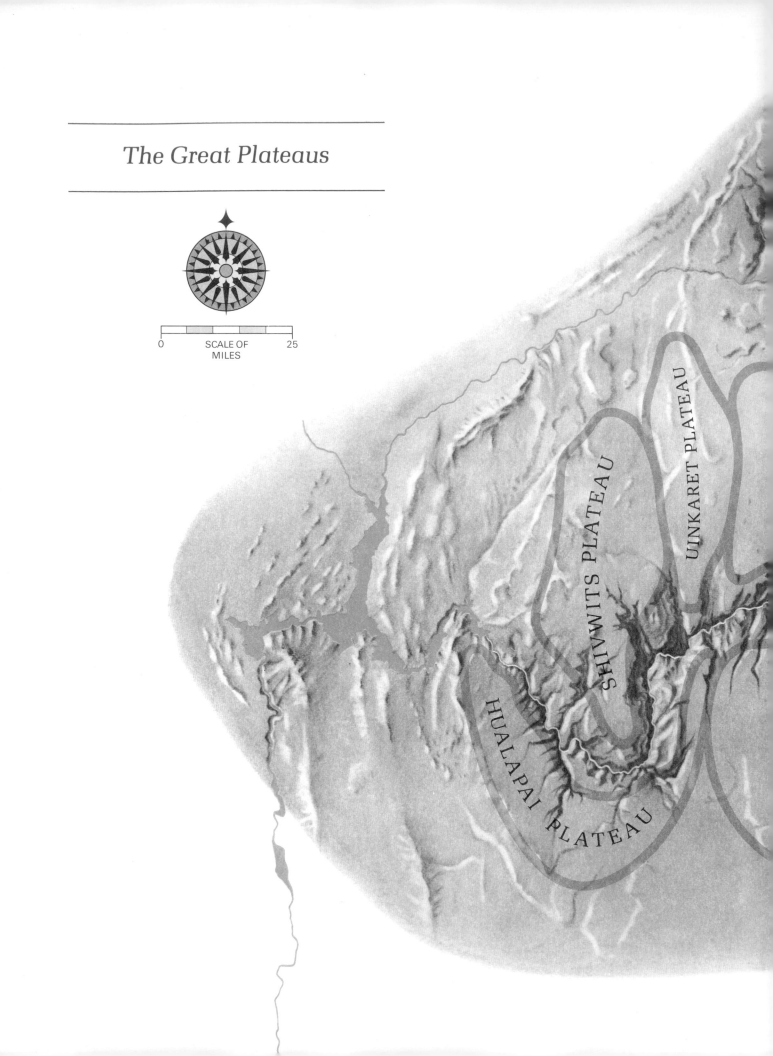

The Great Plateaus

0 SCALE OF MILES 25

HUALAPAI PLATEAU

SHIVWITS PLATEAU

UINKARET PLATEAU

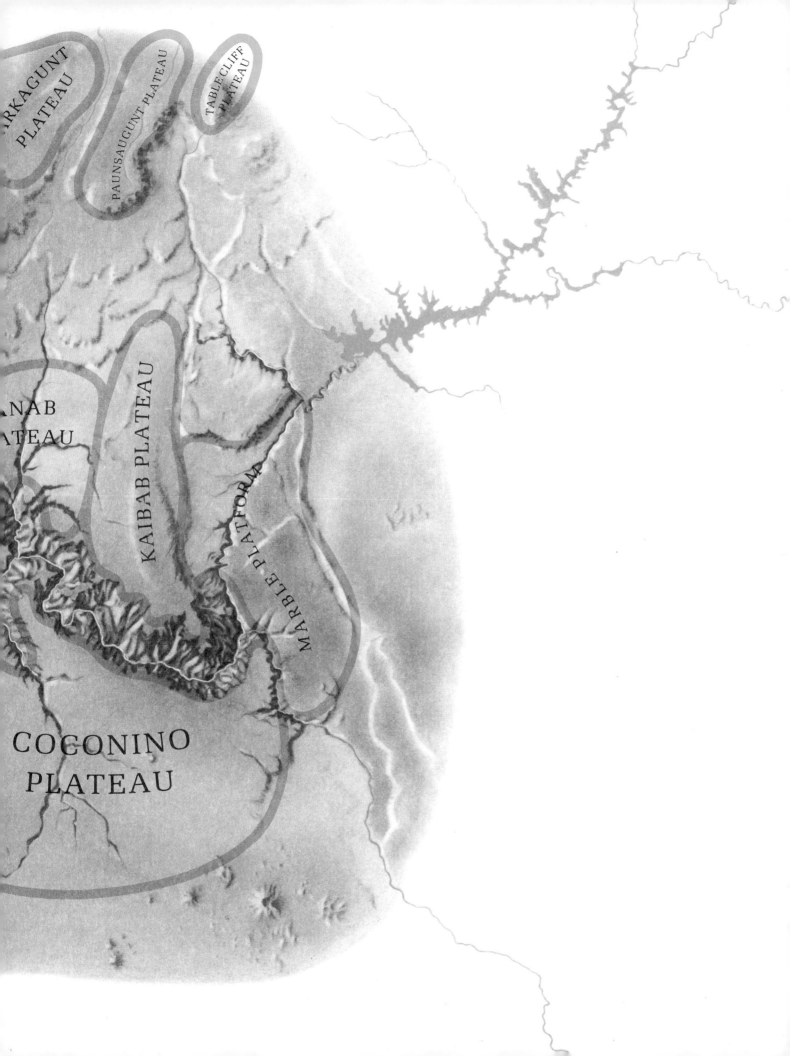

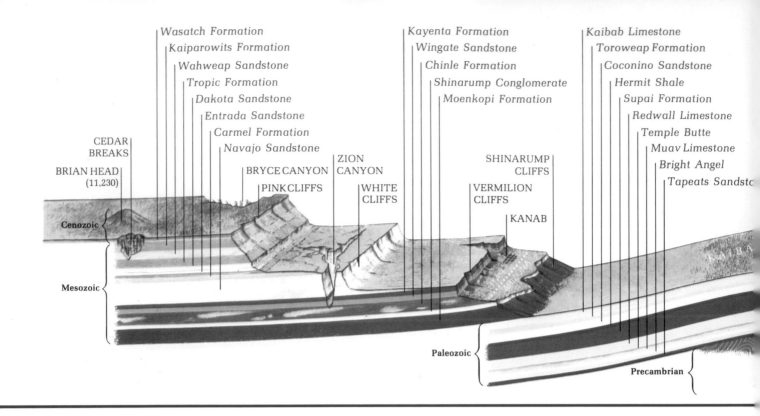

Wasatch Formation
Kaiparowits Formation
Wahweap Sandstone
Tropic Formation
Dakota Sandstone
Entrada Sandstone
Carmel Formation
Navajo Sandstone

Kayenta Formation
Wingate Sandstone
Chinle Formation
Shinarump Conglomerate
Moenkopi Formation

Kaibab Limestone
Toroweap Formation
Coconino Sandstone
Hermit Shale
Supai Formation
Redwall Limestone
Temple Butte
Muav Limestone
Bright Angel
Tapeats Sandsto

CEDAR
BREAKS

BRIAN HEAD
(11,230)

BRYCE CANYON

PINK CLIFFS

ZION
CANYON

WHITE
CLIFFS

SHINARUMP
CLIFFS

VERMILION
CLIFFS

KANAB

Cenozoic

Mesozoic

Paleozoic

Precambrian

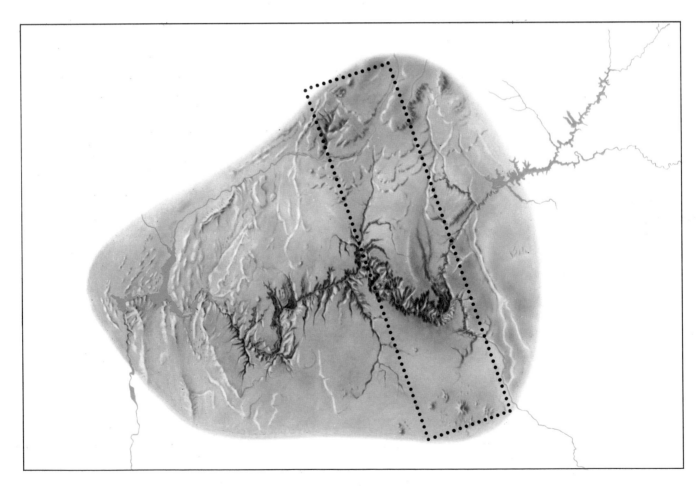

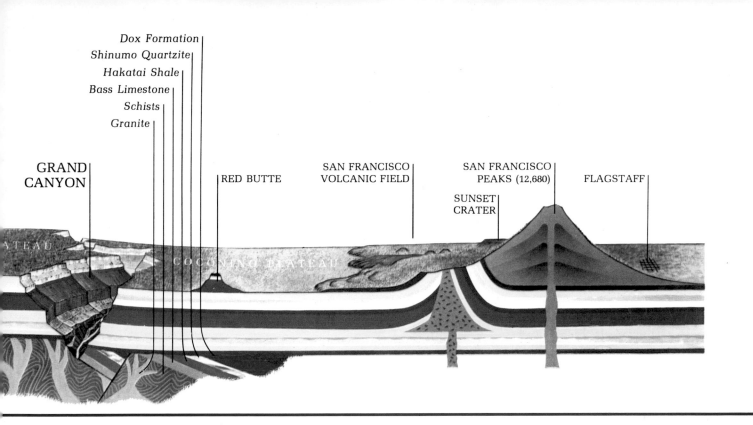

Dox Formation
Shinumo Quartzite
Hakatai Shale
Bass Limestone
Schists
Granite

GRAND
CANYON

RED BUTTE

SAN FRANCISCO
VOLCANIC FIELD

SAN FRANCISCO
PEAKS (12,680)

FLAGSTAFF

SUNSET
CRATER

COCONINO PLATEAU

Schematic Geological Cross-Section

A profile across a billion and a half years of time. Not all strata or formations are shown. Diagram at left indicates location of cross-section above.

posed. Hard rocks are resistant to erosion and will form precipitous angular escarpments which may rise hundreds or even thousands of feet. But softer rocks erode more rapidly and they form steep, ledgy, often talus-covered slopes. Widespread stripping or erosion of the soft rocks accounts for the treads on the canyon staircase and for the flat plateau and mesa tops, benches and terraces seen in Grand Canyon and elsewhere in the district.

Of this land, where wonders are almost commonplace, geologists say that once the architecture of a cliff or canyon wall has been formed it will continuously renew itself in the face of constant erosion. Cliff surfaces, escarpments, and walls retreat as they weather; but in the process they maintain their profiles and will continue to do so until the formation of which they are a part is entirely destroyed. It is a land

of living rock. We can thank the arid climate for preserving the crisp, sharp lines of the Grand Canyon. Where there's little rain, the edge of the strata forming the plateaus and mesas erodes and weathers far faster than the flat tops. Were the climate humid, the sharp angles would disappear, graceful round lines would replace staircase landscape, vegetation would cover the earth, and the Grand Canyon country, with its magnificent, distinctive sculpturing, would not exist. Aridity, let us conclude, is a priceless asset.

Yet water caused it all. The Grand Canyon is the valley of a stream. Creeks and rivers born of rain and melted snow have carved the entire canyon and created elaborate tributary canyon systems reaching back into the plateaus on either side. Many of the long canyon tributaries are rarely visited, even though each is a wonder of erosion—a Grand Canyon on a smaller scale, each, in Powell's words, "a world of beauty in itself."

Even the headwaters, those small, twiglike streams, drop quickly into little canyons of their making and, as they unite with others to form branches, they enter larger canyons. Seldom do canyon country streams break out into the open to lazily meander along. Instead, the Colorado, a young and vigorous river, is hard at work wearing down the

21

Kaibab Limestone

Toroweap Formation

Coconino Sandstone

Hermit Shale

Supai Formation

Redwall Limestone

22

The Strata of Grand Canyon at Point Hansbrough

Kaibab Plateau in the distance.

land. The river has been at it now for some millions of years (though probably not more than ten million), ever since the present "canyon cycle" began as a result of regional uplift and faulting. But even before that time, during the "pre-canyon cycle," streams ancestral to the present Colorado had removed, in places, up to eight thousand feet of sedimentary rock from much of the region, leaving it generally level. On the north, however, as the canyon cycle began, exposures of the strata remained where elsewhere they had been removed—the ancestral Vermilion, White, and Pink cliffs.[1]

Had man been there at the beginning of the canyon cycle he probably would not have had much difficulty traveling about. By the time he did arrive, the present landscape was nearly complete and he found it very difficult indeed to travel across it. The old pre-canyon surface had remained generally level, though by faulting and shifting through much of the district, it had been broken up into huge, slightly tilted blocks. Shallow valleys had become profound canyons and gorges as the rapidly running river had sawed and cut its way deep into the earth and had swallowed the eroded rock of the ever-widening rimlands and the retreating cliffs and escarpments. Spectacular changes in the landscape had occurred through vulcanism. Cinder cones and craters appeared here and there, and in the Toroweap area molten lava had poured over the edge of Grand Canyon, flowing down the river for sixty miles. In the heart of a vast volcanic field the lofty San Francisco Peaks had risen to dominate the skyline in the southern part of the Grand Canyon country.

Man himself arrived in time to see some minor but spectacular changes in the landscape. He was present when Sunset Crater erupted about A.D. 1067. By that time prehistoric men had been wandering about throughout the canyon country for perhaps four thousand years. Hunting for game, for land, for minerals, for edible plants, and for new routes, they must have discovered all of the many vista points—the San Francisco Peaks, the Markagunt and Paunsaugunt, as well as the high places on the cliffs, terraces, and rimlands of the canyons. It was mostly all high country, and when the hunting was good the haze was gone and the air was clear. You could see a hundred miles easily and even two hundred from some places where distant high points stood above the curvature of the earth's horizon. At the canyon rim you could look down deep into the earth and from the same spot you could look up and see the whole sky. It was a land of light, and space, and color.

SOUTH RIM

For ages the popular gateway to the Grand Canyon has been the South Rim. The south rimlands, extending all the way from the Little Colorado River to the mouth of the Grand Canyon, are formed by the Coconino and Hualapai plateaus, two of the seven plateaus facing the great gorge. The best-known approach, of course, is the highway to the South Rim of Grand Canyon National Park, but on this route you travel only a few miles along the rim. If you should want to travel the full length of the rim from the Little Colorado, you should prepare for a hike of something over seven hundred miles! During this walk you would find it necessary to detour several times from the main gorge in order to head lengthy canyon tributaries.[2]

The Coconino Plateau, much the best known of the seven, extends from the canyon of the Little Colorado on the east to the Aubrey Cliffs on the west. The southern boundary, fifty miles from the Grand Canyon, is marked by the vast San Francisco volcanic field, some three thousand square miles in extent and dominated by the tight cluster of summits now known as the San Francisco Peaks.[3] Actually the peaks form the eroded crest line of a single volcanic mountain, and three of them (Humphrey, Agassiz, and Fremont) range in altitude up to twelve thousand

*Its waters laden with lime, the beauty of Havasu Creek is enhanced
by the dams it builds as it flows toward the Colorado. Arizona.*

feet and over, the highest elevations in Arizona. Scattered about through the field are a number of secondary volcanic mountains (Bill Williams, Sitgreaves, Kendrick, Elden, and O'Leary). Over four hundred craters and craterlets, cones and conelets, basalt outcrops and lava flows indicate several different stages of volcanic activity in this land. Some of these look so fresh they appear to have cooled only yesterday.

During late stages of volcanic activity, lava flows reached the Little Colorado River. The beautiful Grand Falls was created when a stream of lava from Merriam Crater flowed into the river, blocking it where it ran through a shallow canyon. When the lava cooled, the river flowed around the edge of the dam, falling back over the canyon wall into its old canyon now filled in part with basalt. Sunset Crater, with fresh-looking lava flows at its base, is a typical crater and has become one of the best known since it was made a national monument. The most recent to erupt, stained pink and red near the rim, the crater at times still seems to glow though its fires have been out for centuries.[4]

Travel north from Flagstaff over U.S. Highway 89. As you leave behind the volcanic formations and the high, forested slopes you descend by a series of broad limestone slopes and sandstone ridges to reach the Little Colorado at Cameron. Now the architecture of mesa and plateau and canyon is everywhere around you. Off to the right in the distance is the low-lying flat top of the Ward Terrace with its beautifully dissected facade. To the left is the brooding face of the Coconino Plateau, here called Gray Mountain, and just above Cameron the Little Colorado enters a canyon which, at its mouth fifty miles downstream, has become a narrow gorge three thousand feet deep.

The Little Colorado is by far the longest tributary of the big Colorado in the Grand Canyon district. Its headstreams reach up to the Continental Divide in western New Mexico and to much of Arizona's Mogollon Rim country. The Petrified Forest, the Painted Desert, and the eastern slopes of the San Francisco volcanic field fall within its basin.

As a river the Little Colorado is not very impressive. Most of the rain and snow falls on the periphery of the basin, evaporating and sinking into the ground or drawn off in irrigation. The basin contracts below Winslow, and at Grand Falls, where you would expect a stream to begin to develop head, you may see only a trickle in a wide, sandy bed.

Even at Cameron the bed of the stream is dry much of the time. But at other times you may see a torrent of red water pouring into the canyon and rolling along, its surface marked by the rhythmic undulations of sand waves. The marvelous open sweep of the Painted Desert westward from the Petrified Forest National Park to Moenkopi Wash, which enters the Little Colorado just below Cameron, will run with color after a summer rain. The colors mix to form a rich, creamy, reddish chocolate flow having very much the consistency of thin paint. A river full of this, falling over Grand Falls, will fill the air with heavy spray, some of which seems to turn to dust in the hot desert light. Reaching the main stream through the beautiful, deep, sharp-edged, jagged gorge, even a small stream of liquid mud from the Little Colorado's Painted Desert will color the waters of the big Colorado all the way to Lake Mead. Except to the Hopi Indians, who for centuries made pilgrimages to its depths, the great gorge of the Little Colorado is perhaps the least known of the major features of the Grand Canyon country.[5]

Drive west from Cameron to Grand Canyon National Park. As you come out on the rim at Desert View and travel west to Grand View Point, you will be crossing the crest of the Coconino Plateau and its northern rim. On a rainy day, you will find it strange to stand on the rim of the canyon a mile deep and to see that the rain-made streams flow away from the canyon and not into it! But this is not an uncommon phenomenon in the canyon country.

What has happened here is that the Colorado River has cut a massive plateau neatly in two. The Coconino Plateau is a southward extension of the Kaibab Plateau which reaches its maximum height on the north side of the canyon some distance from the rim. Thus the North Rim, where the river bisects the plateau, is higher—by a thousand feet—than the South Rim, so the rimlands of the Kaibab slope toward the canyon, while those of the South Rim slope away from it. Therefore, you can drive along the rim

*Grand Falls (upper right) on the Little Colorado River. When a
lava flow from Merriam Crater dammed the Little Colorado
and spilled out across the desert on the opposite banks,
the river found a way around the tongue of hard rocks and fell
back over the old canyon walls to form the falls (above). Arizona.*

for miles without crossing a single tributary gorge.

To the west, beyond the highways of Grand Canyon National Park, the country changes radically. On the western section of the Coconino Plateau water flows toward the Grand Canyon, rather than away from it, and long, profound tributary canyons, heading back on the plateau, may carry perennial streams.

Havasu, or Cataract, Canyon is by far the largest southern tributary of the Grand Canyon west of the Little Colorado River, and it is one of the most remarkable canyon systems in a country where astounding and stupendous gorges are commonplace. Throughout the ages of geological time the main stream and a dozen of its tributaries have cut a maze of canyons out of the plateau.

Havasu Canyon alone is easily fifty miles long, and within this distance the stream drops 3,850 feet before it reaches the Colorado. About ten miles above the mouth big springs burst from the canyon floor, and below this point Havasu Creek widens out to a quarter of a mile or so for about three miles; here the

Havasupai Indians have for centuries made their homes. The Indians dam the spring-fed creek and use its turquoise-blue and lime-laden waters to irrigate their crops. After offering the gift of life to the community, the creek flows on through a rapidly deepening and narrowing canyon, and, after plunging over a series of five waterfalls, reaches the Colorado some seven miles below.

West of the Havasu are the strange and beautiful National and Mohawk canyons. Difficult to reach and seldom visited, long and narrow and closely parallel, these watercourses drain the eastward-dipping back slopes of the Aubrey Cliffs which mark the western limits of the Coconino Plateau.

Running along the line of a fault, a thousand feet high, facing west, the Aubrey Cliffs separate the Coconino from the Hualapai Plateau, the westernmost block on the south side of the Grand Canyon. The Hualapai, forming a great horseshoe, tilts toward and encloses the left side of Colorado River throughout the last hundred miles of the Grand Canyon. It's small

27

as the Grand Canyon plateaus go; it's not more than twenty-five miles anywhere from the outer edge of the horseshoe to the Colorado. Tributary canyons, therefore, are mostly short, but there are so many of them that they have dissected the South Rim into an elaborate succession of points and promontories.

The longest canyons of the Hualapai are full of interest. Prospect Valley at the base of the Aubrey Cliffs is indeed a valley in the more conventional sense. It opens out to the north in a broad avenue approaching the Colorado and reaches the Grand Canyon at one of its narrowest places as a hanging valley, the bed of which is twenty-three hundred feet almost directly above the river. It is the counterpart of Toroweap Valley directly opposite on the north side of the Colorado. Spencer Canyon is one of the longer and more intricate canyon systems. A tributary, Meriwitica (spelled variously), is celebrated in the mythology of the Hualapai Indians as a place of origins. The Hualapais, whose reservation nearly blankets the Hualapai Plateau, have their tribal headquarters at Peach Springs at the head of Peach Springs Canyon. This, a fork of Diamond Creek, is the only tributary in Grand Canyon through which it is possible to drive a wheeled vehicle to the edge of the Colorado River.

From Peach Springs drive west on U.S. 66 through Truxton Canyon to the head of Hualapai Valley. Off to the right, take notice of that line of cliffs running north. These are the Grand Wash Cliffs— gray, knobby, and ledgy. Somehow they don't seem very high. Yet here, where Music Mountain towers almost four thousand feet above the valley, they reach their greatest elevation. Running north to the Colorado River and beyond, the cliffs form the face of the massive, upthrust block of the Hualapai Plateau and the spectacular western edge of the South Rim country of the Grand Canyon.[6]

THE NORTHWARD TILT

Some of the most majestic plateau and canyon landscape in the world is found on the Arizona Strip. All of the country north of the Colorado River—the northwestern corner of Arizona—that's The Strip. Save for the Virgin Mountains astride the Nevada line to the west, The Strip is taken up with five elongated plateaus. Sharply divided by zones of fault and flexure, identified by long lines of cliffs or steep slopes trending north and south, these platforms form the northern rim and face of Grand Canyon. In general they tilt to the north toward the Utah country; but some also dip gently to the east. In geological antiquity when these platforms were being elevated, the western edges were forced up and the eastern edges thrown down. Thus, some of the more prominent lines of cliffs running across the Arizona Strip are the western escarpments, or cuestas, of these remarkable platforms.

All of this means that the southern and western slopes and exposures, cliffs and canyon walls are likely to be higher, bolder, more prominent, and more elaborately sculptured. Because the chapters of the earth's history visible in Grand Canyon are more fully exposed on the north side of the river and because more chapters are to be seen on the north side than on the South Rim, many geologists since Powell's day have favored the northern side as a field of study—the Arizona Strip and the High Plateaus of southern Utah.

A good way to see the plateau and canyon country of the Colorado is by air. If you fly low due east of Las Vegas for about two hundred miles, you will see some of the best of the Arizona Strip—the southern extension of the five plateaus, the North Rim, Marble Canyon, and the Echo Cliffs.

Flying over the chaotic landscape on either side of Lake Mead you can see ahead, in vivid contrast, the flat top of the Shivwits Plateau, first of the five. The long line of Grand Wash Cliffs, a series of precipitous palisades, boldly faces west. Just where the Colorado breaks through them, where the Grand Canyon ends, they rise to over thirty-six hundred feet above the headwaters of Lake Mead. You can see the tilt now, toward the east but stronger to the north. Off to the right, some twenty miles away, you can see the southernmost extension of the Shivwits Plateau—the member opposite the Hualapai Plateau—a narrow penin-

Spencer Canyon, Hualapai Plateau, Hualapai Indian Reservation. Arizona.

sula with the Colorado River bent around it and looking out on a wilderness of canyons unequaled in beauty anywhere along the river.

Next the Uinkaret Plateau comes into view. The great Hurricane Cliffs form its western escarpment. Of all the great dislocations in the earth's crust in the West, Dutton thought none to be "more wonderful or more interesting" than the Hurricane Fault. In a continuous line of cliffs, usually over a thousand feet high, the ledge extends from a point some distance north of Cedar City, Utah, all the way across the Arizona Strip and across the Grand Canyon.

The southern extremity of the Uinkaret, the narrowest of the five plateaus, is nearly covered with a volcanic field which brings an elevated and irregular silhouette to the tabular skyline of the North Rim country. Since the lofty volcanic peaks—Trumbull, Logan, and Emma (known collectively as the Pine, or Sawmill, or Uinkaret Mountains)—as well as some of the lesser volcanic mountains round and about, stand on the southernmost and highest part of the plateau, they may be seen from points north and south a hundred miles away.

Staying on course as you continue your flight eastward you quickly pass over the narrow valley of the Toroweap, the main avenue of approach to Grand Canyon National Monument, which incorporates sections of Grand Canyon at its narrowest. Toroweap Valley and its fifteen-hundred-foot-high cliffs mark the western edge of the Kanab Plateau.

Fly on due east for sixty miles and you will be over the southern tip of the Kaibab Plateau, the highest of the North Rim plateaus. The Kaibab, an elongated upwarp extending all the way across the Arizona Strip and some distance into Utah, rises from two to four thousand feet above the plateaus border-

ing it on the east and west, and its dark, heavily forested crown, running for miles at a height of more than eight thousand feet, dominates the skyline of the eastern part of the Grand Canyon country. To the Paiute Indians it appeared to be a recumbent mountain, and they named it "mountain-lying-down."

Flying over the Kaibab, you suddenly find yourself high above the Marble Plateau, or Platform. The last of the five on your flight from west to east, the Marble Platform is bounded on the south by the deep gorge of the Little Colorado and straight ahead that jagged line of cliffs—the Echo Cliffs—forms the eastern limits.

From your viewpoint high above it, note the black, sharp outlines—the sharpest anywhere to be seen in the Grand Canyon country—of Marble Canyon as it carries the Colorado diagonally across the plateau. Note that the river flows south-southwest against the dip of the surface which is generally north-northeast. Note, too, that canyon tributaries are entering the main gorge facing upstream. By all the signs from above, the Colorado through Marble Canyon should be flowing in the opposite direction! Now you are over the Echo Cliffs, an unbroken escarpment running north and south for seventy-five miles, and you have passed over the five steplike platforms forming the north rimlands of the Grand Canyon.[7]

But there is also a series of platforms, or terraces, separated by prominent lines of cliffs, running generally east and west across the northern periphery of the Grand Canyon country. Powell called them the

San Francisco Peaks from the east. Arizona.

Echo Cliffs at The Gap. Arizona.

Joshua trees at the base of the Grand Wash Cliffs, and the rugged western escarpment of the Hualapai Plateau. Arizona

The Northward Tilt. The Marble Platform bounded by the Kaibab Plateau (dark band, distance), the Paria Plateau (center right), and the Echo Cliffs (foothills, left), is bisected by the jagged Marble Canyon. The Colorado flows against the tilt from the shallow canyon at lower right to upper left where the canyon is over two thousand feet deep. The black, looping line is U.S. Highway 89A which bridges Marble Canyon (lower right). This is the major historic route between Utah and Arizona. When it opened in 1929, the bridge put the crossing at Lee's Ferry, six miles upstream (not shown), out of business.

"Terrace Plateaus." On your return go north and then fly west along the Arizona–Utah boundary. As you travel the hundred miles between Lee's Ferry and St. George, below and to the right you will see piled up a vertical mile of rainbow strata; mostly in Utah, this grand structure is supported by four lines of cliffs which generally face south.

The country tilts toward the north. The lines of cliffs you see are the receding faces of hard, resistant strata, remnants of rock that once covered the entire Grand Canyon country to the south. In other words, more than a vertical mile of rock has been weathered and stripped away from the country you have just flown over, and the structure at hand is all that remains after what geologists call the "great denudation." In ascending order the Shinarump, Vermilion, White, and Pink cliffs, each separated by a wide terrace, form a giant staircase which will bring you up to the high rims of the Markagunt and the Paunsaugunt. Tilting northward, the outer rims of these great plateaus, in several places ranging over ten thousand feet above sea level, form the forested divide between the Great Basin and the Grand Canyon country.

In brilliant bands of color the cliffs find superlative expression in a number of places. Here are a few: Shinarump (also called Chocolate) Cliffs—Lost Spring and Gooseberry Mountains (both flat-topped mesas); Vermilion Cliffs—the breathtaking escarpment of the Paria Plateau and the towers at Short Creek; White Cliffs—the crags, temples, buttes, and massive cliffs of Zion National Park, including the wonderful towering cliffs of the Kolob; Pink Cliffs—the delicate, fretted pinnacles and spires of Cedar Breaks National Monument, Bryce Canyon National Park, and the Table Cliff Plateau.

The three major streams of the northern section of the Grand Canyon district head on the Pink Cliffs which crown the Markagunt and the Paunsaugunt plateaus. The Virgin River drains the southern face of the Markagunt, and it is difficult to believe that so small a stream could do so much. Slicing down through the successive strata, the headstreams have created a masterpiece of erosion, made up of deep slotlike canyons overshadowed by domes, mesas, towers, pilasters, and bosses of delicately colored sandstone. Many of these features are easily seen in Zion National Park, but many more are difficult to reach. The incredible narrow canyon of the Parunuweap, on the main fork, has been traversed by only a few people. Below Zion the Virgin breaks through the Hurricane Cliffs and leaves behind the classic tabular landscape of the Colorado Plateau.[8]

Kanab Creek, a lesser stream than the Virgin, is wholly contained by the Colorado Plateau. The headstreams, reaching up to the Pink Cliffs of the Paunsaugunt, drop down through the White, Vermilion, and Shinarump cliffs through shallow canyons and more or less open valleys. But a few miles below Kanab and Fredonia the creek enters a canyon which gradually deepens, and where the stream enters the Colorado River in the middle of Grand Canyon, it is flowing through an inner, narrow, straight-walled gorge 2,250 feet deep. The outer rim towers above that another sixteen hundred feet, making a vertical distance of nearly four thousand feet. In a region of spectacular scenery the view from the head of the inner gorge down Kanab Canyon is one of the greatest sights of the Grand Canyon country.[9]

On the north and east, the Grand Canyon country is bounded by the Paria River, a weird and wonderful stream heading on the Pink Cliffs of the eastern rim of the Paunsaugunt, most of which comes within the bounds of Bryce Canyon National Park. But when you stand on the rim at Sunset Point in Bryce, look across the valley below. Directly to the east that high promontory—Table Cliff Plateau—stands over ten thousand feet above the sea and an even two thousand feet above you. Table Cliff Plateau is a culminating point both in Utah's High Plateaus and in the Grand Canyon district, and the waters dropping down through its beautifully eroded Pink Cliffs join with those of Bryce in the open Paria Amphitheater.

Then through a succession of narrow, straight-walled canyons, lined with cottonwoods, the Paria makes its fantastic way through the White and Vermilion cliffs and through a tortuous fifty-mile-long gorge across the back of the Paria Plateau. It breaks out into the open for a few miles and then at Lee's Ferry its waters join those of the Colorado to begin the long run through Grand Canyon.[10]

vening light at Bright Angel Point. Across
ne canyon, the South Rim, a thousand feet
ower, is nearly lost in shadow. The San Fran-
isco Peaks on the distant horizon. Arizona.

(Next spread) Table Cliff Plateau, east
across the valley of the Paria River from Bryce
Canyon, is 10,000 feet above sea level, 2,000
feet higher than the rim at Bryce. Utah.

3

Five Faces of Grand Canyon

In the Grand Canyon country the view from the river's edge, from the base of the cliff, from the foot of the mountain, is likely to be the most rewarding. The distant vistas from volcanic peaks, plateau promontories, or elevated canyon rims are often difficult to absorb. Your mind forms a general picture, either lacking in detail, or so full of details that it is confused

and blurred. The view from the rim of Grand Canyon may even seem flat and monotonous, lacking in perspective.

Ride the waters through the Grand Canyon if you want a different view. Light and shadows continually change as you move along; the walls rise in sharp profiles or appear as shadowy silhouettes; the upward

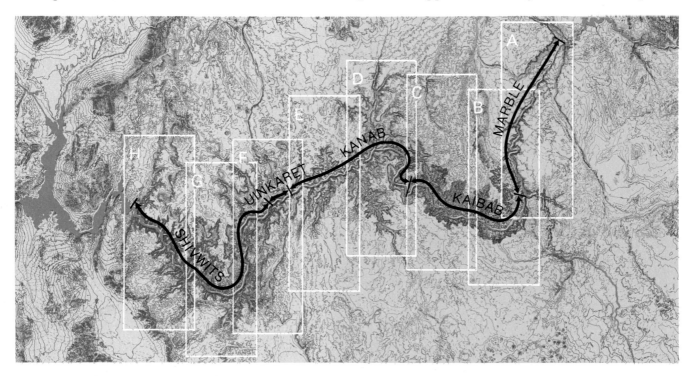

Below the Little Colorado the canyon walls
break away and for fifteen miles the river flows through
the widest part of Grand Canyon. Arizona.

vision into the light reflects back the canyon contour and outline. Since the rims on either side restrict the horizon, you are forced to focus on the part, not the panorama. In the parts you find variety, an ordered and composed variety—each section bears similarity to the next, yet each is different from the last. And there are five divisions of the canyon, each conforming to the bounds of the great plateaus of the north rimlands, and each showing a different face to the canyon voyager. You are close enough to the rock and the water to appreciate the power at work, and you can even come to grips now and then with the marvels and the beauty of its creation. The rhythm and tempo of the water, the rise and reach of the walls, the quality of air and light generate emotion and mood. On the rim you can take it or leave it. On the water you take it.

MILE 0.0

For a mile or two after it breaks through the Echo Cliffs and leaves Glen Canyon, the Colorado sweeps out into the open at Lee's Ferry. This is a marvelous place; it is one of those points in the canyon country where history comes to a sharp focus. At Lee's Ferry you are at once on the edge and the bottom and top of things. The towering Echo Cliffs, upstream and running off to the left, mark the eastern edge of the Grand Canyon district. On the right, the Vermilion Cliffs and the Shinarump Cliffs (here a deep chocolate-brown) rise three thousand feet to mark the base of the "Terrace Plateaus." Here, where the Paria River comes in, you are at the northern extremity of the Marble Canyon Platform; you are at the head of Grand Canyon. Here, for a moment, the waters of the Colorado and the rim of the Grand Canyon reach the same plane. As you push off from Mile 0 to begin your voyage through Grand Canyon you literally step from the rim of the canyon into your boat.[1]

MILE 4.5

The rimrock rises as you descend into Marble Canyon, which forms the upper 61.5 miles of Grand Can-

40

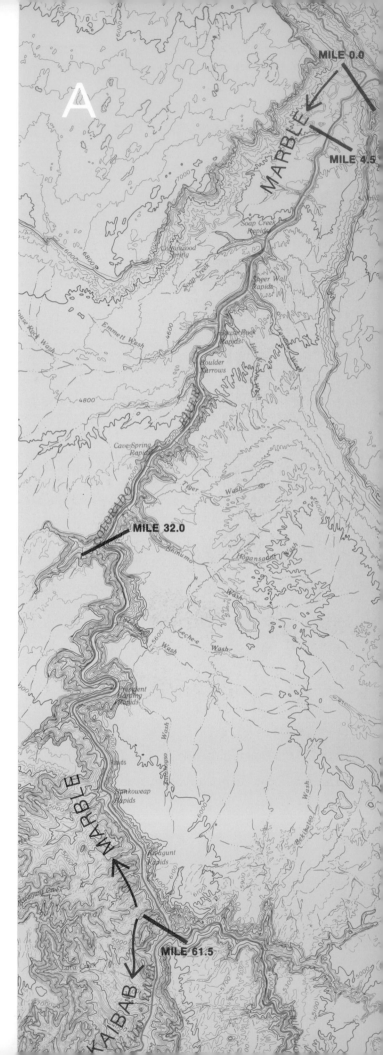

The mouth of Glen Canyon just above Lee's Ferry. Arizona.

Lee's Ferry, Arizona. Looking down the Colorado River from the geological survey camp at Lee's Ferry, August, 1951.

yon, and at this point you see Navajo Bridge, which put Lee's Ferry out of business, spanning a gorge already over four hundred feet deep. And now you begin to see change in the canyon, change of the kind you will notice all the way through Grand Canyon. The strata of which the walls are composed—limestone, sandstone, and shale—determine the profile of the canyon. Since the strata differ in hardness and alternate between resistant and soft beds, the canyon profile takes on the appearance of a staircase. From your viewpoint on the water, it appears as an inverted, truncated pyramid.[2] Thus at Mile 4.5 below Lee's Ferry, the Colorado has already cut down through the hard strata of the Kaibab, Toroweap, and Coconino formations, and the canyon walls are very steep. But at this point the next layer below, the Hermit Shale, soft and easily eroded, comes up; the canyon widens and, as the Hermit rises, slopes appear to relieve the monotony of the cliffs which preserve their form, however, and may be seen as the sharp, capping rim of the canyon. And thus it goes all the way through Grand Canyon—a wonderful and ordered symmetry, in brilliant color.

MILE 32.0

Vasey's Paradise. To reach this point you will have dropped down through another major layer of rocks, the thick Supai Formation, and are well down through another, the great Redwall Limestone, each producing its own characteristic configuration in the canyon profile. If you stop the boat on the right bank where springs burst from the base of the Redwall cliff amidst a tangle of greenery and flowers, you will find yourself at a place named by Powell after the botanist George Vasey.

Could any place be more beautiful? For it is not only the cool spring waters, the green grass and flowers of Vasey's Paradise, not just the river drifting quietly here, rippling over a gravel bar and contained by the nearly vertical cliffs of the Redwall Limestone; not those cliffs alone but the entire, magnificent, colored staircase of successive cliffs towering well over twenty-seven hundred feet above you. Here, only halfway through Marble Canyon, you are in a gorge

The Little Colorado (center) enters the Big Colorado, marking the end
of Marble Canyon section (left). Arizona. Photograph made in 1923.

half a mile deep. From rim to rim it is a little over a mile wide. The canyon is lined with great horizontal bands of color, reminders of the successive layers of rock that you have seen at eye level on your voyage down through the canyon.

Let your eye drop down from the rim over the strata, each with its own characteristic color: gray touched with streaks of red (Kaibab and Toroweap); a clear, broad band of pale buff to bone white (Coconino); brick red (Hermit), red to buff to red (Supai), to the Redwall before you at eye level. The reds predominate, and when summer rains bring an occasional waterfall down over the strata the water is nearly always red.

The Redwall Limestone, a hard cliff-forming stratum about five hundred feet thick and the most prominent stratum throughout Grand Canyon, is bluish gray (prospectors called it the "Blue Limestone"), but its surface in most places is stained and colored red by weathering of the Supai immediately above it. Impressed by the Redwall with its sheer cliffs, cirques and caves, niches and panels, alcoves and royal arches, Powell called it "the marble," and he named the upper part of the Grand Canyon after it.[3]

MILE 61.5

Marble Canyon ends where the Little Colorado, running turquoise-blue normally, but a light chocolate-red in flood, joins the big Colorado as it debouches from a narrow canyon, thirty-three hundred feet deep. To reach the confluence from Vasey's Paradise, you quickly left the Redwall behind and then dropped down through four more strata—rather dull-looking beds ranging in color from purplish and bluish green to tan and brown (in descending order, the Temple Butte, Muav, Bright Angel, and Tapeats formations).[4]

By the time you arrive at the Little Colorado, you have seen close at hand all of those layers of rocks, each of which by its individual character determines the structure and architectural style of the upper levels of Grand Canyon. Distinctive and unique, with its own special quality of beauty, Marble Canyon is only the beginning, the first face of Grand Canyon.

46   *The Redwall Limestone in*
          Marble Canyon, Mile 38.5. Arizona.
          JOHN SANTA (BUREAU OF RECLAMATION)

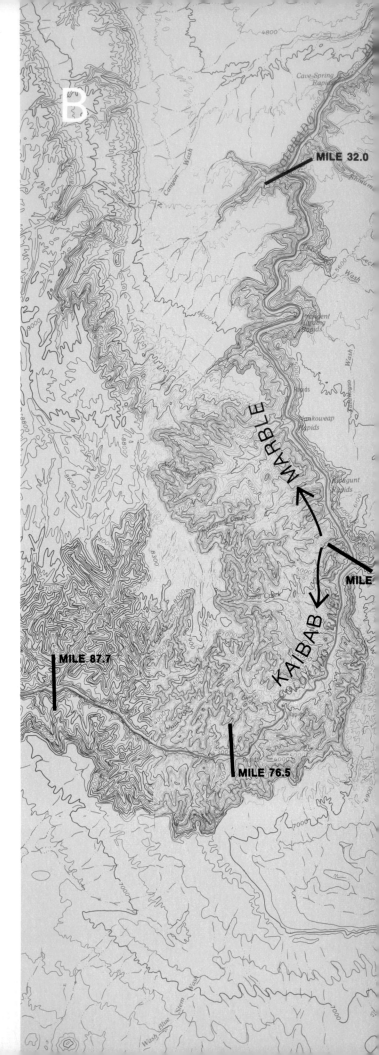

MILE 76.5

Hance Rapids, named after John Hance, prospector.
You will find it exhilarating to ride the river below the
Little Colorado. The canyon walls break away, and
for fifteen miles the river flows through the widest
part of Grand Canyon. The sky is wide again. On the
left, you are treated to magnificent views of the palisades forming the rim of the canyon from the mouth
of the Little Colorado to Desert View. On the right
rises the much more intricate landscape of isolated
buttes and points and pinnacles ("shrines" and "temples" and "castles"), remnants of the highly dissected
face of the Kaibab Plateau which changes in aspect
with every mile.

Strata not seen before are conspicuous throughout this section of Grand Canyon. You will notice that
the beds forming the lower levels of the canyon are
composed of brightly colored rock ranging, top to
bottom, from reddish brown to greenish gray to vermilion to red to white and finally to bluish rock. In
addition, the strata are tilted sloping away from the
horizontal plane of those with which you became familiar in Marble Canyon. That these strata (called by
geologists the Grand Canyon Series of younger Precambrian age) are rather soft and easily eroded accounts for the wide valley through most of this section of the canyon, and the predominantly reddish
color of the rock treats the eye to a blaze of color.

But now, as you move on downstream, the canyon begins to narrow again, the bright color begins to
fade from the rock, and as you drop down over Hance
Rapids you quickly enter the black maw of the somber Upper Granite Gorge, entrenched in the Vishnu
Schist and granitic rocks of older Precambrian age.

MILE 87.7

Bright Angel Creek, named by Powell in 1869. As you
have found out, the Upper Granite Gorge is V-shaped,
steep-sided, cut in dark, forbidding rocks. The river is
swift and narrow and deep—it fills the bottom of the
gorge nearly everywhere from wall to wall—and after

48

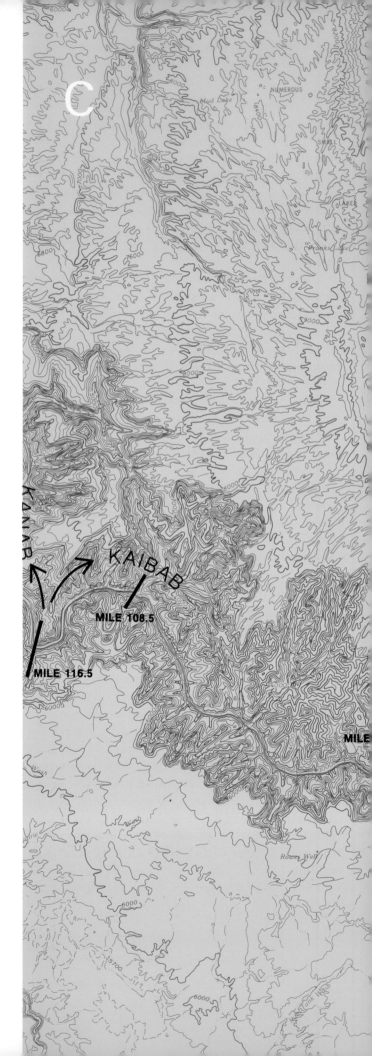

riding some of the most savage rapids in Grand Canyon (Hance, Sockdolager, Grapevine), and coursing through some of its narrowest sections, it is with some relief that you pull up to stop on the right at Bright Angel Creek. The clear waters of the creek, which enter the Colorado through a fairly open canyon, and the fine campsites at its mouth suggest to such travelers that Powell's Bright Angel is a most appropriate name.

Here in the Granite Gorge you have reached some of the oldest rocks exposed in the Colorado Plateau—the basement rocks of the Grand Canyon. In your voyage through the canyon to Bright Angel Creek, you have taken a trip backward through incredibly long eras of the older part of geological time. The walls of the Granite Gorge are something like two billion years old. The basement rocks, and those of the Grand Canyon Series, are of the earliest, or Precambrian, era in the earth's history, and they actually represent at least two ages of mountain building. Neither rock sequence is exposed continuously in the canyon. The Vishnu Schist may represent but the roots of an ancient mountain system which was worn away to a generally level plain before deposition of the Grand Canyon Series began. These strata were subsequently tilted, faulted, and eroded to a plain of uneven surface. All of this took about a billion and a half years, ending 600 million years ago.

During the next 375 million years—the Paleozoic Era of geologic times—the layers in ascending order, from the Tapeats Sandstone to the Kaibab Limestone, were laid down. From your position at the mouth of Bright Angel Creek the combined thickness of all these formations constitutes over a vertical mile of rock, a marvelous cross-section of the earth's history which may be seen to fine advantage from rim to river at the geological museum at Yavapai Point on the South Rim. There, as your eye in seconds sweeps upward from the river to the North Rim, try to imagine another vertical mile or so of horizontal strata piled above that. Then you would have a picture of the region as it was at the end of another geological era in the earth's history—the Mesozoic—which lasted 155 million years and came to an end about 70 million years ago, long before there was a Grand Canyon.

During the Cenozoic—the present geological era—and only in the more recent period of that era has the landscape of the Grand Canyon taken shape. Erosion stripped away the Mesozoic from most of the area, leaving the strata of the upper mile fully exposed on the southern faces of Utah's High Plateaus. The three great lines of cliffs—Pink, White, and Vermilion—together with the lesser beds interspersed between them, will rival in their diversity and variety of color the formations of the lower mile which were exposed when the Colorado River carved the great canyon. During the course of the Cenozoic, vulcanism produced the only upward relief on the tabular skyline by creating volcanos, cinder cones, craters, and lava flows.

This glorious column of rocks—two miles thick—extending from Precambrian to Cenozoic, carries within it the record of the emergence of life from its simplest forms in the older rocks to more complex expressions in the younger rocks. As many have said, the Grand Canyon country is an open book of the earth's history.[5] The story of man's appearance and activity in Grand Canyon country would not take up more than a short paragraph on the last page of the book. As you contemplate the nature of the Grand Canyon universe from your camp at Bright Angel Creek, you might agree that this is about the right amount of space. However, to satisfy man's unquenchable vanity, we will henceforth have much more to say about the last short paragraph than the rest of the book.

In the human history of Grand Canyon, Bright Angel from about the turn of the century has been a "crossroads." Since Powell's day nearly all river travelers have stopped here, at least for a drink of cool, fresh water, and no place on the canyon floor has been visited more frequently. Trails built from both rims to the mouth of Bright Angel opened the way for thousands to ride or hike down the "lower mile" to the waters of the Colorado. In 1909, John Burroughs and John Muir made the trip down the Bright Angel Trail. Muir argued against the trip: *Go up to see*, he said, *not down*. Not to be talked out of the adventure by the Scottish mountain climber, Burroughs persisted and wrote that the trip into the canyon on

(Next spread) Storm clouds over The Dome, an isolated butte on the Esplanade on the north side of the Colorado in Grand Canyon National Monument. A similar formation, Mt. Sinyala, appears in the distance (lower left) on the south side of the canyon. Arizona.

ALLEN J. MALMQUIST

mule-back was worth it "if only to fall in love with a mule."

"It is always worthwhile to sit or kneel at the feet of grandeur," Burroughs wrote, and down in the bottom of the canyon he found exhilarating the upward vision from the "shapeless mass" of the Precambrian, which suggested "chaos and turmoil," to the horizontal strata above it which suggested order and plan. Close at hand he could see the abrupt changes between one geologic age and another: "new colors, new constituents, new qualities."[6] To get personally involved with the great canyon, do it by foot, muleback, or boat.

MILE 108.5

History? Man has been climbing about in the vastness of the canyon, living and hunting and exploring in it for about four thousand years. Here on the right, where Shinumo (Paiute name for the prehistoric inhabitants of the Grand Canyon country adopted by the Powell Survey) Creek comes in, there are ruins and remains. But there are hundreds and even thousands of archaeological sites scattered all through the canyon. Here the early Precambrian rocks have dropped down, the Grand Canyon Series is broadly exposed locally, and open vistas of the canyon at large appear again. Here the last of the route seekers— Robert B. Stanton—planned to build a switching yard for the railroad line he expected to build all the way through the canyons of the Colorado from Grand Junction. Here W. W. Bass came to prospect and built a camp alongside the creek, the waters of which he turned to irrigation, as the prehistoric peoples in the same place had done centuries before. Bass worked out a trail down from the South Rim and up Shinumo Creek to the Kaibab on the North Rim. Over this route he brought dudes into the canyon and developed the first transcanyon tourist business.[7]

MILE 116.5

Elves' Chasm. Once past Bright Angel you leave behind the Grand Canyon known to the millions.

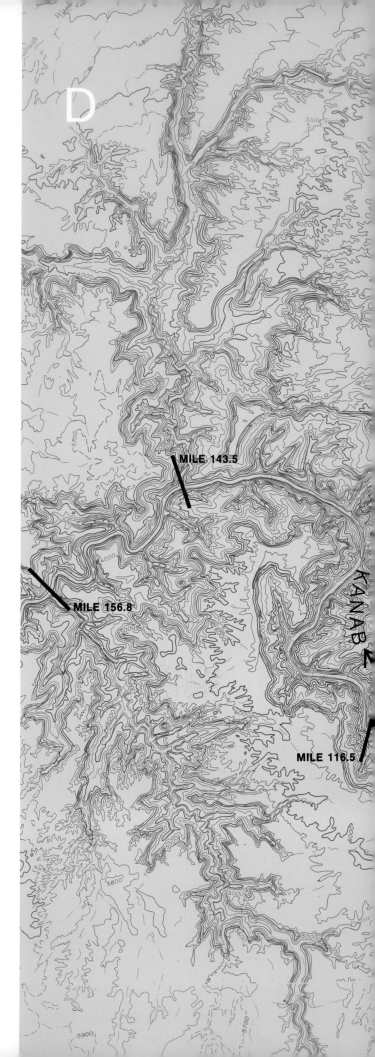

Once past Shinumo Creek you leave behind the Grand Canyon known to the thousands. Less than halfway through you enter a stupendous gorge seen by only a few either from the river or the rim. At Elves' Chasm the Grand Canyon changes radically in character. Just below that point the Precambrian rocks slip out of sight. The wide Tonto Platform, which you can see as a prominent green bench some three thousand feet below the South Rim at Grand Canyon Village, has all but disappeared, and the profile of the canyon now becomes a spectacular, narrow, straight-sided gorge from two to three thousand feet deep. Although not wide at this point, another terrace, or platform, can be seen a thousand feet below the outer rim, its surface a hard layer of the red Supai formation. It becomes miles wide farther west. Dutton named it the Esplanade, and this, together with the profound inner gorge, are the most prominent features of the great canyon for miles below Elves' Chasm.[8]

MILE 143.5

Kanab Creek on the right. Just three miles over the halfway mark. To reach this point you pass through another section where the Precambrian rocks come up again—the Middle Granite Gorge—and a consequent widening of the canyon for a few miles where the Grand Canyon Series is also exposed. But by the time you have reached Kanab Creek, where Powell ended his second run through the canyon in September, 1872, the Grand Canyon has become straight-walled, narrow, and over two thousand feet deep. Above that the Esplanade is widely developed, and from the outer rim of the canyon one may behold a magnificent red platform, several miles in width, bisected by the narrow inner gorge. The monotony is broken by the widely spaced tributary canyons—of which Kanab Creek is the classic example—that cut across the Esplanade and come into the parent stream at grade level. Indeed, this long, narrow, and deep section of Grand Canyon coincides approximately with the width of Kanab Plateau and with the western part of the Coconino Plateau.

The steep, hard walls of the Middle Granite Gorge. Arizona.

53

MILE 156.8

It would be easy to miss the mouth of Havasu Creek, historically one of the most interesting tributaries of the Colorado River in Grand Canyon. It comes in on the left through a narrow slot in a canyon two thousand feet deep. Six miles upstream the Havasupai Indians have lived for some centuries, and near here some of the first significant mining in Grand Canyon took place. In addition to its historic interest, Havasu Canyon, with its perennial stream, its waterfalls, and the abundance of its rich green riparian vegetation set off against the red rock walls, is one of spectacular beauty.

MILE 177.8

Lava Pinnacle. From Kanab Creek you have traveled thirty-seven miles through a canyon swinging from left to right in graceful, looping curves. Scarcely more than half a mile wide, the gorge through this section ranges from two thousand to three thousand feet deep. Best seen from the river level, the walls of the canyon rise very steeply, broken only by narrow, ledgy steps, and in many places the sky is reduced to a narrow arc. One of the finest rim viewpoints in Grand Canyon is the Toroweap overlook (on the north side, in Grand Canyon National Monument, easily reached by automobile). On the level of the Esplanade you may look down a vertical distance of nearly three thousand feet. You can see the lava pinnacle, a column of basalt which forms an island in the river, and within view downstream is Lava Falls, one of the most respected rapids in Grand Canyon.

MILE 179.25

Lava Falls. To reach this point by boat you have dropped in elevation 1,442 feet, a drop of eight feet per mile. You have encountered about eighty rapids, large and small, but many were major rapids by anyone's system of rating. On a rating scale where ten in-

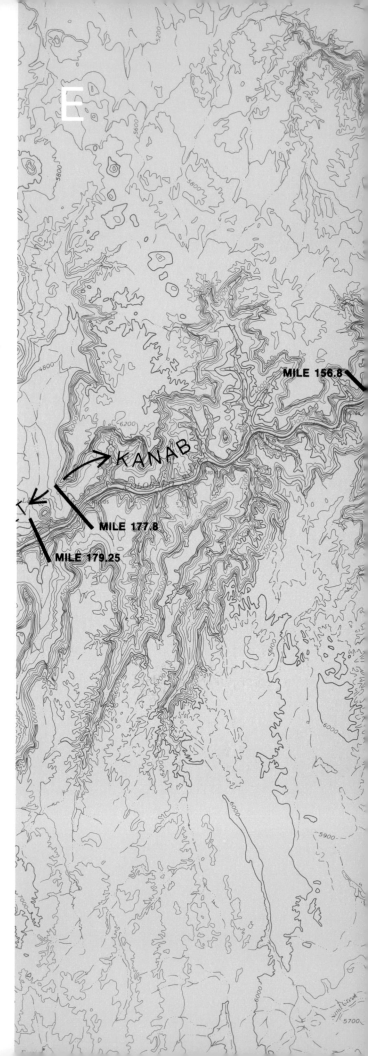

The wide platform of the Esplanade separates the inner
gorge from the outer walls of Grand Canyon, looking
upstream from the North Rim below Boysag Point, Arizona.

dicates maximum difficulty, Lava Falls in the minds of most river men is pegged at ten, rarely at nine. The canyon changes again at this point. In recent geological times, after the river had carved the canyon to near its present depth, lava cascaded over the right rim to dam the river to a height of five hundred feet or more: moreover the liquid basalt flowed on down the gorge for over sixty-five miles before it stopped. The river in time removed most of the lava but interesting remnants remain. The lava pinnacle puts voyagers on notice that Lava Falls is just over a mile below; the falls consist of a rough place where the river drops very sharply over a jumble of black rocks and boulders.

Powell portaged the rapid in 1869 and said little about it. But he was greatly intrigued with the phenomenon of molten rock damming and displacing the river. He took note of the great cone (Dutton named it Vulcan's Throne) perched on the edge of the right rim, one source of the lava flood that filled the gorge. "What a conflict of water and fire there must have been here!" he wrote. "Just imagine a river of molten rock, running down about 2,500 feet into a river of melted snow. What a seething and boiling of the waters; what clouds of steam rolled into the heavens!"[9]

In 1869, Powell had no way of knowing that at Lava Falls he still had a hundred miles to go before reaching the mouth of Grand Canyon.

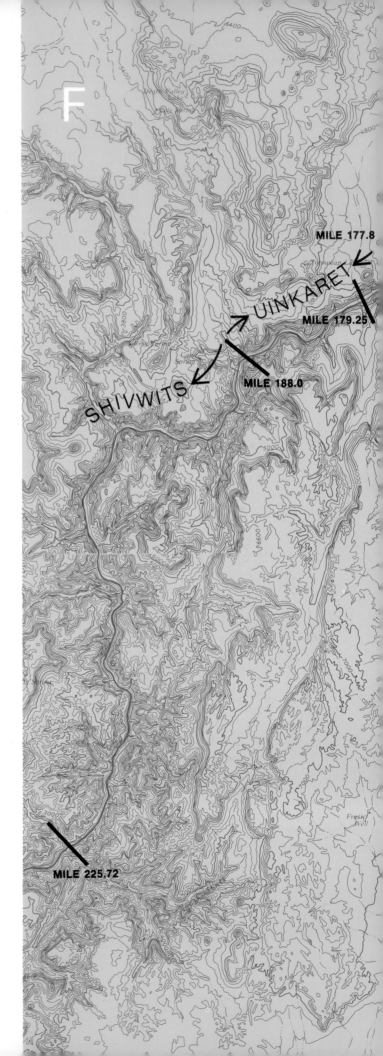

MILE 188.0

Whitmore Wash. For some distance below Lava Falls you will notice on the right side where additional rivers of basalt have poured over the rim. Indeed, these spectacular relics of vulcanism give a very special character to a short section of the canyon, a section that coincides approximately with the Uinkaret Plateau, the scene of so much volcanic activity. Whitmore Wash, which heads on the eastern slope of the volcanic Pine Mountains, has had its course changed (probably more than once) by lava flows, and enters the Colorado just downstream from a flow that reached the river at Mile 187.5.

← SHIVWITS DIVISION →

56

*Ancient lava on the wall of Grand Canyon at the
mouth of Whitmore Wash. Arizona.*

Remnants of the basalt from the Uinkaret Plateau, which flow down the canyon for so many miles, may be seen clinging to the walls here and there on either side of the river. The stream has excavated a new channel which is deeper than the one filled with lava, and in places you will see a section of gravel and sand under the lava that formed the old bed. The erosive capacity of the Colorado River, which is so nicely illustrated in this short section of the Grand Canyon, is quite beyond belief.

MILE 225.72

Diamond Creek. Not far below Whitmore Wash the Colorado starts a big swing to the south around the Shivwits Plateau, bordering it on the right and around the inside of the "horseshoe" of the Hualapai Plateau on the left. Above Diamond Creek, a complex series of faults play interesting tricks with the horizontal strata. Erosion of the walls has been extensive, the canyon widens, and you are treated to a splendid variety of majestic views unlike those in any other section of the canyon. On the north side, the Esplanade narrows, and you can catch an occasional sight of the Shivwits Plateau standing over four thousand feet above you four or five miles away. On the opposite side, the Esplanade has disappeared and there are places east of Granite Park where the rim, over a vertical mile above the Colorado, is visible over the successive strata piled up in huge steps widely separated one from the other.

Diamond Creek, the only place in Grand Canyon where you could bring wagons to the water's edge, was the historic gateway to the lower canyon used by Ives and other early explorers, and by the first tourists. The creek enters the river near the head of the Lower Granite Gorge. As you come down the river after many pleasant vistas through the spectacular canyon country below Whitmore, the hard, granitic rocks of the Precambrian begin to come up—"that dreaded rock," Powell called it. Then, almost suddenly, at the mouth of Diamond, you find yourself in a dark, gloomy gorge several hundred feet deep.

58

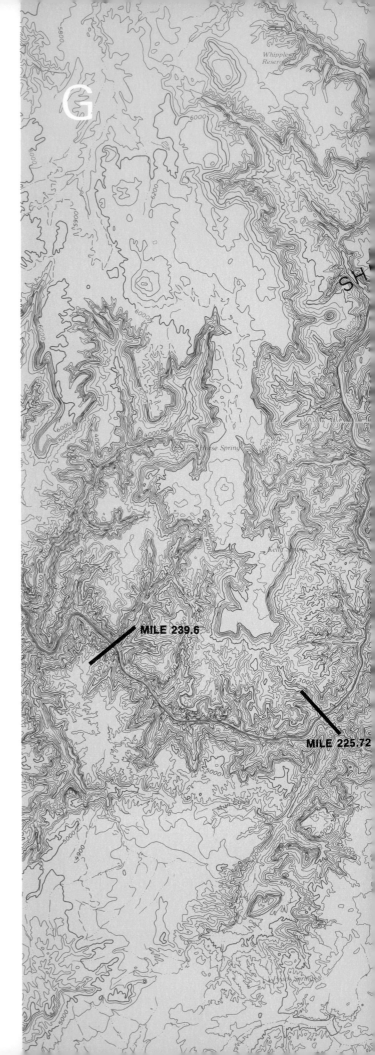

MILE 239.6

Separation Canyon. For thirteen miles from Diamond Creek the Colorado races along through the upper section of the Lower Granite Gorge. It is dark, narrow, and full of rapids; the high, rough, sharp, and very steep gneiss and granite walls brood over a canyon where there are almost no beaches or convenient places to land. The thirteen miles shook the stamina of three of Powell's men—O. G. and Senaca Howland and W. H. Dunn—and when the party reached the rapids at Mile 239.6, their spirit broke. They left the party and headed up a side canyon, intending to walk out to the Mormon settlements. They reached the top of the Shivwits Plateau where they were killed by Indians. The route traveled by the Howlands and Dunn has since been known as Separation Canyon and the rapids as Separation Rapids. The rapids are no longer a threat to travel, as they were silted up when the headwaters of Lake Mead reached this point.[10]

MILE 279.0

The site of Pierce's (Pearce's) Ferry at the end of Grand Canyon near the head of Lake Mead.[11] The lower section of Grand Canyon—the last ninety miles—has been sold short. River travelers, tired from the long run from Lee's Ferry and depressed by the somber and dangerous Lower Granite Gorge, have said little about the lower canyon. The prospect of emerging from the great canyon captured the feeling of many as they traveled the last miles. Senses already dulled by the beauties of Grand Canyon above, who had the capacity to absorb any more?

Powell probably expressed the feelings of most later travelers. He had conquered the "Great Unknown," and upon emerging from the canyon he wrote that, "the relief from danger, and the joy of success, are great. . . . Ever before us has been an unknown danger, heavier than immediate peril. . . . Now the danger is over; now the toil has ceased; now the gloom has disappeared; now the firmament is

The Grand Canyon below 59
Kanab Creek. Arizona.

bounded only by the horizon; and what an expanse of constellations can be seen!"[12]

No, Powell tells you little about the canyon through the last miles, and those who came through in later years have said but little more. Yet the Grand Canyon puts on a majestic face to the end. It is true that the Granite Gorge, which is over a thousand feet deep in places, tightly controls the river for some distance below Diamond Creek, but there is no very wide platform above the Precambrian rocks (as there is in the Upper Granite Gorge), and great cliffs, composed of the same strata you have seen all the way down the canyon, tower in massive promontories over the gloomy inner gorge. Then, about thirty-five miles below Diamond Creek, the Precambrian goes under and the river flows on through a pleasant, open, wide-bottomed canyon. In graceful tiers the cliffs on both sides rise over two thousand feet, and where the river flows through the Grand Wash Cliffs to the open country beyond, the walls soar up to over three thousand feet above the water.

The last ninety miles of Grand Canyon have some of the qualities you have seen in the sections above, but the canyon face is different. The major change is to be found in the numbers of large side canyons; every mile or so one comes in on the left or right. The numerous side streams have breached the walls of Grand Canyon to relieve the monotony that you may have experienced in that long, narrow section through the Kanab Plateau. As Ellsworth Kolb put it, it was like an unbroken avenue above Lava Falls, but below, "the numerous side canyons cut the walls in regular sections like gigantic city blocks."

Somehow in several places through this section Grand Canyon has a relaxed appearance; the walls seem to have settled back and down in quiet repose and peaceful solitude. In the Lower Granite Gorge you are reminded that the Colorado is still hard at work, but otherwise the canyon takes on a mood of magnificent serenity.

Once you have completed the run you will agree that not to have seen the last ninety miles is to have missed some of the very best of Grand Canyon. Robert B. Stanton felt that way; after having traveled five hundred miles of the river's canyons on his rail-

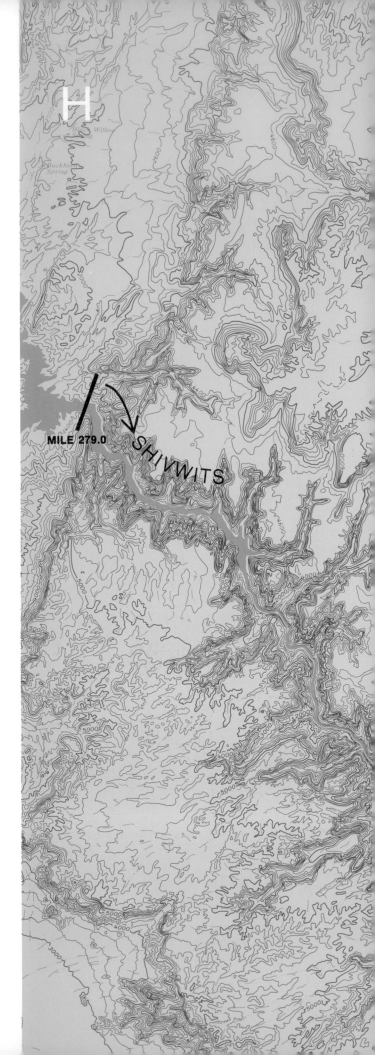

road survey, he wrote that through all these miles the canyons never lost their fascination for him, and the last few miles of Grand Canyon held him "spellbound in wonder and admiration."[13] Who could fail to agree? On the run through Grand Canyon you have been engulfed in beauty for 279 miles.

The Grand Canyon at Mile 244, two miles above the mouth of Diamond Creek. The rim (upper right) stands over a mile above the Colorado. Arizona.

(Next spread) The Grand Canyon was first seen by white men in 1540, when a detachment of Coronado's expedition reached a place on the South Rim near Desert View. From a point covered with low pines, the explorers had a good view of the river and the canyon as it opened out upstream to the north.

THE ROAD

4
Western Mystery

THE GREAT BARRANCA   PUERTO DE BUCARELI
PYRAMIDS OF ZION

5
Golden Gate

RECKLESS BREED · MORMON CORRIDOR
A PRACTICABLE AND ECONOMICAL ROUTE

6
Dixieland

BIG CAÑON OF THE COLORADO
CENTRAL ROAD TO ARIZONA · COTTON MISSION

*A section of the old pioneer road at the base of
the Vermilion Cliffs near Lee's Ferry, Arizona.*

4
Western Mystery

THE GREAT BARRANCA

Within fifty years after Columbus dropped anchor in the New World, a Spanish exploring party had reached the rim of Grand Canyon. Columbus was looking for a new route to the Orient, but when it appeared that he had come upon a land new to Europeans, the Spanish pioneers, with incredible speed, explored the American continents.

Since, as they found, the two continents formed a barrier squarely across any western passage to India, the explorers turned to search for a road through, over, or around this frustrating obstacle to the opening of commerce between Spain and the East. As they swarmed about, they encountered everywhere the Indian tribes. And when, in 1521, Cortés subdued the Aztecs, a new era began in American history.

America now became a land of promise. For the next twenty-five years, Spanish exploring parties ranged far into the interior wilderness of North America. Men looked for new "Mexicos" rather than water passages and commercial routes. They imagined that the way ahead was filled with wealthy and populous cities. They seized upon hearsay and rumor, and were over-credulous of the stories told by the Indians. Thus, the dancing chimera of fabulous places like El Dorado and Quivira, the Seven Cities and the land of Amazons beckoned, promising untold riches in the lands beyond the horizon.

A classic example of the naiveté, bravery, foolishness, and doggedness of explorers in the age of El Dorado was illustrated in the expedition of 1540–1542, sent into the heart of the North American continent and directed by Francisco Vázquez de Coronado. Rumor of populous Indian cities in the distant interior, far north of the frontier settlement in Mexico, so intrigued the viceroy of New Spain that he sent the Franciscan friar, Marcos de Niza, to investigate. The viceroy instructed the friar to take note of everything en route and to look for any indication of water communication between the North (Atlantic) and the South (Pacific) seas, and to report whether the Indians lived in scattered settlements or in villages and towns. Marcos probably traveled as far as the Zuñi villages in New Mexico, and, from some distance, he viewed one of the towns, which he called Cíbola, located in a province of the same name.

The good friar reported just what everyone hoped to hear. Cíbola, he said, "is larger than the city of Mexico," and six other towns were also nearby. Off to the west somewhere was the city of Totonteac, larger even than the seven cities of Cíbola. "It has so many houses and people," Marcos reported, "there is

Mystic Falls below Point Imperial in the Nankoweap Basin, Grand Canyon. Arizona.

Hopi Indians en route to the Grand Canyon salt deposits carved their clan symbols on the rocks at Willow Springs. Arizona.

no end to it."[1] His glowing account was enough for the viceroy—you could trust a friar to be accurate, couldn't you? At the head of a military and exploring expedition of about three hundred men, Coronado was dispatched to conquer and claim the land of the Seven Cities, the kingdom of Totonteac, and other wondrous places.

Coronado reached Cíbola early in July, 1540, but he found none of the glittering wealth reported by Marcos, who very soon found an excuse to return to Mexico.[2] He was committed to continue; if Cíbola was a hoax, probably the real prize would soon show itself on some distant horizon.

The Zuñis pointed the way. Off to the northwest, they said, was the kingdom of Tusayán—which also contained seven towns. Coronado sent Pedro de Tovar to reconnoiter. He reached the Hopi villages of northeastern Arizona but again, disappointment. Where were the cities larger and richer than Mexico? What of the country to the west? The Hopis told their still credulous visitors that there was a large river to the west—the Colorado. Follow down the course of that river for several days' journey, they said, and you would come to a nation of tall people, of giants.[3]

A river west of the Hopis, in the valley of which lived a tall people? Possibly they lived in Totonteac, or another of the fabulous places reported by Friar Marcos. When Tovar relayed the story, Coronado immediately sent out from Cíbola an exploring party of about twelve men under his chief officer, García López de Cárdenas. The explorers stopped by Tusayán where the Hopis offered provisions and guides for the journey ahead.

As it happened, the Hopis were thoroughly familiar with the country lying west of their villages to the Colorado River. They lived on branches of the Little Colorado and knew of the great gorge where it entered the Grand Canyon. For at least two centuries before the coming of the Spaniards the Hopis had gathered salt found on ledges on the left bank of the river, about two miles below the mouth of the Little Colorado in Grand Canyon. To reach that remote spot, the Indians generally traveled by way of Moenkopi and Willow Springs to the north side of the Little Colorado. Then, over a perilous trail in Salt

68

Trail Canyon, they descended nearly three thousand feet to the canyon floor. Thence they walked on down to the mouth of the canyon about seven miles. As a rule they returned by the same route.

The gorge of the Little Colorado and the adjacent section of Grand Canyon was a sacred place to the Indians. The salt-gathering expeditions were pilgrimages. The Hopis performed rites en route, they inscribed their clan symbols on the rocks at Willow Springs, and they placed offerings at wayside shrines. To return with a bag full of salt was evidence that the pilgrimage had been made, and there were varied uses for the precious substance brought back from the canyon at the cost of such enormous effort.[4]

The Hopis' knowledge of the Grand Canyon carried far beyond the region of the Little Colorado. They—particularly the people of Oraibi—were active traders. They traveled west along the South Rim of Grand Canyon to trade with the Havasupais, who lived deep in their canyon home. They were also acquainted with the Hualapais, neighbors of the Havasupais toward the west. Then, along the lower Colorado River in the vicinity of The Needles lived the Mohaves, who probably were the people the Hopis had in mind when they told the Spaniards of the "tall men." The men of this tribe often attained six feet, and they must have seemed gigantic to the Hopis, who seldom reached over about five and a half feet. The trail between Oraibi and The Needles by way of Grand Canyon was an important aboriginal trade route. The Hopis carried pottery and cotton textiles to trade with the Havasupais for red paint and deerskins. Not long after the coming of the white man some important new items were added—woolen textiles, horses, and guns.[5]

Thus, García López de Cárdenas and his party, dispatched by Coronado to explore the country west of Tusayán, had at their disposal the best guides they could have found. It was during the summer—probably August—of 1540, when the Spaniards headed west from the Hopi villages bound for the "large river" and the land of the tall men. Although the documentary sources are brief, the explorers probably followed the Hopi trading trail which crossed over to the south side of the Little Colorado near the present site of Cameron. Their route then paralleled Arizona State Highway 64, and this brought them to the South Rim at Desert View Point, or possibly at one of the other points a few miles west, such as Lipan Point.

The first Europeans to look into Grand Canyon reacted much as visitors have ever since. They guessed about distance, the depth of the canyon, and the width of the river. They estimated quite accurately that the air line distance from rim to rim was about eight or nine miles (three to four leagues). From a point covered with low, twisted pines, the explorers had a good view of the Grand Canyon as it opened out to the north. The Colorado, clearly visible nearly five thousand feet below them, seemed only about six feet (a fathom they called it) wide.

The party spent three days on the rim looking for a way down into the canyon. On the third day Captain Pablo de Melgosa, Juan Galeras, and a third man, these men "being the most agile," found a rough and difficult trail, probably the one which on occasion the Hopis used to reach the salt deposits near the mouth of the Little Colorado. It was somewhat less hazardous than the route via Salt Trail Canyon and the gorge of the Little Colorado, and it was accessible from the Hopi-Havasupai trading trail along the South Rim.

But the Spaniards could not find a way to reach the bottom of the canyon and, after going about a third of the way down, they turned back. The river, they reported, was very much wider than it appeared from the rim. And some of the rocks of the canyon walls, which from above seemed no bigger than a man, they found upon close examination to be higher than the great Giralda bell tower in the city of Sevilla. The explorers pushed on west from the Desert View area toward the land of the tall men, but when their water gave out they returned to the Hopi villages and then to Cíbola, or Zuñi.

Cárdenas had found the western river, but the trip "brought no other results," said Pedro de Castañeda, who wrote about it later. The Spaniards had been unable to reach the land of the tall men, and they had learned nothing of the kingdom of Totonteac or other fabulous places. What these European discoverers felt about Grand Canyon we may only imagine;

the full written report by Pedro de Sotomayor has been lost. The interesting fact does appear, in the brief accounts extant, that the Spaniards referred to the great gorge not as a *cañón* (anglicized to canyon, a word not in use in this sense in 1540), but as a *barranca*, the Spanish word for cliff or precipice, derived from Greek and Latin.[6]

From Cíbola, Coronado turned east to invade the Pueblos of the Rio Grande valley—the province of Tiguex—and he eventually reached Quivira on the plains of Kansas. But there he turned back, disappointed in the meager rewards of the exploration, and he reached Mexico before the end of 1542.

No better luck followed Hernando de Alarcón, who was ordered to keep in touch by sea with Coronado's land party. At about the time that Cárdenas arrived at the South Rim of Grand Canyon, Alarcón reached the mouth of the Colorado. He sailed up the river (which he named the Buena Guía) some distance, but he learned nothing of the whereabouts of Coronado.[7]

Francisco Vázquez de Coronado and Hernando de Alarcón had done some great things. They had found a "new" Mexico though it scarcely matched the splendor of the Aztecs' realm. They had discovered and explored the Colorado River, both at the Grand Canyon and throughout much of its lower course, and had opened routes by land and sea that connected Mexico with the newly discovered lands. In their enthusiasm to beat the luck of Cortés, the explorers had spent more time looking for Indian cities than in probing the wilderness for waterways and straits connecting the North and South seas. The geographical knowledge produced by these early explorers was soon elaborated by imaginative cartographers whose portrayal of the Colorado and other waterways on their maps held out hope to those who continued to dream of finding a western water route from Europe across America to India.[8]

PUERTO DE BUCARELI

Not long after Coronado returned home the great silver bonanzas were discovered on the central plateau north of Mexico City. As men rushed to open mines at Zacatecas, Guanajuato, and elsewhere, the land of Cíbola and Quivira was forgotten temporarily. But, as the mining frontier moved rapidly northward to reach the modern state of Chihuahua, interest in the Pueblo country revived. In 1598, Juan de Oñate led a colonizing expedition to take possession of New Mexico, but Spanish power after that was not extended very far beyond the narrow valley of the Rio Grande. The country to the west, beyond the Zuñi and Hopi villages, remained a mystery for many years. The few who ventured into it usually did so only on a brief reconnaissance to prospect, to search for fabulous places, or to acquire geographical knowledge.

In a notable exploration to the "South Sea," begun in the fall of 1604 and ended in the spring of 1605, Juan de Oñate, by way of the Hopi villages and Bill Williams River, crossed from the Rio Grande to the Colorado, which he named the Buena Esperanza—river of Good Hope. When the Oñate party reached the Little Colorado, the name Río Colorado—from the red color of its waters—was given the stream which the explorers thought was the main river. This appears to be the earliest use of the name Colorado to describe the river, which already had a number of other names. Before turning back, Oñate went downstream to the Gulf of California where he took possession of the river for Spain.[9]

From the Indians along the way Oñate learned of many interesting things which later writers elaborated to such an extent that the land began to acquire an aura to match anything dreamed of during the age of El Dorado. Rumors were heard of a strait connecting the North and South seas, and stories were told of Lake Copala, the ancient home of the Aztecs, and other wonderful places.[10] Despite these beckoning wonders, Spain took little interest in the Colorado River until 1769 when Alta California was colonized, an interest that was intensified in 1776 when Juan Bautista de Anza founded San Francisco.

Even as they planned the Anza venture, viceregal officials in Mexico City knew that the settlements in California were as remote from a supportive base as any in North America. Monterey and Santa Fe were located on about the same latitude. Why not open communication between the two and thus strengthen the coastal settlements? The viceroy instructed the friars of Sonora and New Mexico to investigate this possibility. Little talk now about the imaginary wonders of the wilderness: the good old quixotic days on the northern frontier were passing as Spain faced up to the practical matter of supporting a frontier that extended from San Francisco to St. Louis.

On hand at the right time and place was the right man—Francisco Tomás Hermengildo Garcés. A Franciscan sent to Sonora after the expulsion of the Jesuits, Garcés was assigned to San Xavier del Bac. He got on well with the local Pimas and, wishing to extend the missionary field, he made occasional solitary forays north to the Gila and west to the California coast. In 1775, Garcés accompanied the Anza overland colonizing expedition as far as the Yuma crossing where he struck off by himself. Mindful of the viceroy's instructions, the friar traveled upriver to the land of the Mohave Indians. Turning west, he opened a new route to the Pacific Coast. Not satisfied, Garcés decided to head east from the Mohave villages in an attempt to reach the Hopi towns [11]

In company with some Indian guides, he set out over well-traveled trails that took him through Truxton Wash (Arroyo de San Bernabé) to Peach Springs (Pozos de San Basilio). Going on, he heard of the Havasupai (Jabesuas) Indians, and his guides urged the padre to visit them. "Desirous as I was of seeing more Indians" and of learning about more routes, he followed the guides. The next day, June 20, 1776, Garcés traveled ten leagues ("five leagues east, two northeast, and three north") and "over most difficult terrain" dropped down into Havasu Canyon to the village of the Havasupais.

The first European to visit the Havasupais, Francisco Garcés probably reached their village by way of a foot trail in Hualapai Canyon. At one narrow place he found the trail a little more than three handsbreadth wide with a high cliff on one side and a "hideous abyss" on the other. Some distance farther on, it was necessary for the padre to leave his mule and to go down over one place by a wooden ladder and con-

tinue on foot to the village of Supai, which Garcés named San Antonio. The descent by this old trail has taken the breath away from a good many hardy souls who have attempted it later. [12]

"All the earth here is red," were the words Garcés used to describe the canyon home of the Havasupai Indians. The four-hundred-foot-high walls of the narrow canyon—not much over a quarter of a mile wide in the village area—ledgy and dark red, were carved out of one of the principal red sandstone strata in Grand Canyon—the Supai formation—given this name by geologists because of its classic expression in Havasu Canyon. But even the lighter-colored strata of the two-thousand-foot-high walls of the outer canyon appeared to be red in the early morning and in the late evening light. And Garcés, enjoying the long shadows of a June evening in the village, must have noted the high eastern outer wall, Manakacha Point. The rays of the setting sun colored the sheer cliff a dozen hues of red before the last light on the towering point finally failed.

The padre found the Havasupais friendly and hospitable; he stayed with them five days, and on his return from the Hopi towns he remained six more days. Garcés got on so easily and naturally with Indians that his friend and colleague Father Font said that "he appears to be but an Indian himself." For hours he would sit with them cross-legged in the fire circle. He enjoyed the talk and relished Indian food. [13]

During the first visit the Indians treated him to venison, beef, corn, beans, greens, and mescal, all of which they had in good supply. Garcés noticed that his hosts had cows and branded horses they had brought in from the Hopi towns, as well as other items such as garden tools, hatchets, and red cloth. He estimated that there were thirty-four families in the village. Since some of the Indians were quite light in color, he speculated that this was perhaps owing to their residence deep down in the canyon where the sunlight was limited.

Taking leave of his hosts on June 25, Garcés left Havasu Canyon by the steep Topocoba horse trail up Lee Canyon, which he found "horrifying" and "painful." Camp that night was made among the pines and junipers of the Coconino Plateau, and the next day,

(Next spread) Cliffs and winter storm. Zion National Park. Utah.

HILDEGARD HAMILTON

June 26, after traveling four leagues, Garcés came out on the South Rim; he was very likely the first European since López de Cárdenas (a matter of 236 years) to view the great gorge.[14]

From where he stood on the rim, Garcés could see that the Colorado had cut the canyon through a very large range, or sierra—the Kaibab-Coconino Plateau—that trended north and south. Through this portal the river flowed, and he named it the Pass of Bucareli (Puerto de Bucareli). Thus the Grand Canyon was first named, and at the place where it reached its greatest depth.

Garcés' name was an excellent choice. The Colorado, where it breaks through the eastern wall of the Kaibab Monocline, has formed a huge notch where the wall has been cut away. The full effect of this is best obtained from points some miles directly east of Grand Canyon where the "pass" is clearly visible.

From just where on the South Rim Garcés viewed the canyon is conjectural, but it probably was in the vicinity of one of the points now bearing Indian names (Paiute, Jicarilla, Pima) west of Grand Canyon Village. During that day (June 26th) the padre may have had additional views of the canyon, perhaps in the vicinity of Grand View Point. As he traveled eastward over the Hopi trail, and from points somewhat distant, an occasional glance over his shoulder would have kept in view the Puerto de Bucareli.[15]

On the South Rim, and precisely where millions since have had their first view of the Grand Canyon, Francisco Garcés in 1776 had reached the point where Cárdenas had turned back in 1540. He had closed the gap between that point and the one reached by Hernando de Alarcón on the lower Colorado. He had become acquainted with the tribes of the lower river and had traveled the ancient trade routes by which these tribes communicated with the Havasupais and Hopis. And he had found a road of potential interest to Spain, one closely parallel to the Colorado River and farther north than that opened by Oñate in 1604–1605.

He had, moreover, given a number of first names to the South Rim country and elsewhere. His Puerto de Bucareli commemorated the name of Antonio María de Bucareli y Ursúa, one of the greater viceroys of New Spain (1771–1777), who had been the prime mover in opening the land road between Sonora and California, in sending Anza to strengthen the California settlements, and who had urged the friars to open communication between the isolated northern frontiers of the viceroyalty.[16] The latter objective Garcés had completed almost single-handed; however, he had yet to reach the Hopi villages.

From the South Rim he pressed on over a well-established trail to the Little Colorado, the Indian name for which, he wrote, was Jaquesila (he called it San Pedro Jaquesila) and thence by way of Moenkopi Wash to Oraibi.

Garcés was received so coolly by the Hopis that he gave up plans to travel on to Zuñi. The Indians refused him food, would not accept gifts, and all but ordered him out of the village. He wrote a note to the Spanish missionary at Zuñi, climbed on his mule, and headed back the way he had come, with a smile on his face. The date was July 4, 1776.

Back in his home mission at San Xavier del Bac in September, the peripatetic padre added some lengthy commentaries to his diary. He named the tribes he had visited or heard about and summarized their condition. He offered suggestions for defending the frontier and founding missions, but he had little to say about the route he had opened between California and Oraibi and the South Rim of Grand Canyon. There must be, he remarked, a better way from New Mexico to the coast, and in this he was in agreement with his Franciscan colleague Father Silvestre Vélez de Escalante, missionary in New Mexico, who, at the moment Garcés arrived in Oraibi, was making final preparations to leave on a journey through the Ute country to California.[17]

PYRAMIDS OF ZION

As one of his first assignments in New Mexico, Franciscan Father Escalante spent more than a year in the village of Zuñi. Mindful of the viceroy's interest in locating new routes, in June, 1775, he had journeyed to the Hopi villages to learn what he could

*The South Rim of the Grand Canyon fro
Crystal Rapid, Mile 98.5. Arizon*

about the lands to the west. A Havasupai Indian at Oraibi told him of the difficulties of traveling directly westward from the Pueblo country. There was a high sierra to cross, and the Río Grande de los Misterios (The Great River of Mystery) running west along the base of the range was impassable. The River of Mystery! One more name for the Colorado and a good one it was!

Having developed this information Escalante concluded that a practical route to the coast must be sought through the land of the Utes north and west of Santa Fe. When his superior, Father Francisco Atanasio Domínguez, arrived to make an inspection of the religious establishment in New Mexico, Escalante prevailed upon him to undertake a journey of discovery. The friars set out from Santa Fe on July 29, 1776, and with Bernardo de Miera, expedition cartographer, and a few associates, they made a pioneer traverse through western Colorado and northern Utah to Utah Lake.

There, apparently giving no thought to finding such places as Copala, and other frontier chimera of an earlier day, the Spaniards headed south to reach the latitude of Monterey where they planned to turn west again. A snowstorm early in October caught them not far from Sevier Lake. Rather than risk the uncertainties of continuing on to California, they decided to return to New Mexico. On October 12, near Cedar City, the little band crossed over the divide separating the Great Basin from the drainage of the Colorado River. During the next twenty-seven days the explorers found a way across the northern side of the Grand Canyon country, the first white men to do so.[18]

From the rim of the Great Basin, Domínguez and Escalante worked their way down along the base of Hurricane Cliffs. After the snow and wind of the higher elevations, they were comforted by the mild weather; the trees were still in leaf, flowers were blooming, and they saw some mesquite, found only in warm climates, and grape vines. The discoverers soon reached the Virgin River just below the point where it broke through the Hurricane Cliffs and flowed through Timpoweap Canyon. Taking note of the hot, mineralized springs, Bernardo de Miera named the

stream the Sulphurous River of the Pyramids (Río Sulfúreo de las Pirámides).

It was a good name. On their way to the Virgin, and for some few miles after they left it, the explorers must have caught glimpses of the cliffs and towers and monuments visible to the east. They could have seen West Temple, Mt. Kinesava, South Guardian Angel, and Smithsonian Butte, among others. On his map of the expedition's travels, Bernardo de Miera with some accuracy drew the towers, buttes, and pyramids, the first portrayal of some of the prominent features of Zion National Park and environs.[19]

There is nothing in the contemporary record to indicate that the Spaniards gave the Virgin River any other name than "Río Sulfúreo" or "Río Sulfúreo de las Pirámides," a name that remained on the maps (though not always identified with the Virgin River) for a number of years. The present name was applied sometime after 1776, and it was in common usage when Frémont came along in 1844. He adopted the Spanish form "Río Virgen," but this was subsequently anglicized in part to "Rio Virgin," a name that has proved more popular than "Virgin River."

Domínguez and Escalante described in some detail the life and habits of the Indians they visited. Before leaving the Great Basin they had passed from the Ute (Yutas the Spaniards called them) country into lands occupied by Paiutes (Payuchis, the Spanish name, now the Southern Paiutes), a gentle people who lived in small bands and managed to make a living from the meager natural resources. Near Cedar City Escalante noted that the Huascari Paiutes (Guacaros, as Miera had it on his map) subsisted on piñon nuts, grass seeds, and rabbits. They planted no corn. They dressed poorly. In describing the female attire the diarist said it consisted of buckskin hanging from the waist and this "hardly covered that what can not be looked upon without peril." Along the Virgin River the explorers were in the territory of the Parusis, who watered corn and squash patches with "very well-made" irrigation ditches.

The Spaniards did not linger by the Virgin. Moving south along the Hurricane Cliffs they hoped to reach the Colorado River, but, when some Parusis Indians told them a deep canyon would block their

76

Principal Explorations
and Settlements
1540-1868

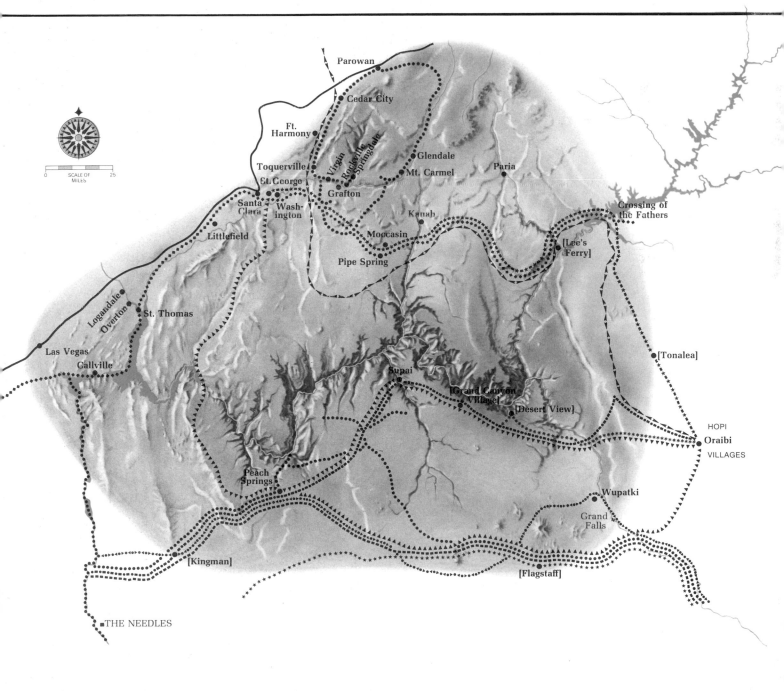

passage, they climbed the cliffs and headed in an easterly direction across the Arizona Strip. They were in open country now. In the clear October air they were within easy sight of the Vermilion Cliffs and the White Cliffs (on his map Miera labeled them the "Sierra Blanca") to the north and the Uinkaret Mountains to the south. From the Yubuincariri, or Uinkaret, band of Paiutes, who did not plant but subsisted by hunting and gathering, the Europeans bought a *fanega* of seeds and a quantity of tunas, or cactus fruit.

The Spaniards reached Kanab Creek about eight miles below Fredonia, and near the Arizona-Utah line they crossed the Kaibab Plateau, at the eastern base of which they happened upon a small Indian encampment. The Spaniards camped for two days with their hosts. For one thing, they needed to recover from an illness caused from eating the seeds and tunas. Escalante observed that Father Domínguez was so "ill from a pain in the rectum" that he could not move. Miera was treated by the Indian medicine man who "doctored him with songs and ceremonies." When Escalante learned of this he condemned such practice as "entirely superstitious" and "contrary to the evangelical and divine law." In his diary he lectured Miera for not knowing better, and he went on to discuss some of the problems of propagating the faith on the New Mexican frontier.

Rested now and "cured," the Spaniards pressed on, and during the next three days they took an easy trail—a half circle—around the base of the Paria Plateau. They watered at House Rock Spring and Jacob's Pools and on October 26, 1776, crossed the Paria River at its mouth (they named it the Santa Teresa) and went into camp on the bank of the Colorado River where they stayed for six days. Although Escalante refers to the Río Colorado, he also called it the Río Grande de los Cosninas (one more name for the great river!) after a contemporary name for the Havasupai Indians.[20]

Domínguez and Escalante were the first Europeans to arrive at the place where nearly a hundred years later John D. Lee established a ferry across the Colorado. Remote and isolated, Lee called the place "Lonely Dell." To the Spaniards who discovered it,

the question was whether they could ever leave it. They found themselves closed in by high cliffs on three sides and they could not ford the river. With a touch of humor they named the spot San Benito Get-Out-If-You-Can (Salsipuedes). Desperate, the friars managed to struggle over the Echo Cliffs at a point about three miles up the Paria and, after several days, they found a difficult ford across the Colorado, later known as the Crossing of the Fathers. Soon on more familiar ground, they headed for the Hopi and Zuñi villages and reached Santa Fe, January 2, 1777.[21]

The three Franciscan friars had done more to extend Spain's claim to North American territory than anybody sent to the frontier since Coronado. Garcés, who applauded the revival of the old passion for discovering and taking possession of new lands, had opened communication between California and New Mexico. Domínguez and Escalante failed to do this on their entrada in latitudes farther north, but they discovered a vast circle of new country in the heart of the Rockies. They had accomplished all of this during the last half of 1776, within six months after Juan Bautista de Anza had laid the foundations of San Francisco.

The Franciscans discovered the Grand Canyon country. Although García López de Cárdenas in 1540 enjoyed the first view of the great gorge, Garcés, Domínguez, and Escalante went much farther than he did. They saw the Grand Canyon at its deepest part and named it, and they reached the water's edge at its head at Lee's Ferry.

They crossed the major streams that fell into the canyon; they caught glimpses of the southern escarpments of Utah's High Plateaus, and they came into full view of the isolated peaks that break the monotony of the flat, angular landscape of the Colorado Plateau—the San Francisco Peaks and Bill Williams Mountain, and the Uinkarets. They laid out these discoveries on maps of surprising accuracy. On his map of the Domínguez-Escalante expedition, Miera even attempted to describe the Grand Canyon when he said the Rio Colorado was enclosed by very steep walls of red rock.[22] They came to know the plant and animal life, the lack of water, the purity of air, and the quality of light. They became acquainted with the

Indians and learned how they survived in a land of great beauty but where the conditions of life were difficult. They named the tribes and reported intertribal relations. They put names on the land. They left a basic set of primary documents descriptive of all these things, and they appraised their discoveries in continental perspective.

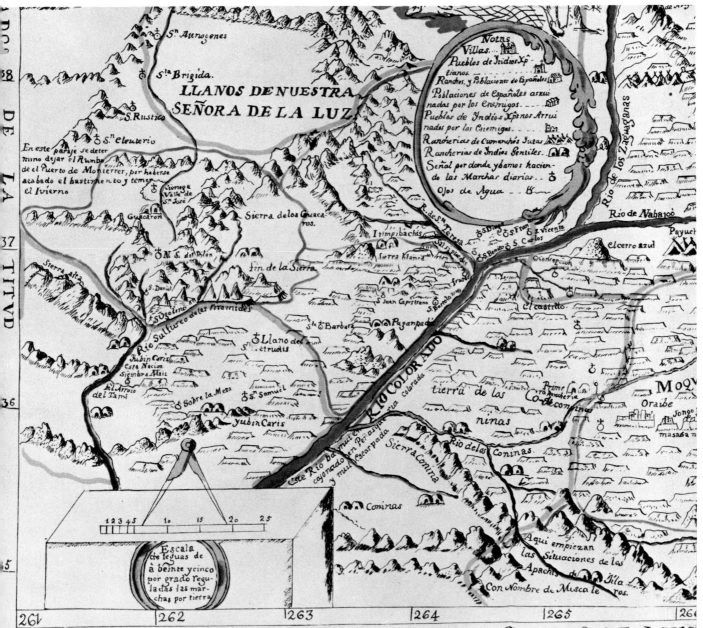

Drawn by Bernardo de Miera y Pacheco in 1778, this map (section) shows the region explored by the Domínguez-Escalante Expedition in 1776, and it is the first to portray the Grand Canyon country in some detail. The "Rio Sulfureo de las Piramides" is the Virgin River; the "R. de Sta. Teresa" is the Paria River; the "Rio de los Coninas" is the Little Colorado; "Rio Colorado" preceded by words descriptive of the Grand Canyon appears in the Marble Canyon section.

5
Golden Gate

RECKLESS BREED

Spanish explorers left the Grand Canyon country in 1778, never to return. In 1810, Spain's American empire began to fall apart in revolution, and her richest possession, the Viceroyalty of New Spain, emerged as independent Mexico in 1821.

If the Spanish discoverers of the Grand Canyon country were concerned primarily with roads to California and India and with the founding of posts and missions among the tribes, those who followed them in the Mexican period were more interested in the economic exploitation of the immediate region. Mexican traders based at Santa Fe and at other points along the Rio Grande began to fan out through the Rockies. And with controls against foreigners now lifted, they were soon joined by enterprising Americans who sought profits from furs.

Few were articulate; probably most were illiterate. But the trappers during the great years of fur trade, which had passed its peak by 1844, were the first to map in accurate detail the middle and southern Rockies, much of the Colorado River system, together with extensive reaches of the Great Basin. Naturally the mountain men first sought out the choicest beaver country, where the animals were

plentiful and the plews fine. The upper Colorado and the basin of the Green were good beaver country, but the great canyons below the confluence of the two streams were pretty tough hunting. Beaver lived in these canyons all right, but the record, such as it is, indicates little trapping in the region of Cataract and Glen canyons and none at all in the Grand Canyon below Lee's Ferry. For a time there was a burst of activity along the lower course of the Colorado below Grand Canyon and in the valley of the Gila.

The trappers were a wild lot of free men who left the bonds of society to romp and roam through Mexican territory—not only following the trails so laboriously discovered by the Spaniards before them, but opening new ones. Among those who left their mark on the southwestern wilderness—Mexico's northwestern frontier—were Sylvester and James Ohio Pattie, father and son, Ewing Young, George C. Yount, William Workman, Kit Carson, Pegleg Smith, Pauline Weaver, Bill Williams, Milton Sublette, Michel Roubidoux, and Antoine Leroux. They were, in Cleland's words, a "reckless breed."[1]

Some of those trappers who traveled between the upper and lower basins of the Colorado were the first after the Spaniards to see the Grand Canyon country. What they had to say about the great gorges, if not vague, was uncomplimentary. The prospect of moving traps and other heavy equipment down precipitous canyon walls held no appeal. James Ohio Pattie and a number of others in early 1826 traveled upstream along the Colorado, skirting the Grand Canyon. Of the river so constricted by the rims and cliffs and canyon walls he said, "These horrid mountains, which so cage it up, as to deprive all human beings of the ability to descend to its banks, and make use of its waters." When Pattie had passed beyond the canyon country he said, "No mortal has the power of describing the pleasure I felt, when I could once more reach the banks of the river."[2]

William A. Ferris opened his account of the trappers' *Life in the Rocky Mountains* (1836) with a short descriptive chapter on the "chanion" of the Colorado below the mouth of the Green River. For two or three hundred miles, he said, the river was confined to a "canal" in places more than a "thousand feet deep." Even those familiar with the great works of nature would "recoil with terror" from a view of the narrow gorge. From the rim, "many a half-starved trapper" has seen what appeared to be a willow-lined brook which in reality was a mighty river. In places the walls were so close together, Ferris added, that the bottoms disappeared. Here the river, compressed to one fourth its width, rushed along like Niagara, and its navigation was impracticable. He also observed that the tributary streams were confined by canyon walls, thus deflecting travel to the open areas back some distance from the Colorado.[3] Indeed, once they had had a taste of the Grand Canyon country the trappers sought ways to bypass it altogether.

The traders, who succeeded in opening a trail from New Mexico to California, felt the same way about the region. From Santa Fe, Antonio Armíjo brought a trading party cross-country to the Crossing of the Fathers in Glen Canyon which he reached in December, 1829. Fording the Colorado, Armíjo then traveled across the Arizona Strip to the Virgin River by a route parallel to that opened by Domínguez and Escalante years before. The New Mexicans went on to California, disposed of their woolen goods in exchange for horses and mules, and returned by the same route early in 1830. The Armíjo venture marked the opening of regular trade between New Mexico and California, a commerce that lasted for years, but

after 1830 the traffic bypassed the Grand Canyon country, since passage through it was slow, rough, difficult, and hazardous.

In the meantime, trappers from Taos and Santa Fe had worked their way across the upper Colorado and Green to the Great Basin, and in 1826 Jedediah Smith of the Rocky Mountain Fur Company opened a trail from Salt Lake to southern California. The route—the so-called Old Spanish Trail—wound about over the map for twelve hundred miles. Until 1848, it was the main trail between Santa Fe and Los Angeles. It reached a northernmost point at the Green River crossing in Utah. Then it followed a southwesterly direction, passing through Cedar City, Mountain Meadows, the lower Virgin River, and Las Vegas. The first party to travel the entire length of the route was led by two American adventurers, William Wolfskill and George C. Yount, who crossed from Santa Fe to California during the winter of 1830–1831, one year after Armíjo's pioneer trading venture.[4]

The trail to California was long, but it had its advantages: it headed the great canyons of the Colorado; it avoided the belligerent Apaches living south of Grand Canyon; it threaded the Ute country and the Utes welcomed trade, especially those living athwart the trail in central Utah. Woolen goods produced in New Mexico, primarily a sheep country, were sold or exchanged for horses in California where they were plentiful. The Utes of central Utah introduced a major trade item—slaves. For woolens or for horses the Utes were happy to exchange Indian slaves, mainly Paiutes, who were taken to either New Mexico or California and sold as domestic servants. The master slaver was the Ute chieftain Joseph Walker (Wakara, Walkara, and other spellings), who remained a powerful figure in the Utah country until some time after the coming of the Mormons, who offered the first serious challenge to his authority.[5] By then, with the arrival of the settlers, the wild, reckless days in the mountains had come to an end.

Even after the opening of the Spanish Trail from New Mexico to California, men still dreamed of finding a water route from the Rockies to the coast. This was thought to be possible because contemporary maps showed a number of rivers between the Colum-

Hikers in Lower Meriwitica Canyon, Hualapai Plateau. Arizona.

Canyons and cliffs of the Kolob section, Zion National Park,
from the site of the pioneer Mormon settlement of Fort Harmony. Utah.

bia and the Colorado flowing from the Rockies to the Pacific. These fictitious streams grew out of some geographical misconceptions entertained by the eighteenth-century Spanish explorers and publicized in the *Political Essay on the Kingdom of New Spain* (1811), written by the eminent scientist Alexander von Humboldt. The explorers had not realized the existence of the Great Basin and had thought that streams flowing westward from the Rockies must reach the Pacific Ocean. Imaginative cartographers of the day, with fragmentary knowledge at hand, simply drew in complete rivers on their maps. One such stream was the San Buenaventura River, actually the Sevier River of Utah, which Domínguez, Escalante, and Micra had discovered and named in 1776.[6]

The prince of dreamers was John C. Frémont. On his second exploration of the West, Frémont was sent by the government to examine and describe the region from South Pass to the Pacific and from the valley of the Columbia to the Spanish coastal possessions. From the Dalles on the Columbia, he turned south, expecting to find the San Buenaventura River. He scaled the Sierra Nevada, traveled southward through the Central Valley of California, and then headed back over the Spanish Trail via the Mojave River, Las Vegas, and the "Rio Virgin." From Little Salt Lake, near the later site of Cedar City, he continued on north and, paralleling the earlier routes of Domínguez and Escalante, and Jedediah Smith, reached Utah Lake in May, 1844.

At Utah Lake Frémont correctly concluded that between the Columbia and the Colorado all Rocky Mountain streams simply had no outlet to the sea; they were contained by a vast interior drainage which he named the Great Basin. Thus he exposed the mythical nature of the geography exemplified by the San Buenaventura and popularized by Humboldt and others. Jedediah Smith and other fur men earlier had established the same fact, but Frémont's widely circulated report, issued in 1845, made it a certainty to the public. If there remained any doubts about the accuracy of these conclusions, the explorer dispelled them during a third expedition which took him from Great Salt Lake to California by way of the Humboldt River (named by Frémont to honor the German scientist he so much admired), Truckee Pass, and the Sierra Nevada.

The findings of the third expedition were summarized by Frémont in his *Geographical Memoir*, published by Congress in mid-1848, which was accompanied by the great map of the trans-Rocky Mountain West drawn by Charles Preuss. It portrayed in detail the entire West from the forty-ninth parallel south to include the possessions newly acquired from Mexico, and from the upper Missouri and the upper Rio Grande and the Continental Divide to the Pacific. The Preuss map was a brilliant documentation of the known facts about western geography. The mythical rivers were gone, and with them passed the illusion of an easy water passage to India. No matter; by 1848, railroads had come of age.

Preuss made it clear at a glance that from the middle latitudes of the United States the principal ways to reach the west coast were by the Oregon Trail down the valley of the Columbia, by the Salt Lake–Spanish Trail paralleling (at some distance) the "Rio Colorado," and by the road directly across the Great Basin following the valley of the Humboldt. Over these roads rails could be laid. The central route would best serve the needs of Oriental commerce, Frémont wrote in the *Geographical Memoir*. San Francisco, he pointed out, was "on the line of communication with Asia." The potential advantages of its great harbor were such that Frémont compared it with Constantinople's Golden Horn, and he named the entrance the Golden Gate.[7]

MORMON CORRIDOR

By the time Frémont's *Geographical Memoir* appeared, gold had been discovered at Sutter's Mill on the American River. The destiny of the West—and of the nation—was dramatically altered by that event. There was less thought now of the Orient as men looked about for the best way to reach golden California. The rush that began in 1848 lasted for ten years. Thousands came by sea, sailed into San Francisco Bay through Frémont's Golden Gate, and then went on to the diggings in the foothills of the Sierra Nevada. More thousands, with the Preuss-Frémont map in their baggage, headed west on the overland trails—the majority took the central route over South Pass, and from there numbers turned south from Fort Bridger. The first waves of this overland tide washed over the Mormon settlements in Salt Lake Valley during the summer of 1849.

Although the members of the Church of Jesus Christ of Latter-day Saints had fled to the Great Basin to rid themselves of punitive neighbors, they knew quite well that total isolation from the world was neither possible nor even desirable. Arriving on the shores of Great Salt Lake in the summer of 1847, the Mormon pioneers very quickly began to establish contact with distant regions. The first was California. Before the end of 1848, Jefferson Hunt, O. P. Rockwell, and others had demonstrated that a route between Salt Lake and Los Angeles—following the Spanish Trail from the rim of the Great Basin—was feasible for wagons. In 1849, Hunt and Howard Egan guided two of the first gold rush parties over the road which soon became known as the Mormon Trail.[8]

The Forty-Niners arriving in Salt Lake found two routes to the gold fields open to them: the shorter road by way of the Humboldt, or the longer, snow-free route by way of southern California. Although the gold rush destroyed Mormon isolation it came as a blessing to the Mormon economy. The rushers brought money, stock, and tools and equipment of all kinds, and this windfall enabled the Saints to extend their settlements rapidly beyond the shores of Great Salt Lake. Indeed, the years 1849 and 1850 were productive enough to finance a decade of growth.[9]

Colonial expansion from Salt Lake early developed a strong southward bent, a trend which continued for years. Always mindful of the importance of an ice-free gateway to the Pacific, the Latter-day Saints founded the first settlements throughout southern Utah, and in much of southern Nevada and northern Arizona. By 1877, when Brigham Young died, the Mormon frontier had nearly encircled the Grand Canyon country.

Late in 1849, Brigham Young sent the "Southern Exploring Company," led by Parley P. Pratt, to spy out the land along the California road, to size up the natural resources and to locate sites for settlements. Pratt went as far south as the valley of the Virgin, but he found it desolate and unattractive, a region "thrown together in dreadful confusion"; it was, in short, he said, "a country in ruins." The area toward the east—the environs of Zion National Park—"was bounded by vast tables of mountains, one rising above another and presenting a level summit at the horizon." On the other hand, the Southern Exploring Company found the country around Little Salt Lake and the adjoining Cedar Valley to be far better for settlement. The soil was good and well watered, grass was plentiful, and timber grew nearby. Moreover, the explorers had found a hill of iron ore, today known as Iron Mountain.

Brigham Young acted promptly to establish a colony in Little Salt Lake Valley. Not only was it athwart the road to California, but the discovery of iron ore was of the highest importance. The Saints had some small stocks of iron, and they were able to acquire more from destitute gold seekers, but this was scarcely enough to meet the needs of the growing Mormon community. When Iron County was established by the territorial legislature, the church organized the "Iron Mission," and called for fifty or more "good and effective men" to undertake settlement of the remote region, over two hundred miles from Salt Lake. One hundred eighteen men, thirty with their families, responded, forming by far the largest colonizing expedition organized by the Mormons since their arrival in the Great Basin in 1847. It was placed under the command of big, genial, and energetic George A. Smith, an apostle of the church. The colonists arrived in Little Salt Lake Valley in mid-January, 1851, and began at once to lay out a fort and settlement which they called Parowan City.

The Iron Mission had no more than arrived and dug in at Parowan than Brigham Young, in February, 1851, named two more apostles of the church, Amasa M. Lyman and Charles C. Rich, to lead a colony to southern California to establish a "stronghold for the gathering of the Saints." This was part of the plan to develop an outer cordon of settlements located strategically at some distance from Salt Lake on the roads leading to Utah. An expedition of 520 people, traveling in several organized companies, reached the coast early in June and went to work to build a typical Mormon settlement on the huge Rancho de San Bernardino. Once these beginnings were made, church authorities planned to secure the corridor by founding a string of settlements between Parowan and San Bernardino.

Meanwhile the Iron Mission was making some progress. A company of miners and iron makers, converts from England, Scotland, and Wales, arrived to form the nucleus of a new settlement near the iron mountain. The location was determined when coal was discovered on the Markagunt Plateau, and Cedar City was laid out at the mouth of Coal Creek in November, 1851. By using a blacksmith's bellows they

Lower Grand Canyon near the mouth of Bridge Canyon. Arizona.

(Next spread) Sky and open space. Shinumo Altar on the Marble Platform east of Marble Canyon. Arizona.

JOHN M. KITCHEN

extracted the first iron—enough "to shoe a horse"—in February, 1852. But a number of problems had to be resolved before much ore was produced. Just as the situation took an optimistic turn, the Walker Indian War broke out and operations had to be shut down.[10]

The war grew out of the inevitable tensions that developed as the Mormons appropriated to their own use the lands in central Utah inhabited by the Ute Indians. Joseph Walker and his brothers, who dominated the Utes in Utah, were alarmed by these encroachments and were enraged when the Mormons attempted to halt the trade in Indian slaves through legislation and even by military measures. The war began in July, 1853, and lasted nearly a year.[11]

The struggle had little effect on Mormon colonization along the Spanish Trail in southern Utah. If anything, it suggested to church officials the need for more missionary work among the Indians. In the spring of 1854, ground was broken for Fort Harmony, located a few miles south of Cedar City, and before the end of the year, the "Southern Indian Mission" had located a settlement on Santa Clara Creek near the Salt Lake–Los Angeles trail, close to the present town of Santa Clara.[12]

The next move was an obvious one. The best water on the Spanish Trail between Santa Clara Creek and San Bernardino came from the abundant springs at Las Vegas. The flow from this source was ample enough to water some patches, or even small meadows ("vegas") of wild grass. Indeed, from the earliest days, travelers over the Spanish Trail had made Las Vegas an important stopping place. Occupation of the site was essential to the security of the Mormon corridor and in April, 1855, a colony of thirty "Indian Missionaries," headed by William Bringhurst, was sent to take possession of it and to establish a colony. Bringhurst was instructed particularly to pacify the Indians and convert them to the Mormon way of life, thus making the Utah–California corridor a safer route to travel.

The missionaries arrived at Las Vegas, then a part of New Mexico territory, on June 14, 1855. They put in crops at once, built a fort, made a treaty with the local Paiute Indians who were friendly, and organized a company of infantry, known as the "Las Vegas

Guards," who celebrated the Fourth of July by firing off three salutes at daybreak.

The colony took on additional importance when a Mormon exploring party discovered some lead deposits near the Spanish Trail some thirty miles southwest of Las Vegas. The first assays showed promise and in February, 1856, Brigham Young sent Nathaniel V. Jones and thirty others to investigate further and develop the mine. A good prospect was found on Potosi Mountain, a quantity of ore was mined, a blast furnace was put in operation on Christmas Day, 1856, and some nine thousand pounds of lead were soon produced from sixty tons of refractory ore. Most of the lead from the Potosi mine, one of the first in what was to become Nevada, was freighted to Salt Lake City and cast into bullets by the church.[13]

In less than ten years the Saints had moved some distance beyond the shores of Great Salt Lake. Determined not to be isolated in their Great Basin kingdom, the Mormons, through a combination of zeal and close cooperation, had opened, colonized, and fortified an all-weather road to the sea. En route they had struck iron, coal, and lead, and had set up primitive industries at Cedar City and Potosi. Their settlements between Fort Harmony and Las Vegas were the first in the Grand Canyon country, which was little better known in 1857 than it had been in 1776. It was in fact as much a mystery as ever; it was still a blank on the map.

A PRACTICABLE
AND ECONOMICAL ROUTE

The rush to California roared on through the 1850s and brought with it demands for new, or at least improved, roads to carry gold seekers across the West and to serve the purposes of supply and communication. The possibility of building a transcontinental railroad was now seriously entertained, and there was a revival of interest in western river travel that focused on the Colorado.

Routes across the Southwest were in particular demand. The Spanish Trail west from Santa Fe was not very satisfactory. It was long and roundabout; it had never been a wagon route except in the western section after 1848, when the Mormons opened it to wheeled traffic. In fact the year 1848 marked the practical demise of the Spanish Trail as a major western road. One of the last to ride the long trail from Los Angeles to Santa Fe was Kit Carson, carrying early confirmation of the discovery of gold in California.[14]

Nearly all the gold seekers who came into the Southwest by the Santa Fe Trail went on to California via southern roads that had been opened through the Gila River Valley during the war with Mexico. The Navajo Indians and the Apaches to the south of them posed a formidable barrier, blocking travel to the west over the Continental Divide from Santa Fe and Albuquerque. Save for an occasional trader or trapper and perhaps some gold rushers on horseback, few had ventured beyond the Hopi villages into the Grand Canyon country since Garcés traveled into it in 1776. Yet, on the map at least, the region along the thirty-fifth parallel through the basin of the Little Colorado and south of the Grand Canyon seemed to promise a direct route from Santa Fe to California and the gold fields. After a temporary peace concluded with the Navajos the U.S. Army's Corps of Topographical Engineers looked into the matter.

The mapping, surveying, and opening of routes and roads throughout the American West owed much to the Topographical Engineers, who operated as an independent unit of the army from 1838 to the opening of the Civil War. Their maps, based on actual exploration, and their reports, often laden with scientific data, revealed the West in all of its complexity. The engineers portrayed the West as it was, not as it was thought to be. Unlike the early nineteenth-century cartographers, they did not abhor white paper; when the engineers found that nothing was known of a region they left it blank on their maps.

The engineers were prompted to act by energetic Lieutenant J. H. Simpson who gathered information from fur men and traders. Richard Campbell of Santa Fe told the engineer he had traveled the route with a pack train in 1827 and had found ample wood, water, and grass. Upon further inquiry Simpson learned enough to suspect that the valley of the Colorado

River might be passable toward the west. The engineer had taken a page right out of Humboldt's *Political Essay on the Kingdom of New Spain*. The learned scientist had suggested the possibility of interoceanic communication by way of the Rio Grande and the Rio Colorado. Frémont had disposed of the fictitious rivers farther north, but what of the Colorado? Everyone knew it flowed west to the Pacific, but who in 1849 knew anything else about it? The traders and trappers of New Mexico said it was "deeply cañoned," but, asked Simpson, was the canyon continuous? The replies he received were not convincing and he recommended an exploration of the western country to settle the mystery of the Colorado. Lieutenant John Parke compiled a remarkable map of the canyon country which clearly revealed that most of it was "unexplored."[15]

Accordingly, in 1851, Captain Lorenzo Sitgreaves was sent to explore the Zuñi River "to its junction with the Colorado, determining its course and character, particularly in reference to its navigable properties. . . . The junction of the Zuñi and the Colorado will be accurately determined. You will then pursue the Colorado to its junction with the Gulf of California. . . ." Although he scarcely fulfilled the latter objective, Sitgreaves carried out a pioneer traverse across the entire present state of Arizona, opening a route that crossed back and forth over the thirty-fifth parallel.

Guided by Antoine Leroux, a mountain man resident in Taos, New Mexico, Sitgreaves left Zuñi Pueblo on September 24, 1851. He soon found that the Zuñi River, "a mere rivulet," was not navigable, and that it did not empty into the great Colorado but into the Little Colorado, "an insignificant stream," also not navigable. The explorers continued on downstream until they came to Grand Falls, "a beautiful cascade," which Leroux said was the head of the canyon of the Little Colorado. Rather than attempt to follow the canyon, Sitgreaves turned toward the San Francisco Peaks and discovered en route the prehistoric ruins now within the boundaries of Wupatki National Monument. He reported "ruins of stone houses of considerable size, and in some instances of three stories in height," located on prominent points scattered across an area of eight or nine miles.

The command passed around the north side of the San Francisco Peaks, and then by way of Bill Williams Mountain, Peach Springs, Truxton Canyon, and Sitgreaves Pass, it reached the Colorado River near the later site of Fort Mohave early in November. Mindful of his instructions, Sitgreaves had planned that from this point he would proceed upstream to the "Great Cañon" and, among other things, determine accurately the mouth of the "Rio Virgin," but rations were short and the animals were exhausted, so he turned downstream to Fort Yuma and eventually reached San Diego.

The Sitgreaves reconnaissance was the first scientific examination of the southern periphery of the Grand Canyon region. The map drawn by Richard H. Kern portrayed the route from Zuñi to the Colorado River with considerable accuracy, and it was extended south to include the basin of the Gila River as surveyed by W. H. Emory. Beyond this, the map included very little that the Sitgreaves party had not observed, and as a result the immediate region of the Grand Canyon was wholly blank.

Sitgreaves felt he could add little information beyond that carried on the Kern map, and his report of the exploration was a disappointing document eighteen pages in length. The captain found the region dull and unexciting. "Almost the entire country traversed," he said, was "barren, and without general interest." The general public thought otherwise. Although Sitgreaves' own account was brief enough, the accompanying report and the large-scale maps published to the world much geographical, ethnological, and scientific information about a region heretofore imperfectly known, and two editions of the work, totaling over five thousand copies, were issued by the Senate in 1853 and 1854.

Included were a number of lithographs made from drawings by Richard Kern showing Indians (Zuñis, Cosninas, Mohaves) and the first views made of Grand Falls on the Little Colorado and the spectacular prehistoric ruins at Wupatki. More important, midway between the Spanish Trail and the Gila River routes, Sitgreaves had located a suitable road across northern Arizona to serve the needs of travel between

the Rio Grande and the Rio Colorado. Thirty years afterward, the route he marked out was followed much of the way by the Santa Fe railroad and even later by the engineers who laid out U.S. Highway 66.[16]

There was more to come. Sitgreaves' report was published at a time when national interest was running high over the prospect of building a transcontinental railroad to connect the populous East with California. Unable to agree whether the road should run through the north, south, or central states, Congress in 1853 authorized the War Department to undertake feasibility surveys to locate "the most practicable and economical route for a railroad from the Mississippi River to the Pacific Ocean." Four routes—two in the south, one in the north, and one through the center—were surveyed by the Topographical Engineers.

Lieutenant A. W. Whipple was ordered to investigate the thirty-fifth parallel route between Fort Smith, Arkansas, and Los Angeles, one of the two southern possibilities; the other, near the Mexican boundary west of El Paso, was surveyed by Lieutenant John G. Parke. Whipple's staff included Lieutenant J. C. Ives, later to explore the Grand Canyon country with his own command, and a number of scientists and specialists, including H. B. Möllhausen, artist-naturalist friend of Alexander von Humboldt. Antoine Leroux served as guide. The expedition reached the Zuñi Pueblo in November, 1853. During the next three months Whipple made a careful study of a belt of country across northern Arizona. He crossed Sitgreaves' trail in a number of places, but in the western area he diverged from it and ran his survey down Bill Williams River to the Colorado. He then turned north along the river, crossed at The Needles, and went on to the coast by the Spanish Trail, or Mormon Road.

Whipple's "Report of Explorations for a Railway Route Near the Thirty-fifth Parallel of North Latitude" consisted of two large quartos in the magnificent thirteen-volume set issued by the War Department to publish the results of the combined Pacific railway surveys. There was a detailed itinerary and description of the route, with colored lithographs from drawings by Möllhausen and others of Zuñi and

Mohave Indians, and the San Francisco Peaks in winter. The volumes also included a long report on the Indian tribes, and there were others on geology, botany, and zoology. A beautifully engraved map showed the areas surveyed, the names applied en route (Cañon Diablo, Cosnino Caves, Red Butte, Leroux Spring, Aztec Pass, The Needles, and others), and the recommended route for a railway which Whipple found to be "not only practicable, but in many respects, eminently advantageous."

Although he did not touch the Colorado River above the Mohave villages, Whipple gave to the public an elaborate geographical, ethnological, and scientific work covering the southern periphery of the Grand Canyon country. Added to this was the *Diary of a Journey*, published by Möllhausen, whose work was filled with observations on geography, Indians, plant and animal life, and on the personnel of the exploring party. Alexander von Humboldt wrote in the preface that the finding of the best route across the western territories would bring important advantages to the "restlessly active" and "enterprising" American people "destined to play an important part in the commerce with China and Japan."[17]

The railroad survey of the central route near the thirty-eighth parallel captured more national attention than the Whipple survey. John C. Frémont, who had plugged up the West's mythical rivers, and his powerful and influential father-in-law, T. H. Benton, former Senator from Missouri, saw in the railroads a golden future for American world commerce which they hoped and expected would flow across the West between St. Louis and the Golden Gate. Disappointed when the official survey of the route was assigned to Lieutenant John W. Gunnison of the Topographical Engineers, Frémont, with private backing, set out on his fifth and last expedition to survey the route himself. Ahead of both Gunnison and Frémont, E. F. Beale, recently appointed Superintendent of Indian Affairs in California, was persuaded by Benton to travel the central route on his way to the new post.

All three parties crossed the Green River at the ford of the Spanish Trail which they followed into the Great Basin. Beale went on to California over the Spanish–Mormon trail. Gunnison was caught up in the Walker War and in October, 1853, on the Sevier River, he and part of his command were killed by Indians. Frémont's party, narrowly missing destruction in the winter snows of Utah's mountains, finally reached the Mormon frontier town of Parowan where the men recuperated before going on across the Great Basin to California.

The death of Gunnison and his men, and Frémont's near disaster, detracted little from the arguments in favor of a central route. G. H. Heap, a journalist who had traveled with Beale, came out with a book entitled *A Central Route to the Pacific* in 1854; the official report of the Gunnison Survey appeared in 1855. And Frémont and Benton continued to urge that the Golden Gate become the western terminus of the iron tracks.

Once the reports of the western railroad surveys were in, it became apparent that there was more than one "practicable and economical" route from the Mississippi to the Pacific, and sectional and political rivalry delayed the decision until the Civil War, when construction on the first transcontinental railroad was finally begun. Completed in 1869, the road did not follow the Frémont-Benton route, though it terminated at the Golden Gate.[18]

The engineers in charge of the Pacific railroad surveys had accumulated much new knowledge about the geography of the American West. Lieutenant G. W. Warren of the Topographical Engineers incorporated this information on his great map of the Trans-Mississippi West, completed in 1857, the best and most accurate map up to that date. But Warren was forced to show some large blank spaces which he marked "unexplored." One of the largest of these incorporated the entire canyon country of the Colorado from the line surveyed by Gunnison across the Green River in Utah to the route followed by Whipple across the Colorado River near the Mohave villages.[19] The engineers, of course, sought to avoid the rough and difficult country—the steep-walled canyons of the Colorado were a much more effective barrier by far than the mountain range. They looked for the easy pass, the low divide, and the gentle slope for a route that could carry commerce from the Mississippi to the Pacific directly and economically.

Dixieland

BIG CAÑON OF THE COLORADO

The Grand Canyon country might have remained a blank on the maps for some time had it not been for the "Utah War," 1857–1858, a conflict that grew out of mounting tensions between the Mormons and federal territorial officials. When relations deteriorated, President Buchanan sent a military expedition of twenty-five hundred men under the command of Colonel Albert S. Johnston to enforce federal authority in Utah. Fearing that the arrival of the army would be followed by mob violence, which the Mormons had come to Utah ten years before to escape, Brigham Young decided to meet the invaders head-on. Mormon guerrillas slowed the progress of the army, which was forced to winter near Fort Bridger, but in the spring of 1858 a truce was negotiated, largely through the influence of Thomas L. Kane, who on other occasions had befriended the Mormons. Johnston's army, however, remained in Utah and some forty miles from Salt Lake City established Camp Floyd, which remained an active post until the outbreak of the Civil War in 1861.[1]

To locate routes to supply the new installation the army sent the Topographical Engineers to the field. Captain J. H. Simpson located a new wagon road from Camp Floyd to the Sierra Nevada; from Santa Fe, Captain J. N. Macomb went to look for a feasible wagon route through the intricate canyon country of southeastern Utah.[2] But the first in the field was Lieutenant Joseph Christmas Ives, who steamed up the Colorado in 1858 to determine the extent of its navigability.

During the decade that had begun with the discovery of gold in California, neither public nor private interests had given much thought to testing the Colorado River as a navigable stream. Sitgreaves, in 1851, had been directed to do so, but he had bypassed the Grand Canyon to explore the lower river. In 1853, when the Pacific Railroad surveyors were marking out horizontal routes across the West, R. B. Marcy, captain of the regular infantry, had suggested an examination of the Colorado from a point on the Green near the Mormon settlements to Fort Yuma on the lower river. Marcy noted that since the day in 1540 when Spanish explorers first viewed it, many "extraordinary and marvelous" accounts had been written about the Colorado River country. Despite this, he said, our knowledge of the region was very limited. A systematic exploration would be in the national interest; it would develop scientific data, information about the tribes, determine the character of the river throughout its entire length, and test its practicability for steamboat navigation. But railroad routes, not rivers, were all the cry in official western exploration at the time, and Marcy's proposal was rejected.[3]

The Utah War put the matter in a different light. The army decided to find out if the Colorado would serve as a military waterway from which troops might be quickly dispatched to interior points. After the founding of Fort Yuma at the mouth of the Gila River in 1851, the army had considered the lower Colorado as a military supply route, and Lieutenant George H. Derby had mapped the river from the Gila to the Gulf of California in 1852. Now, in 1857, Lieutenant Joseph C. Ives of the Topographical Engineers, who had been with Whipple on the railroad survey of the thirty-fifth parallel, was directed to ascertain the navigability of the Colorado above Fort Yuma.[4]

To accomplish his purpose Ives had built a steel steamboat of shallow draft, the *Explorer*. The boat was tested on the Delaware River and then dismantled and shipped to the mouth of the Colorado where in December, 1857, it was laboriously reassembled. On January 11, 1858, Ives left Fort Yuma and steamed up the Colorado. After an adventurous trip of about two months he reached Black Canyon where Hoover Dam now stands. There, at the foot of the canyon, the *Explorer* crashed into a submerged rock. In a skiff Ives worked his way up the canyon and reached the mouth of Las Vegas Wash. He thought it might be the mouth of the Virgin, which he believed would offer easy access to the Mormon road between Salt Lake and Los Angeles. Convinced that he was near the head of navigation and unwilling to risk further upstream travel in the steamboat, Ives turned back downstream to continue the exploration by land. The *Explorer* was sent back to Fort Yuma and, with a party including J. S. Newberry, geologist, F. W. von Egloffstein, artist and cartographer, and H. B. Möllhausen, artist and naturalist (who also had traveled with Whipple), Ives set off eastward following the wagon tracks left by Edward F. Beale.

Topographical exploration by the federal government for trails and roads in the American West was no less important than the railroad surveys. Many miles of roads were built and improved at public expense. By the time the first transcontinental railroad was completed in 1869, a network of wagon

Dr. J. S. Newberry, with the Ives Expedition of 1857-58, was the first geologist to reach the floor of Grand Canyon.

roads, which had been surveyed, improved, or built by either the War or Interior departments, had spread over the West.

One such wagon road across northern Arizona between Fort Defiance and the Colorado was surveyed and built for the War Department by Edward F. Beale, who had traveled the central railroad route in 1853. In September and October, 1857, Beale worked out a location for a road that followed the Sitgreaves and Whipple routes. Beale's caravan, consisting of heavy equipment and supply wagons, was given an exotic touch by the presence of some twenty-five camels and their native attendants. When the camels, introduced by the War Department experimentally as pack animals, reached the Colorado

River, they entered the water and swam across, much to the surprise of some observers.

Beale returned eastward over the road in January and February of 1858 to test it for winter travel. During the spring of 1859 the work of actual construction and improvement was undertaken. The completion of Beale's road directly west from Albuquerque to the California border was the fulfillment of an aim centuries old and ranked in importance with the opening of wagon travel over the Salt Lake–Los Angeles trail by the Mormons ten years before. Beale saw his road as the precursor of the railroad sure to follow. In extravagant terms he praised the thirty-fifth parallel route as having the best timber, grass, water, and grade of any between the western frontier and the Pacific Ocean. He was a forerunner. The Santa Fe Railway and U.S. Highway 66, both main roads across the Southwest, closely paralleled Beale's tracks between the Rio Grande and the Rio Colorado.[5]

Lieutenant Joseph C. Ives and his party headed eastward over the Beale road in March, 1858, to make a further examination of the Colorado. Mindful of his mission to test the navigable quality of the river, Ives planned now to take a look at the "Big Cañon" country some distance above the point reached by the *Explorer*. On April 1, the explorers topped a swell at the head of Peach Springs Canyon, a major tributary of Diamond Creek which bisects the Hualapai Plateau, where a "splendid panorama" burst into view. North of them the rugged walls of the canyon framed the towering Shivwits Plateau beyond, across the Colorado on the north side of Grand Canyon. "The famous 'Big Cañon' was before us; and for a long time we paused in wondering delight," Ives wrote, "surveying this stupendous formation through which the Colorado and its tributaries break their way."

For three weeks the explorers examined the country between Diamond Creek on the west and Havasu Canyon on the east. As they descended Peach Springs Canyon the scenery became "wilder and grander." The rude huts of the Hualapai Indians stood in strange contrast to the monumental architecture of the canyon with its "gaping chasms" and "colossal piles." On April 3, Ives reached the floor of the Grand Canyon at the mouth of Diamond Creek where he found the Colorado rushing through the rock-studded channel like a mill-race.

The day was spent in an examination of the locality. During the descent to the river from the head of Peach Springs Canyon, Dr. J. S. Newberry had a splendid opportunity to study the exposed successive strata forming the canyon walls, and now, in the bottom of the "Great Cañon of the Colorado," he completed a geological cross-section extending from the hard Precambrian rocks of the Lower Granite Gorge upward to the top of the plateau.

Leaving the river the explorers climbed out of Peach Springs Canyon by way of a steep eastern fork which brought them out on a point where by eye they could follow the course of the Colorado as it swept clockwise in a great southern horseshoe bend around the Shivwits Plateau. Overlooking the apex of the bend they could see north and northwest up both prongs of the horseshoe over a bewildering canyon landscape. Newberry thought the view was particularly grand and he wrote of it: "The course of the Colorado was visible for nearly a hundred miles, and the series of Cyclopean walls into which the mesas of different elevations have been cut by that stream and its tributaries formed a scene of which the sublime features deeply impressed each member of our party."

Traveling northeast now and generally on the trail followed by Garcés in 1776, Ives soon found himself in a pine forest on the high western edge of the Coconino Plateau. A few miles northeast of Frazier's Well, on a lookout on a sixty-six-hundred-foot-high divide sloping east to Havasu Canyon and north to Mohawk and National canyons, he stopped to absorb another "sublime spectacle" which included the rounded volcanic Pine Mountains on the Uinkaret Plateau north across the river (Ives named them the North Side Mountains), and the San Francisco Peaks to the east, snow-covered and "sharply defined against the sky."

During the next few days reconnaissance parties explored north, east, and west. With one group Ives visited Havasu Canyon and from a point on one of the ledges they could see the village of the Havasupais (or Yampais, as they called them), probably the first white men to do so since Garcés. Eastward the explorers reached the rim of Havasu Canyon from another angle. Ives marveled at the extent and magnitude of this great canyon which had so cut up the plateau that it resembled a "vast ruin." Ives led another group north to the rim of the Grand Canyon, probably by way of the high mesa between Mohawk Canyon and Prospect Valley, while a second party, traveling west on foot, reached a point overlooking Granite Park where the rim of the canyon was over a mile above the river. Finding their way blocked by canyons and "impassable obstacles," except toward the southeast, the explorers headed in that direction and reached the San Francisco Peaks before the end of April.

The intricately eroded façade of the Ward Terrace overlooking the Painted Desert near Cameron. Arizona.

Ives did not see the Grand Canyon anywhere above the mouth of Havasu Canyon. From the San Francisco Peaks he traveled on eastward to the Little Colorado (or Flax River, as he called it), and from the mouth of Canyon Diablo with a small detachment he headed north across the Painted Desert—which was named on the spot by Dr. Newberry—to the Hopi villages and thence to Fort Defiance where the expedition was disbanded.

The examination by Ives of the big triangle of country between Diamond Creek and Havasu Canyon was one of the classic explorations of the Grand Canyon country. Ives had seen more of the Grand Canyon than any white man before his day, and he wrote of it with the excitement of one who had seen some wonderful places. But the practical bent of a mind trained at West Point reined him in almost apologetically when feeling bubbled up. He wrote: "The region explored after leaving the navigable portion of the Colorado—though, in a scientific point of view, of the highest interest, and presenting natural features whose strange sublimity is perhaps unparalleled in any part of the world—is not of much value." Later in the report he said, "It is 'altogether valueless,'" and in another passage, "ours has been the first and will doubtless be the last party of whites to visit this profitless locality. It seems intended by nature that the Colorado River, along the greater portions of its lonely and majestic way, shall be forever unvisited and undisturbed. . . ." This was a thought echoed by H. B. Möllhausen who wrote that this "terribly beautiful wilderness" might, for coming centuries, "remain a secret to mankind."

Ives' *Report Upon the Colorado River of the West*, issued in quarto in an edition of 11,000 copies by the Government Printing Office in 1861, was one of the best books done by the Topographical Engineers in all of the western explorations. Ives' narrative, clear and readable, was followed by a number of scientific papers. Full-page lithographs done from sketches made by Egloffstein, Möllhausen, and Ives depicted dramatic scenes and landscapes. Colored lithographs of Indians including Mohaves, Hualapais, and Navajos were included. In addition, Egloffstein made eight panoramic sketches of landscapes along the way which appear in the book as foldouts, and he prepared two beautiful maps using a specially designed process; one showed the Colorado River to the head of navigation, and one depicted the extent of the exploration in the Grand Canyon country.[6]

Ives gave the world its first good look at the Grand Canyon. There it was—beautiful in its detail, even though "profitless." Dr. Newberry, the first scientist to reach the canyon, wrote a treatise on the geology of the Colorado Plateau which became the foundation work for subsequent studies. But the full-page lithographs of the "Big Cañon" were so grotesquely exaggerated as to give the public a warped and distorted view. These, done by J. J. Young from sketches made in the field by Egloffstein, portray the canyon as a narrow, dark, straight-walled crack, reminiscent of one of the more somber illustrations of Dante's *Inferno*. Such views undoubtedly influenced the public's concept of the Grand Canyon for decades. As late as 1914, humorist Irvin S. Cobb would write that his "preconceived conception" of the Grand Canyon—one most people had before they saw it themselves—was that of "a straight up-and-down slit in the earth, fabulously steep and fabulously deep; nevertheless, merely a slit."[7]

Ives had discovered much about the Colorado and the lower part of Grand Canyon, but the region above Havasu Canyon remained a blank, little better known than it was in Coronado's time. One basic geographical misconception about it grew out of the exploration and was nicely documented on the Egloffstein map. From their high lookout point, back on the western rim of the Coconino Plateau, the explorers had imagined that the main gorge of the Colorado, which they could follow for an "enormous distance," was in fact the canyon of the Little Colorado and that the main river, which they may have identified with the gorge of Kanab Creek, came in directly from the north. This error, however, was quickly corrected on the maps—drawn by Egloffstein also—incorporating the results of the Macomb expedition into southeastern Utah in 1859.

The Macomb and Ives explorations into the canyon country of the Colorado River were complementary. Both were organized to discover possible military routes from peripheral regions into the heartland of the Mormon country. Ives found that the Colorado up to Black Canyon was navigable, but that river travel through the Big Cañon was scarcely feasible. Macomb found that the canyon lands of southeastern Utah were practically impassable to land travelers.

Ives and Macomb together found out enough about the Colorado River to put to rest, at least for a time, the idea that the canyon country could ever serve as a westward passage to the sea. But their reports, including the pioneer geological studies by J. S. Newberry, who was also geologist to the Macomb expedition, made known many details about a wonderful region. Men thereafter began to take much more interest in the land itself than in just finding a way through it.[8] Even as Ives was writing that the Big Cañon country "shall be forever unvisited and undisturbed," the Mormons were already moving into it from small settlements along the Virgin River.

CENTRAL ROAD TO ARIZONA

The Utah War, 1857–1858, disrupted colonization on the outer Mormon frontier. As Johnston's army approached late in 1857, the Saints could only guess at the final outcome of the impending conflict. There was danger that they might be forced once again to leave their homes and flee. In any event it would be better, church officials thought, if the distant frontiers were contracted. Accordingly, the colonists in the outer cordon settlements were instructed to come back to Utah. Defense of the kingdom would be easier if the Mormons were not widely scattered, and the strength of a whole people would be present were another exodus forced upon them. Consequently, the colonists in San Bernardino, Las Vegas, Carson Valley, and other places moved back to the inner cordon settlements.

The Saints who trekked in from San Bernardino and Las Vegas generally settled in the first Utah towns they reached on the Salt Lake–California Trail: Santa Clara, Cedar City, and Parowan. But, in a country where the life-supporting resources were limited, the new arrivals put a severe strain on the land which could only be relieved by finding new areas suitable for settlement.

Although he abandoned San Bernardino in California, Brigham Young set about to find another corridor to the sea. The Utah War made it imperative to have a substitute for the Salt Lake–Southern California route. Young was quite as much interested in the problems of supply and communication as the United States Army, who threatened to surround his Great Basin kingdom.[9] Like the army, Young turned to the Colorado River as one of the best possibilities.

The Mormons must have looked upon the Ives expedition, which appeared at the time that Johnston's army was en route to Utah, as another phase of the military invasion of their territory. Missionaries working among the Mohave Indians spied on Ives and watched his movements as he worked his way upriver to Black Canyon.[10] The Mormon press printed exchanges from other western newspapers reporting the expedition's progress. On July 28, 1858, the *Deseret News* reprinted an article from the San Francisco *Alta California,* which stated that the Colorado was navigable for a distance of 335 miles to the mouth of the "great kanyon" (Black Canyon), just below the mouth of the Virgin River. An earlier issue of the *News* carried a letter from E. F. Beale to the Secretary of War in which he suggested using camels in the Utah War!

All of this was important news to the Saints, and Ives had no more than left the river before Brigham Young sent George A. Smith to explore along the Colorado below the mouth of the Virgin River and look for suitable locations for settlements. Smith left Cedar City in March, 1858, and traveled down to the Beale crossing, but he failed to find any very good sites, and plans for colonizing in that quarter were postponed when it appeared the war was not going to be one of armed conflict.[11] If the people were to be forced into exodus Young knew that every possible escape route must be found. What of the possibility of crossing the Colorado and heading south and east into central Arizona (then the Territory of New Mexico), inhabited only by Navajo and Hopi Indians?

Corral and cliffs in Kanab Canyon above Kanab. Uta

The entire canyon country of the Colorado downstream from the crossing of the Spanish Trail at Moab to the mouth of the Virgin River was unknown to the Mormons when the Utah War opened in 1857. Now in 1858, Brigham Young sent Jacob Hamblin, president of the Southern Indian Mission, to find a way across the wilderness and to open relations with the Hopi Indians. Living on the picturesque mesas drained by northern tributaries of the Little Colorado, the Hopis from Coronado's day had long been of interest to the white men. Ives had been their most recent visitor in the spring of 1858. The Mormons probably learned of the Hopis first from the Utes, notably Chief Walker and his band, who traded with them on occasion.[12]

Jacob Hamblin and party left Santa Clara late in

Natural Arch in the Kolob section, Zion National Park. Utah.

October and headed across the Arizona Strip. As no one had traveled the region, Chief Naraguts of the Kaibab band of Southern Paiutes and several of his men were taken along as guides. The explorers skirted the bold southward-facing escarpment of the Vermilion Cliffs and reached Pipe Spring on the second night. This watering place, one of the best and most easily accessible springs in the Grand Canyon country, had been known to the Indians for centuries, but Hamblin and his men were possibly the first whites to see it. It may have been on this occasion that the spring acquired its name. "Gunlock" Will Hamblin, brother of Jacob and a good man with a gun, on a bet shot the bottom out of Dudley Leavitt's pipe at twenty-five yards without breaking the bowl. Straightaway, the story goes, the place was called Pipe Spring.[13]

Moving on eastward by a trail closely parallel to that taken by Domínguez and Escalante in 1776, the Mormons forded the Colorado at the Crossing of the Fathers and went on to Oraibi. They were well received by the Hopis who served up a banquet of stewed meat, *piki* bread, beans, and peaches. The explorers visited the other Hopi towns and with great interest took note of everything they saw. Four missionaries remained behind to preach, and Hamblin and the others returned to Santa Clara by the same route they had taken on the way out.

Brigham Young sent a second expedition to the Hopis in October, 1859, and again Jacob Hamblin was put in charge. Provided with a large supply of trade goods, Hamblin planned this time to build a boat and ferry the Colorado at the mouth of the Paria, but he failed to make the crossing there and again forded the river upstream at the Crossing of the Fathers. Still a third expedition under Hamblin was sent in the fall of 1860, but at Tonalea, not far from Oraibi, the party encountered some hostile Navajos who killed George Albert Smith, Jr., son of the Mormon apostle.[14]

Smith's death was the first casualty in an impending conflict between two moving frontiers, one white, one Indian. The Mormons, based along the Virgin River, were moving eastward to undertake missionary work with the Hopis and to search for suitable homelands south of the Colorado. They en-

countered a vanguard of Navajo Indians who were moving westward into the canyon country of the Colorado to escape the military power of the United States. The Navajos had been troublesome since 1846 when the Americans first arrived in New Mexico and, despite the founding of Fort Defiance in 1851, they had maintained their warlike state. During the years 1858–1860, several military expeditions ranged north and west of Defiance, the main result of which was to drive the hostiles into retreat and hiding in the wilderness of canyons draining into the Colorado. Some of these Indians stopped Hamblin's party on November 2, 1860, and killed young Smith.

This did not end the trouble; within five years the Mormons themselves were at war with the Navajos. Nor did it end Mormon interest in a mission to the Hopi Indians, but it deflected their approach, and a new route south of the Grand Canyon was soon found.

Jacob Hamblin deservedly is well remembered as one of the heroes of the Mormon frontier. He arrived in Santa Clara on the Virgin River in 1854; thereafter, he served his church in the Grand Canyon country for twenty-nine years as missionary, explorer, colonist, and peacemaker. His first three trips to the Hopi towns opened the way for Mormon settlement of the Arizona Strip. He closed the gap between the Mormon settlements on the Virgin River and the ancient Hopi villages, and the trail he opened (later elaborated by Hamblin and others) became the main road between Utah and Arizona, paralleled today by the major trunk highway U.S. 89.

By 1860, most of the Grand Canyon country was enclosed by three major routes: the Spanish–Mormon trail bounded it on the west between the Virgin River and Las Vegas; the Hamblin trail between the Virgin River and the Hopi villages bisected the northern part of the region; and the Beale road between the Little Colorado and the Grand Wash Cliffs formed a southern boundary. Thus, the dream of Coronado, Oñate, Garcés, Domínguez and Escalante, Ives and Macomb had been realized. A triangle of roads had been opened to serve the needs of those who wanted to pass through to reach lands of greater promise beyond. But as the frontier closed on neighboring re-

(Next spread) *Summer storm over the Grand Canyon from the South Rim above Granite Park. North of the canyon Mt. Dellenbaugh, on the Shivwits Plateau, shimmers in the light. Arizona.*

C. GREGORY CRAMPTON

gions the canyon country began to take on something of a glitter of its own to the farmer, stockman, lumberman, and prospector, and these same routes served the needs of the exploiter.

COTTON MISSION

The Mormon villages on the southern rim of the Great Basin and on tributaries of the Virgin River were the first beginnings of permanent settlement in the entire Grand Canyon region. Parowan, Cedar City, and Fort Harmony, located under the shadow of the Markagunt Plateau, standing high on the eastern skyline, and Santa Clara, located at the southern base of the brooding, gray bulk of Pine Valley Mountain, formed an original nucleus of colonies from which the Mormons pushed into the sandstone wilderness of the Colorado River.

Both over ten thousand feet in altitude, the Markagunt and Pine Valley Mountain receive much winter snow, and the melted water drains off in creeks and forks to form the Virgin River. Living, running water was the basis of life in the arid West. Even though its waters were confined mostly to narrow canyons and to long valleys of little breadth, the Virgin River offered to those displaced Mormons, pulled back in 1857 from the outer cordons, the best chance of finding a place to farm and to live.

Explorers went out to look for suitable lands. Jesse N. Smith and a party of eleven were sent from Parowan to explore the headwaters of the Virgin River in search of places where "cotton would grow." During August and September, 1858, Smith covered a big circle of country in a traverse which included the Markagunt Plateau and Long Valley on the east, or main fork, of the Virgin. Unable to pass through the narrow Parunuweap Canyon the explorers topped out on the south rim, where they worked their way through a confusing and baffling network of tributary canyons only to be rimrocked on Shunesburg Mountain and South Mountain, which overlooked the mouth of the North Fork of the Virgin where it issued from Zion Canyon to join the main stream. They could

see the lofty towers on both sides of the mouth of Zion Canyon and they could follow the course of the Virgin River for fifteen miles as it flowed westward through a narrow, open valley bounded on either side by spectacular mesas, benches, buttes, and crags. And they could see here and there a few acres of flatland along the banks edged with cottonwoods.

Backtracking, the explorers found a passage down through the Vermilion Cliffs and worked their way along the base of these cliffs and of Gooseberry Mesa to reach the lower end of the valley they had seen from Shunesburg and South mountains. From a base camp some of the men hiked up the river to the mouth of Zion Canyon and then the entire party pushed on, dropped down over the Hurricane Cliffs, and reached the settlement of Toquerville which had been founded the preceding spring.

Jesse N. Smith and party had made a first examination of the main branches of the Virgin River east of the Hurricane Cliffs. The east fork, in Long Valley, was a clear, pure stream, Smith reported, but he was not impressed with the main stream below the mouth of Zion Canyon. The water was muddy from summer rains, and there were only about six hundred acres of bottomland suitable for cultivation. The Virgin, he observed, meandered back and forth across the narrow valley, and there were signs of heavy floods. With the rise of a few feet, the river would sweep over all the bottomland for miles, he predicted.[15]

Water. Bottomland. Floods. These Mormon pioneers were interested in the productive capability of the land and not in the beauties of the landscape. That Smith had seen some of the most beautiful parts of the Grand Canyon region was not evident in his report. To him it was just a poor country, and he could agree with one who had preceded him to the mouth of Zion Canyon that, as a farming area, "nothing could be made of it." But to the Mormon bent upon extending the kingdom of God in the wilderness, a few acres and a little water spelled opportunity.

During the years 1857–1860 the basin of the Virgin River began to fill up with settlers, many from the abandoned settlements in California. Between the mouth of Zion Canyon and the Hurricane Cliffs three small villages were started—Virgin City, Grafton, and

Adventure. The latter name was appropriate recognition of the reality of pioneer life along the Virgin—it was indeed a hazardous experience. As Jesse N. Smith had predicted, the settlers were forced to do battle with the river. At once the source of life, its floods brought death and destruction. Many indeed were to discover that the Virgin, wild, free, and capricious, was very slow to respond favorably to the touch of man.

If the valley of the Virgin was a tough place to make a living, the climate below Zion Canyon was warm and benign. West of the Hurricane Cliffs the river was less than three thousand feet above the sea, and warm-weather crops—including cotton—would grow. Experiments in raising cotton had begun along the Santa Clara in 1855 and these were encouraging enough to prompt the Mormon Church to send more settlers to step up production. A number of the cotton pioneers were converts from the southern states, and before long the valley of the Virgin was being called Utah's "Dixie."

With the coming of the Civil War, which cut off cotton supplies from the South, the cotton experiment in Dixie took on fresh significance. In May, 1861, within a month after the fall of Fort Sumter, Brigham Young and other church officials visited southern Utah. They found the settlements scattered and pitifully small. Convinced that enough cotton could be grown along the Virgin River to supply the Mormons' needs, Young, at the semiannual conference of the church in October, 1861, named and called over three hundred family heads from the central districts in Utah to colonize the Virgin River country. Over seven hundred Latter-day Saints responded to form the Cotton Mission.

Mormon settlement of the often inhospitable regions beyond the Salt Lake Valley was accomplished in large measure by means of the mission which, by 1861, was a well-developed institution of frontier expansion. Missions were formed not only to propagate the faith but to colonize new regions, open relations with Indians, or engage in a specific economic activity like the manufacture of iron or the growing of cotton. The Mormon Church called its members to serve in building a broad, temporal foundation and an eco-nomic self-sufficiency, to support its ecclesiastical goals. Thus the advance of the Mormon frontier in the West was a product of planning and spirited co-operation. This was in contrast to the general course of American frontier expansion which was primarily the product of individual voluntary effort.

The Cotton Mission to southern Utah was large and impressive. Those picked to go were stable, self-reliant citizens possessing a wide variety of skills, and two apostles of the church, George A. Smith and Erastus Snow, joined the mission as permanent settlers. Late in November, 1861, an advance company selected a townsite located between two volcanic ridges and a short distance north of the Virgin River. It was the place where Brigham Young earlier in the year had predicted a city would be built with "spires, towers, and steeples." The place was named St. George.

Most of the members of the mission were on the land by the end of 1861. The majority settled at St. George, but others moved in to strengthen the struggling colonies elsewhere along the Virgin. A group of over thirty Swiss families was also called to join the Cotton Mission, and they settled at Santa Clara, five miles west of St. George. The church hoped to produce not only cotton but other warm-weather crops like sugar, wine, tobacco, figs, almonds, and olives. Wine and tobacco were high on the list, but cotton was foremost. To strengthen the Virgin River settlements and to ensure a steady flow of produce, the church issued a series of calls which brought some three thousand people to southern Utah by the end of the decade.

The settling of Dixie was a basic part of a larger plan which called for the opening of a corridor to the sea via the Colorado River, an idea which Brigham Young and the church authorities had entertained since 1858 when Ives had steamed up Black Canyon. St. George and the settlements along the Virgin might easily become the principal gateway from the outside world to the Mormon empire and a base for further colonial expansion.[16]

During 1862 and 1863 Jacob Hamblin made two more journeys to the Hopi villages, going out both times by way of the Grand Wash Cliffs and the south side of Grand Canyon. On the second he found a good crossing at the mouth of Grand Canyon, where Harrison Pearce later established a ferry (altered in common usage to Pierce's Ferry) and thus opened a new route between Utah and Arizona. The Mormon explorers got a good look at the country south of the Grand Canyon and the basin of the Little Colorado which seemed to offer the best possibilities for settlement, and good relations with the Hopis were furthered.[17]

Meanwhile developments along the Colorado below the Grand Canyon were bringing within reach the Mormon dream of a water road to the sea. Thanks to the expanding military and mining activity along the river, steamboat navigation had passed the experimental stage by 1864. Fort Mohave had been established in 1859 at Beale's Crossing, and the mining camps at La Paz and El Dorado canyons were booming. The Colorado Steam Navigation Company, which had largely monopolized the trade during its ten years on the river, was then operating three large steamboats to supply these and other points. In 1864, William H. Hardy established a ferry and a landing at Hardyville, a few miles above Fort Mohave. Early in November he sent a circular to the citizens of Utah inviting their trade. Merchandise, he wrote, could be delivered at Hardyville at just slightly over San Francisco prices, which were far lower than those in Utah owing to the high overland freight rates.

Brigham Young saw an opportunity for the Mormons in these developments, and with characteristic vigor he acted to open a connection with the steamboat-carrying trade on the Colorado. In November, he appointed Anson Call to head a party to locate a road from St. George to the Colorado River and to build a warehouse and landing at the head of navigation. Call found a suitable place at the mouth of Callville Wash, a point on the north bank of the Colorado about ten miles above Black Canyon, where Ives had been stopped. Optimistic that a corridor from Salt Lake to the sea would soon be opened, the Deseret Mercantile Association, consisting of Utah merchants, was chartered to handle the river commerce. The association named Anson Call agent on the Colorado and then it went to work opening a road to the river. A town

named Callville was laid out, and a stone warehouse was built.[18]

To secure the road between St. George and Callville and to extend settlement to new areas where warm-weather crops could be grown, Brigham Young issued a call for his people to occupy the lower valley of the Virgin and also the Muddy River, a tributary draining the Moapa Valley. Consequently, Littlefield on the Virgin and St. Thomas and Logandale on the Muddy were settled between the fall of 1864 and the spring of 1865, the first foundations of another colonial venture—the Muddy Mission.[19]

Through 1865 and 1866 there was much enthusiasm in Utah over the prospects of the Colorado corridor, and this was mirrored by the merchants of San Francisco who hoped to dominate the river commerce. But there were abundant difficulties. The new settlements in Dixie and on the lower Virgin had disturbed and displaced the Indians who rose in rebellion in 1865 and threatened the population and

commerce. The shipping lanes faced financial and navigational difficulties. Once goods were deposited at Callville, the poor roads to the Utah settlements caused breakdowns and long delays. Despite these problems, many tons of freight reached Utah via the Colorado River route. However, by 1867 the Union Pacific and Central Pacific were rapidly closing the gap, and when the rails were joined at Promontory, Utah, in May, 1869, the dream of a commercial corridor to the sea by way of the Colorado River vanished.

But the settlements scattered along the Virgin River from Zion Canyon to St. Thomas remained as expressions of the Mormon move south. They suffered from Indian troubles, isolation, political difficulties, and economic depression, but, nonetheless, they became the bases from which the frontier spread eastward across the Arizona Strip and the northern portion of the Grand Canyon country, a region which came to be largely dominated by Mormon interests.

The coming of the railroad brought to an end the long quest for a river road to the Pacific. Since the time of Coronado, the Colorado had figured in these dreams. Many of those who reached the river's banks had been more interested in a way through the region it drained than in the huge basin itself. Yet who in 1869 knew very much about the river and its magnificent canyons? No one had traveled on the Colorado very far, certainly not through the canyon country. It was literally a great unknown. But in May, 1869, John Wesley Powell and a party in four boats pushed off from Green River station on the newly completed Union Pacific to explore the mysteries of the great canyons of the Colorado from Wyoming to the mouth of the Virgin River.

Grafton, on the banks of the Virgin River just below the mouth of Zion Canyon. The Mormon settlers who pioneered the region found the Virgin unruly and capricious, its spring and summer floods a frequent threat to life and property. Photo made in 1941. Utah.

THE WATER

avasu Falls on Cataract Creek in Havasu Canyon. Arizona.

Powell of the Colorado

VOYAGE INTO THE UNKNOWN

After the Civil War the opening of the West proceeded with remarkable speed. Waves of eager exploiters washed over the land between California and the Great Plains, seizing upon the mines, the soil, the range, the forests, and the water. Overrun by these newcomers, the Indians rose in vain rebellion to protect their way of life. By the turn of the century the invasion had spent itself, and the Indians found themselves confined to reservations.

During twelve of the early postwar boom years four separate public surveys were undertaken to map, explore, study scientifically, and describe systematically the West beyond the hundredth meridian. The bulky reports on geology, geography, biology, ethnology, and archaeology, and the charts and maps and pictorial material issued by these surveys publicized the West and helped to speed not only its exploitation but the nation's understanding of it.

The War Department sent Clarence King to survey the region traversed by the Union Pacific–Central Pacific along the fortieth parallel. The Department of the Interior commissioned F. V. Hayden to head the U.S. Geological and Geographical Survey of the Territories, and he carried out elaborate explorations in the Rocky Mountains north of the area examined by King and south of it into Colorado and neighboring territories.

A third survey grew out of the two voyages on the Colorado River led by John Wesley Powell who, during the years 1869 and 1871–1872, explored the great canyons of the Colorado and the Green from Green River, Wyoming, to the foot of Grand Canyon, as well as some of the adjacent country. A fourth survey, under the War Department, was directed by George M. Wheeler of the Corps of Topographical Engineers. Wheeler touched the western and southern sections of the Grand Canyon region and competed in some areas with the Powell Survey.

Powell fought for the Union in the Civil War and lost his right forearm at Shiloh. He was discharged with the rank of major, a title he used the rest of his life. After the war Powell became a professor of geology at Illinois Wesleyan University, and from this base in 1867 and 1868 he made geological excursions to the Rocky Mountains where he became interested in the Colorado River. The Colorado, where it flowed through Utah and Arizona, was still a mystery, the region it drained largely unexplored. No one by 1868 had traveled the river any great distance, and it was known only at a few crossing points. What of the rumors of dark canyons, whirlpools, and high waterfalls? Powell decided to find out by being the first to

eparation Canyon. The Colorado River, running from right to left (across lower alf of photograph), dropped over a rapid formed by debris pushed into the river y two cross canyons. Rather than risk any more rapids, three of Powell's men ft the 1869 expedition to walk out to the settlements. They reached the hivwits Plateau (top of photograph) where they were killed by Indians. Arizona.

run the Colorado. But his interest was more in science than adventure. The canyons, he said, would be a geological "book of revelations" and he determined to read the book.

Powell's two voyages of discovery constitute the most celebrated chapter of Colorado River history.[1] The first began at the Union Pacific Railroad bridge across the Green River at Green River Station, Wyoming, where on May 24, 1869, ten men started out in four boats. Three months and six days later six men landed two boats at the mouth of the Virgin River after having traveled over a thousand miles through a canyon wilderness virtually unknown before.

After spending nearly two months running the great canyons of the Green River the explorers reached the confluence of the Green and Colorado on July 16. They explored the beautiful "Land of Standing Rocks" on both sides of the river and then went on down Cataract Canyon, one of the roughest sections of water on the entire trip. A week later they came out on smooth water at the mouth of a muddy stream which Powell called the Dirty Devil. Now for 169 miles the explorers rested on their oars as they drifted along on placid water through Glen Canyon. On August 4, the party reached the mouth of the Paria River at the head of Marble Canyon.

Next day, "with some feeling of anxiety," as Powell wrote, the explorers entered a "new cañon." Indeed in 1869, the Colorado above the Paria was better known than it was below. Spanish padres, Mexican packers, government surveyors, and Mormon missionaries had crossed it and mountain men had trapped its waters. But below the Paria the white men knew nothing of the Colorado as it flowed through Grand Canyon beyond what a few might have seen from rim viewpoints. Ives, of course, had reached the canyon floor at the mouth of Diamond Creek. The apocryphal raft trip through Grand Canyon by James White in 1867 has intrigued historians, but it added very little to the sum total of knowledge.[2]

With all its fast water and heavy rapids, Marble Canyon required five days' travel. Powell admired the canyon scenery, all on a "grand scale"—the beautiful colors of the canyon walls, the water-worn limestone, "all polished and fitted with strange devices, and embossed in a thousand fantastic patterns," and which gleamed in "iridescent beauty" in the sunlight. He spoke of Vasey's Paradise with its springs and fountains "covered with mosses, and ferns, and beautiful flowering plants." He particularly noted the alcoves, chambers, and caves so characteristic of the Redwall Limestone, and the side canyons often containing pools of clear, cool spring water.

On August 10, Powell reached the mouth of the Little Colorado and the end of Marble Canyon, 61.5 miles below the Paria.[3] Here for three days the men rested, took astronomical observations, salvaged the best of their spoiling food, and made ready to enter the "Great Unknown," as Powell called the canyon ahead. "We have an unknown distance yet to run, an unknown river yet to explore," he wrote. Eager to be on their way, but beset by moods of anxiety and misgiving, the voyagers went on down the great canyon.

They had 218 miles to do. The river soon forced itself upon them; there was less time to admire the "gigantic scenery," and the moodiness intensified. By the end of the first day they had reached the head of the Upper Granite Gorge. By now Powell had learned that "hard rocks have given us bad river; soft rocks, smooth water." They now faced a narrow V-shaped canyon cut by the Colorado through the hardest rocks they had yet seen—the Precambrian granite.

The first rapid inspired awe. "The cañon is narrower than we have ever before seen it; the water is swifter; there are but few broken rocks in the channel; but the walls are set on either side, with pinnacles and crags; and sharp, angular buttresses, bristling with wind and wave-polished spires, extend far out into the river," Powell wrote. Lining, portaging, running, Powell and his men laboriously worked their way through the "solemn, mysterious" canyon, down through "these grand, gloomy depths," past some of the worst rapids in Grand Canyon—Hance, Sockdolager, Grapevine. Bradley wrote that August 14 was the "wildest day" on the water so far; what a "frightful sea" one rapid was!

On the afternoon of August 15, the party stopped at the mouth of a "clear, beautiful creek, coming down through a gorgeous red cañon." After the muddy waters of the Colorado—made darker by

*"House Rock" at House Rock Spring, on the Utah-Arizona
road. Named by the Powell Survey in 1871. Arizona.*

115

Sunset Crater. Arizona.

runoff from summer rains—that stream seemed so inviting and the sandy beach at its mouth so pleasant that Powell named it Bright Angel. Powell, son of a Methodist minister, may have felt conscience-stricken that he had recognized the devil upstream in Glen Canyon when he had named a muddy little stream the Dirty Devil. Bright Angel soothed the conscience as its clear waters comforted the man.[4]

The explorers spent two days at Bright Angel. They dried out, fashioned some new oars from a seasoned pine log, and checked over the supplies and equipment. There was enough food—musty flour, dried apples, but plenty of coffee—for ten days. The boats were battered and shaken, the barometers were useless, the canvas was rotten, all the rubber ponchos had been lost, half of the party was without hats, no one had an entire outfit of clothing, and there was not a blanket apiece to go around. Hoping that the worst places had been passed, and that his party could get out of the canyon in less than ten days, Powell pushed on to make all haste possible.

But they were still in the "granite prison" and progress was slow, back-breaking, and the nearly incessant rains helped to break down morale. At one point where the men were making a long portage Powell climbed out of the Granite Gorge to try to get some bearings, but though he reached a place high above the river still there was "more canyon above than below" and ahead, nothing but a "labyrinth of deep gorges." On this climb Powell had to study geology on the run, and there were only minutes to appreciate the picture of summer rain clouds playing about in the gorges. He wrote, "But somehow I think of the nine days' rations, and the bad river, and the lesson of the rocks, and the glory of the scene is but half seen."

Once out of the granite the going was smoother and faster. Although there were few quiet stretches of any distance, they made good time. On August 25, they reached Lava Falls, lined them, and made a run for the day of thirty-five miles. Next day, another run of thirty-five miles.

Mid-morning of the twenty-seventh the party reached the head of Lower Granite Gorge where the river was narrowly confined to the "black, hard walls." With anxiety and misgiving Powell went on. Right at the entrance, at the mouth of Diamond Creek, a portage was necessary. This was where Ives, eleven years before, had observed that the river rushed through the gorge "like a mill-race." Through one heavy rapid after another the three boats coursed along at better than ten miles an hour. At about eleven o'clock the explorers stopped to look over a rapid which filled the entire canyon from wall to wall. It was one of the worst they had seen. They spent the rest of the day investigating the fall—there was no way to line around it; the only choice was to run it.

The big rapid broke the spirit of three men—O.G. and Seneca Howland and William Dunn, who decided to separate from the expedition and walk out to the Mormon settlements. Next morning, with one boat left to them, the three men watched as the rest of the party successfully ran the rapid. Rather than follow they turned their backs on the river and started up a watercourse, since known as Separation Canyon.[5]

Separation Rapids, 239.5 miles below the mouth of the Paria River, was not as bad as it looked. The two boats came out of it right side up, and the six men hurried on into the unknown. Six and a half miles below Separation they came to an even worse place —Lava Cliff Rapid. They attempted to line but when one boat broke loose and went through without mishap, the other ran it. The worst was over. They were soon out of the Granite Gorge; the canyon opened up, the river was still swift, but there were no more rapids of any consequence.[6]

At noon on August 29, the battered explorers passed from the towering walls of Grand Canyon out into open country. Camp that night in a thicket of mesquite was sweet. "The relief from danger, and the joy of success, are great," Powell wrote. And the river rolled by *silently*. The danger was over, the gloom was gone, the toil had ceased, and there was still enough food for two or three more days! Continuing on downstream next day the explorers passed two Indian camps, and after noon they arrived at the mouth of the Virgin River where they found some Mormons fishing.

Man has known the Grand Canyon for over 3,000 years. The open canyon between the mouth of the Little Colorado and the head of the Upper Granite Gorge was much visited and numbers of prehistoric remains are to be seen there. Located near the mouth of Comanche Creek, the ruined structure in the foreground was built by Indians of the Pueblo III culture, 1100—1150 A.D. Arizona.

Wukoki ruin, Wupatki National Monument. San Francisco Peaks in the background (lower right). Arizona.

John Wesley Powell and the five who stayed with him—Walter H. Powell (J.W.'s brother), George Y. Bradley, J. C. Sumner, William R. Hawkins, and Andrew Hall—had conquered the great canyons of the Green and the Colorado. Indeed it had been a voyage into the unknown. By his voyage Powell had dissipated much of the mystery of the Colorado. He had found out that though the river was navigable it would scarcely serve as a commercial channel. Even as he left the river he began to develop plans to put the canyon country on the map. But elation was dampened by the news of tragedy. Upon reaching Salt Lake City en route east the major learned that the three men who had left the expedition at Separation Rapids had been killed by the Shivwits Indians.[7]

BLACK SAND

In Salt Lake City, on the evening of September 21, 1869, in the assembly rooms of the Thirteenth Ward of the Church of Jesus Christ of Latter-day Saints, Powell gave his first public lecture on the canyons of the Colorado. He regaled his audience with incidents and adventures encountered during the trip; he articulated some of his first thinking on canyon country geology; he described the prehistoric ruins seen at several places along the way and speculated on the character and origins of those who had built them. Powell had discovered some impressive Indian-made structures in Glen Canyon and some lesser sites at the mouths of the Little Colorado, Bright Angel and Shinumo creeks in Grand Canyon.[8]

Why had these ancient people sought the canyon depths to build their homes? Were they the ancestors of the Pueblo Indians who lived in houses of similar construction? Were they related to the Aztecs, as Humboldt had suggested in his *New Spain*? Powell was much intrigued by the riddle of the ruins, but he was more interested in living Indians, and during the course of subsequent field investigations in the Colorado River region he devoted much time to the study of ethnology, leaving archaeology to others. The awesome canyons posed a formidable barrier to archaeo-logical investigation, and students of prehistory have generally avoided the region until recent times. Modern archaeologists, working systematically and traveling by boat and even helicopter, have pieced together the broad outlines of the aboriginal prehistory of the Grand Canyon country.

The earliest man-made remains yet discovered are small animal figurines fashioned of split willow twigs, found in remote and isolated caves deep in the Grand Canyon where they were left by prehistoric hunters possibly four thousand years ago. Archaeologists identify the figurine makers with the Desert Culture, or Desert Archaic, whose remarkable and ingenious people, inhabiting much of the arid West, developed a way of life based on foraging in a land where the range of foods was varied but sparse.[9]

The figurine makers left their rugged hunting ground long before the beginning of the Christian era, and centuries passed before humans again appeared in the Grand Canyon country. By A.D. 700, men who probably stemmed from the same roots as the old Desert Archaic, but now more culturally sophisticated, were again roaming the canyons. These people, called Anasazi (from the Navajo word for the "ancient ones") by the archaeologists, were the ancestors of the modern Pueblo Indians. They were less dependent on hunting and gathering and sought patches of ground where they could put in crops.

The Anasazis entered the region in large numbers after about A.D. 1000—during a period called by students Pueblo III—and in the canyons and on the rimlands for the next 150 years they built hundreds of stone and adobe structures to serve as dwellings, storage space, and ceremonial rooms. Nearly all the most prominent ruins date from this time. Not the least important locale was the lower valley of the Virgin where, about the mouth of the Muddy River, a large population settled and built the famed Pueblo Grande de Nevada, or Lost City.

Two other peoples, also stemming from the Desert Culture, lived along the southern reaches and periphery of Grand Canyon. The Cohoninas ranged from the Hualapai Plateau to the San Francisco Peaks, and to the east of them lived the Sinaguas. They were contemporaries of the Anasazis, and their

(Next spread) The Inner Gorge of the Colorado at Grand Canyon National Monument. Looking east, upriver, over ancient lava flows and Vulcan's Throne. Cinder cone on the left. Lava Falls, one of the most respected rapids in Grand Canyon, appears in the sunny spot on the river at middle right. Arizona.

ALLEN J. MALMQUIST

East Rim trail, Zion National Park. Utah.

West Rim trail, Zion National Park. Utah.

culture was heavily influenced by them. For reasons not yet clear, the Anasazis and the Cohoninas, if not the Sinaguas, abandoned the Grand Canyon region near the turn of the thirteenth century. There was a prolonged drouth before 1300, but there were probably other forces behind the exodus.

Life in the Grand Canyon country was difficult, and the ancient ones had to develop efficient ways of hunting, gathering, and farming just to survive. They were living in a desert, and a high one, where the snows and rains were scanty. Water. Water was the key to life in the region. Beyond the hundredth meridian, the West generally is semi-arid and dry, but the canyon country is arid and drier. Only the highest elevations—the High Plateaus of Utah, the Kaibab and Uinkaret plateaus, and the San Francisco Peaks—receive more than twenty inches of rain annually. The rest of the country receives half that or even less.

Precipitation of course varies with altitude. The extremities of relief within the region, ranging from elevations in excess of twelve thousand feet (San Francisco Peaks) to a low of twelve hundred feet (Lake Mead), serve to produce bands or zones of rainfall and climate. Climb, if you will, from the depths of Grand Canyon to the top of the San Francisco Peaks and you will pass from a dry, hot desert to a cold, treeless surface suggestive of the Arctic regions. The dramatic variety of climate in the Grand Canyon country suggested the life-zone concept to C. Hart Merriam, who identified seven distinct zones of vegetation. His findings, published in 1889, have since been found applicable elsewhere.[10] Thus, in a land of local, mini-climates, few generalizations about the weather will apply everywhere.

The Indians learned that regional diversity of climate produced an abundant variety of plants and animals. Deer lived on the tree-covered peaks and plateaus, antelope roamed the open places, and desert bighorn sheep grazed on and below the rocky rims and canyon ledges. Rabbits flourished in bushy areas, and wild turkeys throve among the pines of the lower levels. The aboriginal menu·was enriched by a number of products harvested from wild plants: piñon nuts, cactus fruit, and mescal (the roasted butt of the agave plant), and seeds and berries including mesquite, catclaw, and yucca.

In addition, where dependable water sources were found, the prehistoric Indians grew corn, beans, and squash in small irrigated plots. From a rather extensive catalog of wild animals and plants, and domesticated crops, the Indians also derived materials for building, clothing, and trade, and the manufacture of tools, weapons, and baskets. From the earth came stone for weapons, jewelry, and building, clay for pottery, salt for seasoning and commerce, and red and black paint for personal ornamentation and trade.

Although the natural resources available to the canyon country Indians were varied, few were found in abundance. Consequently, hunting and food gathering, based upon a thorough knowledge of the environment, were well organized and efficient. A good balance existed between the resources of the land and the dependent population; however, water and farm lands were very limited, and when radical changes in natural conditions and weather occurred, the lives of the aborigines were profoundly affected.

This can be dramatically illustrated. About A.D. 1067, Sunset Crater, east of the San Francisco Peaks, erupted in a burst of violent activity and for some time blew out clouds of ashes and cinders. The local Sinaguan Indians fled from their homes in terror, but when the crater had quieted they cautiously returned to assess the damage. They found their homeland and an area eight hundred square miles in extent had been covered with a mantle of black sand. They dug out, rebuilt, and planted corn in the cinder-covered fields. Probably to the surprise of the planters, the crops that year were the best ever. The black sand and ash had provided a mulch which conserved water and improved the yield. Moreover, someone discovered that corn would grow almost anywhere under the black mulch! What had looked like disaster had turned into bonanza. Where there had been but few suitable acres before the eruption, now there were comparatively unlimited lands where crops would grow.

This welcome news was not lost on nearby desert dwellers who rushed in to take up land in the black sand country. The Sinaguans prospered and their

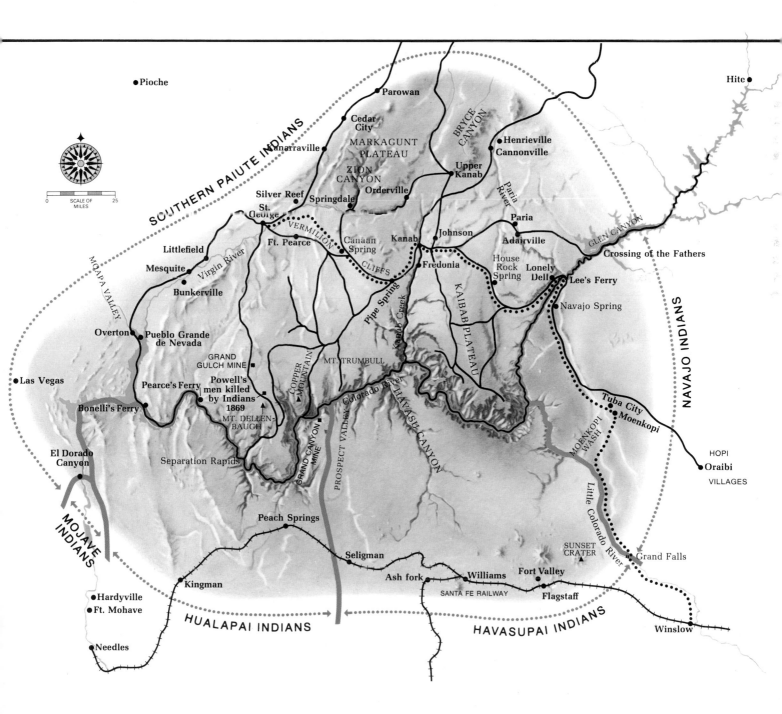

Opening the Land
1869-1890

Explorations by John Wesley Powell
and the Powell Survey, 1869-1873
The Honeymoon Trail
Approximate Range of Indian Tribes

Pioche

Hite

Parowan

Cedar
City

MARKAGUNT
PLATEAU

BRYCE
CANYON

Henrieville
Cannonville

Kanarraville

SOUTHERN PAIUTE INDIANS

ZION
CANYON

Upper
Kanab

Silver Reef

Springdale

Orderville

Paria
River

St.
George

VERMILION

Paria

Adairville

GLEN CANYON

Littlefield

Ft. Pearce

Canaan
Spring

Kanab

Johnson

CLIFFS

Crossing of the Fathers

Mesquite

Virgin River

Fredonia

House
Rock
Spring

Lonely
Dell

Lee's Ferry

Bunkerville

Pipe Spring

Navajo Spring

MOAPA VALLEY

Kanab Creek

Overton

Pueblo Grande
de Nevada

KAIBAB PLATEAU

NAVAJO INDIANS

GRAND
GULCH MINE

MT. TRUMBULL

Las Vegas

Pearce's Ferry

COPPER MOUNTAIN

Powell's
men killed
by Indians
1869

Colorado River

HAVASU CANYON

Tuba City

Moenkopi

Bonelli's Ferry

MT. DELLEN-
BAUGH

MOENKOPI WASH

HOPI

El Dorado
Canyon

Separation Rapids

GRAND CANYON MINE

PROSPECT VALLEY

Little Colorado River

Oraibi

VILLAGES

MOJAVE
INDIANS

Peach Springs

SUNSET
CRATER

Grand Falls

Seligman

Williams

Fort Valley

Kingman

Ash fork

SANTA FE RAILWAY

Flagstaff

Hardyville

Ft. Mohave

HUALAPAI INDIANS

HAVASUPAI INDIANS

Winslow

Needles

SCALE OF
MILES
0   25

culture flourished. Through trade and close association with other peoples they enriched their own way of life. From the Anasazis they adopted the multi-stoned apartment houses and from the Hohokam people, whose central territory was the valley of the Gila River, they learned a ball game played on a large, paved court.

For two hundred years the black sand around Sunset Crater supported a number of villages, or pueblos, before the land gave out. Through the years the high spring winds gradually swept the light ash and cinders into drifts and canyons, thus denuding the level places and the water-saving mulch. Crops became poorer, then failed altogether as the land reverted to its original state. More and more farmers were forced to leave this prehistoric dustbowl, and by the middle of the thirteenth century the Sinaguan villages had been abandoned and were falling into decay. Imposing ruins, such as those in Wupatki National Monument, in the heart of the black sand country, remain to commemorate the extremity of life in a region of great beauty but of limited natural resources.

Even though the canyon country was marginal at best, there were a few places that would support limited numbers of people. Not long after the departure of the ancient ones the ancestors of the modern Indians moved in: the Havasupais and Hualapais occupied Cohonina territory; the Hopis took up lands around the Moenkopi area; the Southern Paiutes appropriated the Arizona Strip and the High Plateaus. Some of the moderns appear to have been less dependent on farming and they found it possible to survive in a meager environment by making fuller use than their predecessors of the varied resources. When the first white settlers moved in, they found the Indians living in balance and harmony with the supporting environment.[11]

The white man upset the equilibrium. The Mormons were the first to create imbalances, and armed conflicts—such as the Walker War, 1853–1854—resulted. After this disturbance, the presence of the Paiutes along the trail to California suggested the need for missions to pacify the Indians. The Mormons established the Southern Indian Mission in the Virgin River basin in 1854, followed by the settlement of Las Vegas the next year.

Despite some hostilities the Indians and Mormons generally got on well. When it came to utilization of the natural resources the white man was much more efficient than the Indian. With his dams and plows and tools and draft animals he could make the land produce a surplus where the Indian grew only enough for himself.

The Paiutes, however, were dismayed by the increasing numbers of whites. Although they enjoyed the larger harvests, the converts had to work shoulder to shoulder with the industrious missionaries to produce them. They tired of this as of the exhortations to prayer, to cleanliness, and to "improvements" in their way of life. The Paiutes soon began to long for the old ways, and by 1856 they were again painting themselves and abusing their women as they had before the Mormon missionaries arrived. As time passed they became ever more restless.[12]

The Navajo Indians also felt pressure from the white men. The Athapascan-speaking Navajos and Apaches were latecomers to the Southwest. Nomadic intruders rather than descendants of older prehistoric cultures, they settled near the Pueblos in northern New Mexico, learning from and preying upon them. During the Spanish period these tribes extended their range westward. By the time they came under American rule in 1848 the Navajos' homeland was centered at Canyon de Chelly in the Chuska Range. From there they roamed and raided from the Rio Grande to the San Francisco Peaks. The Apache bands in the meantime had broken away and moved into the region south of that dominated by the Navajos.

To stop their raiding the United States Army campaigned against the Navajos intermittently from 1846 to 1864, when a portion of the tribe surrendered and agreed to removal. But many escaped American force by fleeing to the slick rock and canyon country of the Colorado River between the San Juan and the Little Colorado. Jacob Hamblin and his party, while on the third expedition to the Hopis in November, 1860, encountered some of the hostile Navajos, who killed George A. Smith, Jr. This was the first incident opening a decade of hostility between the Mormons

ass and sage at Wupatki National Monument. When Sunset Crater erupted
out A.D. 1067 and spread ash over the countryside, the desert land held the
visture then, and became more productive. Prehistoric farmers throve for 200
ars in the black sand area, but as the soil eroded away the Indians departed,
iving their towns and villages to fall into ruins. Arizona.

and the Navajos, who, for a time, found ready allies in the Paiutes.

During the early 1860s the Mormon frontier expanded notably. The Cotton Mission, with St. George as its capital, grew apace. New settlements were established along the Virgin from Springdale in Zion Canyon to St. Thomas at the foot of the Moapa Valley. The Saints did not reoccupy Las Vegas; for a time during the Civil War this adobe compound abandoned by the Mormons in 1857 was designated as Fort Baker, but it was never garrisoned and remained a fort in name only.[13] From Dixie the Mormons moved eastward and planted settlements at the base of the High Plateaus and on the Arizona Strip. Pipe Spring, Moccasin, Glendale, and Kanab were all located at springs and along streams long used by the Indians.

As the white population increased, the Paiutes saw their water and food supplies endangered, and they grew sullen and hostile. In 1865, the Utes in central Utah rose against white domination and opened a conflict known as the Black Hawk War. Encouraged by this the Paiutes on the Arizona Strip, with some help from the Navajos, struck out at the Mormon intruders. Late in 1865 and early in 1866 the Indians raided the settlements and killed J. M. Whitmore and Robert McIntyre at Pipe Spring, and Joseph, Robert, and Isabella Berry near Short Creek.

The Mormons abandoned their villages on The Strip. Fort Pearce (usually spelled Pierce), a turreted structure, was built near St. George to guard the eastern approaches to the Virgin Valley. The Iron Military District of the Utah Territorial Militia, with headquarters at St. George, opened a campaign against the marauders. In mid-September, 1866, a company of cavalry commanded by Captain James Andrus, was sent to the field to make a reconnaissance of the country along the Colorado from the Kaibab Plateau to the mouth of the Green River. Andrus planned to examine the crossings of the Colorado to learn all he could of the country, to chastise the enemy, and to try to reconcile any Paiutes of a friendly disposition.

The militiamen conducted an important exploration which carried them around the eastern base of the Paunsaugunt Plateau and to the top of Boulder Mountain. They were quite probably the first whites to see the castellated rims of the Paunsaugunt, including the formations in Bryce Canyon and those of the Table Cliff Plateau. From the volcanic eastern rim of Boulder Mountain they were treated to magnificent vistas of the slick rock country sloping off to Glen Canyon of the Colorado. And they spied out the lands opening the way for Mormon settlement east of the High Plateaus. There was one encounter with the Navajos when Elijah Averett, Jr., was ambushed and killed.[14]

The war dragged on; armed patrols guarded the routes leading from the Navajo country to the Mormon settlements. Jacob Hamblin, one of the principals in manning the guard, labored to strengthen the Mormons' friendship with the Paiutes. At best, however, the loyalty of the several bands, notably those remote from the Mormon settlements, remained uncertain.

August 28, 1869. Three men, O. G. Howland, Seneca Howland, and William Dunn, stood on the right shore and watched as the two boats bounced through the billowing waves of Separation Rapid. Rather than follow in the boat left to them, the three turned their backs on the Powell expedition and the Colorado and started up Separation Canyon. Powell and the rest made it through Separation Rapids and were out of the Grand Canyon in two days. The Howlands and Dunn walked into a war.

A straight-walled, three-pronged canyon, Separation heads on the western side of the extreme southern tip of the Shivwits Plateau. By way of the eastern fork of the canyon the hapless trio climbed out to the top of the plateau. Hoping to reach the Mormon settlements along the Virgin River, the men traveled for miles across the relatively flat surface of the plateau through piñon-juniper forest, occasionally coming out into the open in parklike meadows bordered with stands of yellow pine. There was little to guide them. A symmetrical mountain formed by lava, later named Mt. Dellenbaugh by the Powell Survey, appeared off to their left. They may have climbed it to take their bearings. Continuing north a few miles, the Howlands and Dunn reached the vicinity of the present Parashont Ranch where all three were killed by the resident Shivwits Indians, a band of Southern Paiutes.[15] They were casualties in a frontier struggle, a conflict aggravated by the poverty and barrenness of the land. But the conflict had run its course by the end of 1869, and Powell himself was able to assist in ending it the following year.

THE ROMANTIC VISION

John Wesley Powell in 1869 may have conquered the "great unknown" but he had only begun to read the "book of revelations." Everything he had seen in the Colorado River canyon lands fed his interest and fired his imagination. Within a year he was back in the Grand Canyon country. Powell's trip through the great canyons of the Colorado caught national attention, and to continue his work of exploration he obtained an appropriation from Congress, and with it promises of continued support. Thus was inaugurated the Geographical and Topographical Survey of the Colorado River of the West—the Powell Survey.

During the first year Powell planned to make a reconnaissance of the lands adjacent to the Colorado River, a move preliminary to a second trip through the canyons. He headed for southern Utah and the Arizona Strip, since he wanted to find out what had happened to the Howland brothers and William Dunn. His party rendezvoused at the edge of the meadows on upper Kanab Creek. Here Powell met Jacob Hamblin, who had been engaged as guide and had brought with him a number of Kaibabit Paiutes along with their chief, Chuarrumpeak, or Chuar.

During the month of September, Powell explored and described some of the grand features of the region. He climbed through the Pink Cliffs to the rim of the Paunsaugunt Plateau. From Pipe Spring he headed across the Arizona Strip, climbed the Uinkaret Mountains, and reached the floor of Grand Canyon by a steep trail down Whitmore Canyon.

After returning from the Grand Canyon, Powell and Hamblin met and talked with some of the Shivwits Paiutes and learned that they had indeed killed the Howland brothers and Dunn. They had heard from an Indian living across the Colorado that the three white men were miners who had killed an Indian woman in a drunken brawl. They knew that no one had ever come down the river before; so the men were thought to be guilty and were ambushed and riddled with arrows. The Shivwits apologized for the mistake and promised Powell a peaceful reception in their country whenever he wished to return.

Having discovered a route into Grand Canyon by which he could supply a river expedition, and having obtained assurances of peace from the Indians, Powell prevailed upon Jacob Hamblin to guide him to the Hopi villages he so much wanted to see. Leaving the rendezvous camp on upper Kanab Creek on October 1, the party crossed the Kaibab Plateau at about the latitude of Jacob Lake, skirted the Vermilion Cliffs, and arrived at the mouth of the Paria River where an advance party had built a rude ferry. Men, supplies, and equipment were floated across on this, the first boat crossing of the Colorado at the place where two years later John D. Lee established a ferry. Powell had located another route by which he could supply a second expedition through the canyons of the Colorado.[16]

Within a few days Powell and Hamblin reached Oraibi, the westernmost of the Hopi villages in what Powell called the "Province of Tusayan," the name used by Coronado's men over three centuries before. He spent nearly two months studying the Hopis and their way of life. During this time Hamblin prevailed upon the major to go with him to Fort Defiance, where, with the Navajo chiefs, the two men worked out peace terms ending the ten-year-old Navajo–Mormon war.

Jacob Hamblin returned to the settlements to report the news. With him traveled a headman of Oraibi Pueblo, Tuba, and his wife, on a visit of several months among the Mormons. The trip produced an enduring friendship between the chief and his hosts. With the war at an end the way was open for the Mormons to undertake a new southward thrust across the Colorado into lands bordering those of the Hopis and Navajos.

After 1870 only a few incidents marred the peaceful relations between the Indians and whites in the northern part of the Grand Canyon country.[17] As

Jacob Lake on the Kaibab Plateau. Arizona.

elsewhere on the American frontier, the Indians had been overpowered and lost the battle. And, as elsewhere, they soon found themselves confined to reservations.

Leaving the land of the Hopis and Navajos, Powell went east to prepare for a second exploration of the Colorado. The second voyage, which began at Green River, Wyoming, on May 22, 1871, was largely a duplication of the first, but it was better equipped, and much more time was taken to study out the canyons. The expedition did not reach the mouth of the Paria until late October, 1871. At that point the party left the river and began to map and explore the Arizona Strip and the lands at the southern and eastern bases of the High Plateaus. Working through the winter the members of the expedition—Powell, A. H. Thompson, W. C. Powell, F. S. Dellenbaugh, F. M. Bishop, E. O. Beaman, J. K. Hillers, S. V. Jones, and A. H. Hattan—laid out a base line extending nine miles south of Kanab. From this line the men began mapping by triangulation, and this work took them to the Kaibab and Uinkaret plateaus. Powell succeeded in reaching the Colorado at the mouth of Kanab Canyon and thus found another route to supply a river expedition. A. H. Thompson, who was in charge of the survey in Powell's absence, made a notable traverse of the rough canyon country north of the Paria River to the Dirty Devil.

While the survey was in progress, Powell went east to obtain the necessary appropriations and then returned to resume command of the river trip through Grand Canyon. Leaving the mouth of the Paria on August 17, the voyagers found the Colorado unseasonably high. The rough water so severely buffeted the boats that Powell decided to end the river trip at the mouth of Kanab Canyon, which the party reached on September 7. Systematic mapping of the country north of Grand Canyon was now resumed, and by mid-February, 1873, a preliminary map was completed covering the entire region from Grand Wash to the Echo Cliffs and north to the base of the High Plateaus. Next, A. H. Thompson began mapping the High Plateaus and the western part of the Glen Canyon country, and during the next five seasons this was carried northward through Utah to the Wyoming and

Colorado boundaries. At the same time Powell, G. K. Gilbert, and Clarence Dutton made detailed geological studies of the Uinta Mountains, the Henry Mountains and the High Plateaus, and the Grand Canyon.

Before 1875, the public knew little about the Powell Survey. The major had written brief official reports and some of the expedition members had published newspaper accounts about the river trips and the land explorations. In 1875 Powell published two series of articles in *Scribner's* and in *Popular Science,* a number of which, with some changes, were included in his *Exploration of the Colorado River of the West and Its Tributaries Explored in 1869, 1870, 1871, and 1872,* also issued in 1875.

In these works he wrote of the two river trips and of the progress of the land survey up to the completion of the mapping of the Grand Canyon country. The major's handling of the river and some of the land explorations was anything but good history. He made a composite report of the voyages, but there was no mention of the personnel of the second trip, and certain facts about the survey were changed to heighten dramatic effect.

John Wesley Powell always regarded his explorations as investigations made in the spirit of science rather than in the name of adventure. As a consequence his writings were mainly scientific in tone, but he developed an easy, direct style, and when he wrote of the Grand Canyon country he often used words exuberantly, imaginatively, and with romantic effect. One frequently encounters passages full of feeling and exultation which recall the excitement he felt while exploring a beautiful, pristine wilderness.

Powell described the view from the White Cliffs as "a painted desert—not a desert plain, but a desert of rocks cut by deep gorges and relieved by towering cliffs and pinnacled rocks, naked rocks brilliant in the sunlight." He described a view of the Vermilion Cliffs: "When we were out a few miles, I looked back and saw the morning sun shining in splendor on their painted faces. The salient angles were on fire, and the retreating angles were buried in shade. I gazed and gazed until my vision dreamed, and the cliffs appeared a long bank of purple clouds piled from the horizon high into heaven."

The view from the summit of Mt. Trumbull on the Uinkaret Plateau inspired Powell to write: "A vision of glory! Peaks of lava all around below us; the Vermilion Cliffs to the north, with their splendor of colors; the Pine Valley Mountains to the north-west, clothed in mellow perspective haze; unnamed mountains to the south-west towering over cañons bottomless to my peering gaze; and away beyond, the San Francisco Mountains lifting their black heads into the heavens."

The cliffs bordering Moenkopi Wash called forth these words: "These cliffs are rocks of bright colors, golden, vermilion, purple and azure hues, and so storm-carved as to imitate Gothic and Grecian architecture on a vast scale. Outlying buttes were castles, with minarets and spires; the cliffs, on either side, were cities looking down into the valley, with castles standing between. . . ."

By these efforts Powell was attempting to do what he knew to be impossible. Words could never express the wonders of the canyons, which would tax even the reproductive efforts of the graphic arts. However, he employed photographers on the second voyage and on the subsequent land surveys. E. O. Beaman, James Fennemore, and John Hillers were hired in succession. The best work was done by Hillers, who stayed with the survey the longest. Photographs taken by these men were made into stereopticon views and these found wide public sale.

Some of the photographs were used as the subjects for drawings by various artists including Thomas Moran, whom Powell introduced to the Grand Canyon in 1873. Moran's sketches and drawings, in the romantic style characteristic of his landscapes, appear throughout the pages of Powell's works on the canyon country.

If Lieutenant J. C. Ives had given the public a good view of the southwestern corner of the Grand Canyon country, John Wesley Powell had exposed the entire northern half of it. In words and by graphic art and maps, he introduced the world to a land he obviously loved with passion, and it was a love he never lost. In 1895, he published *Canyons of the Colorado,* which was drawn mainly from his earlier pieces published in 1875. But he did write a special chapter on the Grand Canyon for the book. Once again he tried to capture in words the "grand effects" of "the most sublime spectacle on earth." The alternating beds of sandstone resemble "vast ribbons of landscape" and the "colors of the heavens are rivalled by the colors of the rocks. The rainbow is not more replete with hues. But form and color do not exhaust the divine qualities of Grand Canyon. It is a land of music." Again: "The glories and the beauties of form, color, and sound unite in the Grand Canyon—forms unrivalled even by mountains, colors that vie with sunsets, and sounds that span the diapason from trumpet to tinkling raindrops, from cataract to bubbling fountain."[18]

When it came to the Grand Canyon country, Powell, the scientist, was a most romantic expositor of the unrivaled beauties of the land of living rock.

Eagle Arch, Johnson Canyon. Utah.

Desert Bonanza

HOME ON THE COOPERATIVE RANGE

Those attempting to make a living from the arid lands of the Grand Canyon country were not inclined to relish the beauty of its landscape. John Wesley Powell might write of the "land of music," but the literature of Mormon pioneering in Dixie is quite devoid of such feeling. John Taylor, the third president of the Church of Jesus Christ of Latter-day Saints, wrote of the "little, forbidding, barren places" his people had colonized. This was a good thing, he concluded, for the growth of his church. He went on, "We are a very small people, and we are in the midst of a very large people. We occupy these valleys among these rugged mountains, and we dwell in deserts. . . . it is hard sledding. But wherever there is a habitable place, Latter-day Saints are living on it, and consequently living in these little places, they control the mountains and the country."

John Taylor wrote this in 1881,[1] and by that time throughout the northern half of the Grand Canyon country Mormon colonists had taken up every "little, barren place" with sufficient water, and they had pushed south to colonize the basin of the Little Colorado. The border wars between the Mormons and the Utes, Paiutes, and Navajos, 1865–1870, caused a se-

vere recession of the Mormon frontier in southern Utah and the neighboring parts of Arizona and Nevada. Once the war was over, expansion resumed and the frontiers were extended to new areas in the country between the Virgin and the Little Colorado. Indeed, during the period 1870–1883, the Mormons established their primacy in one of the most rugged frontiers anywhere in the West.

Pioneer life in the Grand Canyon region was anything but easy. As an example consider those people who formed the Muddy Mission and settled in the Moapa Valley in the lower basin of the Virgin River. In some ways life here was not as difficult as in other areas in the Mormon kingdom. The Muddy River, formed by large springs, was not subject to rampaging floods like the Virgin. Irrigation water could be taken out through canals and ditches without fear of washouts.

The hot summer climate was disagreeable to some people and insects abounded. Malaria was common and numbers of settlers died from this and other diseases. Building materials were scarce, and the little settlements were made largely of adobe, not unlike the prehistoric Indian structures, which lined both banks of the lower valley. Transportation problems were severe, since roads scarcely existed. Travelers between St. George and the Muddy found it necessary to cross the quicksand bed of the Virgin

The cliffs of Mt. Kinesava, Zion National Park, tower 3,500 feet above the Rockville cemetery. Utah.

River many times. This was bad enough in low water; at high water it was nearly impossible. The Indian troubles farther north during the Black Hawk War were mirrored to some extent along the Muddy, but the local Paiutes seemed content to steal the settlers' cattle.

Remote, isolated in the extreme, the Muddy Mission contributed little to the cotton experiment, and once the dream of a corridor to the sea by way of the Colorado River vanished, the settlements languished. The missionaries spent their energies largely in developing a subsistence economy. With little outside income, they were on the edge of poverty most of the time and constantly starved for manufactured goods they could not afford.[2]

The worst trouble to plague the Mormons along the Muddy was political in character and resulted from boundary changes involving Utah, Nevada, and Arizona. When the first colonists arrived, the Moapa Valley was in Pah-Ute County, Arizona Territory, county seat at Callville, but in 1866 Congress gave the western part of the county to Nevada. Nevada promptly organized Lincoln County to include the new territory, but there was some doubt whether the Muddy River settlements actually fell within its limits. A boundary survey in 1870 showed that they did indeed. Nevada then required payment of back taxes and current assessments in specie, a demand which few of the Saints on the Muddy could meet.

The end of the mission was in sight. Faced with confiscation of their property unless they paid Nevada taxes, most of the colonists elected to leave the valley and move back to Utah. Under the direction of James Leithead and Daniel Stark the exodus began on February 1, 1871. Within ten years, however, the Mormons began to return to the Muddy and, accepting citizenship in Nevada, restored and rebuilt St. Thomas, Overton, and Logandale.[3]

Only a few had remained behind during the exodus of 1871, among them Daniel Bonelli, who moved to the mouth of the Virgin River, where he established a ferry. Bonelli was the first "booster" of the Virgin River country, and for many years Bonelli's Ferry was a main crossing of the Colorado. A small village grew up there known as Junction City, Junctionville, and finally, Rioville, which boasted a post office.

Upstream from Rioville on the Colorado, at the very mouth of Grand Canyon, another ferry was put in operation in 1876 by Harrison Pearce at the point where in 1863 Jacob Hamblin had found a good crossing. About midway between Pearce's (also known as Colorado Crossing) and Bonelli's, Mike Scanlon established another ferry in 1881.[4] During the 1870s and 1880s a number of mining districts were opened in Utah, Arizona, and Nevada, and the ferries were in frequent service as miners rushed about from one camp to another. Some of the Mormon migrants heading for Arizona used these crossings—notably Pearce's—but most of them crossed at Lee's Ferry, at the head of Grand Canyon, 279 miles upstream.

Meanwhile back in Dixie, the Saints began to resettle ground lost during the Indian war and to occupy new areas. East of the Hurricane Cliffs the Saints had holed up at Virgin and Rockville. Before 1870, a string of small settlements had come into

Pioneer log cabin at Paria settlement on the Paria River. Utah.

existence along the Virgin River between the mouth of Zion Canyon and the Hurricane Cliffs—Zion, Springdale, Northrop, Shunesburg, Rockville (originally Adventure), Grafton, Duncan's Retreat, Virgin City. Amidst a glorious profusion of mesas, buttes, temples, crags, cliffs, and under the lofty towers of Zion Canyon, they continued to do battle with the capricious Virgin River which annually washed out dams, ditches, and other works of man, and carried away the precious soil along its banks.

John Wesley Powell and the members of his survey might say, "Nothing can exceed the wondrous beauty of . . . Zion Valley," while the artist Thomas Moran captured the sublimity of the landscape in watercolors. The pioneer watching half of his farm go downstream in a flood had a different reaction. He could agree with John Taylor, his church president, who said, "Our mountains have very large feet." There were many mountains and not enough tillable soil. The canyon country of the Virgin River may have had great beauty but most of the practical men facing the harsh reality of making a garden in a sandstone wilderness were scarcely affected by the landscape at all. Some were touched by it though. Isaac Behunin, one of the earliest settlers in the great canyon, was excited by the grandeur of the place and named it Zion. However, when Brigham Young visited Zion Canyon about 1870 he thought the name inappropriate and said it was not Zion. And for a time the canyon, to the literal-minded, bore the name "Not Zion."[5]

Long Valley, above Parunuweap Canyon on the eastern fork of the Virgin River, had been evacuated during the Indian war, and it was here that most of the exiles from the Muddy Mission settled in 1871. The abandoned villages at Winsor and Berryville were now renamed Mt. Carmel and Glendale, respectively. Trouble continued to plague them. Grasshoppers ate the first wheat crop and frost killed the corn. Many were poverty-stricken and in rags. There was not

Stone fort at Pipe Spring National Monument.
Photograph taken about 1908. Arizona.

enough housing. Measles swept through the valley and carried off numbers of children. No wonder that these desolate Long Valley pioneers were ready to embrace an experiment in communal living instituted by the Mormon Church in 1874.

The United Order, proclaimed by Brigham Young in 1874, presaged by the Mormon cooperatives, was a further attempt to make the Mormon kingdom self-sufficient and to combat the depression brought on by the national panic of 1873. The depressed prices of farm products were keenly felt in the southern Utah communities so distant from the cash market.

The Saints were asked to cooperate in all forms of labor and enterprise with the goal of eliminating individual profit-making, establishing complete self-sufficiency, and human equality. In launching the order at St. George, Brigham Young probably realized that the "perfect society" which he envisioned would have a better chance of success where cooperation had been a necessary concomitant to survival. The ideal was widely adopted in southern Utah where it took several forms. In most communities it became a cooperative effort of persons engaged in a common enterprise such as farming or herding. One of the more important achievements of the order was the building of the temple at St. George, the first Mormon temple to be erected in the West. In enterprises of this kind the participants pooled their time and resources to carry out the single objective at hand, but they continued in the private ownership of property, including lands and homes. However, a few communities adopted a complete apostolic communism where all real and personal property was deeded to the community. The most interesting of these was Orderville in Long Valley.

The Mormons, who had suffered hardships on the Muddy and poverty in Long Valley, entered the United Order with a determination bordering on desperation. The most zealous laid out a new town, Orderville, three miles up the valley from Mt. Carmel. Land, animals, farming equipment, food, and supplies were all turned over to a municipal corporation governed by articles of agreement.

Members of the order lived in apartment houses built around the town square with a hall in the center where everyone dined together. Farms, gardens, orchards, herds, and shops and mills were all communally worked and the products pooled. The surplus was sold in neighboring communities to build up a reserve. Members withdrew food and supplies from common stocks upon need. Newcomers were invited to join, and by 1880 about seven hundred people were living in the experiment.

The United Order in Long Valley lasted ten years, which was nearly seven years longer than it survived elsewhere. The decline came about through overpopulation. Membership grew so large as to overload the area's resources. The youthful members became discontented. Outside influences also had a weakening effect. The opening of the mines at Silver Reef near St. George in 1876 produced millions of dollars, but little of this wealth reached Orderville. Those in the order were held up to ridicule by their neighbors and called old-fashioned because they persisted in using homemade products instead of manufactured clothing and goods from the outside. Then in the early 1880s most of the community leaders were driven underground by the antipolygamy crusade. In 1885, the order was dissolved and the common property was distributed among the hundred-odd families who had stayed with the experiment. The community continued, however, and most of those who participated remember the experience as a happy one. Indeed, Orderville today likes to refer to itself as the "United Order town."[6]

Zeal for living in the United Order in Dixie was uneven, and when it began to die out certain families moved away to perpetuate the experiment elsewhere. On the Virgin River midway between Dixie and the Muddy, Bunkerville was settled in 1877 by one such group; within three years Littlefield and Mesquite were established nearby.[7] After many vicissitudes—Indian war, political action, depression, floods—the Saints finally had staked out all the irrigable acres of the desert river from Zion Canyon and Long Valley to Bonelli's Ferry. By 1880, the Virgin River belonged to the Mormons.

As the decade of the 1870s opened, the Grand Canyon country was still a quiet wilderness, largely undisturbed and unexploited. But the pioneer was soon to leave a deeper mark. For one thing the virgin range was a veritable bonanza. The first settlers in the Grand Canyon region, the Mormons were the first to utilize the range lands. Herds, of course, were found in all the settlements and cooperative herding was a common feature in the distinctive Mormon village, especially during the years of the United Order.

Cattle and sheep became increasingly important in the economy of the pioneers in the southern Utah region, after the coming of the Pacific Railroad which brought Utah products within range of the national market. Moreover, the opening of mines in the inter-mountain West created an outlet for foodstuffs close at hand. These conditions produced a rapid growth of the livestock industry in Utah, which coincided with the explosive expansion of cattle grazing throughout the West following the Civil War.

The Mormons profited heavily from the beef boom. Although there was a substantial amount of private enterprise, several of the largest outfits in southern Utah were cooperatives. In a number of these the Mormon Church participated in part to en-sure the care and profits from livestock paid to the church as tithing, a common practice at the time.

The Mormon cooperatives ranged cattle and sheep all over the Grand Canyon country from the North Rim to the highest meadows of the Markagunt and the Paunsaugunt plateaus. Perhaps the largest outfit operating in the region was the Canaan Co-operative Stock Company, organized in 1870. Head-quarters were set up at Pipe Spring. Chosen as man-ager, Anson P. Winsor supervised the building of a strong fort at the spot. Begun in 1870, and completed in 1872, the cut-stone structure, which is today the principal building at Pipe Spring National Monu-ment, was called at the time "Winsor Castle." Not long after this the company's operation was trans-ferred to Canaan Spring in a cove at the base of Ver-milion Cliffs, a few miles west of Short Creek. Pipe then became the headquarters for another coopera-tive, the Winsor Castle Stock Growing Company, organized in 1873.

There were others. The Kanarra Cattle Company from Cedar Valley grazed stock across the Markagunt and Paunsaugunt plateaus. As early as 1874 cowboys of this outfit were herding cattle along the rim of Bryce Canyon and wintering stock in the bottoms along the Paria River where Cannonville and Henrie-ville were later founded, and the Orderville United Order acquired a number of ranches and cattle from its members and put a herd on the Kaibab Plateau about 1877. Stock was wintered in House Rock Valley at the eastern base of the plateau and the summer range centered at DeMotte Park, a beautiful mea-dow in the conifer forest on top of the plateau.[8]

Bonanza in grass. For a few years the companies made big profits. The Canaan Company declared a dividend of nearly forty percent in less than two years after its founding—but it was too good to last. Elsewhere in the West, where the grass was heavier, the profits held up longer, but in the desert country the pristine range was sparse and it was soon seri-ously depleted from overgrazing. The cooperatives began to disappear after 1890, to be replaced by indi-vidual ranchers. In 1895, B. F. Saunders bought out the Canaan Company and acquired certain other prop-erties on the Arizona Strip, most of which were later sold to the huge Grand Canyon Cattle Company. Preston Nutter, a non-Mormon, also acquired a num-ber of properties, including some from B. F. Saunders, and for years was the biggest cattleman on the western part of The Strip.[9]

The pioneer stockmen were the first to become intimately familiar with the northern half of the Grand Canyon country. They identified every acces-sible spring, waterhole, wash, and stream throughout the region. They located timber resources, discovered minerals, and sized up the country for its agricultural possibilities. But they found the farming potential poor indeed. Nearly every place with a few irrigable acres had either been staked out before the Indian wars, or else occupied very soon thereafter.

All the settlements and villages were established about the base of the High Plateaus which provided the water necessary for their survival. Kanab, Upper Kanab (later Alton), Johnson, and Scutumpah (also Clarkston), on Kanab Creek and its tributaries, and Cannonville, Paria, Adairville, and Lee's Ferry, on the Paria River, were the main links in the Mormon fron-tier east of Long Valley and Pipe Spring.

Looking downstream at Lee's Ferry on the Colorado. The original ferry site was upstream out of view. Wagons on the left approach had to cross the tilted formation known as Lee's Backbone. To bypass this rough haul a dugway (visible

Throughout the entire region from the Virgin to the Paria there was little room for local expansion. The first settlers had taken up most of the land, and after the 1870s few new settlements were started. An exception was Fredonia, eight miles south of Kanab in Arizona, begun in the mid-1880s as a refuge for a number of polygamous wives in flight from aggressive federal marshals bent upon enforcing the Edmunds Act of 1882 which made a crime of "unlawful cohabitation."[10]

In the northern half of the Grand Canyon country the limits of the frontier were probably reached before 1890; after that, settlement was even retracted. The size of the herds had to be cut in the face of overgrazing and drouth. Streamside settlements were plagued with floods, and some, like Paria, had to give up the ghost. It was a hard land in which to make a living; the resources were limited and one could not live on the scenery. For a time the pioneers made it blossom, but they often left the land in worse condition than they found it, precluding further expansion. "What," asks Karl Larson, "of the barren waste that once was a desert in bloom?"[11]

HONEYMOON TRAIL

In their misuse of the environment the pioneer Mormons were little different from their contemporaries elsewhere in the West. The progression of the Mormon frontier, however, was quite a different phenomenon from frontier expansion elsewhere which, as a rule, was haphazard and the product of individual enterprise. Working cooperatively, and often under direction from ecclesiastical authority, the Mormon frontiersman consciously extended the boundaries of the kingdom at whatever cost to himself. Individuals stood together on the "cutting edge of civilization" as part of a whole, planned movement.

The move south from Salt Lake City—the opening of a corridor to the Pacific, and the establishment of a central road into the Territory of Arizona—had been planned.[12] Brigham Young had foreseen the basin of the Little Colorado as a field for colonization

near the water's edge) was built in 1898 and used until the ferry closed operations in 1928. The Paria River comes in on the right (center) and the towering ramparts of the Paria Plateau are in the background. Arizona.

since 1858 when Jacob Hamblin first visited the Hopi villages. Once peace was made with Navajos and the country between Dixie and the Colorado River settled, the Mormons were ready to colonize the Little Colorado. And when they were forced to abandon the Muddy Mission in Nevada, and as the federal campaign against polygamy gained momentum, Young determined to act. The Little Colorado would not only absorb surplus population but it could serve as a base for further expansion southward even as far as Mexico. The first move was to establish a ferry across the Colorado at the mouth of the Paria where both Hamblin and Powell had found a feasible crossing. The job was undertaken by John D. Lee, who opened regular ferry service in January, 1873.

Lee's Ferry is certainly one of the most beautiful places in the Grand Canyon country and one of the most historic. There the Colorado breaks through the towering Echo Cliffs which mark the end of Glen Canyon. It courses along for two miles between open banks and then plunges over the boulder delta at the mouth of the Paria River to be swallowed by Marble Canyon. At the head of Grand Canyon, it was the only place for 279 miles downstream where a wheeled vehicle could be brought to the water's edge.

Domínguez and Escalante in 1776 had found that the Colorado could not be forded at the mouth of the Paria so they had gone on upstream to the Crossing of the Fathers. That ford had served the Santa Fe traders and the first Mormon expeditions to the Hopis. Later Jacob Hamblin rafted the river at Lee's Ferry, and in 1870, with lumber from the Kaibab, Powell and Hamblin built the first crude ferry, the *Cañon Maid,* on which the party crossed the river. The next year Powell ended his run through the upper canyons there; before he returned in the summer of 1872 to resume the voyage into Grand Canyon, John D. Lee had arrived.

Lee, in hiding for complicity in the Mountain Meadows massacre, had learned of the remote spot on the Colorado from Jacob Hamblin, and with one of his wives, Emma, he moved there in December, 1871. Emma named the place "Lonely Dell." The towering cliffs and mesas, the bare sand and rocks, scarcely suggest the word "dell," but the place was remote and lonely enough. Lee put up a house, dammed the Paria, and planted crops. Through the year 1872 he occasionally ferried people across the river using a crude raft, possibly the *Cañon Maid,* and at times Powell's *Nellie Powell,* left behind by the major on the Grand Canyon run of that year. Regular ferry service began in January when the *Colorado,* built of local timber, was christened. Thus was opened a new way across the river, replacing the historic Crossing of the Fathers upstream.[13]

Once the ferry was ready at Lonely Dell, Brigham Young acted quickly. A call was issued for colonists to go to Arizona and fill the Little Colorado Mission, which was placed under the direction of Horton D. Haight. The missionaries—109 men, six women and a child—assembled at Pipe Spring and in fifty-four wagons began the trek. For nearly two hundred miles they had to pick their way along, making a road as they went. Only a few wagons had ever been taken to Lee's Ferry before, and the tracks were not always

C. GREGORY CRAMPTON

Inscription at House Rock Spring.
A record of the first attempt by the Mormons
to colonize the Little Colorado. Arizona.

visible. From the open valley of Kanab Creek the colonists wound along the ledgy, rocky western slope of the Kaibab Plateau. On top they had to traverse a thick forest of piñon and juniper which snared animals and tore canvas. Then they jolted and bumped down the eastern slope of the Kaibab, which was steeper than the western slope. Through House Rock Valley and along the base of the Vermilion Cliffs they pulled through deep sand, headed washes and deep gulches, and finally arrived at the mouth of the Paria.

Lee's Ferry was a natural, but difficult, crossing of the Colorado. The approach to the right bank from the west was easy enough, but on the left bank a ridge dipping sharply upstream rose almost vertically from the river's edge. The first ferry crossing was upstream from the base of the ridge, forcing travelers to cross the barrier, which soon acquired the name "Lee's Backbone."

At Lee's Ferry the pioneers of 1873 found themselves at the end of the road. On the opposite bank there was only a horse trail. The steep, slick rock surface of Lee's Backbone wore out animals and tempers. Once on the crest, the colonists had to switchback the wagons down over a talus slope covered with blocks of sandstone. Making their way along the base of the Echo Cliffs, the pioneer band headed side canyons opening into Marble Canyon, and plugged doggedly along through washes, over barren hills, and across the Painted Desert. Finally, they reached Moenkopi where there was a good supply of spring water. In traveling the seventy miles from Lee's Ferry the trekkers had consumed twenty-six days—less than three miles a day! Going on to the Little Colorado, they found its bed nearly dry and the region bleak and barren—a disappointing climax to their efforts. Discouraged by the prospects of settlement in so desolate a place, the missionaries regretfully gave up and headed back over the long, dry road to the settlements. Camped at House Rock Spring near the head of House Rock Valley, one of them laconically

The lower crossing at Lee's Ferry, Arizona. Travelers avoided Lee's Backbone by taking this crossing, but it could only be used when the river was low. In operation, 1878-98. View of the right bank, Paria Plateau, background.

143

144

Looking north along the Echo Cliffs, marking the eastern edge of the Grand Canyon country. Springs at the southern end of the cliffs (lower right), near the Indian village of Moenave, provide some water for irrigation. Arizona.

wrote on the rocks "To Arizonia and Busted June 6 A.D. 1873."[14]

Through a trek as difficult as any yet taken by the Utah Mormons, these pioneers had opened a road to the Little Colorado, and the church was determined to add the region to the kingdom. Scouting parties under Daniel W. Jones and James S. Brown, sent out in 1875, reported favorably, and the next year the church organized a new mission of two hundred men to settle the Little Colorado. The vanguard, under Lot Smith, reached Sunset Crossing, near present-day Winslow, in March, 1876. During the next four years traffic over the Utah–Arizona road was fairly constant as the Saints actively settled the new land; by

The mineralized sandstones of Silver Reef were found in the upturned strata to the left of the nose of the Virgin anticline. The Virgin River (lower center) flows at a right angle across the formation. Utah.

1880 most of the Little Colorado towns—Brigham City, Sunset, St. Joseph, Taylor, Obed, Woodruff, and other places—had been founded, and the Mormons were firmly established in northeastern Arizona. By the same time the celebrated Hole-in-the-Rock colonizing expedition had established a foothold in southeastern Utah.[15]

Among those frequently seen on the pioneer road were honeymooners from the Mormon settlements on the Little Colorado. The young people, married by a justice of the peace before starting out, made the long journey to St. George to have the ceremony solemnized in the temple which had been completed in 1877. The newlyweds would fit out a wagon covered with heavy canvas supported by hickory bows. A small iron cook stove was also a space warmer, and a forty-gallon water barrel was slung on the outside of the wagon. About mid-November the couples began the trip—generally several wagons traveled together. Observers reported that the wagons crept along in no apparent haste. Camps were made early and struck late, and sometimes at the good watering places like Moenkopi, Navajo Spring, and House Rock Spring, the travelers might camp for two or more days. Arriving at St. George, they spent the winter in the warm Dixie sun and returned to the Little Colorado in April.[16]

The Mormon push south into Arizona resulted in the permanent settlement of Moenkopi and environs, which became an important way-station and watering place on the road between Utah and the Little Colorado. With numerous springs flowing from aquifers in bluffs and cliffs, and with living water in the nearby wash, Moenkopi was an oasis in a bleak but colorful desert. Prehistoric Indians had lived here, and Garcés in 1776 found some Hopis engaged in seasonal farming. Later a few Utes, Paiutes, and Havasupais dwelt in the area, but the coming of the Navajos in the 1850s discouraged further settlement until the Mormons made peace with those Indians. During the 1870s small Mormon colonies were established at Moenkopi and at nearby Moenave and Tuba City, named after the friendly Hopi Chief Tuba. The Mormon presence was reassuring to the Hopis who moved to the area in some numbers and began build-

ing a village on the banks of Moenkopi Wash. The Mormons and the Hopis lived side by side, but not without friction as both peoples competed for the limited local resources.[17]

The vital link on the Utah–Arizona road was Lee's Ferry. After Lee's death in 1877, the Church of Jesus Christ of Latter-day Saints acquired the site and provided regular service until 1910 when ownership passed first to the Grand Canyon Cattle Company and finally to Coconino County, Arizona, in which it is located. The ferry remained in service until 1928 when it was replaced by Navajo Bridge, built across Marble Canyon six miles downstream.[18]

SILVER REEF

Silver Reef, sixteen miles from St. George, was the biggest bonanza ever found in the Grand Canyon region. It is unique in American mining history, the only place where commercial amounts of silver ore have been found in sandstone. The metal was located in beds of folded and eroded sedimentary rock adjacent to the great Virgin Anticline, one of the more conspicuous physiographic features in Dixie. Between 1875 and 1909, when the mines shut down, about eight million dollars' worth of metal had been produced.

The first discovery of silver float was made in 1869 near the small Mormon farming community of Leeds. The Harrisburg Mining District was organized in 1874, named for another Mormon village near Leeds. The camp of Silver Reef, however, did not attract much attention until the following year, when William Tecumseh Barbee discovered rich silver ore on Tecumseh Hill. Some of it, shipped to smelters in Salt Lake and in the nearby mining town of Pioche, Nevada, assayed over five hundred dollars a ton. When the news leaked out there was a rush of miners, many of them from Pioche—the "Pioche Stampede"—and the Silver Reef boom was on. The period of greatest production occurred in the decade between 1877 and 1888, when operations by the major companies ceased. After that, some intermittent min-

Ruins at Silver Reef, big bonanza of th
Grand Canyon country. Uta

ing by lessees continued until 1909. The camp was virtually quiescent until 1950, when the uranium boom revived interest briefly in the silver ore, which contained minor amounts of copper, uranium, and vanadium.[19]

The discovery of precious metal at Silver Reef brought a flood of Gentiles to Dixie, and this alarmed the Mormons. It had a corrosive effect on the United Order, but turned out otherwise to be something of a blessing. The Cotton Mission had not prospered. The planters along the Virgin had to cope with a niggardly and hostile environment, Indian troubles, distant markets, and unstable prices, and many turned to subsistence farming to survive.

To bolster the flagging Dixie economy the Mormon Church in 1867 began the construction of a tabernacle in St. George. When completed eight years later the splendid structure had cost over a hundred thousand dollars. Before the tabernacle was finished, ground was broken for a temple. Dedicated in April, 1877, this dignified and stately structure was the first temple to be built by the Church of Jesus Christ of Latter-day Saints west of Nauvoo, and it had cost about half a million dollars. Just as these "public

works" were finished, the mines were opened at Silver Reef.

The Silver Reef rush provided an excellent cash market for all kinds of produce, fruit, hay, and stock, and Dixie wine was always in demand. There was a good market for lumber, firewood, and rock salt which came from deposits mined by prehistoric Indians along the lower Virgin River. Good wages could be made working in the mines, and handsome profits could be gained in freighting. In similar ways the Mormons in southern Utah had benefited from the mining boom in Pioche, Nevada, but Silver Reef, right in their own front yard, was an even greater boon. By the time silver production began to taper off in the late 1880s, the Dixie towns had achieved a stability not characteristic of the first fifteen years of the Cotton Mission.[20]

For the region at large, Silver Reef had a most important effect. The discovery of silver in sedimentary formations opened up the entire Colorado Plateau to prospecting. Men who walked over sandstone without looking now began to ask themselves: "If silver was found in one sandstone outcropping why not silver, or even gold, in another?"

9
Opening the South Rim

GOLD RUSH

Gold in Grand Canyon! Few miners in the 1860s would have seriously considered prospecting on the Colorado Plateau since it was believed that precious metals were not to be found in sedimentary rock. This was true up to 1871 when Powell made his second run through the canyons. When the expedition reached the Crossing of the Fathers in October, Pardyn Dodds and two prospectors, George Riley and John Bonnemort, were on hand to meet them. Dodds had been engaged by Jacob Hamblin to meet the boat party with much-needed supplies. They queried Powell's men about the prospects upriver but received disappointing replies. While waiting for the expedition to arrive, however, they had panned out a little gold from the river sands at the crossing.

Dodds, Riley, and Bonnemort were briefly employed by Powell to assist in the land survey. During the last days of 1871, Powell, with Dodds, Riley, and John Stewart, explored Kanab Canyon as a possible route to supply the river trip the following year. From the Colorado River sands at the mouth of Kanab Creek, Riley panned out a few colors, but the gold was extremely fine, like flour. When the men returned to Kanab the gold discovery was reported to the world

over the wires of the Desert Telegraph.[1]

Gold in Grand Canyon! The rush was soon under way. By February, 1872, hundreds of hopeful prospectors, mainly from Pioche and the mining districts to the west, were arriving at Pipe Spring and Kanab in wagons, on horseback and muleback, and on foot. Buying butter and beef in the Mormon villages, and leaving their vehicles behind, they plunged down Kanab Canyon. As in most gold rushes, many arrived consumed by the fever but improperly equipped and supplied, and with little knowledge of mining. The rush lasted four months before the bubble burst.

The gold was there. You could raise color from the river sand almost anyplace. But the work was hard, the returns exceedingly small. Kanab and Pipe Spring were the nearest supply points; there was little game in the depths of Grand Canyon. Firewood was scarce. Prospectors scrambled about up- and downstream from the mouth of Kanab Canyon, looking for better diggings. George Riley worked his way up the Colorado as far as Tapeats Creek, which he called Surprise Valley, but nowhere did the prospects pan out. By June, as the river began to rise with the spring runoff, the rush was over.

The rush had not been limited to the Kanab Creek area in Grand Canyon. Men reasoned that gold might be found in more than one place in the great gorge. During the first six months of 1872 prospectors

adder up the face of the Redwall Limestone,
uilt to reach mining prospects 258 feet above
le floor of Havasu Canyon. Arizona.

reached the river by way of Grand Wash, Diamond Creek, Whitmore Wash, and probably by other routes. Beginning in March a number of miners went to Lee's Ferry to work the gravels at the mouth of the Paria, but they met with indifferent success. Some went on to the Little Colorado to prospect, and at least one party started down Marble Canyon on a raft. It broke up in the rapids ten or fifteen miles downstream, John D. Lee reported, and the men nearly lost their lives.[2]

Even if no bonanzas had been located in the 1872 excitement, gold had been found at a number of places in Grand Canyon. The disappointed miners naturally pondered about the origin of the metal. In 1866, R. B. Marcy of the United States Army had published *Thirty Years of Army Life on the Border* and had suggested that an exploration of the canyons of the Colorado might yield mineral wealth. Taking note that precious metals had been found both east and west of the Colorado basin, he asked, "Is it not, therefore, probable that the walls of this gigantic crevice will exhibit many rich deposits?" In other places, the miner had to make open cuts or sink shafts to explore his prospect. In the Grand Canyon the exploratory work was already done for him. He could look upon the canyon as a great open cut extending for nearly three hundred miles in which the strata of rocks were laid bare to the depth of a mile or more. Marcy ventured to predict that the "huge gulch" might "yet prove to be the *El Dorado* for which the early Spanish explorers so long and fruitlessly sought."[3]

Marcy might have added that good prospects had been opened earlier in the lower basin of the Colorado below Grand Canyon. In 1858 placer gold was discovered on the lower Gila River, and within a few years a number of new districts were located upstream from Yuma on the Colorado. Particularly good diggings were found at La Paz, and at El Dorado Canyon about thirty-five miles south of Las Vegas. The most spectacular discoveries, however, were made in 1863 in the region between Wickenburg and Prescott in central Arizona. The latter place, named after the historian William H. Prescott, quickly rose to prominence. It was designated the territorial capital when Arizona was created from the western part of New Mexico in 1863. Fort Whipple was established nearby

in 1864; it was named after Lieutenant A. W. Whipple, who had conducted the railroad survey across northern Arizona ten years earlier.

Hard-rock mining soon replaced placering in most of the pioneer districts, and the surplus miners moved on to prospect elsewhere. By 1871 a number of new districts had been organized along the western periphery of the Grand Canyon country from the Prescott–Wickenburg area to Pioche in Nevada. The Potosi mines, near Las Vegas, had been reopened, and the news of rich ore had brought a rush to the Cerbat Mountains, the first range west of the Grand Wash Cliffs in Arizona, where locations had been made as early as 1865. Among those who helped to extend the mining frontier were soldiers on furlough from Fort Mohave and Fort Whipple.[4]

Whether or not they read Marcy, a good many prospectors in the 1872 rush began to explore the walls of Grand Canyon and the adjacent plateaus, looking for the sources of the river gold. They found very little gold but did turn up some silver and copper prospects. In June, 1873, Charles Spencer located the "Moqui" quartz claim in Havasu Canyon where he found good silver prospects in the Redwall Limestone about three hundred yards below Havasu Falls. In 1877, Spencer and Daniel O'Leary located another silver prospect on the south side of the Grand Canyon just below the mouth of the Little Colorado. Still other locations were recorded in Grand Wash Cliffs south of the Colorado.

The Mormons on the north side of the river prospected for minerals as they grazed stock on the Arizona Strip. In June, 1873, Richard Bentley, Samuel S. Adams, and others discovered a copper prospect, in the "Bentley Mining District." This, soon to be called the Grand Gulch mine, was located on the crest of the Grand Wash Cliffs about fifteen miles north of the mouth of Grand Canyon. In 1875, the "Copper Mountain Lode" was located between the fork of Parashont and Andrus canyons in the Mt. Trumbull Mining District. Records of production from these prospects are few, but a smelter was put into operation at the Grand Gulch mine in 1878.[5]

The Grand Canyon prospecting of the 1870s was but a prelude to the excitement that swept over the

Looking upstream from travertine dams in the canyon of the Little Colorado River, seven and a half miles from the big Colorado. Arizona.

Colorado Plateau when the significance of Silver Reef was understood. As millions in silver bullion poured from the sedimentary rock in that booming camp, prospectors swarmed over the Grand Canyon country looking for another such find. Those who had preceded them had found enough good prospects to suggest that the canyon lands indeed might contain a new El Dorado.

The 1880s opened with a burst of prospecting and mining; an excitement was generated that lasted more than twenty years. North of the Grand Canyon many new claims were staked in the Bentley and Mt. Trumbull mining districts. Prospectors worked their way from Parashont Canyon and Copper Mountain around the base of the Shivwits Plateau to the Grand Gulch mine, posting locations as they went. They dropped down through canyon tributaries of the Colorado and even prospected the Precambrian rocks of the Lower Granite Gorge. However, development work during this decade was mainly localized in the Copper Mountain and Bentley districts.[6]

But there was more excitement along the South Rim as prospectors explored the cliffs and canyons from the Little Colorado to Music Mountain. Wide publicity was given the South Rim when the Beckman and Young party, late in 1879, reported a discovery of

Prospector's cabin in the Grand Canyon at the mouth of the Little Colorado, Arizona.

carbonate of lead in Havasu Canyon. The Prescott *Arizona Miner* for January 22, 1880, optimistically heralded the find as "a Leadville in Arizona," referring to the wealthy mining camp in the Rockies then at the height of production.[7] The discovery in Havasu received more publicity when Beckman and Young returned to explore the canyon further. On April 1, 1880, one of the party, Daniel W. Mooney, fell to his death when he attempted to let himself down by a rope over a cliff near a cataract, since known as Mooney Falls.[8]

Havasu (Cataract) Canyon was alive with prospectors through the 1880s while other districts along the South Rim, west of there, were opened at the same time—Pine Springs, Prospect Valley, and Music Mountain. Although there was less activity east of Havasu, the Little Colorado Mining District, covering the area between the San Francisco Peaks, Black Falls, Willow Springs, and Gray Mountain, was organized formally on April 3, 1880, with Seth B. Tanner, chairman.[9]

The amount of actual mining and development work done by the prospectors during the 1880s is not easily determined. No one, however, discovered a Leadville or another Silver Reef. After preliminary exploration, few of the prospects showed enough good ore to justify further development. Most of the claims were located in the roughest country, on the ledges, or the breaks of the rims and plateaus, or deep in the canyons, remote from settlements, timber, and water, and distant from what few roads there were. Under these conditions only exceptionally rich ore, and a sizable quantity of it, would produce a profit.

Extensive mining was done in Havasu Canyon where good prospects were found in the Redwall. Some of the principal operations were confined to a short section of about two miles in length below Havasu Falls and included Mooney Falls and the tributary Carbonate Canyon. This was surely one of the most dramatically located mining areas in the entire Grand Canyon region. The inner canyon of Havasu was only half a mile wide at Mooney Falls and over thirteen hundred feet deep. Between the two falls the Redwall rose in perpendicular walls over 250 feet in height. Some men prospected with Winchest-

Smelter chimney at the Grand Gulch Copper Mine on the Arizona Strip. Discovered in the 1870's, it was one of the earliest "sandstone bonanzas" in the Grand Canyon Country.

"Struck it rich." The Coconino Silver Mine, Havasu Canyon, 1883. Arizona.

ers. Shooting off some of the outcroppings of the Redwall they retrieved enough chips to learn that the upper part of the strata contained rich deposits of lead and silver. While some built precarious trails to the inner canyon, others prospected the cliffs with ropes and derrick. To reach one of the prospects, miners about the turn of the century built an iron pipe ladder up the face of the west wall of Havasu Canyon. An observer who saw it in place years later likened it to a gigantic fire escape—258 feet high! It was, he said, "the greatest ladder in the world."

Mining in Havasu required scaling walls, building ladders, derricks, and trails, and hauling the best of the high-grade out of the canyon on burros. After that it had to be freighted to distant smelters. Adding the cost of supplies and equipment, ore that would pay elsewhere would be almost valueless in Havasu. The canyon was a magnificently beautiful place to mine, but it was a difficult spot to make a fortune. Havasu produced no bonanza kings.[10]

The prospects elsewhere in the Grand Canyon country were not much better. West of Prospect Valley on the very rim of Grand Canyon, Ridenour, Hardy, Tillman, and Spencer located the "Grand Cañon" mine, a copper and silver prospect in a "sandstone formation," in March of 1880. Assays made later from other mines in the vicinity ran up to eighty percent copper. Some thought this was the district discovered about 1873 by John D. Lee.[11]

By 1883, it was clear that as a mining field the canyon lands of the Colorado offered little promise. In that year, though, Cass Hite discovered placer gold in Glen Canyon above Lee's Ferry and a substantial rush subsequently developed.[12] Even more encouraging for those with prospects along the southern rimlands of Grand Canyon was the coming of the Santa Fe Railroad in 1883.

WEST FROM SANTA FE

1876. Follow the Beale road west from Canyon Diablo to Truxton Wash. Not a single settlement of more than a cabin or two appears in two hundred miles. For a hundred years the South Rim country had been crossed by transients. Garcés, Aubry, Sitgreaves, Whipple, and Beale had worked out a number of parallel routes followed by traders, overlanders, Mormon scouts, couriers, mail carriers, and prospectors. However, by the end of this year, the course of the future had been set. The railroad was coming.

One transcontinental railroad was scarcely enough to satisfy the needs of the burgeoning West after the Civil War. Even before the Union Pacific-Central Pacific rails were joined in 1869 Congress had chartered the Atlantic and Pacific to build a line from Missouri along the thirty-fifth parallel through New Mexico to the west coast. Not to be outdone by this legislation General William J. Palmer of the Kansas Pacific Railroad made an instrumental survey for his line from Kansas through New Mexico and Arizona to California. Palmer followed the thirty-fifth parallel and marked out a route close to the one laid down by Whipple. Palmer and C. C. Parry, geologist and naturalist of the survey, echoed Whipple in their praise of the route for a trunk line railroad. They extolled the "magnificent pine forests," the "beautiful grassy valleys and parks," and the undeveloped mining country of the Arizona section. Palmer also wrote of the recreational potential. The most attractive place of summer resort on the entire line of the road, he noted, was the area around the San Francisco Peaks. "It has every attraction; health, scenery, sky, water, elevation, climate, and proximity to the greatest natural curiosity known on this continent—the 'Grand Cañon' of the Colorado River, from which it is distant some 40 or 50 miles." Palmer's *Report of Surveys Across the Continent in 1867–'68*, published in 1869, touched a note seldom heard before in the Grand Canyon country: an appreciation for the beauty of the landscape.[13]

Although tourists were notably absent, by 1876 the riches of the South Rim country were being exploited. Prospectors from the west had opened mines in the canyon itself. Sheepmen had discovered the Plateau's virgin ranges and were grazing herds about Bill Williams Mountain and the San Francisco Peaks. The first few settlers had already arrived, and the prospects of a railroad quickened interest in the economic potential along the proposed route.

One who touted the opportunities was Samuel W. Cozzens, who early in 1876 published a book on Arizona and New Mexico, entitled, *The Ancient Cíbola, the Marvelous Country*. Cozzens lectured in New England on the splendid prospects awaiting settlers in this land, the "Ancient Cíbola" of Coronado, and he floated a colonization company to promote settlement in the valley of the Little Colorado along the line of the railroad.

In and around Boston, Cozzens recruited about a hundred men who took the train and headed west for the promised land. At the end of the tracks they bought wagons and went on to their destination, only to discover that the Mormons had beaten them to the spot by a few weeks and were already breaking ground. Rather than mingle with the Mormons, and disappointed with the prospects of desert farming, they pushed on west. Encamped at the base of the San Francisco Peaks on July 4, 1876, the Bostonians celebrated the nation's centennial by running up a flag on a pine tree stripped for the purpose. The immigrants then went on to Prescott where they found employment. When the railroad reached their centennial camp site in 1882 the stripped pine was still standing; this suggested the name Flagstaff for the station opened nearby.[14]

The rails were slow to arrive. The Kansas Pacific built into Colorado rather than into the Southwest. The Atlantic and Pacific foundered in the Panic of 1873, but early in 1880 a half-interest in the company was acquired by the aggressive Atchison, Topeka and Santa Fe Railroad whose tracks had already reached Santa Fe and Albuquerque. The agreement called for rapid construction of the line from Albuquerque (Isleta) to California under the federal charter held by the Atlantic and Pacific. Graders went to work before the end of 1880, and by August, 1883, A&P tracks had been laid to the left bank of the Colorado opposite Needles, California, a distance of about 578 miles. The company then bridged the Colorado and linked its rails with those of the Southern Pacific which had already laid track to Needles. A road with transcontinental connections was completed across the southern periphery of the Grand Canyon country.[15]

The coming of the rails along the route of Coronado, Garcés, Whipple, Beale, and Palmer not only provided a new western road to the Pacific but vitalized the whole of northern Arizona. A variety of entrepreneurs followed the tracks, and some of the construction camps along the route soon became the most prominent towns in the northern part of the territory: Holbrook, Winslow, Flagstaff, Williams, Ash Fork, Seligman, Kingman; all but the middle three were named after persons identified with the railroad. The line operated under the name Atlantic and Pacific until 1897 when title shifted to the Santa Fe Pacific. In 1903 the name of the parent company— Atchison, Topeka, and Santa Fe Railway—was extended over the route.[16]

Since the railroad brought the national market within easy reach the cattlemen were quick to follow as tracks were laid across the pristine grasslands of northern Arizona. For every mile of track built in New Mexico and Arizona the company had been awarded a grant of twenty odd-numbered sections of land, and these were sold at bargain prices. The Aztec Land and Cattle Company, also called the Hashknife from the shape of its brand, bought a million acres from the A&P between Holbrook and Flagstaff and developed the biggest spread in the region. Fort Valley, a beautiful park at the foot of the San Francisco Peaks, a few miles north of Flagstaff, was the base of operations of the Moroni Cattle Company. This outfit, later called the Arizona Cattle Company, or the A1 after its brand, was organized by John W. Young, a son of Brigham Young, who had graded roadbed and supplied ties during construction days on the A&P. In 1881, Young built a fortified camp, called Fort Moroni, and this became the ranching headquarters for the cattle operation which spread out over an extensive range north and west of Flagstaff.

Sheepmen, like William Ashurst, who had run their herds in the region before the coming of the railroad, now appeared in greater numbers. For example, E. B. Perrin, sheepman and land speculator, bought over 250,000 acres from the A&P in the Flagstaff area by 1887. And there were numbers of others, sheepmen and cattlemen, big and small, whose stock ranged across the railroad lands—and the even-

The Grand Canyon at Shinumo Creek. Arizona.

numbered sections of the public domain—from Holbrook to Kingman and north from the railroad to the rimlands of Grand Canyon.

The last seven years of the decade witnessed a speculative scramble for the grass of the South Rim country. By 1890, businesslike procedures had replaced the adventurous gambling which had wrecked some of the big outfits like the Hashknife and A1. The Babbitt brothers, who arrived in Flagstaff in 1886, illustrated this new breed. The brothers went into cattle and sheep, branding their stock with a CO Bar. With careful management of range and water they prospered from the start. Their empire grew as they picked up the wreckage of the A1 and some of the Hashknife, and within a few years the Babbitt's CO Bar was the largest outfit on the northern Arizona range.[17]

Lumber interests, too, appeared with the arrival of the railroad. Edward E. Ayer of Chicago, who had been in Arizona during the Civil War, opened the first sawmill in the South Rim country at Flagstaff in 1882. He formed the Arizona Lumber and Timber Company which he sold within a few years. With the fortune made from Arizona Lumber he assembled a distinguished library of books pertaining to the Indians of the Americas, a collection which he donated to the Newberry Library in Chicago.[18]

The arrival of the rails also inaugurated a new era in Grand Canyon mining. The southern sector of the Colorado Plateau was now easy to reach. Supplies and equipment could be brought in at less cost and ore hauled to the smelter at a cheaper rate. After 1883, many new claims were staked in the Grand Canyon, particularly on the southern side of the Colorado.[19]

The opening of the South Rim country brought with it enough arrivals to justify the formation of a new county. In 1891, Coconino was separated from Yavapai and the county seat was located at Flagstaff. Farther west, Mohave's county capital, which had moved about from place to place, finally came to rest

in 1887 at the railroad town of Kingman. Together the two counties entirely blanketed the Arizona part of the Grand Canyon country.

Meanwhile another breed had appeared, not to brand, log, or dig, but to see, admire, and enjoy. Coming by train and stage the first tourists had arrived at the South Rim of Grand Canyon.

TO ROAM SO FREE

The coming of the white man was a shock to the Indians of the Grand Canyon country. The intruders, without leave or ceremony, killed the game, plowed the soil, built roads, took the water, cut the forests, and their animals depleted the range. For the first three hundred years there was little conflict because the white men came as transients—explorers, survey-

ors, scouts—who were not given to plundering the earth. But the situation worsened when the settlers arrived.

The Paiutes in Dixie were the first to have to share the resources of the land with permanent neighbors who moved in to settle among them. No frontier lay open to the Paiutes to escape the intruders. The Navajos were more fortunate. As military pressure mounted against them in the 1850s many moved west into the canyon country of the Colorado. They even crossed the river to raid the Mormon outposts. The Paiutes and Navajos, in a brief, informal alliance, attempted to hold back the encroaching whites but in the ensuing "war," the Paiutes were quickly enveloped. For several years longer the Navajos raided, but in 1870 they agreed to peace with the Mormons.

South of the Grand Canyon the pattern was repeated. The Pai tribes—already differentiated in the popular mind as Hualapai and Havasupai, but actu-

Gathering of Navajo Indians near Cameron, about 1900. Arizona.

ally a single people—occupied literally all of the South Rim country from the Little Colorado west to the Mohave territory. The Havasupais utilized the area eastward from Havasu Canyon, and the Hualapais inhabited the land extending west of there to the Black Mountains. Beyond, in the valley of the Colorado River below Black Canyon, lived the Mohave Indians and their neighbors the Chemehuevis, an offshoot of the Las Vegas band of Southern Paiutes.

Although a few violent incidents occurred involving the passage of transients through their territory, these Indians were generally tolerant of travelers until the building of the Beale road. A road meant more traffic. This aroused the temper of the Mohaves who in August, 1858, badly mauled a train of California-bound immigrants as they were encamped on the east bank of the Colorado. As a consequence, the United States Army established Fort Mohave near Beale's Crossing. After another raid or two, the Mohaves settled down to peaceful coexistence with the whites, a policy in large part owing to the remarkable Chief Irataba.[20]

The Hualapai bands avoided any spectacular confrontations with the whites until the prospectors began flooding across their lands in the 1860s. In 1866, one of their chiefs, Wauba Yuma, was shot by a Prescott freighter. They erupted in protest to wage the "Hualapai War." The Indians attacked the mining camps in the Cerbat range and the Hualapai Mountains to the south. Army regulars under the command of Lieutenant Colonel William Redwood Price were sent from California to subjugate them. Operating from Fort Mohave, with the assistance of detachments from Fort Whipple, Price carried on a war of attrition. The Indians had to accept a final peace in 1869. A military post was established at Beale's Springs, near the later site of Kingman, and in the same year, 1871, a small reservation for the Hualapais was established at the same place. Defeated and demoralized, the Indians at Camp Beale's Springs stood in line waiting for rations as they watched their ancestral hunting lands being overrun by the aggressive foreigners.

A worse life was in store for them. In the spring of 1874 about six hundred Hualapais were "removed" to the Colorado River Reservation near La Paz. The reserve had been established in 1865 for all tribes in the Colorado River basin. Accustomed to a free life of hunting in the open mountain ranges and the high Hualapai Plateau, the Indians found themselves crowded together on a low, hot reservation where they were expected to become farmers. Many sickened and died, while others longed for their homeland where the horizons were distant and there was space to live. After a year of confinement the Hualapais fled back home—to subservience. As the war ended, the whites in ever larger numbers came to prospect and mine. They appropriated the range and the water. The Indians became wage earners in the mines and ranches, and hangers-on, homeless wanderers in their own land.[21]

Their condition worsened; by the fall of 1879 many were near starvation. Perhaps grateful that the Hualapais had been an ally in the Apache wars, the United States Army began issuing rations to the destitute ones. Aware that the coming of the railroad would only compound their tragedy, the Indians themselves requested a reservation. In June, 1881, Lieutenant Colonel William Redwood Price, Sixth Cavalry, their enemy in the Hualapai War of 1867–1869, traveled through Pai territory to study local conditions.

During the war, the Hualapais and Price had developed a mutual respect, and in a council held near the head of Milkweed Canyon the Indians told the officer that "the country over which we used to roam so free" had been appropriated by the white men. They feared that the coming of the railroad would bring more men who would take up the few springs remaining. The Indians requested that a reservation embracing the larger part of the Hualapai Plateau be set aside for them. That land, they said, could never be of any great use to the whites; there were no mineral deposits; there was little arable land; there was little water, and the country was so rocky and void of grass as to be unsuitable for grazing. Give us a reservation, they implored, "while there is still time."

Price earnestly recommended to his superiors that the reservation be established. After further study and survey, Major General O. B. Willcox, in

command of the Department of Arizona, agreed, in the interest of "humanity toward these Indians" and to protect the frontier from more war. He endorsed the recommendation in January, 1883, and the reservation was established by presidential order.[22]

The Hualapais had salvaged at least part of their traditional homeland from the encroaching whites. The great, deep, and isolated canyons draining into the Colorado—Meriwitica, Spencer, Peach Springs, Granite, Mohawk (or Moho), National, and Prospect Valley—were theirs. During the 1874–1875 captivity and under white pressure later, many of them had found refuge in these remote fastnesses.

The eastern Pai, or Havasupai, were less fortunate. Prospectors had entered their canyon home as early as 1873, and after rich ore was found near Havasu Falls in 1879, they came as a flood. General O. B. Willcox visited the Havasupais in the spring of 1880 and recommended a reservation for the Indians to avert conflict with the miners. A reserve was confirmed to them in 1882, but it was limited to the canyon floor and consisted of only 518 acres, in contrast to the Hualapai reserve of 997,045 acres. None of those lands over which they used to roam, along the South Rim to the Little Colorado, was included in the reservation.[23]

The Navajos fared much better. From their homeland in the Chuska Mountains they pushed their frontier vigorously westward into the redrock country of the Colorado. They swept around the Hopi villages and engulfed the Hopis and Mormons at Moenkopi and Tuba City. The San Juan slowed them on the north. They met resistance from the Atlantic and Pacific Railroad and the cattlemen on the south, but toward the west the Navajos did not stop until they reached the rim of Marble Canyon and the gorge of the Little Colorado.

The Navajo frontier movement is perhaps unique in American Indian history. As the Indians moved into the eastern perimeter of the Grand Canyon country they obtained extensions of their reservation to incorporate the areas of occupation. By 1884, the reserve had been extended to Marble Canyon, and later extensions increased the size to about fifteen million acres, making it the largest Indian reservation in the United States.[24]

North and west of the Colorado the Paiutes, unable to compete with Mormon frontiersmen, were crowded off their homelands and forced to live as dependents of the whites, or removed to reservations. During the last half of the year 1873, John W. Powell and G. W. Ingalls had been named by the Department of Indian Affairs as special commissioners to study the condition of the Paiutes in the canyon country and the Great Basin. They found that, deprived of their favorite valleys and ranges, the Paiutes could no longer live by hunting and gathering.

The Indians recognized the folly of contending against the whites and asked for a reservation of their own. The commissioners recommended that the Southern Paiutes be placed on a large reservation so located as to include the lower valley of the Virgin and Muddy rivers. But the Indians were slow to move, and in 1875 the reservation was reduced in size to a mere thousand acres located on the Muddy River in the upper Moapa Valley. Most of the Paiutes remained where they were and lived on near their old homes dependent upon and subservient to those who had dispossessed them.

Two reservations for the Paiutes were subsequently established—the Shivwits Reservation, near Santa Clara in Utah, and the Kaibab Reservation near Pipe Spring in Arizona. By providing some economic opportunities, these helped to alleviate the burden of living alongside an alien, though generally tolerant, people. By about 1900, however, the native aspects of Paiute life had all but disappeared.[25]

The white conquest of the Pai tribes and the Paiutes was not only a cultural shock, it also left the Indians a powerless minority in their own land. When an Indian Messiah appeared who promised to restore life to the deceased, to bring back the game, and to rid the country of white oppressors, both peoples were ready to embrace the doctrine. Restoration of a paradise lost would follow, they thought, if true believers engaged in prescribed ritualistic dancing. The Ghost Dance movement which swept across the West in 1889 (actually a revival of an earlier craze), followed upon the revelations of one Wovoka, a Northern Paiute. The revival spread to the Paiutes north of the Grand Canyon who passed it on to the Pai tribes.

The Hualapais in particular accepted the new faith, and in 1889 they began to dance for the return of happier days. For two years the Indians danced, but the millennium did not come. Disappointed, they accepted the missionaries of several Christian sects whose millenary promises extended to all men. By propagating the faith, promoting education, and doing good works, the missionaries who labored among the Indians of the Grand Canyon country tempered the blow, if they did not fully relieve the shock of conquest.[26]

The Indians of the Grand Canyon country had lived in harmony with the land that supported them. They did little to change the face of nature. They were at one with the earth and could not easily survive under the impact of those who exploited it.

The Havasupai Indians live in the inner gorge of Havasu Canyon. Below the village of Supai and the farming area, Havasu, or Cataract Creek, drops over five waterfalls before reaching the Colorado. Navajo Falls in center. Arizona.

163

THE BEAUTY

he confluence of Deep Creek and the North
ork of the Virgin River, Zion National Park. Utah.

10
Grand Ensemble

WHEELER'S RIVER OF THE DESERT

A few of those bent upon conquest of the Grand Canyon wilderness were in turn mastered by the magnificence of its landscape. One such was Lieutenant George M. Wheeler, Army Corps of Engineers. Prompted by the Indian wars in Arizona, the army in the spring of 1869 sent Wheeler to locate a feasible route for moving troops from the Central Pacific Railroad through eastern Nevada to the head of navigation on the Colorado. The officer carried his reconnaissance to the mouth of the Virgin River, and thence to Callville, which he found abandoned, and El Dorado Canyon.

Wheeler published a lengthy report descriptive of the 1869 exploration. It was full of details about routes, mining districts, Mormon settlements along the Muddy, and the crossings and navigability of the Colorado River. While encamped at Callville he found the canyon scenery "the most wild, picturesque and pleasing of any that it has ever been my fortune to meet." Elsewhere he found the "River of the Desert, winding its way through steep and sterile cañons, and again through arid and long and extended deserts," was anything but interesting. Of El Dorado Canyon he wrote, "When we looked back

upon it for the last time no sense was touched save that of relief."[1]

Whether or not he realized it, the "River of the Desert" and the arid country of southern Nevada had touched the young engineer deeply. Wheeler wrote of his desire to visit the "Grand Cañon" while encamped at the mouth of the Virgin, but his party was too worn out to proceed upstream. Within two years Wheeler was back to explore the Grand Canyon.

Powell's trip in 1869 had captured the imagination of the nation, and both the King and Hayden surveys were enlarging the scope of their operations. Wheeler argued with his superiors for still another western survey. Geology was important, he said, but what was needed more, particularly in the face of the growing Indian threat, was a detailed topographical map of the West, one delineating economic, artificial, and cultural features as well as surface configurations. His arguments found ready acceptance and won him direction of what soon became the United States Geographical Surveys West of the Hundredth Meridian, popularly known as the Wheeler Survey.

Wheeler took to the field in the spring of 1871 with a goodly staff including geologists, topographers, a photographer, and a reporter, and a complement of officers and men. His purpose was to map and to gather information about the tribes and the natural resources. He was to give careful and particular at-

The magnificent serenity of Grand Canyon below the Lower Granite Gorge. Arizona. "The canyons of the Colorado," wrote Lt. George M. Wheeler of the U.S. Geographical Surveys west of the hundredth meridian, "stand without a known rival upon the face of the globe."

tention to mining developments. Returning to the scene of his 1869 reconnaissance, he stayed in the field from June until December and mapped a belt of country from Elko on the Central Pacific Railroad through southern Nevada and northwestern and central Arizona to Prescott and Wickenburg. Death Valley and vicinity in eastern California and a small part of southwestern Utah were also included in the exploration.

Easily the most dramatic part of the season's work was Wheeler's upriver trip on the Colorado from Fort Mohave to the mouth of Diamond Creek in Grand Canyon. The party started on September 12 with three specially made boats and a small barge supplied by the quartermaster at Fort Mohave. It was an incredible and difficult journey of thirty-one days. Pushing, pulling, poling, and paddling, the expedition traveled about 225 miles, averaging less than eight miles a day.

Once within Grand Canyon the going was much slower. Traveling upstream for fifty-three miles Wheeler managed to work his way over Lava Cliff Rapids, Powell's Separation Rapids, and through the fast water of the Lower Granite Gorge above Separation. Wheeler had planned fifteen days for the Grand Canyon exploration, but found it required twenty-four days to travel those fifty-three miles—just over two miles a day! The upriver party consisted of twenty men including Wheeler, P. W. Hamel, topographer, G. K. Gilbert, geologist, T. H. O'Sullivan, photographer, and six Mohave Indians. While most of the men left the river at Diamond Creek a few of them returned the two boats to Fort Mohave—which they reached in five days! What a wild ride they must have had down through the Lower Granite Gorge and through Separation and Lava Cliff rapids!

Wheeler had some practical objectives in mind. He had explored that section of the Colorado upstream from Las Vegas Wash to the mouth of Diamond Creek, which Ives in 1857–1858 had not seen. Thus he had determined the "absolute limit of navigation, a question not settled by Ives," and he concluded, "The furthest practical head of improved navigation must remain permanently at the foot of the Grand Cañon." And he concluded, "The exploration of the Colorado River may now be considered complete."

Justification enough. The idea of the Colorado River as a western highway died hard. But Wheeler had taken a good look at the Grand Canyon, which he had missed seeing in 1869. The excitement he felt in fighting his way up the canyon reminds one of Powell's account of his 1869 voyage downstream. This line of Wheeler's could have been written by Powell: "The cañon cut out by this stream is the most romantic I have ever examined among the varied scenes of years of mountain life." In a final volume, the *Geographical Report,* summarizing the ten-year achievements of his survey, Wheeler referred again to the canyons of the Colorado: "They stand without a known rival upon the face of the globe, and must always remain one of the wonders, and will, as circumstances of transportation permit, attract the denizens of all quarters of the world who in their travels delight to gaze upon the intricacies of nature."

There is little of this feeling expressed in Wheeler's *Preliminary Report* of the survey's operations in 1871, which devotes much space to mining and other matters. But men at the time were much more interested in mineral potential of the region to the west than they were in romantic images of the Grand Canyon landscape.[2]

THE MOST SUBLIME

Wheeler's *Geographical Report* was the last of the summary volumes published by the great western surveys. The work of Wheeler, King, Hayden, and Powell in the decade from 1869 to 1879 was an achievement of national significance. The published reports, maps, and heavy quartos on geology, ethnology, paleontology, and biology provided the world with a reference library covering much of the West beyond the hundredth meridian. All of the surveys touched parts of the basin of the Colorado. Powell and Wheeler explored and studied the northern and western parts of the Grand Canyon country. Together they mapped and assembled a mass of scientific data

Strawberry Point on the high southern rim of the Markagun Plateau is one of the headwaters of the Virgin River. Utah

about the region which Ives and Macomb a few years before had found to be practically unknown.

Powell's exploration of the Colorado River canyons was but a prelude to the work of his survey which for ten years was largely confined to the Colorado Plateau. Many of the ideas and concepts which he developed later in works on geology, ethnology, land classification, and reclamation were conceived on the river trips and during the first years of the survey. He saw the whole region as few have since, and he employed a corps of brilliant field assistants to study and report. His own articles in *Scribner's* and *Popular Science*, and the report on the *Exploration of the Colorado River of the West*, all published in 1875, were but the first of a number of notable works stemming from the survey.

Powell's *Report on the Geology of the Uinta Mountains* (1876) contained a broad analysis of the geological provinces of the Colorado Plateau; Grove K. Gilbert contributed a celebrated *Report on the Geology of the Henry Mountains* (1877); Powell and others wrote a *Report on the Lands of the Arid Region* (1878, 1879), a pioneer study of the classification and use of land in the desert West with particular reference to conditions in Utah; Clarence E. Dutton wrote a classic *Report on the Geology of the High Plateaus of Utah* (1880), and another on the geology of the Grand Canyon district (1882).[3]

Enthralled by the beauty of the red-rock landscape, Dutton wrote like a poet. He felt that those who studied the plateau and canyonlands of the Colorado should report in a style to match their vision. Normally in writing conventional scientific monographs, the "ascetic discipline is necessary. Give the imagination an inch and it is apt to take an ell," and accuracy of statement is imperiled. "But in the Grand Cañon district there is no such danger," Dutton wrote. "The stimulants which are demoralizing elsewhere are necessary here to exalt the mind sufficiently to comprehend the sublimity of the subjects. Their sublimity has in fact been hitherto underrated. Great as the fame of the Grand Cañon of the Colorado, the half remains to be told."

Dutton acted on his own advice. He studied geology more from the plateau tops than from canyon bottoms and from the lofty rims he came upon scenes and panoramas "to exalt the mind." For him the view southward over the Grand Canyon country from the rimlands of the Markagunt was one of the "sublime spectacles" of the plateau country. In midsummer, "standing among evergreens, knee-deep in succulent grass and a wealth of Alpine blossoms, fanned by chill, moist breezes, we look over terraces decked with towers and temples and gashed with cañons to the desert which stretches away beyond the southern horizon, blank, lifeless, and glowing with torrid heat."

Describing the more immediate scene, Dutton wrote of the great masses of rock starting up from terraced platforms. The intricate upper basin of the Virgin River—especially Zion Canyon—was spread out like a map over three thousand feet below him. "The great cliffs—perhaps the grandest of all features in the region of grandeur—are turned away from us, and only now and then are seen in the profile in the flank of some salient. Among the most marvelous things to be found in these terraces are the cañons; such cañons as exist nowhere else even in the Plateau Country."

Dutton described the grand scenes along the rimlands of the Paria amphitheater. Of the intricate, castellated formations now in Bryce Canyon National Park he wrote: "The glory of all this rock-work is seen in the Pink Cliffs. . . . The resemblances to strict architectural forms are often startling. . . . Standing obelisks, prostrate columns, shattered capitals, panels, niches, buttresses, repetitions of symmetrical forms. . . ." He thought the "crowning glory" of the Paria amphitheater was the Table Cliff Plateau on its northeastern arc. "Standing 11,000 feet above sealevel and projected against the deep blue of the western sky. . . . Such glorious tints, such keen contrasts of light and shade, such profusion of sculptured forms, can never be forgotten by him who once beheld it. This is one of the grand panoramas of the Plateau Country and typical in all respects."

The great plateau and canyon country indeed does have the power to exalt the mind, but Dutton warned: "To the eye which is not trained to it and to the mind which is not inured to its strangeness, its

(Previous spread) Table Cliff Plateau, east across the valley of the Paria River from Bryce Canyon, is 10,000 feet above sea level, 2,000 feet higher than the rim at Bryce Canyon. Utah.

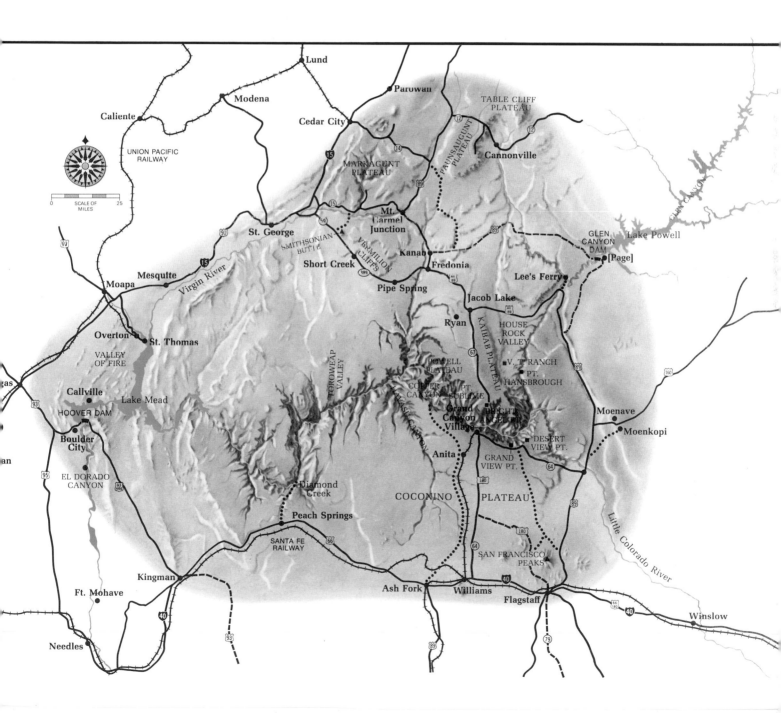

The Tourist Focus
1883-1940

••••••••••••••• Main Tourist routes no
                 longer used extensively
─────────────   Major Highways
─ ─ ─ ─ ─ ─ ─   Highways built after 1940

Lund

Modena

Caliente

Parowan

TABLE CLIFF
PLATEAU

UNION PACIFIC
RAILWAY

Cedar City

Cannonville

MARKAGUNT
PLATEAU

PAUNSAUGUNT
PLATEAU

SCALE OF
MILES
0   25

Mt.
Carmel
Junction

St. George

SMITHSONIAN
BUTTE

VERMILION
CLIFFS

GLEN
CANYON
DAM

Lake Powell

Kanab

[Page]

Mesquite

Virgin River

Short Creek

Fredonia

Lee's Ferry

Moapa

Pipe Spring

Jacob Lake

HOUSE
ROCK
VALLEY

Ryan

Overton

St. Thomas

VALLEY
OF FIRE

TOROWEAP VALLEY

KAIBAB PLATEAU

V. T. RANCH
PT.
HANSBROUGH

Moenave

Callville

Lake Mead

POWELL
PLATEAU

COPPER
CANYON

PT.
SUBLIME

HAVASU CANYON

Grand
Canyon
Village

BRIGHT
ANGEL CR.

Moenkopi

HOOVER DAM

Boulder
City

EL DORADO
CANYON

DESERT
VIEW PT.

Anita

GRAND
VIEW PT.

Diamond
Creek

COCONINO   PLATEAU

Peach Springs

SANTA FE
RAILWAY

SAN FRANCISCO
PEAKS

Little Colorado River

Kingman

Ft. Mohave

Ash Fork

Williams

Flagstaff

Winslow

Needles

desolation and grotesqueness may be repulsive rather than attractive, but to the mind which has grown into sympathy with such scenes it conveys a sense of power and grandeur and a fullness of meaning which lay hold of the sensibilities more forcibly than tropical verdure or snow-clad Alps or Arcadian valleys."[4]

Late in the autumn of 1880, Dutton and W. H. Holmes rode past the base of the Vermilion Cliffs from Kanab Creek to the Virgin River. As they moved along, the "walls increased in altitude, in animation, and in power," reaching a climax in the great towers of Short Creek, standing twenty-three hundred feet above the plain. The geologist wrote of the effects of light and shadow in a land where naked rock dominates the landscape. When the sun is high the scenery is robbed of much of its grandeur. "The effects of foreshortening are excessive, almost beyond belief, and produce the strangest deceptions: separated masses seem to be superimposed; grand fronts become flat and are troubled with false perspective; . . . proportions which are full of grace and meaning are distorted and belied"; the cliffs seem to "wilt and droop"; even the "colors are ruined."

"But as the sun declines there comes a revival. The half-tones at length appear, bringing into relief the component masses; the amphitheaters recede into suggestive distances; the salients silently advance toward us. . . . The whole cliff arouses from lethargy and erects itself in grandeur and power as if conscious of its own majesty. Back also come the colors, and as the sun is about to sink they glow with an intense orange vermilion. . . . But the great gala-days of the cliffs" are those when sunshine and storm wage an "even battle" over the masses of rock, diffusing the light, toning down the glare, and revealing the stately cliffs in perspective "so that the mind can grasp them."

Continuing on westward, Dutton and Holmes crested a low pass between Smithsonian Butte and Eagle Crags. The scientists found themselves at the head of a slope dropping sharply down fifteen hundred feet to the Virgin River. From this point they had an unimpeded view directly into the mouth of Zion Canyon. "There flashed before us a scene never to be forgotten," wrote Dutton in his classic book on the Grand Canyon. He predicted: "In coming time it will, I believe, take rank with a very small number of spectacles each of which will, in its own way, be regarded as one of the most exquisite of its kind which the world discloses."

Dutton was right. The view before him, seen through the clear autumn air, was easily one of the grandest anywhere in the canyon country. Dominating the slopes beneath the geologists were ledges and projections and strata of rock alive with color—chocolate, maroon, purple, lavender, magenta, and toned white. Running nearly north and south the walls of Zion were of extraordinary beauty in the slanting light of morning and evening. From their vista point, Dutton and Holmes could see the clusters of cliffs and temples and towers rising over half a mile high on either side of the gorge. "There is an eloquence to their forms which stirs the imagination with a singular power, and kindles in the mind of the dullest observer a glowing response," in Dutton's glowing words.

The explorers enjoyed a magnificent view of the Towers of the Virgin, the highest of which was the West Temple standing thirty-six hundred feet above the river. Dutton wrote: "Directly in front of us a complex group of white towers, springing from a central pile, mount towards the clouds. Out of their midst, and high over all, rests a dome-like mass, which dominates the entire landscape. It is almost white, with brilliant streaks of carmine descending its vertical walls. . . . Here nature has changed her mood from levity to religious solemnity, and revealed her fervor in forms and structures more beautiful than anything in human art." Of Zion Canyon, he said that nothing could exceed its "wondrous beauty."[5]

When it came to the magnificent landscapes of the Grand Canyon country Dutton could shift easily from rigid scientific analysis to poetic appreciation; his works on the High Plateaus and the Grand Canyon were splendid combinations of geology and belles lettres. Happily he put to paper his subjective responses and emotional reactions and the world may be grateful that his manuscript was written in advance of any manual governing style in geological publications. Dutton admitted that his writing was "effusive" at times but justifiable since the Grand Canyon was more than a match for any imagination.

During the course of their studies in 1880, C. E. Dutton and W. H. Holmes reached the north side of the Grand Canyon at the foot of Toroweap Valley. In the Toroweap, Dutton's scientific mind read the secrets of the cliffs, faults, uplifts, dikes, cinder and basaltic cones, and lava flows over sandstone—"it would be difficult to find anywhere else in the world a spot yielding so much subject matter for the geologist," certainly not "in the midst of such dramatic and inspiring surroundings."

The poet—"the fancy is kindled as the eye wanders"—could write: "Wonderfully rich and profuse are the pinnacles and statues along the upper friezes" of the Toroweap Cliffs. Dutton was very fond of architectural metaphor. In this land of living rock he was struck by the similarity of the "architecture displayed in the profiles." Exposed strata presented the same appearance everywhere. He could find nothing comparable in ordinary mountain masses whose "formless and chaotic crags" were only "big and rough." On the other hand the profiles of the plateau and canyon country were "definite, graceful, architectural, and systematic."

The architectural appearance of the great formations, so fully articulated by Dutton, was recognized by others—hence the many "temples" and "towers" and "thrones" scattered about all over the map. Dutton himself started the trend toward "heroic nomenclature." At the foot of Toroweap and on the very brink of Grand Canyon stands a six-hundred-foot-high basaltic cinder cone. This the geologists climbed for a view of the country all around. Three thousand feet below them they could see the white water of Powell's Lava Falls. The main chasm Dutton enlikened to the nave of a church and the valley of Toroweap and its counterpart on the opposite side of the canyon—Prospect Valley—as the arms of the transept. The cone on which they were standing was situated almost exactly at the intersection of the axes of nave and transept. "We named it," Dutton wrote (alas), "Vulcan's Throne."

Leaving the Toroweap, Dutton and Holmes next saw the Grand Canyon from the lofty rims of the Kaibab. The "supreme views" were those obtained from the long promontories of the plateau jutting out into the canyon. One of these the geologists named Point Sublime, for, wrote Dutton, "sitting upon the edge we contemplate the most sublime and awe-inspiring spectacle in the world." Nearly fifty miles of the deepest part of the gorge was revealed to them, about twenty-five miles on either side. Toward the east they could see as far as Cape Royal and Zuñi Point on the North and South rims, respectively, and toward the west Powell Plateau on the north side and the rimlands overlooking Fossil Bay on the south were visible.

Dutton devoted an entire chapter in his "Grand Cañon District" to a description of the panorama from Point Sublime: the recessed alcoves and amphitheaters; the jutting promontories ending in "magnificent gables with sharp mitred edges"; dozens of buttes of gigantic proportions surpassed but slightly in "nobility of form, beauty of decoration, and splendor of color" by the Temples of the Virgin in Zion Canyon.

He singled out the buttes to represent everything that is "forcible, characteristic, and picturesque" in the rock forms of the plateau country. "They are always bold and striking in outline and ornate in architecture. . . . They command the attention with special force and quicken the imagination with a singular power." Oriental architecture seemed to come to Dutton's mind as he wrote of Grand Canyon buttes; he left behind names like Vishnu's Temple (the "finest butte of the chasm") and Shiva's Temple (the "most majestic in aspect").

"The Grand Cañon is the sublimest thing on earth," the geologist wrote, not alone by "virtue of its magnitudes," nor by the rich architecture of its buttes and walls "displaying their richly-molded plinths and friezes, thrusting out their gables, wing-walls, buttresses, and pilasters, and recessed with alcoves and panels," nor of the color and "tone and temper" of the landscape which constantly varies. It is sublime "by virtue of the whole—its ensemble."

As with the landscape of the High Plateaus Dutton warned that the Grand Canyon was new to the mind of the world—"a great innovation in modern ideas of scenery, and in our conceptions of the grandeur, beauty and power of nature." Therefore those whose perceptions of natural beauty had been trained in the Alps, Italy, Scotland, or New England might be shocked at such a landscape. The Grand Canyon country must be dwelt upon and studied if the "meaning and spirit of that marvelous scenery" is to be understood. But time spent in study and contemplation would be richly repaid, Dutton promised. He criticized the notion which pictured the canyon as a "deep, narrow gash in the earth, with nearly vertical walls, like a great and neatly cut trench," a notion given "much color" by the first drawings of the canyon done by Egloffstein and published in the report of Lieutenant J. C. Ives. "Never was a great subject more artistically misrepresented or more charmingly belittled," he wrote of Egloffstein's mischief.

Even more than Powell, Dutton was as sensitive to the beauty of the landscape of the Grand Canyon and the High Plateaus as he was to the natural forces which had created them. We may be grateful that he encompassed both elements into his great monographs. Classics in geological literature, they contained in brilliant prose pictorial descriptions of an awesome and wonderful land and one new to the mind of man. Dutton found nature communicative in the arid plateau country and he shared with the world the full range of its message.[6]

GRANDEUR REVEALED

While geologists and other scientific men described and explained the nature of the Grand Canyon country, the photographers and artists employed by Wheeler and Powell revealed segments of it. They complemented very nicely both the artistic and literal inclinations of the scientists. Though he had not discovered it, Powell was the first to penetrate deeply into a new land. The excitement he felt in probing the "Great Unknown" of canyon and plateau, with all of their "great innovations" in landscape, never left him. Yet he was a scientist at heart. If he felt moved to romanticize at times he could also speculate accu-

rately about geological origins. And Powell chose illustrators who nicely served his dualistic vision of the canyon country.

When it came to ensuring a steady flow of federal appropriations Powell knew that one good picture was worth many words. He hired E. O. Beaman as photographer for the second river trip; when Beaman quit early in 1872, his work fell to James Fennemore and Clem Powell and finally to John K. "Jack" Hillers, a member of the party, who learned the business from the ground up. Hillers then became the photographer of the Powell Survey, continuing in the same capacity with the U.S. Geological Survey until 1900.

Jack Hillers made many fine views of the canyon country; he accompanied Powell and Ingalls during their investigation of the Great Basin and plateau tribes in 1873 when he had many splendid opportunities to photograph the Indians, especially the Southern Paiutes. Powell used Hillers' photographs to good effect. He had many of them made up into stereoscopic slides. Numerous sets were given to the federal officials; many more were sold to the public and thus the canyon country and its native inhabitants were graphically presented to a wide popular audience. Only a few of the Hillers photographs appeared in the publications of the Powell Survey; some were made into woodcuts, and a number were used as the basis for illustrations done by the English-born artist Thomas Moran.[7]

Ferdinand F. Hayden also knew the value of publicity, and in 1871, when his survey explored the Yellowstone country, Thomas Moran was one of the artists to go along. Moran was enthralled by the western landscape, its lavish scale, vivid colors, and brilliant light. His watercolors helped persuade Congress to create Yellowstone, the first national park, in March, 1872, and that body later bought from the artist a huge (five by twelve feet) canvas of the "Grand Canyon of the Yellowstone," for which it paid him ten thousand dollars.

Thus Thomas Moran's reputation as a western landscapist was already made when he responded to John Wesley Powell's invitation to see the Grand Canyon country. During July and August, 1873, he visited Zion Canyon, the Vermilion Cliffs, and the

Grand Canyon at Toroweap and the Kaibab. From a point on Powell Plateau Moran sketched out the details for another five-by-twelve canvas. He entitled it the "Grand Chasm of the Colorado," and again Congress paid him ten thousand dollars for the work, which was hung in the Capitol with the "Grand Canyon of the Yellowstone." Both paintings were exhibited at the Centennial Exposition at Philadelphia in 1876.

In the centennial year Louis Prang of Boston published in folio fifteen chromolithographic reproductions of Moran's western watercolors in a book written by F. V. Hayden, *The Yellowstone National Park and the Mountain Regions of Portions of Idaho, Nevada, Colorado and Utah*. The reproductions, faithful to Moran's brilliant coloring, were magnificently done. One is of Zion Canyon and bears the title, "Valley of Babbling Waters, Southern Utah." Hayden's accompanying text describes the scenery of southern Utah and along the Colorado and its branches as among the "most remarkable and grand in this or any other country." Even though the Mormons were already making a precarious living from it, Hayden went on to say that "this great country," rich in scenes like those of Moran's "Valley of Babbling Waters," must ever be "dedicated to nature, for it can never be inhabited by man. It is unique, grand, barren, and desolate."

Thomas Moran caught all of this in his art. He was able to portray the "splendor and grace of Nature's architecture," as Dutton was to say later, and to captivate the public with his treatment of the "great innovations." In the mid-seventies he turned out a large number of illustrations which helped to mold the popular concept of the canyon country. Most of these were woodcuts based primarily on photographs made by Jack Hillers. They appeared in the second volume of W. C. Bryant's sumptuous *Picturesque America* (1874), in Powell's popular series in *Scribner's* (1875) and in his *Exploration of the Colorado River of the West* (1875). Then the beautiful Prang volume of chromolithographs appeared in 1876. The American people, as they approached their centennial, must have begun to develop an awareness of the grandeur of the canyon landscape.

Thomas Moran's greatest work was done in color. He responded confidently and competently to color, strong light, and mood and tone, and he succeeded in capturing the natural grandeur of a land which has frightened away most artists. He was a romantic, an idealist; he sought the essential character of the canyons without becoming literal and topographical. He established local orientation in the foreground of his pictures where the rocks were "so carefully drawn that a geologist could determine their precise nature." As he moved back in the scene he rearranged the buttes and cliffs and pinnacles to suit his wish, but he preserved the architecture and the profiles. Thus Moran's "Grand Chasm of the Colorado" and the "Valley of Babbling Waters" are not literal landscapes, but they are nevertheless easily identifiable with Grand and Zion canyons.

Scattered clouds, characteristic of summer

W. H. Holmes of the Powell Survey.

storms in the Southwest, usually appear in Moran's canyon country pictures. The clouds and cloud shadows lent height and distance and a vastness of scale. And with these effects he caught the sense of mystery which most observers have felt in some way envelops the great canyons; with color he conveyed the power of nature to the senses of his viewers. Moran's paintings and watercolors were melodious works of art and they beautifully illustrated what Powell meant by the "Land of Music."

Moran, the foremost pioneer artist of the Colorado Plateau, lived until 1926 and returned frequently to the Grand Canyon. It was one of his favorite places, and some of his best oils and watercolors were done after 1900. He is unsung now, but his romantic vision influenced the way many people for two generations looked at the Grand Canyon country, a region "flooded with color and picturesqueness," a land of "beauty and grandeur," a wilderness beyond compare.[8]

W. H. Holmes, too, had been with the Hayden Survey before he joined Powell's team of scientists studying the Colorado Plateau. With Hayden in the Yellowstone and in Colorado and Wyoming, Holmes served as geologist and illustrator. He developed a technique for drawing rock forms and whole ranges of mountains that complemented the work of survey photographer W. H. Jackson. Holmes' panoramas in some respects went beyond the camera as scientific illustration, for he accentuated essential texture, structure, and profile, and eliminated the extraneous and superfluous. He was at the opposite pole from Moran who idealized the landscape. Holmes interpreted the landscape, but he did so literally. A geologist could read the rocks in a Moran foreground; in a Holmes panorama he could read a structure forty miles distant.

After his work on Utah's High Plateaus, Clarence E. Dutton could appreciate the illustrations done by Holmes; and when he headed for the Grand Canyon in 1880 he saw to it that W. H. Holmes went along as assistant geologist. Holmes was the right man in the right place. What he learned with Hayden he brought to perfect expression on the North Rim of the Grand Canyon. As Dutton looked on, Holmes tackled the towers of the Vermilion Cliffs at Short Creek, the Temples of the Virgin in Zion Canyon, and the Grand Canyon from Toroweap and finally, from Point Sublime. With the eye of an artist Holmes selected the essentials from the intricate architecture and then rapidly and deftly sketched them—with scientific accuracy.

W. H. Holmes' panoramas of the Grand Canyon, beautifully lithographed in green and in sepia tones, were published in the folio atlas accompanying Dutton's "Tertiary History." To open the atlas to any of its double-page panoramas, as Stegner writes, "is to step to the edge of forty miles of outdoors." Those of the canyon from Toroweap and Point Sublime are almost as breathtaking as the view itself, and even more literal. Holmes eliminated haze, and his rims and buttes, alcoves and amphitheaters are as clear in the distance as they are in the foreground. He avoided Moran's idealization; his drawings were done with scientific clarity and topographical accuracy, yet they are among the most beautiful illustrations ever made of the Grand Canyon country. They must have been very appealing to the scientific side of John Wesley Powell.

Indeed, the "Tertiary History of the Grand Cañon District" was an appropriate finale to the field studies undertaken by the Powell Survey. With the accompanying atlas it was one of the most beautiful works ever published about the Grand Canyon country. The text, in Clarence Dutton's rhapsodic prose, is interspersed with illustrations by Hillers, Moran, and Holmes, and a number of the geological maps are done in colors.[9]

Actually, in 1879, the four western surveys had been consolidated to form the U.S. Geological Survey; Clarence King was named the first director. At the same time, John W. Powell was named to head the new Bureau of American Ethnology, a branch of the Smithsonian Institution, and he held this post to the end of his life. In 1881, King resigned from the Geological Survey and Powell was appointed to the position, which he occupied until 1894. Powell's interest in the Colorado Plateau never waned, but he sent others to the field while he went on to his greatest achievement—to enlist government support for scientific study—which resulted in the publication of many papers on geology, ethnology, irrigation, reclamation, and conservation.[10]

Ten years after the consolidation of the surveys Captain George M. Wheeler published his *Geographical Report,* a heavy and lengthy quarto summarizing a decade of western exploration by his field parties. He gave ample attention to the Colorado Plateau where he had operated at times in all but open competition with the Powell Survey. He included a full report of his upriver exploration of the Grand Canyon in 1871 and a summary of the expedition of 1872 when a detachment of his men made a reconnaissance of the country between the Virgin and Paria rivers. These sections of the book are fully illustrated with a number of pictures made from photographs by T. H. O'Sullivan and William Bell, and of engravings of the mouth of Parunuweap Canyon, the Crossing of the Fathers, and Bryce Canyon made from sketches by John Weyss. Like Powell, Wheeler at an earlier date had published stereoscopic slides and mounted copies of the O'Sullivan and Bell photographs; these were much superior to the illustrations made from them in Wheeler's summary report. The

Weyss illustrations are grotesque and show none of the artistry of those made by Moran and Holmes.

Wheeler included a chronological summary of the exploration of the Colorado River from 1539 to 1872. Most of those on his list had sought practical goals—a road, the exploration of resources; Wheeler himself was the last to test the river in Grand Canyon for its navigability. With the coming of Powell and Wheeler a new emphasis began. Indeed, both men held to practical objectives: to catalog resources, study native peoples, to describe and delineate the nature and origin of the land itself. They did these things and they put the Grand Canyon country on the map. But at the same time they brilliantly revealed a wilderness of wonders unknown before; they saw the region as a whole and they endowed it with philosophical values. Powell and Wheeler (whose contribution was comparatively minor) wrote a textbook of marvelous things seen and felt. For anyone seeking to experience these things himself, theirs is still the best introduction.

Angel's Gate, Grand Canyon National Park. Arizona.

"Mysterious" is the way many people have described the Grand Canyon. Arizona.

Desert snowstorm over the Grand Canyon. Arizona.

The Pullman Frontier

DENVER, COLORADO CANYON AND PACIFIC RAILROAD

Robert Brewster Stanton also set out to conquer the Grand Canyon and was in turn vanquished by it. Like George M. Wheeler he was an engineer in search of a passage to India. Wheeler sought a water road, Stanton a railroad. Powell's celebrated voyage and the publications of the Powell and Wheeler surveys had focused much attention on the Colorado River and the idea of building a railroad along the stream from the Rockies to the sea probably had occurred to several people. In the 1880s the railroad fever was at its height in the West; competing lines were building across mountain ranges and deserts to reach the Pacific and the markets en route and beyond. Why not construct a line along the Colorado River which on the map appeared to be the easiest grade west from the Continental Divide?

Why not indeed? S. S. Harper, who had prospected along the Atlantic and Pacific line in northern Arizona, thought it a feasible idea, even though he had seen the Colorado River but once—at Lee's Ferry. He found a ready listener in Frank M. Brown of Denver, a Colorado and California promoter, who was eager to get into railroads. The two men studied the reports of Ives and Powell; in Washington, Brown discussed the plan with the major who, startled, pronounced it "quite impracticable." Otherwise they found no serious obstacles, and the promise of riches was more than a match for any negative arguments. There was a fortune to be made. Colorado coal in California would command premium prices. Resources along the line would be developed and the canyon country scenery would attract more paying customers.

Early in 1889, the Denver, Colorado Canyon and Pacific Railroad Company was organized to capitalize on Harper's idea. Frank M. Brown, president, set about energetically to make a survey of the route. Robert Brewster Stanton was appointed chief engineer in charge, to determine the engineering feasibility. Stanton had already made something of a name for himself in railroad engineering. Among other positions he had worked on the Atlantic and Pacific in Indian Territory and more recently he had built the Georgetown Loop on the Union Pacific in Colorado.

Adventure was assured and disaster invited by the outfit Brown ordered for the survey. The boats were but fifteen feet long and clinker-built of thin, red cedar planking. Brown thought it best not to be burdened with "cumbersome boats" of larger dimension, for the light boats would be easier to portage. No life preservers were provided.

With Brown in charge, the surveyors left Green River, Utah, on May 25. The going was easy until they reached Cataract Canyon on the Colorado just below the mouth of the Green River where the survey began. In that savage forty-mile stretch of water two boats were lost along with most of the cooking gear and supplies, but Stanton managed to carry the instrumental survey through to Hite at Dandy Crossing in Glen Canyon. At that point the party was divided. Brown and Stanton hurried on to make a reconnaissance of the canyons ahead, leaving behind a crew to carry the survey through Glen Canyon.

At Lee's Ferry the advance party loaded on fresh provisions and plunged into Marble Canyon. On July 10, the second day out, Frank M. Brown was drowned when his boat capsized just below Soap Creek Rapid. Tragedy struck again on July 15 when Harry C. Richards and Peter M. Hansbrough capsized and drowned in a bad rapid twenty-four and a half miles below Lee's Ferry. Saddened by the losses the five men remaining drifted on down to the mouth of South Canyon just above Vasey's Paradise. There they wisely decided to quit the river; caching their supplies at "Point Retreat," they walked out to the V. T. Ranch and safety.[1]

Undaunted by setbacks and tragedy Stanton was determined to see the survey completed and the railroad built. He assumed control of the company's field operations, raised enough money to buy a new outfit, and before the end of the year was back on the river. With three sturdy oak boats, twenty-two feet long, and specially fitted with safety features, including life preservers, Stanton put in at the mouth of North Wash in Glen Canyon. Twelve men made up the party, of which three were veterans of the first trip. With special food brought along for the occasion Stanton treated his crew to an elegant Christmas dinner at Lee's Ferry, and on December 28, 1889, the surveyors once more tackled Grand Canyon.

Marble Canyon dealt them more hard luck. On New Year's day the photographer, F. A. Nims, broke his leg and had to be carried out. Some ten miles below Point Retreat, where the river makes a sharp horseshoe bend, the party came upon the decomposed remains of Peter Hansbrough. After a simple

Robert Brewster Stanton in the middle section of Grand Canyon while making the 1890 railroad survey. Arizona.

burial ceremony Stanton named the great butte on the inside of the bend Point Hansbrough, in memory of his associate.

Slowly and laboriously the engineer carried his "instrumental reconnaissance" down the canyon, making but a few miles a day. He had to stop to study the canyon; sketches, surveys, and photographs were made at difficult points and particularly at side canyons where bridging might be required. Stanton saw to it that almost every mile was photographed, in order to argue graphically the feasibility of the route before skeptical backers of the line. With Nims gone, Stanton himself assumed the duties of photographer.

Unbelievable though it seems, R. B. Stanton found a route over which—or so he argued—rails could be laid all the way through Marble Canyon! This is the way he classified the necessary construction through this division, consisting of 62.51 miles of tracks: .05 miles over level bottom land; 26.51 miles over rough talus slopes of loose and solid rocks; 27.35 miles of "cliff bench work—sandstone and marble"; .75 miles of "heavy embankment in river"; 2.37 miles of tunnel. The engineer compiled similar figures for the entirety of Grand Canyon (and for the canyons above Lee's Ferry).

The railroad crew spent nearly all winter surveying the Grand Canyon. There were few serious mishaps below Marble Canyon. One boat, already badly damaged, was smashed to pieces in Horn Creek Rapid, and this put an overload on the two remaining craft. But Harry McDonald left shortly afterward to prospect the North Rim and three more departed at Diamond Creek. The surveyors were out of the canyon on March 17, and on April 26, 1890, they reached a point very close to tidewater in Mexico where the river survey was terminated. By instruments and careful study Stanton had surveyed nine hundred miles of the Colorado—the distance from the mouth of the Green River to the Gulf of California.

Armed now with facts, figures, statistics, maps, surveys, and nine hundred photographs, Robert B. Stanton set about to win financial backing for the railroad. The proposed route from Grand Junction to tidewater—at San Diego—was feasible and practicable, he argued. Construction and maintenance costs would be less than the other transcontinentals. Nowhere would the grade exceed one percent. The road would be ice-free and could even be operated by electricity generated by the river's water power! The resources of the canyon country—minerals, timber, and the produce of the land—would find ready markets, and the scenic values of the route were high, he argued.

The railroad got no further than the survey. The board of the Denver, Colorado Canyon and Pacific Railroad found no funds to continue; they may well have been skeptical of the academic stance of the doughty engineer. He denied that the scheme was impossible or impracticable, and expressed with firmness his views on its positive economic feasibility. Probably his most interested audience was composed of delegates to the annual meeting of the American Society of Civil Engineers, who heard him read a paper on the "Availability of the Cañons of the Colorado River of the West for Railway Purposes." Even at the peak of the railroad boom, however, the idea found no takers.[2]

Without financial backing for this project Stanton turned to other enterprises, the largest and most dramatic of which was gold mining in Glen Canyon. He had staked out some gold placers on his second trip through that canyon in 1889. Ten years later he returned as head of a mining company, staked out the entire canyon (169 miles in length!), and installed a bucket dredge to recover the placer gold. The dust was too fine—it floated right through the dredge machinery—and the project failed.[3]

Robert B. Stanton was obsessed by the canyon country of the Colorado. He regarded the railroad survey as one of the most meaningful experiences in his life. He was the first after Powell to make the long run through the canyons below Green River, Utah. His study and survey of the canyons—the first with utilization as the objective—were much more thorough than Powell's and the pages of his meticulously kept notes are much more numerous. His work had greatly extended the scope of knowledge about Powell's "Great Unknown." At any rate it must have been satisfying to him to know that his survey of the river would assure him a prominent place in the river's long history—hopefully on a par with Powell, the man with one arm. Stanton had only one good arm, his right, but that hadn't held *him* back either.

Unlike Powell, Stanton was slow to publish. He felt he must write about his experiences, but he wanted them to be seen in the perspective of time and the river's history. In 1889, George M. Wheeler had published a two-page chronology in his *Geographical Report,* the only historical account of the river. Stanton finally decided to write a history of his own; he labored for fourteen years and brought forth "The River and the Canyon," a manuscript of over a thousand folio pages devoted to a history of the exploration, navigation, and survey of the canyons of the Colorado from 1539 to about 1914. The work, written "from the standpoint of an engineer," was completed in 1920, but it was never published.[4]

In his history Stanton devoted an appropriate space to the railroad survey. He wrote that for him the great canyons held a double meaning: he looked at them as a place to build a railroad, but he also saw them "in their beauty, in their grandeur, in their sublimity," and at times he gave himself up to "their mysterious influences." He dwelt at some length on the sublimity of the Grand Canyon and at times his prose rivaled Dutton's, whom he admired more than Moran. He admitted that Moran's "Grand Chasm of the Colorado" was the work of a master but, he wrote, "It does not move. It is quiet. It is still. The Grand Canyon is never still, it is never quiet. It is a living, moving being, ever changing in form and color. . . . How can such a shifting, animated glory be caught and held on canvas?"

Stanton's description of the "birth of a canyon day," which he witnessed from the towering summit of Osiris Temple, is as good as anything in the poetic prose of Dutton or Powell. The engineer never tired of the canyons. Near the end of the survey, he wrote: "I stood, in the last few miles of the Grand Canyon, spellbound in wonder and admiration, as firmly as I was fixed in the first few miles, in surprise and astonishment."[5]

Within his own lifetime Robert B. Stanton witnessed some changes in the history of the canyon. During the railroad survey in Grand Canyon, he had seen only one person, a prospector near the head of the Upper Granite Gorge. Writing very near the end of his life he mourned the passing of the wilderness. "Alas! today," he exclaimed in anguish, there are hotels on the South Rim, tourists arrive in Pullman cars, and they look at the canyon while they "sip French champagne and smoke Havana cigars." Stanton had taken a proprietary interest (as others have before and since) in the Grand Canyon. He was one of its discoverers. It was his, and he would not have it profaned.

"I would not build a fence around the Grand

BILL BELKNAP

Wild burros in the Grand Canyon at the water's edge at Mile 214. Arizona.

Canyon and keep the tourist out. No, not at all. But with my fondness for the wilderness and the desert, and my love for what is so falsely called the solitude of the Grand Canyon, I have always felt that 'civilization' should never have approached it. I would not deprive anyone of the joy of seeing such a marvel—even from an aeroplane, if he wishes, but, it seems to me, to really appreciate such a country one must see it, as one can only do, by wandering among its pinnacles and its gorges just as they were—untouched by the hand of man—years ago."

Is this the man who would have built a railroad through the canyon and turned the power of the river to run it? In the concluding paragraphs of "The River and the Canyon" Stanton gave his answer. "Every engineer—possibly there are exceptions—is possessed of two beings. With one he loves Nature for Nature's sake, loves it as God made it and gave it to us; with the other he follows Telford's definition of the profession of an engineer—'being the art of directing the great sources of power in Nature for the use and convenience of man.'"[6] Here, nature and the canyon had won.

COPPER BOOM

The completion of the Santa Fe in 1883 and Stanton's railroad survey stimulated prospecting throughout the canyon country, especially along the South Rim. During the twenty years between 1880 and 1900, thousands of claims were staked in the Grand Canyon and on the uplands on both sides of the river. Some of the more notable discoveries were made on the Kaibab Plateau, at Lee's Ferry, and in the Grand Canyon between the Little Colorado and Shinumo Creek.[7]

Some of Stanton's men on the railroad survey had taken more than a passing interest in the mineral potential of the Grand Canyon. Felix Lantier, the lone prospector the surveyors had met, fed their enthusiasm with glowing accounts of gold, silver, and copper. Harry McDonald, who left Stanton to prospect, turned up in Denver where he argued convincingly of the mineral potential of the canyons and helped to organize the Colorado, Grand Canyon Mining and Improvement Company. The prospectus announced that the firm planned to mine and operate toll roads, ferries, and hotels. As an initial venture a prospecting party was organized with James S. Best in charge. In two boats of the basic Stanton design, eight men, four of them veterans of the Stanton railroad survey, started from Green River, Utah, intending to prospect through Grand Canyon. The party lost one boat in Cataract Canyon but managed to reach Lee's Ferry in August, 1891. Four of the group went on by horseback

Grand Canyon tourists on the South Rim about 1901. Arizona.

Grosvenor Arch in Butler Valley on a branch of the Paria River. Utah.

to explore the Kaibab and Bright Angel Creek, which they reached on foot from the North Rim.

Coming hard on the heels of the Stanton survey, the Best expedition attracted some attention in the regional press. Considerable interest focused on Bright Angel Creek; allusions were made to a "lost mine" found there. Best and company did stake a few claims, near Jacob Lake and elsewhere, but these amounted to very little. When some of the men returned from the wilds they said much more about the fine hunting on the Kaibab and the scenes of "wild enchantment" along Bright Angel Creek than they did about the meager prospects of the region.[8] Nonetheless the Stanton railroad survey and the activities of the Best party advertised the canyon country as a promising field.

The Mormons continued to be the most active prospectors in the North Rim country. Many of the family names of the pioneer settlers of Dixie and southern Utah were signed on claims staked on the Kaibab, "under the sand rocks"—that is, below the rim of Grand Canyon—and elsewhere on the Arizona Strip. The best mines developed on the north side were copper deposits found near Jacob Lake and Lamb's Lake on the Kaibab. Shortly after 1900 a smelter was built at Ryan, at the western base of the plateau, to refine ore from these and other locations. Farther west, the mines at Copper Mountain and Grand Gulch were intermittently productive.[9]

All other conditions being equal, the proximity of the Santa Fe railroad was assurance that the Grand Canyon mining rush would be localized along the South Rim; as it turned out, some of the best prospects were found south of the river. Numbers of those prominent in Grand Canyon history appeared in the rush of the nineties—W. H. Ashurst, Peter Berry, S. B. Tanner, John Hance, N. J. Cameron, Ralph Cameron, D. L. Hogan, L. D. Boucher, E. J. Babbitt, W. O. O'Neill. W. W. Bass, S. B. Rowe, and others.[10]

The first ten staked claims in the Grand Canyon at various times from 1890 to early in 1893, and they made enough possible discoveries to boom the field. The influx of prospectors was large enough to justify the formation of the Grand Canyon Mining District, organized at "Cottonwood Camp" on February 20,

1893, by W. H. Ashurst and P. D. Berry. But the Panic of 1893 engulfed the nation in the spring, and the depression stifled canyon country prospecting during the mid-1890s. Recovery late in the nineties coincided with a jump in the price of copper, and the canyon country came on strong once again. Among the later arrivals was William "Buckey" O'Neill, who in 1897 staked a number of claims along the canyon rim in the vicinity of "Cyclorama" Point north of Rowe's Well, one of the few rimland watering places.[11]

The prospectors went almost everywhere—they located claims in side canyons, rimlands, plateau tops, mesas, and the great gorge itself. Areas that had been raked over lightly in the 1870s and 1880s were combed now more thoroughly. To reach prospects in the canyon, the miners built new trails from the South Rim and restored others. Some of these were extended across the river to the north side and a number of horizontal routes were worked out.

Beyond the joy of living outdoors in a land of magnificent vistas, the miners found little to reward them for their pains and hard work. Although other minerals were found (including asbestos of good quality), most of the mines were copper, and the price of this metal tended to fluctuate dramatically. A few rich pockets and deposits were found, but most of the prospects showed lean, low-grade ore. Given the cost of hauling this (by burro to the rim, by wagon to the railhead) to the smelter, a drop in the price of copper would spell ruin to a marginal operation.

To cut costs the Grand Canyon miners talked of a railroad—one to connect the mainline Santa Fe with the South Rim. The tourist-minded towns of Flagstaff, Williams, and Ash Fork also promoted the idea. While others talked, Buckey O'Neill acted. Among other prospects O'Neill had located some copper claims about fourteen miles south of the rim at a place he called Anita. He thought the ore rich enough to attract some development capital, and he interested Lombard, Goode and Company, a Chicago engineering firm. In 1898, the company bought O'Neill's mining interests and set about to build a smelter in Williams and a railroad from that point to the South Rim by way of the Anita mine. By 1900, the Santa Fe and Grand Canyon Railway (not affiliated with the

Santa Fe system) had reached Anita, but production at the mine had fallen off; the company found itself in financial trouble and in August, 1901, sold out to the Atchison, Topeka and Santa Fe Railway Company. The Santa Fe quickly completed the line; the first scheduled train from Williams reached the South Rim on September 20, 1901.

Mining in the Grand Canyon country remained a high-risk venture. Much capital was invested, few fortunes—if any—were made. The copper boom of the 1890s was based upon an inflated market. When prices skidded after the turn of the century none of the canyon country mines could compete with the big producers elsewhere and operations were shut down. The smelter at Williams, completed by Lombard, Goode and Company, was little used, if at all. The better mines were reopened at later times when metal price increases suggested the possibility of profit. The most productive mines on the south side of the canyon were the Grandview, opened by Pete Berry and N. J. and Ralph Cameron, the Orphan mine, located by Dan Hogan, and the mines in Copper Canyon worked by W. W. Bass. The Anita and adjoining mines, the mines in Havasu Canyon, and others to the west in the Hualapai country were at times profitable producers.[12]

The miners did much to direct the course of history in the Grand Canyon country. They were the first to become microscopically familiar with large sections of it—particularly the great canyon. They put names on the land; they found out ways to get about in difficult country; they built a network of roads and trails and brought rails to the rim of the canyon. They added a new dimension to the wildlife of the canyon: burros, escaped from captivity, or turned loose, roamed the canyon wild and free. As a rule the prospectors were not very articulate, but they did help to advertise the wonders of the region—notably the South Rim. They came to find that the scenery was more productive than the mines. There was more gold in the pockets of the tourists than in the rocks of the canyon. They became guides, travel agents, hoteliers, and helped to set the course of tourist travel to the Grand Canyon. And the pattern cut out by 1901 has changed very little to the present day.

DUDES

The publications of the Powell and Wheeler surveys, the art of Thomas Moran, Stanton's railroad survey of the Colorado canyons, and the mining rushes widely advertised the wonders of the Grand Canyon country. Upon completion of the Santa Fe Railway, and even before, tourists in small numbers came to see for themselves. Very few saw the scenes portrayed by Powell, Dutton, Moran, and Holmes because the early sightseers were confined to the South Rim country. None of Powell's men had visited the southern side of Grand Canyon, and Wheeler had described only the

W. W. Bass, Grand Canyon miner, poet and guide.

part of it below Diamond Creek. At hand to greet the visitors along the South Rim were numbers of miners and prospectors who showed them how to get about and what to see.

A young ethnologist from the Smithsonian Institution, sojourning at the Zuñi Pueblo, was the first of the tourists to arrive. Frank Hamilton Cushing learned of the Havasupais from the Zuñis. They told him of the "marvelous country toward the sunset" and of the Indians who lived deep in a canyon, the trail down which, they said, was a "whole day long." Cushing wanted to see the canyon dwellers whose quiet lives had been disturbed recently by miners. On horseback and with a Zuñi guide he followed the ancient trading trail by way of the Hopi villages and

"Grub time" in camp at the mouth of Diamond Creek. Photograph made in 1883. Arizona.

thence to the South Rim and Topocoba Hilltop.

Cushing arrived in June, 1881, scarcely a week after Lieutenant Colonel W. R. Price had surveyed a projected reservation for the Indians. The first ethnologist to visit these isolated people, Cushing described the Havasupais who were still living as they had for centuries. Within a decade after his visit— certainly by 1900—the native ways of the Havasupais had been permanently changed by contact with the white man. In a small way Cushing himself contributed to this end. He was a tourist; that his journey was an adventure, he freely admitted. His interesting account of the trip, "The Nation of Willows," appeared in two issues of the *Atlantic Monthly* in 1882. Cushing's article is recognized as a valuable ethnological record, but it is also a significant document in the travel literature of the Grand Canyon country. Thenceforth, first the few and then the many canyon-bound tourists with enough time tried to schedule a visit to the Havasupais.[13]

In November, 1884, General George Crook, commander of the army forces in Arizona, made a "tour" of duty from Fort Whipple to the canyon home of the Havasupais, which he was anxious to see, and the Grand Canyon. Captain John G. Bourke chronicled the reconnaissance and produced a document comparable to Cushing's in its ethnological importance. Crook left Havasupai Canyon by the Hualapai Trail, went out to the rim of Grand Canyon overlooking Diamond Creek, near where Ives had been in 1858, and then entrained for the base at Peach Springs.[14]

Crook's tour coincided with the opening of commercial tourist travel in the western section of Grand Canyon. Peach Springs station on the Santa Fe was but twenty-five miles from the Colorado River and it was the only place in the Grand Canyon below Lee's Ferry where wagons could be taken to the water's edge. Ives had reached the canyon floor by way of Peach Springs Canyon and Diamond Creek, and Wheeler's upriver party in 1871 had exited by this route. It was a natural tourist gateway as J. H. Farlee recognized in 1884 when he built a wagon road of sorts from the railroad to the river and erected a public house at the confluence of Peach Springs Canyon and Diamond Creek, two miles from the Colorado.

194

Peach Springs Canyon, a fork of Diamond Creek, was the route taken by Lt. J. C. Ives to reach the floor of Grand Canyon in 1858. Once the Santa Fe Railway was completed in 1883, some of the first tourists used this route to reach the floor of Grand Canyon. It is the only place in the entire length of the canyon where wagons and automobiles can be taken to the water's edge. Arizona.

Some of the first tourists to see Grand Canyon made use of Farlee's services. One of the earliest travelers by this route described Farlee as stage driver, road owner, guide, landlord, and cook. He would meet the trains—both east and west trains arrived between two and three in the morning. After providing a "tolerable" breakfast at the station, Farlee would convey his customers down the canyon in a four-horse three-seated "stage," built upon the "buckboard principle." Farlee's "hotel" was described as a four-room board "shanty," two bedrooms above and a single room and a kitchen below. For tourists in a hurry the proprietor would make the round trip to the river in a day; probably few stayed more than two or three days.

Some of the most spectacular landscapes of Grand Canyon grace the lower canyon but, seen from the water's edge at the mouth of Diamond Creek, they are not so evident. The somber walls of Lower Granite Gorge dominate the scene. The early tourists found they could see it all in an hour or two—certainly a morning spent scrambling about was enough. Farlee's "Grand Canyon Stage Line" was a pioneer tourist enterprise in the Grand Canyon country, but it lasted only a short while. For six or seven years he handled seventy-five, maybe a hundred, sightseers a year; but after that, business dwindled and Farlee succumbed to the competition working out of Flagstaff, Williams, and Ash Fork.[15]

East of Peach Springs and the Hualapai country a few tourists before 1890 had reached the Grand Canyon from the raw little towns along the Santa Fe, but after 1890, when the copper rush boomed the South Rim, there was much more travel, and regular services soon became available. In 1892, a subsidiary of the Santa Fe Railway opened triweekly stagecoach service from Flagstaff to the canyon. Travelers over the line the first two weeks numbered company officials, foreign visitors, and journalists, including Charles F. Lummis; also among the passengers was artist Thomas Moran, making his first trip to the South Rim.[16]

These and other early tourists told the world of their experiences. "For the first time in its history," Charles Lummis wrote, "this sublimest wonder of the earth is really open to all sight-seers . . . at its noblest point." Lummis himself had seen the canyon before and called it simply, "the grandest gorge in the world." He soon changed this to "the greatest thing in the world" and urged Americans to see their own country before going abroad. J. G. Lemmon, a botanist, described the panorama of the canyon and the great plateaus of the Arizona Strip as he saw them from the summit of Mt. Agassiz, one of the San Francisco Peaks. Studying the canyon strata close at hand, and with Dutton's work in mind, he counted up to fifty architectural and sculptural forms. In one of the better articles of the day, Lemmon finally admitted that this canyon was "too vast, too varied, too sublime, too appalling for adequate description."

Virginia Dox exclaimed: "In all the wide, wide world there can be nothing more wonderful and beautiful." Charles Dudley Warner spoke of the canyon as a "new world." Our "education in scenery" has been of a "totally different kind," and only long familiarity with the canyon would perfect one's comprehension of it. Echoing Dutton he wrote, "I think the mind needs training in the desert scenery to enable it to grasp the unique sublimity of the Grand Cañon." A party composed of thirty-six members (mainly Europeans) of the fifth International Geological Congress visited the canyon in September, 1891; they possibly needed less instruction in geological scenery than most tourists but, nonetheless, they were accompanied by experts. Arriving in Flagstaff in two palace Pullman cars, the party by chartered stage reached the South Rim where they were lectured by John Wesley Powell, Director, U.S. Geological Survey.[17]

Although most tourists in the nineties took the stage line from Flagstaff, W. W. Bass and Sanford Rowe, operating from Ash Fork and Williams, carried a good share of Grand Canyon passengers. As the traffic increased, accommodations were built along the rim between Grandview Point and Havasupai Point, a distance of about thirty-five miles. Most of these facilities were operated by miners—Hance, Berry, Cameron, Boucher, and Bass—who came to find tourists more lucrative than prospecting, but others as well—Buggeln, Thurber, and Rowe—got into the business. The accommodations and services

Camp at Mile 185.5 in lower Grand Canyon. Arizona.

were as varied as the character of the proprietors. John Hance at Grandview Point regaled the customers with tall tales about himself and the canyon. Bill Bass at Havasupai Point took the canyon more seriously; miner, photographer, poet, he offered a wide range of services including transportation, lodging, and guided trips to Havasu Canyon and across Grand Canyon to the Kaibab Plateau.[18]

The stages were a prelude to the trains. When the rails reached the edge of the canyon, the tide of tourists gained momentum. Some of those who had seen the canyon before hoped such an influx would never happen. The railroad would "profane creation's masterpiece," wrote Charles Lummis. He then followed a line heard many times since his day: "The coming of

the mob will kill the joy of those with souls. For when a glory of nature is absolutely facile to the herd, it reeks with their inanity and is never again the same. Cheapened sublimity is no more sublime." Harriet Monroe had rejoiced in the dusty stage ride and the rough accommodations and was happy that "one of the glories of the earth was still undesecrated by the chatter of facile tourists." A few miners "burrowing for copper" supplied acceptable local color.[19]

The railroad brought more travelers to the canyon than ever before, but they did not come in "herds." It cost money to travel. The lengthy excursion was beyond the reach of the many—the "facile" tourists. The new element was the dude who would ride in the cars all the way or not at all. For him the

train—the Pullman frontier—was the cutting edge between civilization and wildness.

By 1901 the Grand Canyon was taking shape in the public mind. Many visitors of the 1890s had written descriptive articles. The stage lines had published extensive promotional literature, particularly the Flagstaff route backed by the Santa Fe. The 1893 edition of the company's brochure, written by C. A. Higgins, was illustrated by Thomas Moran, H. F. Farny, and F. H. Lungren. Karl Baedeker included a section (and map) on stage coach travel to the canyon in his 1899 handbook to *The United States,* and in 1900 George Wharton James published *In and Around the Grand Canyon,* the first book written by a tourist for tourists. Professional photographers had reached the South Rim to record in black-and-white objectivity what so many tourists had tried unsuccessfully to capture in words. Henry G. Peabody, one of the best landscape photographers, issued his first album in 1900. Those who could not travel to the canyon could listen to lectures about it by John L. Stoddard and Burton Holmes.[20]

The Santa Fe delivered its passengers to the door of the Bright Angel Hotel perched on the rim of the canyon near the head of Bright Angel Trail. The hotel had been started in 1896 by J. W. Thurber of the Flagstaff stage line and acquired by the railroad in 1900, and it was now expanded to accommodate the rising flow of tourists. Around and about the end of the tracks Grand Canyon Village took shape and boasted of a post office in 1902. Adjoining the Bright Angel, the Santa Fe built the sumptuous El Tovar Hotel. This rustic hostelry, named after one of Coronado's lieutenants, opened in 1905. It was operated by Fred Harvey, already famous across the Southwest as a hotelier and purveyor of good meals served by attractive waitresses in crisply starched white and black uniforms. The pioneer phase of South Rim tourism had ended![21]

The first generation of canyon country tourists, following the miners to the canyon, had largely confined their sightseeing to the narrow, thirty-five-mile segment of the South Rim between Grandview and Havasupai points. What they saw from there and from the depths below the rim *was* the Grand Canyon to them, and by talk and print and photography they created a kind of popular image of the gorge which with time became indelible. Not much more than what you can see from this section of the South Rim defined the bounds of Grand Canyon National Park. Those who created the park included the area known to the tourists and very little more. It took the general public a long time to understand that the Grand Canyon did not begin nor end where the arbitrary boundaries of the park crossed the Colorado River.

Brian Head (altitude 11,229 feet) towers over Cedar Breaks National Monument on the western rim of the Markagunt Plateau. Utah.

12

The Insistent Earth

Thanks to the vigorous expansion of the Mormon people the frontier of settlement and exploitation reached the northern part of the Grand Canyon country a decade or two before it touched the South Rim. The district described and portrayed by Powell, Dutton, Holmes, Moran, and Hillers was far away from any railroad, and as a consequence it became a popular pleasuring ground only after the automobile became a reality. Tourists came late to the North Rim.

John W. Young, a son of Brigham Young and canyon country entrepreneur, made one dramatic attempt to open the North Rim to tourism. In the late 1880s, Young, representing the Mormon Church in England, attempted to interest the English aristocracy in the Kaibab as a sporting area and hunting ground. When some curiosity was shown, Young induced Buffalo Bill Cody, who was then in England with his Wild West Show, to act as guide for the English sportsmen and to replenish the stock for his exhibition at Young's V. T. Ranch on the Kaibab.

One day in November, 1892, Buffalo Bill and a party of English noblemen, American army officers, sportsmen, and assorted businessmen and capitalists stepped off the west-bound train at Flagstaff where they were met with teams and carriages by Dan Seegmiller of Kanab. Outfitted with an "arsenal" of the latest and most improved weapons, the party set out to see the Grand Canyon, hunt the Kaibab, and explore the North Rim. Seegmiller drove his charges first to Hance's Camp on the South Rim. From there it was a long, bumpy, jolting ride of nearly a hundred and fifty miles to Lee's Ferry. Next came the steep, rocky eastern slope of the Coconino Plateau; the ford of the Little Colorado at Tanner's Crossing; the soft, sandy tracks across the Painted Desert; then ledgy, broken trail under the shadow of the Echo Cliffs; and finally Lee's Backbone. Beyond the ferry they traveled fifty miles across Houserock Valley, through deep sand, low hills and hummocks, and rocky washes. Bone-tired and shaken, the travelers finally reached the V. T. Ranch at the eastern base of the Kaibab.

It was probably the longest, roughest ride most of the visitors had ever had. No accounts of the trip have been found to indicate what members of the party may have thought about the delights of viewing an unparalleled landscape in the clear November air. But the hunting was good on the Kaibab. At a point above Bright Angel Creek, the visitors turned their backs on the Grand Canyon and posed for photographs. On the spot they named the place MacKinnon Point in honor of H. MacKinnon, bart., "Col., Gren.

Buckskin Gulch, a tributary of the Paria River, heads on the Pink Cliffs, flows in a spectacular canyon through the White Cliffs, bisects the north end of the Kaibab Plateau and enters the parent stream through this narrow slot on the Utah-Arizona boundary.

Gds." London, who had killed the first buck on the Kaibab. In honor of the "guide," someone proposed that the yawning canyon tributary of Bright Angel just below them be named "Buffalo Bill's Colosseum." The name, which would have been quite as appropriate as the nearby Oza Butte and Manu Temple, did not stick, however, and MacKinnon Point has since been renamed to honor the artist Gunnar Widforss.

The English lords declined the invitation to invest in the Kaibab as a hunting ground and tourist center for sportsmen and sightseers. Rather than take the long road back to Flagstaff, the party went out through Kanab and the Utah settlements where the roads were better. The Kaibab, they agreed, was simply "too far away and too hard to reach."[1]

And that is the way matters stood for some time. The Kaibab—the North Rim—"was too far away and too hard to reach." It would help, some believed, if the Arizona Strip belonged to Utah. Very soon after achieving statehood in 1896, the Utah legislature introduced bills in Congress calling for the annexation of the region north of the Grand Canyon; further attempts were made in 1902 and in 1904, but the matter, which aroused much antagonism in Arizona, was dropped when Arizona became a state in 1912.[2]

With eyes on the burgeoning growth of South Rim tourism, a few enterprising Utahns—among them Dan Seegmiller, E. D. Woolley, and David D.

William F. Cody's party at the V.T. Ranch, 1892. An English lord rests on the hitching rack on the left, Buffalo Bill on the right. Arizona.

Rust—tried to overcome isolation and bad roads and develop tourist travel to the North Rim. Woolley organized the Grand Canyon Transportation Company to open cross-canyon traffic from the North Rim to the Santa Fe railroad on the South Rim. The company built a trail through Bright Angel Canyon, strung a cable over the Colorado, and constructed a trail out of the Granite Gorge to connect with the Bright Angel Trail at Indian Gardens. Later called Phantom Ranch, the construction camp near the mouth of Bright Angel Creek was made ready for tourists. The route was opened in 1907, but the customers were few. The North Rim could scarcely compete with the South Rim when the nearest railhead was over two hundred miles from the canyon's edge.

The hunting on the Kaibab was one of the greatest attractions of the North Rim country. For centuries before the coming of the white man the Indians had harvested deer on the plateau, and the Mormon pioneers had called it Buckskin Mountain. Conservationist Senator Reed Smoot of Utah, who had visited the Kaibab in 1905, thought it wise to protect the herds and got a bill through Congress to this effect. President Theodore Roosevelt signed the bill on November 28, 1906, creating the Grand Canyon Game Reserve within the Grand Canyon Forest Reserve.

The Grand Canyon Forest, proclaimed by President Benjamin Harrison in 1893, was the first move made by the federal government to protect the area from uncontrolled exploitation. National park status for Grand Canyon had been advanced earlier by Harrison when he was Senator from Indiana, but three separate bills with this objective failed in Congress. The park idea gained some momentum with the coming of the railroad. Cries of overcommercialization were heard and grew louder after 1905, when the deluxe El Tovar opened its doors. Theodore Roosevelt agreed. In 1903, he had traveled by train to the South Rim where in an oft-quoted speech he said that the Grand Canyon is "the one great sight which every American . . . should see." Do nothing to spoil its "wonderful grandeur," he counseled, "leave it as it is. You cannot improve upon it. The ages have been at work on it, and man can only mar it."

Roosevelt used the power of the presidency to back up his convictions. The game reserve was one move. On January 11, 1908, he established Grand Canyon National Monument, one of sixteen such reservations ordered by Roosevelt under authority of the Antiquities Act of 1906; others peripheral to the Grand Canyon country were Natural Bridges, Petrified Forest, and El Morro, or Inscription Rock. Monument status meant that no further private entry or appropriation of lands within the reservation boundary would be permitted.

There were a few voices who argued that the greatest wonder of the continent should be a national park, but they were shouted down by local interests who had opposed the forest reserve, and who feared that the grass and timber and minerals and water would be locked up for all time. Yellowstone and Yosemite were more popular with visitors than Grand Canyon. Verdant nature was more attractive to most Americans and other visitors than the desert country of the Southwest. Some time would have to pass before the bleak, naked rocks of the Colorado Plateau and its leafless, bizarre canyons would gain full stature as a pleasuring ground.

Nevertheless, by 1912, when Arizona became a state, local opposition to the park idea had been surmounted by a growing national interest in the canyon. President William Howard Taft had visited the South Rim in October, 1909, an event that attracted as much publicity as Roosevelt's earlier visit. Meanwhile a continuing flow of articulate visitors and artists had created an enduring popular image of the canyon that even today governs the vision of many visitors.[3]

Looking down upon the canyon from the railroad terminal Joaquin Miller asked himself if any place he had seen was "as full of glory, as full of God." John Muir assured wilderness lovers that in the presence of such stupendous scenery the locomotives and trains on the canyon rim were no more disturbing than the hooting of an owl in the lonely woods. William Allen White said that "this cañon some day must have its special meaning for mankind. . . ." Dr. T. M. Prudden called the Colorado Plateau the "World's Masterpiece." Lilian Whiting labeled the Grand Canyon the "Carnival of the Gods." Arizona's own historian Sharlot M. Hall wrote of "Beautiful Havasu" Canyon and its Indian dwellers and described a "Christmas at Grand Canyon." John Burroughs depicted the glorious and different views to be obtained from the bottom of the canyon. And George Wharton James issued a new guidebook, *The Grand Canyon of Arizona; How to See It,* which included a chapter on "Three Ways of Spending One Day at the Canyon."[4]

Meanwhile on the north side of the canyon, hunting had kept the Kaibab Plateau in the public view. When the Grand Canyon Game Reserve was set aside, James T. "Uncle Jim" Owens was appointed warden to protect the deer and kill off mountain lions and other predators. Owens had come into the North Rim country with C. F. "Buffalo" Jones in 1906 to establish a preserve for the disappearing bison and to experiment in breeding these animals with cattle. With a special permit in hand Jones pastured his buffalo near Bright Angel Point on the Kaibab, but the forest did not agree with the animals and they were moved to the treeless range of House Rock Valley.

The experiment in producing the hybrid "cattalo" was anything but successful, and Jim took a job in the forest as government warden and hunter. Lions were so plentiful he was soon collecting big money in bounties and guiding cougar-hunting parties. Among them was tenderfoot Zane Grey, who left a dental practice in New York and came out to hunt and rope lions with Buffalo Jones. Enthralled with life in the open, Grey promptly launched a writing career with a biography of Jones, *The Last of the Plainsmen* (1908). He then turned to fiction; the world bought millions of his western novels, many of which were set in the canyon country of the Colorado. Theodore Roosevelt visited the canyon again in 1913 and hunted lions with Owens on the North Rim before going on to visit Rainbow Bridge.[5]

River travel on the Colorado had increased since Stanton completed the railroad survey in 1890. In 1896 George F. Flavell and Ramon Montos ran the canyons of the Colorado from Green River, Wyoming, to the Grand Wash Cliffs, in a simple flat-bottomed skiff, a feat duplicated within a few months by Nathaniel Galloway and W. C. Richmond, and later in 1907 by Charles Russell and Edwin Monett. Frederick S. Dellenbaugh, who had been on Powell's second river trip, did much to stimulate interest in the river when in 1902 he published *The Romance of the Colorado River,* a historical narrative from Coronado to Stanton. This was followed in 1908 by *A Canyon Voyage,* a detailed narrative based on his diary of the second Powell expedition.

Julius F. Stone, who had been associated with Stanton in the Glen Canyon gold-mining venture, became much interested in the river and in 1909 engaged Nathaniel Galloway to pilot his party through the canyons from Green River, Wyoming. Stone carried along copies of Powell's *Report* and Dellenbaugh's *A Canyon Voyage* as guidebooks. His party, which included S. S. Dubendorff and R. A. Cogswell, completed the run to Needles.

In September, 1911, Ellsworth and Emery Kolb, who had been landscape photographers on the South Rim for ten years, set out from Green River, Wyoming, on a photographic trip through the canyons. They relied heavily on information supplied by prior voyagers and completed the run to Needles in January, 1912. To supplement the photographic record, which included the first motion pictures, Ellsworth Kolb wrote a straightforward narrative account, liberally illustrated with photographs taken on the "big trip," *Through the Grand Canyon from Wyoming to Mexico,* published in October, 1914. In August, the *National Geographic Magazine* had published a long article by the Kolbs on their "Experiences in the Grand Canyon," illustrated by some of their best photographs taken over the preceding decade. Public interest in the Grand Canyon, which has grown steadily for years, was reflected in and heightened by Ellsworth Kolb's book and the magazine article.[6]

And by the artists. During these years Thomas Moran was doing some of his best work and could be seen occasionally along the South Rim sketching on viewpoints not far from El Tovar. Other artists and illustrators courageous enough to tackle the canyon appeared, among them Louis Akin, Maxfield Parrish, and William R. Leigh. The Santa Fe Railway used the work of a number of southwestern painters in its promotional advertising. And the U.S. Geological Survey

A summer evening at the Grand Canyon near El Tovar Hotel.
The view familiar to the millions. Arizona.

had published the beautiful maps drawn by François E. Matthes to facilitate interpretations of the canyon scene. For those visitors who liked to study geology from the Pullman car window, the survey in 1915 published a guidebook of the entire route of the Santa Fe Railway from Kansas City to Los Angeles, which included a special section on "A Side Trip to the Grand Canyon of the Colorado." [7]

Clearly, the national mood was right for a Grand Canyon national park; the bill to establish it was advanced through Congress by Arizona's Representative Carl Hayden and Senator Henry Fountain Ashurst, son of one of the canyon's pioneer miners, and in February, 1919, the nation acquired its seventeenth national park. "The Grand Canyon belongs to the world," said Representative Louis C. Cramton of Michigan.[8]

The boundaries of the new park, nowhere very far from the rims, enclosed the canyon from the mouth of Nankoweap Creek to the mouth of Havasu Creek, just over one third of Grand Canyon. But it was the best-known section, the one most visited. Since the 1880s, nearly all travelers had seen the canyon only from the rimlands of the Coconino or Kaibab plateaus. By 1919, the remainder of the great canyon—the other two thirds—scarcely existed in the popular mind, and the new park set precise boundaries to this narrow vision; the Grand Canyon was Grand Canyon National Park.

SEE AMERICA FIRST

The beautiful country sweeping back from the North Rim of the Grand Canyon to the breaks of the High Plateaus had been portrayed in superlatives by Powell, Dutton, Holmes, Moran, and Hillers, but its recreational development lagged behind that of the South Rim and even today, except for a few places, it is very little visited. The entire area, of course, was remote from any railroad, and for forty years after the building of the first transcontinental railroads shaped the economic destiny of the West.

But the railroad needed some incentive to build,

and in all of southern Utah, southern Nevada, and Arizona north of the Colorado, the settlements were few and the resource base poor. On the other hand, the historic Mormon Trail between Salt Lake and Los Angeles offered a practicable route from the central West to the coast, a possibility that became increasingly attractive as railroad competition increased in the 1880s and 1890s.

The completion in 1905 of the San Pedro, Los Angeles and Salt Lake Railroad—the "Salt Lake Route"—built by copper-king Senator William A. Clark and the Union Pacific (who merged their separate, competing interests in 1903) did much to enliven the economy along the way. However, there was very little fanfare when on January 30, 1905, the last spike was driven near Jean, a point about thirty miles southwest of Las Vegas. Before the coming of the railroad Las Vegas had been a very small place—a way station and watering place on the road between Utah and California. In 1882, Archibald and Helen J. Stewart acquired such properties as there were at the place, including the old Mormon fort. After her husband was murdered, Helen Stewart presided over affairs at Las Vegas Rancho until 1903 when she sold the property to William Clark.

After that, Las Vegas changed almost overnight from a sleepy ranch to a busy, booming railroad town where sagebrush quickly gave way to tents and buildings. The town formally began in May, 1905, when the railroad auctioned off lots as the first trains arrived. Southern Nevada grew rapidly following completion of the railroad, and in 1909 Lincoln County was divided to form Clark County with the seat of justice located at Las Vegas.

The Salt Lake Route kept to the west of the main pioneer settlement established along the old Mormon Trail in Utah and Nevada, but stations like Milford, Lund, and Modena in Utah, and Caliente and Moapa in Nevada, soon were serving an extensive hinterland. Among other places a number of spurs and branch lines were built to Cedar City, Iron Mountain, St. Thomas, and in later years to Boulder City and Hoover Dam.[9]

Probably those most appreciative of the arrival of the rails were the Mormon residents along the

Tourists in a bus operated by "Intelligence Tours" admire the Great White Throne, Zion National Park. Utah

One of the first trips by automobile to the North Rim of Grand Canyon.

Muddy. When a spur line was completed from Moapa to St. Thomas in 1912, a genuine celebration took place. A last spike, fashioned of copper from the Grand Gulch mine, was driven, a barbecue was held, and the festivities were presided over by a queen chosen for the occasion. For Mormons along the Muddy the railroad meant the end of nearly fifty years of difficult, isolated pioneering in a land hostile to the hand of man.

The new railroad between Salt Lake and Los Angeles opened up a tourist route, the potentialities of which were appreciated by Salt Lake City, which now found itself the hub of a system of railroads extending in six directions. Fisher S. Harris, enterprising secretary of the Salt Lake Commercial Club, saw an opportunity. Bring out the eastern tourists and let them help "build up a greater West." Harris and the Commercial Club came out with a slogan: "See Europe if you will but see America first." To advance the cause, the Commercial Club called a three-day "See America First" conference in Salt Lake City. At the closing session on January 27, 1906, a "See America League" was formed, with Fisher S. Harris as executive secretary, and commissioned to find ways and means to bring west "the money that now flows from modern millionaires to Europe."

The idea was born too soon. For a time the western railroads—notably those serving Salt Lake City, and particularly the Salt Lake Route—pushed patriotic tourism, but the pattern of travel to the Grand Canyon country was little changed by the new promotion. Public interest was not deflected very far from the railroad at the South Rim. See America before Europe? Since the 1890s, Charles F. Lummis had been chiding his countrymen for their "unpatriotic slighting" of the United States. Lummis opened his book, *Some Strange Corners of Our Country,* with a chapter on the Grand Canyon—"The Grandest Canyon in the World"—in which he lectured those "thousands of un-American Americans" who went to Europe annually "to see scenery infinitely inferior to our own, upon which they have never looked." In 1895, Lummis became editor of the *Land of Sunshine,* a Los Angeles periodical which he dedicated to boosting California and the Southwest. The irascible

Lummis frequently used a long editorial whip to thrash the American bent on globetrotting before he had seen America. Writing of the Grand Canyon in 1898, he said: "Probably the time will come when the Americans who know enough to go and see it will number more than a few score a year."

Indeed, before the war, travel was light. Travel was costly and few responded to Lummis' editorial lashings or to the propaganda issued by the See America First League. One editor commented that many Easterners "would be glad to show their devotion to the See America idea if given money for expenses."[10] Once the European war was over, the American people, disillusioned with foreign entanglements and the war's aftermath, headed for the open spaces in their own land to get away from it all. They were ready to see America first, and see it they did—in their automobiles.

The first automobile—a steam-driven machine owned by Oliver Lippincott, Los Angeles artist—had reached the South Rim in 1902, and in 1909, E. D. Woolley, active promotor of the North Rim, and his brother, E. G. Woolley, Jr., had driven two cars across the Kaibab Plateau to the North Rim. These were adventurous, even hazardous, trips, and the motorists who followed them during the next few years suffered frequent breakdowns and flats and found themselves occasionally stuck in mud or sand.[11]

But the automobile came of age during the war, and for a decade after it a new breed of pioneers washed over the land. The cost of travel was brought within reach of nearly everybody. Packed in the touring car the entire family could travel for the price of one person. The tourists traveled the open road to enjoy the thrill of individually controlled mechanized travel, to learn about America, and to visit the national parks, most of which were remote from centers of population.

Looking for information about the nation's playground the prospective postwar tourist would have discovered that the National Park Service, established in 1916, was administering a number of areas scattered over the map. Stephen T. Mather, the first director of the service, was determined to bring these to the attention of the people. "This nation is richer

(Next spread) The richly colored Precambrian rocks (Grand Canyon Series) in Lava Creek on the north side of the Colorado, Grand Canyon National Park. Arizona.

PHILIP HYDE

in natural scenery of the first order than any other nation," he wrote, "and is serenely ignorant of the fact." Mather dedicated *The National Parks Portfolio,* published in 1921 (third and expanded edition), to the American people and challenged them by saying that, "Some of our finest national parks here pictured you probably have never even heard of."[12]

The *Portfolio* portrayed twenty-four scenes of Grand Canyon National Park (none of the North Rim) which nearly everyone must have recognized, and six of Zion National Park, which the author described as "the latest scenic discovery of America," and which very few people recognized. Mather was right; who had ever heard of Zion? Isolated and remote from the lanes of commerce, southern Utah east of Dixie, and the Arizona Strip, had grown slowly since the 1890s. Tourists would have strengthened the local economy, but only a few wandered into the region, and most of them were bound for the North Rim. Few had come to visit the great canyon described by Dutton, drawn by Holmes, and painted by Moran. Fittingly enough, Zion was "rediscovered" by one of Powell's men.

In the 1870s, F. S. Dellenbaugh, youngest member of the Powell Survey, had mapped around Zion Canyon and seen the great towers from a distance, but he had never entered it. In 1903, he returned, took up residence in Zion Canyon, painted some canvases, and wrote a descriptive article, "A New Valley of Wonders," published in the January, 1904, issue of *Scribner's Magazine.* Dellenbaugh had already distinguished himself as a historian of the Colorado River, and the article, illustrated with many of his own photographs, attracted national attention. It was the most important first step leading in 1909 to the creation of Mukuntuweap National Monument. Mukuntuweap was the local Paiute name for the canyon, which Powell had adopted in his 1875 *Report.*

The national monument suggested to railroad officials and citizens of county and state the possibilities inherent in the landscape close at hand. In a burst of enthusiasm, perhaps in part generated by the "See America First" movement, the people of Utah began to appreciate the magnificent attractions of the sandstone wilderness in the southern part of their state. They had been slow to see the aesthetic quality

in a landscape where the range was sparse and the soil was poor. The agony of pioneering in so mean a land had dulled their appreciation of its beauty.

Their interest had resulted in the establishment in 1908 of Natural Bridges National Monument in southeastern Utah, and now, Zion. Governors of the state visited it, local organizations plumped for roads. Travel writers visited Zion and Cedar Breaks, and rediscovered Bryce Canyon, which the Wheeler Survey had first described and portrayed. When the National Park Service was created, Stephen T. Mather and his assistant Horace M. Albright took note of the publicity about Utah's scenic areas and worked with Utah Senator Reed Smoot to secure passage of a bill in 1919 changing the status of Mukuntuweap National Monument to Zion National Park. There was more to come. In 1923 and 1924, Bryce Canyon National Park

Frederick S. Dellenbaugh, youngest member of Powell's second expedition, 1871-72, whose books popularized the Powell Survey and the history of the Colorado River. Photo made at Zion National Park, 1929. Utah.

212

Navajo home and the towering Echo Cliffs. Arizona.

213

and Pipe Spring and Wupatki national monuments were added to the scenic and historic reservations of the Grand Canyon country. Grand Canyon National Monument, adjoining Grand Canyon National Park on the west, Cedar Breaks National Monument, and Kolob National Monument, adjoining Zion National Park, were all added between 1932 and 1937.[13]

Zion and southern Utah were brought into national focus in 1923 when, at the suggestion of Senator Smoot, President Warren G. Harding visited the park late in June, shortly before his death. Harding was enthralled by the park, and his remarks to local audiences about "Utah's magnificent scenery" were published widely across the nation.[14]

Harding's party had traveled by the Union Pacific to Lund and thence to Cedar City over the newly completed branch line. The branch was formally

dedicated on September 12, 1923. Speeches were made by Senator Smoot, Stephen T. Mather, President Heber J. Grant of the Church of Jesus Christ of Latter-day Saints, Harry Chandler, proprietor of the Los Angeles *Times*, and others. A "golden rail" was laid in place, and Utah's Governor Charles R. Mabey and other officials drove the last spikes which had been fabricated of iron some sixty years before in the pioneer foundry at Cedar City.

Knowing that the rails would never be extended beyond Cedar City, the Union Pacific in 1923 organized the Utah Parks Company, a subsidiary designed to develop tourist travel beyond the railhead to the High Plateaus and the North Rim country. The company bought out the pioneer entrepreneurs—W. W. Wylie, who operated tent camps at Zion and North Rim, and the Parry brothers, who ran buses between

E. C. LARUE (U.S. GEOLOGICAL SURVEY)

214

Cranking up. U.S. Geological Survey party at Lee's Ferry, Arizona, 1921. Man has been able to see with clarity the river as a unity, if not the landscape created by it. In the 1920's the states of the Colorado River developed much concern about utilization and control, and by the Colorado River Compact they divided up the flow of water among themselves.

Balanced rocks along the Lee's Ferry road have attracted photographers since the 1870's. The Echo Cliffs on the opposite side of Marble Canyon appear in the background. Arizona.

215

Rhythmic patterns in cross-bedded sandstone, Zion National Park. Utah.

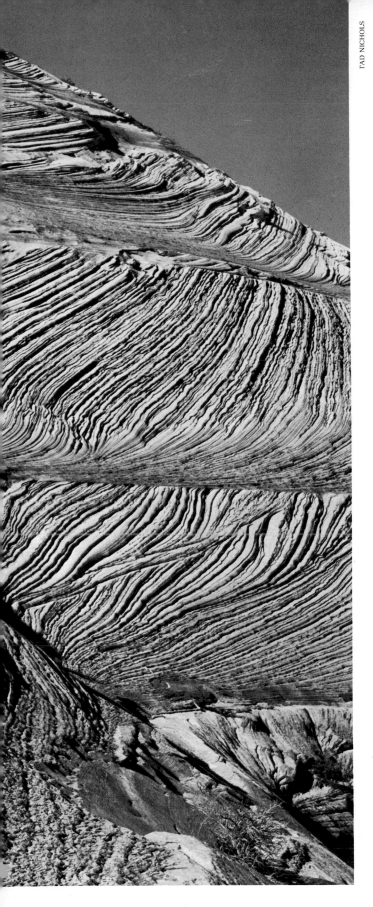

the railhead and the parks—and built comfortable, rustic hotels at Zion, Cedar Breaks, Bryce, and North Rim, all of which were in operation before the end of 1928. The Grand Canyon Lodge on Bright Angel Point on the North Rim was a deluxe hostelry within sight of the El Tovar, about eleven airline miles across Grand Canyon on the South Rim.

The Utah Parks Company and the Union Pacific publicized and popularized the parks and monuments on the north side as Fred Harvey and the Santa Fe had done for the South Rim. The companies carried on a campaign of national advertising and this was complemented by travelers who published their own accounts of the wonders of the North Rim country. The Page Company of Boston launched a "See America First" series of substantial travel books, of which three touched upon the scenery of the Grand Canyon country. *Utah, The Land of Blossoming Valleys* (1922) and *Arizona the Wonderland* (1927) were written by George Wharton James, who already had two books on the Grand Canyon to his name. *Wonderlands of the American West*, published in 1925 by Thomas Murphy, contained chapters on Grand and Zion canyons illustrated with colored reproductions of paintings by Thomas Moran and other artists.

These books and others, like J. Cecil Alter's *Through the Heart of the Scenic West,* and numbers of articles and newspaper accounts, and the railroad promotion, together with the works of professional photographers and Utah painters—including J. B. Fairbanks and H. L. A. Culmer, an admirer of Moran—put the northern part of the Grand Canyon country on the traveler's map. By the mid-twenties the tourists were arriving by the thousands. To handle the crowds, the Utah Parks Company, in the summer of 1926, began operating a daily autobus service from Cedar City around a loop to Zion, North Rim, Bryce, and Cedar Breaks, and by 1929, a variety of package tours, including mule-back trips across Grand Canyon, was available.[15]

By the end of the 1920s a system of unpaved roads on both sides of the Colorado River had been developed, connecting the parks and monuments of the Grand Canyon country with regional trunk highways. The American public embraced the automobile with

(Next spread) The head of Lake Mead reaches into the mouth of Grand Canyon in the distance. Looking eastward from a point near the Nevada-Arizona boundary.

C. GREGORY CRAMPTON

almost passionate fervor, and after World War I road-building scarcely kept pace with the demands of a nation on wheels. States and sections cooperated in designating sea-to-sea highways and "trails," and associations and automobile clubs supported road-building and road-marking and publicized attractions and facilities along the routes. During the twenties over a dozen such major roads appeared on the map. Two of them skirted the Grand Canyon country. Across northern Arizona the National Old Trails Road—Washington to Los Angeles, later designated U.S. Highway 66 and Interstate 40—closely paralleled the route of Garcés, Whipple, Beale, and the Santa Fe Railway. On the western periphery the Arrowhead Trail, also called the Zion Park Highway—Salt Lake to Las Vegas and Los Angeles, later designated U.S. Highway 91 and Interstate 15—paralleled the old Spanish–Mormon Trail and the Union Pacific Railroad.

The historic Utah–Arizona road, opened by Domínguez and Escalante, and Jacob Hamblin, became a major highway—later U.S. 89—when, in 1929, the Grand Canyon, or Navajo Bridge, was put across Marble Canyon below Lee's Ferry, and in 1930, when the spectacular Zion-Mt. Carmel highway was opened. Thus, the entire Grand Canyon country was enclosed by trunk roads—a "magic circle," one writer said—making it accessible to a nation on the move.[16]

With good hotels and other facilities to serve them, tourists in their cars flooded into the parks, and by 1926 they exceeded in number (as they have ever since) those who came by rail and bus. In 1930 over a hundred thousand people traveled to the South Rim by auto; by 1940 the figure was over a quarter of a million. They braved dirt and gravel roads for ten years or so before they were greeted by hardtop. Over the pavement, which represented the shortest distance between any two given parks, the automobile tourist lost touch with the land. He experienced only that part of the country he could see en route, and as he moved faster and faster, the distant vision blurred. He became less and less aware of the great country as he sped over it, and he soon saw only the segments—the national parks, called by one of the "See America First" writers the "civilized wildernesses."[17]

THE DAM AND LAS VEGAS

Utilization. Through the centuries man has attempted to turn the resources of the Grand Canyon country to his own use. Some made it pay, others did not. The Colorado River defeated those who sought to make of it a water road to the western sea or to lay tracks through its canyons. There were no broad acres of tillable land. The Mormons quickly took up the irrigable banks of the Virgin, Paria, and Kanab, and the farmers' frontier became static, or nearly so. Beyond Silver Reef on the western periphery, the prospectors found no bonanzas. The graziers and the timber merchants profited, notably so after the coming of the railroad. Community life was limited to a few Mormon villages at the base of the High Plateaus and to a string of towns generated by the railroad along the southern periphery. Save for the Navajos, who acquired the eastern part of the region, the Indians for the most part lost out.

The pioneer exploiters rarely showed much appreciation for the beauty of the land, but they did become intimately familiar with it, and before the formation of the parks they served as guides to those who wanted to see for themselves the wonders of the sandstone country described by Powell and other government men. Indeed, the landscape itself has since become one of the region's biggest economic assets.[18]

The greatest obvious resource was the Colorado River, and as the states within its basin grew, men began to talk of ways in which its waters could be brought to maximum use for irrigation and power. Data on the potentialities of the river were compiled by E. C. LaRue of the U.S. Geological Survey. His "Colorado River and Its Utilization" (1916) showed that the lower-basin states were using far more river water than the states of the upper basin. In order to ensure equitable and full development of the resource the seven states of the Colorado River basin, in 1922, worked out a formal compact.

The Colorado River Compact divided the water of the river between the states of the upper basin and

*Site of the Mormon town of St. Thomas is exposed when the
waters of Lake Mead are drawn down to a low level. Nevada.*

The 1923 Survey of the Grand Canyon. E. C. LaRue
photographing Vasey's Paradise. Arizona.

those of the lower basin, the point of division being fixed at Lee's Ferry. The agreement quieted the matter of title to the water, it established the basis for future agreements between the compact states, and it opened the way for federal construction of large multipurpose projects. The first of these was authorized in 1928 with the passage of the Boulder Canyon Project Act.

Completed in 1935, Hoover Dam, built across the mainstream, closed the book on the wild, free days of the Colorado. Henceforth it would be domesticated, harnessed, controlled, regulated, and utilized. The waters of Lake Mead, rising behind the dam, quietly obliterated places reminiscent of some of the larger themes of the river's history. The dam itself was built in Black Canyon where Ives had stove in the *Explorer*. Callville went under, along with Bonelli's and Pierce's ferries, and the Mormon town of St. Thomas. The prehistoric "Lost City," or Pueblo Grande de Nevada, was engulfed. At maximum level the waters of Lake Mead reached forty-four miles into Grand Canyon and drowned Powell's Separation Rapids.[19]

The western periphery, much like the rest of the Grand Canyon country, had enjoyed a slow-moving, easygoing,· romantic history involving only a few people trying to make a go of it in a desert wilderness. But the great dam changed all of that. Las Vegas, way station on the Spanish-Mormon Trail to Los Angeles, sprang into more vigorous life with the coming of the railroad, and was dramatically transformed when the dam was built and Lake Mead was created. Boulder City, the government town, close to the dam, was born of the project, but Las Vegas profited most from the construction years.

The nation took great pride in the huge hydro-electric project. The dam was another example of something dear to the American—once more, he could say, nature has been conquered for human use. Thousands came to watch the construction, and millions have since arrived to marvel at American in-

High power lines and contrails, Hoover Dam. Nevada.

223

genuity, technology, and science. But visitors also found spread out before them a vacationland of great charm and beauty. In 1936, the Lake Mead National Recreation Area—the first of its kind—was formed, granting to the National Park Service jurisdiction over public use of the shoreline and waters of the reservoir (and later of Lake Mohave, the reservoir behind Davis Dam, sixty-seven miles downstream). The lake—115 miles long with 550 miles of shoreline at maximum pool—brought within easy reach a desert wonderland compounded of blue water, exotic vegetation, bizarre land splotched with great patches of brilliantly colored rocks, and some of the most awesome sections of Grand Canyon, all of it laved by clean, dry air.

The building of the dam and the formation of Lake Mead stimulated some interest in the Grand Canyon and in river travel. Until the signing of the Colorado River Compact very few voyagers had made the Grand Canyon run. In 1923, the U.S. Geological Survey sent a party directed by C. H. Birdseye to locate dam sites and survey the full length of Grand Canyon. This activity was nationally publicized, and the resultant set of detailed large-scale maps and profiles provided the first reliable guides for navigating the hazardous river. Clyde Eddy ran the canyon in 1927; Haldane "Buzz" Holmstrom soloed in 1937; soon thereafter Norman Nevills began running commercial trips, but as late as 1949 scarcely a hundred persons had boated the entire length of Grand Canyon. Most of those with boats confined themselves to the placid waters of Lake Mead, and only a few of them took time enough to explore the lower reaches of Grand Canyon.

Many a tourist who'd never before headed west beyond the hundredth meridian discovered on his visit to Hoover Dam that the arid lands were hospitable, not hostile. The scenery was beautiful, the water sports exciting. Las Vegas seized upon this potential and provided attractions of its own to complement those of the dam and Lake Mead. The first resort hotel went up in the 1930s. Capitalizing on desert climate, gambling, live shows, and the easy informality of the frontier West, Las Vegas thereafter grew meteorically to become an entertainment capital second

Grand Canyon abstraction. Arizona.

Merriam Crater in the San Francisco volcanic field. Arizona.

to none, as the area at large became one of the most popular tourist centers in the West, in the public view almost a world in itself.[20]

QUIET WILDERNESS

Seen first by Europeans in 1540, hunted in and occupied by Indians some thousands of years before that, the Grand Canyon region is one of the oldest in the United States, yet one of the least known. History has coursed around it or through it along a few narrow roads. The waters and the canyons have deflected man and segmented his view of the land. Even those intimately familiar with one part will most likely know nothing of the adjoining sections. Most tourists see only the prominent viewpoints in the national reservations easily accessible from the three main-line highways—thirty-five miles of the South Rim, Bright Angel Point and Cape Royal on the North Rim, the floor of Zion Canyon, the rims of Bryce and Cedar Breaks, Lake Mead. But these are only the parts of a whole, the roads connecting them, the frames for a single picture.

Back from the highways and away from the towns, the magnificent rest of it—great pockets of wilderness—stretch away under a splendid, silent sun. Shivwits, Parunuweap, Tatahotso, Sinyala, Meriwitica, are these familiar names?

The Grand Canyon country is full of surprises mostly missed by the highway traveler who has forgotten what a mile is but does know that sixty miles is the distance you can cover in an hour. To those of slower pace, the plateaus and canyon country reveal themselves. There is order and symmetry and rhythm in the landscape, yet the variety of forms and aspects—its sights and sounds and smells—is infinite. It is, in Prudden's words, the "insistent earth."

The sweep and open sky of the Arizona Strip; the primeval solitude of Kelly Point; the birth of a thousand-foot-high waterfall after a Grand Canyon rainstorm; the sweet coolness of an early morning in June on the high desert; the beckoning welcome of a single cottonwood in a dry wash; white sand beaches in red canyon country; the glamour of Wupatki.

The lush, long-stemmed sego lilies growing up through the dead sage; Hermit Rapids; the brilliant red cap on West Temple; the prehistoric calmness of Moenave; the jagged rim of the Little Colorado's gorge; the rhythmic look of the Petticoat Hills; the smoke and smell and dust of falling rock; the sleek, fat, wild burros who've never worked a day in their lives; blue-green copper ore in white sandstone; the soft, rounded hills of the Painted Desert; Pipe Spring.

Evening clouds painted pastel pink by light reflected from red sandstone; the giant Joshuas along the Grand Wash Cliffs; the wonders of pink granite and coral pink sand, of travertine dams and lava cascades; the parks of the Kaibab; the Grand Canyon filled with fog; Navajo sheep pens on Blue Moon bench; Prospect Valley; the thread of fertility which is a rivulet of muddy water.

It was tough, beautiful country, and few men dared to try to take the measure of it, describe its meaning, or identify its mystique. Garcés, Hamblin, Powell, Holmes, Moran, Stanton. Captivated by the "magnificence and towering mystery" of the Grand Canyon, Ferde Grofé, in more recent times, was impelled to set to music his impressions. "I saw color," he wrote, "but I 'heard' it too." The result was his "Grand Canyon Suite," introduced in 1931 by Paul Whiteman's orchestra and since played round the world. Great pictures in tone, paint, and words have been rare enough. As Irvin Cobb said, "God made the canyon, but he didn't make any words to describe it." Few have developed a passion for the great canyon country of the Colorado, probably because it was too powerful for most men and they feared impotence.

Those who called it a wasteland were deaf to the eloquence of the rocks; the pageantry of light and color seems to have escaped them. In the future, as the cacophony of a complex and crowded world increases, these people, it is easy to predict, will disappear. Back in 1935, J. B. Priestley wrote of the Grand Canyon: "Even to remember that it is still there lifts up the heart."[21] We will hear this repeated as more men discover in the Grand Canyon country one of the grandest natural entities in the world, one where they can set their own words to the music all about them.

The Narrows of Zion Canyon. Utah.

Notes

1

Grand Canyon Country

1 My Grand Canyon country is somewhat smaller than the Grand Canyon section of the Colorado Plateau as defined by modern physiographers. I have not included the area south of the Santa Fe Railway and Highway 66 between Flagstaff and Peach Springs. That country drains away to the south into the Verde and Bill Williams rivers, the heads of which breach the Mogollon Rim. This long escarpment, which trends south-southeast across Arizona and into New Mexico, separates the Colorado Plateau from the basin-and-range physiographic province to the south. I include only the rimlands of Utah's high Markagunt and Paunsaugunt plateaus. My definition is pretty close to what C. E. Dutton of the Powell Survey called the "Grand Cañon District" (1882).

The High Plateaus section of the Colorado Plateau as defined by geographers and geologists is a much larger area than mine. Following C. E. Dutton's lead (1880), they include all the elevated tablelands extending from the heads of the Virgin River on the south to the heads of the Price River on the north, which dominate the landscape along both sides of the divide separating the waters of the Colorado from those flowing into the Great Basin.

Hunt (1967), Chapter 14, excludes the Paria River–Marble Canyon area from the Grand Canyon section of the Colorado Plateau, but I find this difficult to accept. See also C. B. Hunt (1956 and 1969). Fenneman (1931) and Atwood (1940) indicate the changes in geographical description of the Colorado Plateau since the time of the Powell Survey.

2—On Powell and Powell's men as namers see Stegner (1954), 191–198; the same material appeared in (1953).

3—Names attached to watering places and settlements by the Southern Paiute in the Kanab–Kaibab region are discussed in detail by Kelly (1964), 5–21. See also two articles by Palmer (1928) and (1933). On Havasupai names see Spier (1928), 91–100, 304–315, 322.

4—Done to some extent on historical principles, the place names of the three states are covered by Averett (1962), Leigh (1961), and Granger (1960). The U.S. Work Projects Administration publications issued in 1940 and 1941 under the auspices of the state writers' projects are all helpful, but they tend to lose their importance as one moves into the historically rich but sparsely inhabited Grand Canyon country.

A number of names I have included have been chosen more or less at random from maps, notably from the topographic quadrangles published by the U.S. Geological Survey and grazing maps published by the U.S. Bureau of Land Management. A number are in local usage and do not appear on any maps.

5—In their influences on the public the three beautiful topographic quadrangles issued by the U.S. Geological Survey—Bright Angel (1903), Vishnu (1907), and Shinumo (1908)—deserve to rank with the drawings of the Grand Canyon made by W. H. Holmes of the Powell Survey. The topography of the first (and the best) was done by F. E. Matthes, of the third by Richard T. Evans, and the two together worked out the topography on the Vishnu sheet. Using these three sheets (and that of a fourth—the Supai sheet, which was not published separately) as a base and holding to the same scale and style, Richard T. Evans prepared the *Topographic Map of the Grand Canyon National Park* in two halves, published in 1927 and reprinted since. The same style was employed on the *Topographic Map of the Grand Canyon National Monument*, surveyed in 1934–1936 and published in 1944. Matthes and Evans (1926) have written a detailed history of the mapping of the canyon, 1902–1923.

Matthes' use of the "heroic style" in Grand Canyon nomenclature was not at all pleasing to everyone. In response to the objection that the Grand Canyon has been peopled with "unnaturalized foreigners," he wrote (but apparently did not publish) that "we compliment inanimate nature when we christen its imperfect mountain shapes for the noblest works of man's own genius." The François Matthes "Place Names in Grand Canyon" file is in the Na-

Mescal plant (Agave Utahensis), used by the Indians for food, grows along the rims and ledges of Grand Canyon. Twin Point, Shivwits Plateau. Arizona.

tional Park Service reference library at Grand Canyon; in it his defense of "heroic" nomenclature is elaborated. It appears in this file that Evans (and Mrs. Evans) were equally responsible in the matter.

Van Dyke (1920), 15, is one of the few in print who has registered objection to the "heroic" style in Grand Canyon nomenclature. Davis (1901), 115, is one of the few geologists to do so.

More recently the park area and much of the Grand Canyon country has been covered by the fifteen-minute topographic quadrangles issued by the U.S. Geological Survey.

One of the finest graphic portrayals of Grand Canyon National Park and Grand Canyon National Monument and environs is by Hamblin and Murphy (1969); the illustrations by William L. Chesser are reminiscent of the style of W. H. Holmes.

Living Rock

1—There is an enormous body of literature devoted to the geology of the Colorado Plateau. Since the explorations of Ives and Powell the corps of geologists attracted to the plateau country has grown steadily. Powell (1875 and 1876), together with Dutton (1880) and (1882), are pioneer and basic studies. Although some of the conclusions of these pioneer scientists still stand, others have been modified by later students. The splendid collection of papers honoring John Wesley Powell on the hundredth anniversary of his exploration of the Colorado River, 1869–1969, will long be a basic text on the geology of the river and the Colorado Plateau. The papers written by Mary C. Rabbitt, Edwin D. McKee, Charles B. Hunt, and Luna B. Leopold, under the title "The Colorado River Region and John Wesley Powell," were published as U.S. Geological Survey *Professional Paper* 669 (1969). The geological history of "Chapter V," the Cenozoic era, the most recent era, extending back at least fifty million years, is not yet fully understood. The evolution of the Colorado River in the Grand Canyon district has been the subject of recent studies by Hunt (1956), McKee and others (1967), and Beal (1967).

Although I have cited in this chapter a number of supporting sources, the interpretation I offer of the landscape of the Grand Canyon country is mainly my own, based on personal knowledge gathered by boat, jeep, and plane.

2—I am not aware that anyone has attempted such a hike. J. Harvey Butchart, Professor of Mathematics, Arizona State University, Flagstaff, has literally hiked thousands of miles in Grand Canyon, more so by far than any other human being, and his knowledge of the trails in the great gorge is intimate. Some of his knowledge is reported in a number of articles published between 1958 and 1968.

Fletcher (1967) made a first trip afoot, and alone, through the Grand Canyon from Havasu Creek to Nankoweap Creek, and it would be wise for anyone planning an extended hike in the Grand Canyon country to read his book. Fletcher, who took two months for his walk, came to grips with the reality of Grand Canyon as only a few have done.

3—Usage has varied in some of the regional nomenclature. In

his classic geological study, Robinson (1913) consistently uses the single term "San Francisco Mountain" to describe the mass, but these days San Francisco Peaks (sometimes Mountains) is more commonly heard. The San Francisco Plateau is an older name for the Coconino Plateau; the former term, when used at all, is now usually restricted to the San Francisco volcanic field and immediate environs.

4—Colton (1967) has summarized the present state of knowledge about the cones and their lava flows, a subject treated lightly by Robinson. Colton and associates have found 422 volcanic vents in the field and have located them all, together with their lava flows, on the two charts accompanying this work. See Toll (1970), a popular article on the San Francisco Peaks and other volcanic areas.

5—Colton and Baxter (1932 and later editions), Strahler (1944), Butchart (1965).

6—Oddly enough, there have been very few comprehensive geographical or geological studies of the South Rim. Herbert E. Gregory, of the U.S. Geological Survey, who published so many good papers on the Navajo country and on the plateau and canyon country of southern Utah (see bibliography), seems to have had no counterpart in the South Rim area. See Darton (1910), Lee (1908), Twenter (1962), Darton and others (1915).

Books which interpret geology for the masses have broadened their approaches to include other areas, but they focus primarily on the parks. See Darton (1917), McKee (1931 and later editions), Maxson (1962), and Beal (1967).

7—Where zones of faulting and flexure cross the Grand Canyon, counterpart cliffs are found on the South Rim, but the maximum exposures, save for the Grand Wash escarpment, are to be seen on the North Rim. In the Grand Canyon country there are, of course, a good many subsidiary faults and minor displacements which have produced complexities in the relief and drainage patterns. A number of these are readily to be seen on such a flight as I have described above. In painting the portrait of so intricate a country I have not attempted to portray all the wrinkles.

Upon the foundations laid down by Powell (1875 and 1876), and Dutton (1880 and 1882), later students have built up an imposing body of knowledge about the northern portion of the Grand Canyon country. A convenient recent listing of them and their works is to be found in the bibliography of McKee and others (1967).

Longwell (1928) is a good introduction to the "chaotic landscape" west of the Grand Wash Cliffs. See Noble (1914), Strahler (1945), and Koons (1945) for descriptions of the North Rim country.

8—John W. Powell's description of the Colorado Plateau, Chapters I–IV, in his *Canyons of the Colorado* (1895), reissued by Dover Publications in 1961, is as good as there is, and I have relied on it heavily for the country north of Grand Canyon. Any historian or geographer will appreciate the papers published by Herbert E. Gregory. As a geologist he was very much interested in these subjects, as his works will show. Almost a quarter of the pages of his papers on the Kaiparowits region and on the Zion Park region are taken up with these matters before he moves into technical geology. Gregory's works, issued in 1916, 1917, and 1951, nearly blanket Utah's High Plateaus and adjacent parts of Arizona. See Ives (1947) on the hinterland of Zion National Park.

9—Although it is a natural and fairly easy way into the Grand Canyon from the north and has been used by scientists and others to some extent, there is very little descriptive literature about Kanab Canyon below Fredonia. One of the most spectacular of the Grand Canyon tributaries, it remains one of the least known to the public. McKee (1946) refers to traverses by Powell, Walcott, and Gilbert, and to his own geological explorations of the canyon in 1941. McKee agrees that the view from the rim of the inner gorge "down Kanab Canyon is one of the really *great* sights" within the Grand Canyon region. A recent hike through the canyon, with splendid photographs by Melvin Goldman, is reported by Rosalie Goldman (1964).

Malmquist (1968) takes you on a hike down Kanab Canyon and Bridge Canyon.

10—The Paria River is the natural boundary between the Grand Canyon country and the canyon lands of southeastern Utah and northeastern Arizona, which is the subject area of my *Standing Up Country* (1964), a companion to this volume. Beyond the works of H. E. Gregory, cited in note 8, there is little in the literature descriptive of the Paria River and its beautiful canyon.

Five Faces of Grand Canyon

1—Naturally, geographically, geologically, and by action of the Board on Geographic Names, the Grand Canyon is a single canyon extending 279 miles below Lee's Ferry. In a letter on July 25, 1968, J. O. Kilmartin of the Board on Geographic Names advises me that the Board's decision in the matter, given on February 4, 1925, is still in effect. LaRue (1925), 9, reported the decision and adopted the usage. The Marble Canyon section extends from Lee's Ferry to the mouth of the Little Colorado, a distance of 61.5 miles, river measurement.

2—The canyons of the Colorado, extending downward from a level plateau, suggest a system of inverted mountains, an idea advanced by Gregory (1917), 117, and perhaps by others, and adopted by Peattie, ed. (1948).

3—The Redwall Limestone was named by Gilbert (1875), 177. As this great strata formed the most distinctive feature of the canyon, Powell named it Marble Canyon. The Redwall contains no marble proper; Powell used the term in its structural and architectural sense. See Powell, *Exploration* (1875), 76, and (1895), 241. See Wilmarth (1938) for the origins of geological names in the Grand Canyon country.

4—An excellent mile-by-mile guide to the geology of the entire canyon from Lee's Ferry to Lake Mead is Hamblin and Rigby (1968-1969). Volume III of Simmons and Gaskill (1969) emphasizes geologic features in Marble Gorge and Grand Canyon. Belknap (1969) has reproduced in handy format the river maps issued by the U.S. Geological Survey in 1923. Using sections of the U.S.G.S. topographic maps covering the area, Péwé (1969) has published a mile-by-mile guide to the geology and geography of the river from Lee's Ferry to Bright Angel Creek. Although the technical terminology is dated, a good guide to the rock structure of the lower levels of the Grand Canyon from Lee's Ferry to Grand Wash Cliffs is Moore

(1925), 125-171. Cooley (1967) is a useful work. The very interesting book by Julius F. Stone (1932) is a record of a trip through the canyons of the Colorado in 1909 from Green River, Wyoming. More than half of the book is taken up with photographs of the canyons and with accompanying commentary by W. T. Lee of the U.S. Geological Survey. The beautiful Sierra Club book by Jett (1967), with color photographs by Philip Hyde, touches on Marble Canyon, which forms a part of the western boundary of the Navajo reservation. See also Cooley, Harshbarger, and others (1969).

5—Those who have written about the Grand Canyon as a textbook in earth history number far more than those who have written about its human history. But, as with so much writing about the Grand Canyon country, the popular literature of geology frequently focuses on the park areas to the exclusion of the rest of it. McKee (1931 and later editions) does touch the whole area. See Deal (1967), Maxson, (1962), Schellbach (1955), Shelton, (1966). Gregory, *Zion Park Region* (1950) covers the subject for the stratigraphy of the High Plateaus. Cooley, comp. (1967), and Stokes and Hintze, comps. (1961-1963), are very useful guides to the field identification of the formations.

6—Burroughs (1911). Essayist, biographer, drama critic, and naturalist Joseph Wood Krutch took the mule trip and produced one of the best books on the Grand Canyon (1958).

7—One of the more articulate visitors to travel the Bass Trail and live in Bass Camp was George Wharton James, whose book (1900) did much to popularize the great canyon.

8—On the geological reasoning in explanation of the Tonto Platform and the Esplanade, see Noble (1914), 73-75.

9—Powell, *Exploration* (1875), 94-95.

10—In September, 1967, there was only the slightest ripple at Separation Rapids. For some years now the reservoir level of Lake Mead has been down below the level of these rapids. Should this condition continue, and as the river gradually flushes out the silt, the rapids might come back to life.

11—The reservoir fluctuates, of course, and the location of the headwaters varies accordingly. At its maximum level of 1,221 feet above sea level Lake Mead would extend into Grand Canyon to about Mile 235. In early September, 1967, the headwaters were in Grand Wash Bay not far from the Nevada line, and the river was running placidly at Pierce's Ferry between high banks of sand deposited when the lake was at higher levels. See note 10.

12—Powell, *Exploration* (1875), 102-103.

13—A number of articulate people have made the run through Grand Canyon. Ellsworth L. and Emery C. Kolb made a photographic tour which they began at Green River, Wyoming, in September, 1911, and completed at Needles in January, 1912. In his good, straightforward account of the trip (1914), Ellsworth Kolb devotes two chapters to the run from Kanab Canyon to Needles, California. This is better than par for coverage of the lower canyon. Both the book and an earlier article by Ellsworth L. and Emery C. Kolb (1914) have early photographic coverage of the canyons from the water level, but there is little below Lava Falls.

In 1923, the U.S. Geological Survey, with Emery C. Kolb as head boatman, carried out a water-power and dam-site survey of the Colorado from Lee's Ferry to Needles. Surely every possible dam site was found and fully reported by LaRue (1925), whose work also contains much detailed information on the great canyon; the emphasis was on dam sites and not landscape. Freeman's two works, both published in 1924, touch on the 1923 expedition.

Julius Stone's account of his 1909 voyage (1932) contains a few pages about and a few photographs of the canyon below Lava Falls. In 1927 Clyde Eddy and a crew of college men made the run through from Green River, Utah, and his book (1929) is an excellent account of the trip but, as with so many voyagers, he focuses on the water and the rapids and not the general landscape.

Even the Sierra Club, in its "beautiful, biased" book by Leydet (1964), will not admit there's a thing to be seen below Separation Rapids, or, for that matter, below Bridge Canyon (Mile 235), the head of Lake Mead at maximum level and the site where the Bureau of Reclamation had planned a dam. Malmquist (1968), takes you on a hike down Bridge Canyon and Kanab Canyon.

One of the most detailed examinations of Grand Canyon ever made was undertaken by Robert B. Stanton, who surveyed the great gorge, 1889–1890, in the interest of building a railroad from Grand Junction, Colorado, to tidewater. Stanton took photographs almost every mile of the way to prove graphically the feasibility of the route, and his survey notes carry much detail. These survey notes, together with a liberal selection of the photographs, are scheduled for publication under the editorship of Dwight L. Smith and C. Gregory Crampton. R. B. Stanton's own summary of the venture has been edited by Smith (1965), and his account of the lower ninety miles is as good as there is.

I have cited a number of sources in this chapter, but the interpretation I offer of the canyon landscape is my own, based on personal knowledge gained from riding the waters, from jeep and truck travel to numerous points on the rim, and from flights over the canyons in light planes.

I am not aware that anyone before has attempted to identify the faces of Grand Canyon. It seems to me that there are five of them, but others might find as many as seven or eight.

Western Mystery

1—Much has been written of the exploring expedition directed by Francisco Vázquez de Coronado. The basic contemporary documents, including the instructions to and the report of Friar Marcos, have been newly translated and gathered into one volume by Hammond and Rey (1940). Winship's work (1896) has not lost its value. Castañeda's narrative has also been reproduced by Hodge (1907).

2—Hodge (1937) identifies the Zuñi village of Hawikuh, now in ruins, with the town first visited by the Spaniards.

3—I am following here Castañeda's account of the Coronado exploration. Both Winship (1896), 489, and Hammond and Rey (1940), 215, translate Castañeda's words, *"gentes muy grandes de cuerpo grande,"* as "people with very large bodies," which could be translated as "very big," or "tall," or even "giants."

4—The extent to which the gorge of the Little Colorado figures in Hopi religious belief is not fully understood by non-Hopis. The canyon has been identified with the Hopi emergence myth. On the floor of the gorge, two miles below the mouth of Salt Trail Canyon, there is a thirty-foot high travertine dome, open at the top, built up by a spring of yellowish water. This has been identified with the *sipapu*, or opening, whence man emerged from the lower world to people the upper world. Don C. Talayesva in Simmons, ed. (1942), 232–246, tells of his experiences in making his first ceremonial expedition to the canyon of the Little Colorado; the mythology of the Grand Canyon salt deposits is explained, 433–435. See also Titiev (1937), O'Kane (1950), 116–119, and Schwartz (1966). Waters (1963), 25, relegates the Grand Canyon to a minor place in the Hopi symbolism of the emergence.

Euler (1967), 70, states that since 1300 the Hopis have made periodic salt-collecting expeditions to Grand Canyon. Davis (1959), 1–4, describes the *sipapu* and the salt deposits along the Colorado on the left bank at Mile 63.8. See also Eiseman, Jr. (1959).

5—Spier (1928), 245–248, details the trade route from Havasu Canyon to Oraibi. See Colton (1960) for a summary of prehistoric commerce. Spencer and Jennings and others (1965), 265, state that the "outstanding physical characteristic" of the Mohaves "was their tall stature, many males standing six feet tall."

6—The brief facts covering the discovery of Grand Canyon are found in four paragraphs in Pedro de Castañeda's account and in two in the anonymous *Relación del Suceso*, both in Hammond and Rey (1940), and in Winship (1896). The Winship translation was included in Hodge, ed. (1907), and in Cutter (1964).

The exact route followed by the discovery party from the Hopi villages to the Grand Canyon is conjectural, but the Indian guides most certainly stayed on established trails. One of these passed under the Coconino Rim (paralleling Arizona Route 64). I am confident, after an examination of the area, that the old Indian trail must have followed the Lee Canyon drainage, which parallels Coconino Rim, right up to Buggeln Hill on the very edge of Grand Canyon. But the Spaniards wanted to see the river, so the Hopis took them out to the rim somewhere between Desert View and Moran Point. The Spaniards probably covered several miles of the rim during the three days they were looking for a trail down into the canyon. Hughes (1967), 19–20, brings the Cárdenas party out to the South Rim between Desert View and Moran Point. Bolton (1949), 138–142, concludes that Cárdenas must have reached the Grand Canyon at Grand View Point. In some notes he gathered for an article on the subject, Matthes (1902–1936) concluded that the discovery party reached the rim at Desert View, or Navajo Point, and he gives his reasons for this conclusion.

Bartlett (1940) analyzes two possible routes from Hopi villages to Grand Canyon. Euler (1967), 70, notes that the Hopi Indians reached the salt deposits below the mouth of the Little Colorado by what later became the Tanner Trail, heading on Lipan Point.

Some writers on the discovery have been misled by what I think is an error in the Castañeda text. Castañeda says (Hammond and Rey [1940], 215) that the settlements (meaning those of the Havasupais and perhaps the Mohaves) "were more than twenty days away" (round trip) from the Hopi towns. In the next sentence he states that when the Cárdenas party had marched for twenty days, they came to the river. The text is undoubtedly defective here. The *Relación del Suceso* is more accurate; the author states that Cárdenas went about fifty leagues (about 125 miles) west from the

Hopi town to reach the river; this is very close to the trail distance between Oraibi and Desert View.

Those who have accepted Castañeda's figure of twenty days' travel west of the Hopi villages have found it necessary to take the discovery party much farther west than the vicinity of Desert View. Winship, who published the Castañeda narrative in 1896, concludes in an article (1900), 274, that the discovery was made in the vicinity of Cataract, or Havasu Canyon. Day (1940), 141-145, has the party making a searching investigation of the South Rim as far west as Havasu Canyon. Dellenbaugh (1902), 32-35, takes the explorers west beyond this to the vicinity of Diamond Creek. Bancroft (1889), 1-5, carries the discovery party north into Utah to the vicinity of the mouth of the San Juan River; by so doing he adds 236 years to the history of that state which in other accounts begins in 1776.

It is also possible that the Hopis guided the Spanish party to the rim of Marble Canyon past the salt trail leading into the canyon of the Little Colorado, but this seems unlikely, as this route would not take the discoverers west to the Havasupais and Mohaves. However, as Castañeda remarks (Hammond and Rey [1940], 216), upon returning from the canyon the Hopi guides obtained salt crystals from a point near a waterfall. This suggests that the Indians may have made a salt-gathering expedition of the exploration and this argues for the Little Colorado route. James (1910), 198, writes that Hopi Indians with whom he talked placed the Cárdenas discovery on the rim of Marble Canyon above the mouth of the Little Colorado.

Winship, and Hammond and Rey translate the word *barranca* as "canyon." However, "canyon," which derives from *cañón*, with the meaning that we now attach to it, is of very recent usage. Corominas (1954), I, 648-649, finds that the origin of the word *cañón* is uncertain, with no documented usage established until 1834. Mathews (1951), 262-263, cites a number of examples of the use of the word, mainly in the West and Southwest after 1834, but none before. Bentley (1932), 114-115, finds the word "canyon" to be completely naturalized, but the word *"barranca"* is also in common use, 100-101. Even today in Mexico and Spanish America, the word *barranca* is more frequently encountered than the word *cañón*.

The beautiful Giralda tower in Sevilla, begun by the Moslems and elaborated during the Renaissance, stands about three hundred and twenty feet high, overlooking the city which was Spain's port for the Americas.

7—Alarcón's report of the 1540 expedition is found in Hammond and Rey (1940), 117-155. Francisco de Ulloa in 1539 had reached the mouth of the Colorado River and may be credited with its discovery, but it was Alarcón who the next year carried out the first exploration of the stream. See Wagner (1968), 20-21, 30-39.

8—The geographical and historical significance of the Coronado-Alarcón explorations is set out in Winship (1896), 403-413, Wagner (1968), 30-39, and Wheat, I (1957), Chapter II.

9—The voluminous contemporary documents covering Oñate's conquest and colonization of New Mexico have been assembled, translated, and edited by Hammond and Rey (1953), 2 vols. A remarkable record of the trip was made by Father Francisco de Escobar whose diary appears on pages 1012-1031.

10—Tyler (1952) and Hammond (1956).

11—Coues, ed. (1900), 2 vols., is elaborately annotated (with some notes on Indian tribes by Frederick Webb Hodge) and it is not likely to be replaced for some years. Another version of the Garcés diary translated from a contemporary manuscript other than the one used by Coues is Galvin, ed. (1965). This work contains few notes, and no revision of Coues' interpretation is attempted. The two translations differ substantially at a number of points. A brief résumé of the diary from a printed edition in Spanish is found in Bancroft (1889), 382-383. The work of Garcés in opening the road to California and his association with Juan Bautista de Anza is treated by Bolton (1939). The intimate chronicler of the second Anza expedition, Father Pedro Font, gives us some warm, human insights of Garcés as a missionary. See Bolton, ed. (1931).

12—Eighty-two years later Joseph C. Ives and a small party went over the same trail. One should compare his full account of the adventure (1861), 104-109, with a brief one by Garcés in the Coues or Galvin editions for June 20, 1776. Coues' annotations of the Garcés diary from the Mohave country to the Havasu Canyon are particularly full. He was on active duty as an army medical officer stationed at Fort Verde when, in June, 1881, in a company commanded by Lieutenant Colonel William Redwood Price, he entered the canyon, though he used the Kla-la-pa Trail which enters Havasu Canyon about twenty-two miles above the Indian village. Even though he had firsthand knowledge of the area, Coues does not specifically indicate that Garcés used the Hualapai Canyon route. Casanova (1967) briefly describes five of the seven or more horse trails entering the canyon and notes early visitors who used them. The Hualapai Canyon Trail is now the principal entryway to Havasu Canyon. One can drive a car to Hualapai Hilltop about eight miles from Supai Village. Horses—but no vehicles, of course—can negotiate the entire distance.

13—Bolton (1931), 121. Font's characterization of his fellow missionary was made after he had seen him in action in the Yuma country, but the same traits must have endeared him to his hosts, the Havasupais.

14—Garcés traveled five leagues during the day. Within two leagues south of the Supai village he had turned east and started up; within another three leagues he had topped out and camped among the junipers and pines on the Coconino Plateau. Casanova (1967) states that Garcés went out by the Moqui, or Hopi, Trail which ascends Moqui Trail Canyon some fifteen miles above Supai. It is about four miles from the mouth of this canyon to the rim where the trail tops out, making in all nineteen to twenty miles (between six and seven leagues), and this is too far if we are to accept Garcés' distances.

15—It is difficult to follow the padre during his ride on June 26. He traveled eight leagues during the day and at the halfway point stopped to view the canyon. But his distances coming out of Havasu Canyon are uncertain. (See note 16.) Coues (1900), II, 351, has him viewing the gorge from the vicinity of Canyon Spring in the apparent vicinity of Grand View Point; Coues, however, has difficulty in following the padre from Havasu Canyon. On the 25th, Garcés came out of Havasu Canyon and traveled some distance before camping among the pine and junipers. Next day he traveled four leagues (about ten miles) when he reached the Grand Canyon overlook. I am inclined to locate him at a point west of Grand Canyon Village; Coues locates him to the east of it.

As almost any diarist does, Garcés probably went back occasionally in his diary and added new information to clarify points and changed sentences and passages. I am inclined to think that he added the name Puerto de Bucareli after leaving the South Rim. From points directly east and for miles distant the Puerto de Bucareli looks like nothing so much as a sharp-edged pass. The "pass" is certainly easier to see at a distance than it is on the rim of the canyon.

16—Given the number of senseless names that have been applied to the natural features in Grand Canyon, it is indeed unfortunate that the first name for the canyon, and one that is both fitting and historically appropriate, has not been perpetuated.

17—See both the Coues and Galvin translations of the Garcés diary for his "reflections." Garcés did not learn of the Domínguez-Escalante exploration until it had left Santa Fe. His letter written to the missionary at Zuñi reached Escalante's hands before the expedition left Santa Fe. The background documentation of the Domínguez-Escalante expedition is found in Adams and Chavez, trans. and eds. (1956), 270–308.

18—Bolton, trans. and ed. (1950), is the best edition of the remarkable diary written by Vélez de Escalante; included is a separate report by Bernardo de Miera and a map by him in colors of the country explored by the expedition. The diary and related documents (together with some valuable maps, including three by Miera) have been edited by Auerbach (1941 and 1943). A brief summary of the Escalante diary, edited by Philip Harry, appears in Simpson (1876). Harris (1909) contains another version of the diary.

19—The Miera map in Bolton (1950) contains much valuable information not found in the Escalante diary.

20—Bolton's interpretation of the route taken by Domínguez and Escalante I find to be accurate in nearly every detail. He retraced much of the trail himself, and his detailed notes take up about half of his work (1950). His delineation of the route from Beaver Valley, through St. George Basin and across the Arizona Strip to the Crossing of the Fathers, was published in 1928. There is nothing in the Escalante diary to suggest that the party traveled as far south as the Uinkaret, or Pine Mountains, or that it reached Pipe Spring, the most historic watering place on the Arizona Strip. Miera's portrayal of the White Cliffs, his Sierra Blanca, is quite as accurate as his handling of the towers of Zion.

Garcés used the term "Jabesua" to describe the Havasupais, but the names Cosnina or Conina, given to these Indians by the Hopis, had been known to the Spaniards since the seventeenth century. See Schroeder (1953) and Whiting (1958), 55–60. Escalante in his diary uses the name a number of times. Bernardo de Miera, on his map of the expedition's travels, assigns the name Río de los Coninas" to the Little Colorado rather than to the main stream, the Río Colorado.

Escalante gives us much valuable information about the Southern Paiute bands encountered from Cedar City to the Virgin River and across the Arizona Strip. For modern ethnographic studies of these Indians, see Kelly (1934 and 1964), and Palmer (1933).

21—The Spanish party with great difficulty located a ford upstream from Lee's Ferry. The details are in Miller (1958); Crampton (1960).

22—Of a location coinciding with the Grand Canyon at the mouth of the Little Colorado, Miera wrote these words on his map: "Este Río ba mui encajonado en Peñasqueria colorado y mui escarpada." Note the word cañón is not used. Miera's map is one of

the finest documents produced by the Domínguez-Escalante expedition. The maps made by Pedro Font, illustrating Garcés' travels, are less detailed than Miera's. See the frontispiece in Coues (1900), I, and the map opposite page 102, in Galvin (1965). See Wheat, I (1957), Chapters V–VI, for the cartographical contributions of Font, Miera, and their contemporaries.

Golden Gate

1—Cleland (1952) complements Chittenden (1902), but the fullest study is Weber (1967).

2—Pattie's *Personal Narrative* appeared first in 1831; a later edition is Goetzmann (1962). There is scarcely enough information in the Pattie *Narrative* to locate the trapper very accurately in his travels through the Grand Canyon area, and the route remains conjectural. See Kroeber, ed. (1964). See also Camp, ed. (1966). Yount and a trapper party in 1827 traveled along the south side of Grand Canyon between the Mohave villages and the Little Colorado. At some point they went down to the "Big Cañon" of the Colorado, possibly by way of Peach Springs Canyon, but the route they followed is by no means clear. Stewart (1966) reviews Anglo-Indian contacts, 1826–1851.

3—Phillips (1940) has edited W. A. Ferris' *Life*. This edition contains a map of the Rockies drawn by Ferris in 1836; he shows the "chanion" of the Colorado, but it is apparent from the map that the author was not as intimately acquainted with the canyon lands as he was with the better beaver country farther north. Another edition of the Ferris work, edited by Auerbach and Alter, was also published in 1940.

4—In their history of the *Old Spanish Trail* (1954), Hafen and Hafen have synthesized prior scholarship and have added much new material. The trail, of course, was not opened until well after the beginning of Mexican rule (1821–1848) and might be called more appropriately the "Old Mexican Trail." The pioneering venture of Antonio Armíjo is mentioned and his agonizingly brief diary is reproduced.

There is no lack of material on the life, times, and exploration of Jedediah Smith. Morgan (1953) and Dale (1941) are works of solid scholarship. Sullivan (1934) includes the journal of Smith's 1827 southwestern expedition which followed the same route as the 1826 trip. Recent scholarship throws new light on Wolfskill and Yount; see Wilson (1965) and Camp, ed. (1966).

5—Hafen and Hafen (1954) have assembled information about the Indian slave trade. See Creer (1949), Snow (1929), Bailey (1966). The notorious Walker has found two biographers: Bailey (1954) and Sonne (1962). Bailey (1966) is a fictionalized biography.

6—The mythical rivers were an important incentive to western exploration. See Crampton (1952), Crampton and Griffen (1956), Cline (1963), Wheat, I (1957), Chapters V–VI. An analysis of Humboldt's map appears in Crampton (1958).

7—Summaries of Frémont's expeditions appear in a hundred books. His interest and that of his father-in-law, Senator Thomas

Hart Benton of Missouri, in discovering a transcontinental river route has not been appreciated. This helps to explain Frémont's search for the San Buenaventura River, which otherwise seems rather naive. One should consult Frémont (1845 and 1848). A new edition of the *Memoir* with introduction by Nevins and Morgan, with a facsimile of the Preuss map, was published in 1964. See Cline (1963), 208, for discussion of Frémont's geographical ideas, and Volumes II-III of Wheat (1958-1959) for his cartographical contribution. Gilbert (1933) brings broad perspective into his study. Warren (1861) had much to say about "hypothetical geography."

8—The eventful history of the Jefferson Hunt wagon train to California, and of the several groups that at one time or another were a part of it, or defected from it, has been assembled by Hafen and Hafen, eds. (1954); the authors also reproduce Howard Egan's original diary which differs from the printed journal edited by W. M. Egan (1917). Smith (1958) is a biography. Reeder (1966) is a full and detailed work.

9—In his splendid book, Arrington (1958), Chapter III, analyzes the beneficial effects of the gold rush on the struggling Mormon economy.

10—I have followed the work of Hunter (1945), Chapter V, on the Pratt exploration and subsequent colonization. See also Creer, ed. (1940) on the San Bernardino colony, and Muir, I (n.d.). Ricks (1964) is a scholarly review of theory and processes. Owing to the importance of iron in the pioneer life of Utah, the beginnings of the industry are fully reported in the *Deseret News*, which had begun publication at Salt Lake on June 15, 1850. Indeed, the newspaper is a primary source of information for the move south by the Mormons and the opening of the corridor to California. The history of the Iron Mission is given by the authors above; for the local viewpoint see Dalton (n.d.), and G. Larson (1951?). The economic history is summarized by Arrington (1958).

11—The Walker War is a central event in early Utah history and accounts of it appear in the general histories. It is nowhere better told than in A. L. Neff's *History* edited by Creer (1940), 370-382. Paul Bailey and Conway B. Sonne, Walker's biographers, tell the story from the Indians' side. Curtailment of the Indian slave trade as a factor in the war is discussed by Bailey, *Indian Slave Trade in the Southwest* (1966), 155-172, and by the Hafens (1954), 259-283. Peace was concluded in May, 1854, and in less than a year the colorful Chief Walker was dead.

12—The history of the Mormons' move south into the valley of the Virgin has been well told by A. Larson (1961), 1-80. See Chapter VIII, "The Mormon Corridor," in Hunter (1945). The original site of Fort Harmony was some few miles south of the later settlement. The two are distinguished locally as "Old" and "New" Fort Harmony. For detailed data on the founding and subsequent history of Mormon towns and settlements, Andrew Jenson's *Encyclopedic History* (1941) is a convenient source.

13—The details on Mormon beginnings at Las Vegas have been extracted from reports by William Bringhurst and others in the *Deseret News*, July 18, 25, and August 8, 29, 1855. Based on contemporary sources, Jenson compiled a "History of the Las Vegas Mission" (1925-1926), covering the period from 1855 to 1868. See also Dumke (1953). Edwards (1965) carries the subject into the 1890s. Arrington (1958), 127-129, reviews the Mormon mining at Potosi; see also Hewett (1931), 69-71.

14—Vinton, ed. (1930), is one of the best accounts of travel over the route. Hafen and Hafen (1954) reproduce the diary of Orville C. Pratt who made the trip from Santa Fe to Los Angeles in 1848.

15—Goetzmann (1959) is a scholarly assessment of the national significance of the contribution made by the Topographical Engineers. G. K. Warren's "Memoir . . . Giving a Brief Account of Early Exploring Expeditions Since A.D. 1800" (1861) includes those of the Topographical Engineers through 1857. The Warren "Memoir" and a summary of expeditions, 1857-1880, are found in Wheeler, I (1889), 513-745.

A good index of the numbers of California-bound Argonauts traveling trails west of Albuquerque is the record on El Morro, or Inscription Rock, where very few names other than those identified with military expeditions appear for the years 1849-1858. See Slater (1961).

J. H. Simpson's *Journal* with drawings by Richard and Edward Kern (1850) is a primary document of great value. His recommendations for further western exploration are found in the conclusions of the report. Frank McNitt has done a service to scholarship by reissuing the work (1964).

16—Sitgreaves' *Report* was issued in 1853 by the 32nd Congress and reissued by the 33rd Congress the following year. Goetzmann (1959), 244-246, and McNitt, ed. (1964), 214-227, have summaries of the Sitgreaves expedition. Bender (1952) is a survey of the development of military policy. Wallace (1955) emphasizes the artistic and scientific contributions made by Robert Kern. Leroux has found a biographer, Parkhill (1965). The explorations of Sitgreaves and Whipple are summarized by Bender (1934).

The "Map of the Territory of New Mexico," compiled from many sources by Second Lieutenant John G. Parke of the Topographical Engineers, was issued by the War Department in 1851. Parke, assisted by Richard H. Kern, depicted a great extent of territory from the heads of the Pecos and Arkansas rivers to the Great Basin, showing the Colorado a point above the crossing of the Spanish Trail to the mouth of the Gila. Parke extended the mouth of the Green River down to about 35°30′ north latitude, almost on the parallel of Flagstaff! This error, which indicated the current lack of knowledge about the Colorado River canyon country, was copied on a number of maps issued subsequently. It was corrected by the Ives and Macomb surveys. The Parke map is reproduced by Wheat, III (1959), who assesses its importance.

17—The published reports of the several railroad surveys are found in *Reports of Explorations and Surveys to Ascertain the Most Practicable and Economic Route for a Railroad from the Mississippi River to the Pacific Ocean* (U.S. War Department, 1855-1861), 12 vols. in 13. The set, often referred to as the *Pacific Railroad Reports,* is a bibliographical nightmare. Whipple's "Report" appears in Volume III (1856), along with reports on the Indian tribes and a geological report. Volume IV of the set includes botanical and zoological studies; part of the zoological report appears in Volume X. The maps are to be found in Volume XI. Foreman (1941) has edited the Whipple itinerary. See also Conrad (1969) and Albright (1921) for a summary review of all the surveys. H. B. Möllhausen's work was published in German and translated (1858), 2 vols. For the artistic productions of the Pacific Railroad surveys, one should consult the splendid study by Taft (1953), Chapter 1; he devotes Chapter 2 to H. B. Möllhausen.

Before setting out from Albuquerque, Whipple obtained some practical geographical information from F. X. Aubry, Santa Fe trader, who from California, July 10–September 10, 1853, crossed northern Arizona along the thirty-fifth parallel and recommended his route as practicable for a railroad. The next year he brought wagons over the same route. See Bieber, ed., with Bender (1938), and Wyman (1932). In the Grand Canyon region the trader's name, though misspelled, is perpetuated in the Aubrey Cliffs.

18—See Albright (1921) for details, but consult Goetzmann (1959 and 1966) for studies in the national significance of these explorations. Beckwith (1855) wrote up Gunnison's report. The book by Heap has been newly issued and edited by Hafen and Hafen (1957). Carvalho, who traveled with Frémont on the last expedition, wrote an account first published in 1857 and newly edited by Korn (1954). Frémont's western explorations are summarized by F. S. Dellenbaugh (1914), and by Nevins (1955).

19—Warren's map, together with his "Memoir to Accompany Map," appear in Volume XI of the *Pacific Railroad Reports* (1861). The map is a cartographic landmark and his memoir concisely summarizes western exploration, 1800–1857. The map is reproduced and its significance set forth by Wheat, IV (1960), 84–91.

Dixieland

1—There is an abundant literature of the Utah War. See Furniss (1960) and Bender (1952) for scholarly summaries; and Hafen and Hafen, eds. (1958), for contemporary accounts.

In a number of ways the war was beneficial to Utah's economy, a matter discussed fully by Arrington (1958), but in the war hysteria generated by the coming of Johnston's army may be found the basic explanation of the infamous massacre at Mountain Meadows where a company of over a hundred California-bound emigrants from Missouri and Arkansas, offensive and insulting in their behavior toward the Mormons as they traveled south through Utah, were killed by fanatical Mormons and some Indians in September, 1857. Quite probably the last word on the subject has been written by Juanita Brooks, herself a Mormon, whose wise, scholarly, and balanced *Mountain Meadows Massacre* (1950; second edition, 1963) explains the affair as a natural product of war hysteria.

2—Simpson's *Report* (1876) and Macomb's *Report* (1876) are both significant works in the literature of the Colorado River canyon country. Simpson's book included a synopsis of parts of Escalante's diary of the Domínguez–Escalante expedition of 1776, by Philip Harry.

The matter of federal military involvement in Utah had come up earlier when in 1854 Lieutenant Colonel Edward J. Steptoe was ordered to investigate the circumstances surrounding the killing of J. W. Gunnison and some of his railroad survey party the year before. For this, and other matters relating to strategic and logistical operations in Utah, 1854–1859, see Jackson (1952), Bailey, ed. (1965), and Miller (1968).

3—In an unpublished letter dated June 30, 1853 (National Archives, Record Group 77), R. G. Marcy urged the Colorado River expedition and applied for the command. In print (1866), he continued to urge exploration of the "Big Cañon."

4—The history of navigation on the Colorado has attracted a number of scholars. One of the best studies is Leavitt (1943). Woodward (1955) discusses the pre-Ives exploration of the Colorado by George A. Johnson. See also Sykes (1937).

5—Jackson (1952) is a scholarly study of federal road-building, 1846–1869; Chapter XI is devoted to the history of "Beale's Wagon Road," 1857–1859. Beale's official reports (1858, 1860) are detailed documents. See Jackson (1952), 367–369, for additional references to the Beale road, the camel experiment, and biographical works.

6—Chapters VII–IX in his *Report* (1861) contain Ives' narrative of the exploration of the Grand Canyon country; see also the introductory letter, pp. 5–6. Newberry devotes forty-five pages to the geology of the region. The method used by Egloffstein in constructing the maps will be found in Appendix D. Ives has attracted very little scholarly attention. Wheat, IV (1960), 95–101, has reproduced the Egloffstein maps with some comment. See Goetzmann (1959 and 1966) for a broad perspective on Ives.

Möllhausen's work (1861), 2 vols., is an important supplement to the Ives book. David H. Miller has supplied me with a translation of Möllhausen's entries for the dates April 3–19, 1858, when the expedition was exploring the Grand Canyon. Taft (1953) devotes an entire chapter to Möllhausen's western art. See D. L. Ashliman (1967) for additional matter on Möllhausen and other German travelers. See also Wallace (1955).

7—Irvin S. Cobb (1914), one of the most popular humorists of his time, devotes two chapters to the Grand Canyon; see p. 29 for his "preconceived conception" of the canyon.

8—I have discussed the importance of the Macomb expedition of 1859 in my *Standing Up Country* (1964), 59–64. J. N. Macomb's *Report* was delayed by the Civil War and did not appear until 1876. However, the Egloffstein map, in the same style as the map of the Ives exploration, was issued separately in 1864. See Wheat IV (1960), 142–143, where it is reproduced and discussed.

9—The effect of the Utah War is fully discussed by Arrington (1958), Chapter VI. See also Ricks (1964).

10—Thales Haskell, in disguise, even spent a night on board the *Explorer*, and he gives his account of it in his journal, reproduced in part by Smith, comp. (1964), 28–30. Jacob Hamblin mentions the episode in his autobiography written by James Little (1881), 52–53. Ives (1861), 88–91, has some interesting comments on the incident and upon Mormon activities among the Colorado River Indians. See also Woodward (1955), 106–116.

11—News stories of Ives' progress up the Colorado were widely copied. The *Deseret News* carried exchange news stories on Ives on June 9 and July 28, 1858, among other dates. The Beale letter appeared in the issue on June 2. See Smith (1970) and Hunter (1939 and 1945).

12—The first thrust by the Mormons into southeastern Utah in 1854–1855 was turned back when Ute Indians destroyed the Elk Mountain Mission at the later site of Moab on the Spanish Trail. See Crampton (1964), Chapter 6.

See the works by Bailey (1954) and Sonne (1962) for reference to trading expeditions by Walker to the Hopi Indians.

13—The pipe episode is not very well documented, but it's very much a part of the folklore of the Arizona Strip. McClintock (1921), 98, credits the story to A. W. Ivins, who was probably drawing on local tradition.

14—Jacob Hamblin has found two biographers: Bailey (1948) and Corbett (1952), both of whom have relied heavily on Little, *Jacob Hamblin* (1881), the explorer's dictated autobiography. See also Juanita Brooks (1943) and Creer (1958). Juanita Brooks has edited the journal of Thales Haskell (1944), 69–98, who is deserving of a full-length biography. A start has been made by Smith, comp. (1964). There is material on the 1858 expedition in the Ammon M. Tenney papers in the L.D.S. Church Historian's Office Library, Salt Lake City.

15—The important exploration by Jesse N. Smith seems to have escaped the notice of local historians. His manuscript reports, dated September 22 and October 6, 1858, are in the L.D.S. Church Historian's Office Library, Salt Lake City. Another version is contained in Jesse N. Smith's *Journal* (1953). Except for the hike upriver to Zion Canyon, the route followed by Smith in 1858 had already been explored in 1852 by a party directed by J. C. L. Smith and John Steele, who should be credited with the actual discovery of much of the region. The report of that exploration was published in the Salt Lake City *Deseret News*, August 7, 1852. See Woodbury (1944), 141–143.

16—As might be expected, the settlement of the Virgin River and the history of the Cotton Mission has been studied extensively. To my mind the best work on the subject is Larson (1961); see also his *The Red Hills of November* (1957), which is a history of the Cotton Mission. Larson has based his works on sound material and, as a long-time resident of St. George, he has an intimate familiarity with the region, its people, and their history. See also Reid (1964), Bradshaw, ed. (1950), Woodbury (1944), and Brooks (1961). Very little attention has been given to the Mormon mission as a frontier institution. A brilliant study by Charles S. Peterson (1967) includes a chapter on the mission with particular reference to the Mormon frontier in southern Utah and the basin of the Little Colorado. The work is scheduled for early publication. James G. Bleak, contemporary historian of the Cotton Mission, prepared a running chronology of the mission, "Annals of the Southern Utah Mission," a highly informative work which has never been published. The original is in the library of the L.D.S. Church Historian's Office, but abridged copies, including one in the Utah State Historical Society, exist elsewhere. A penetrating study of Mormon history with emphasis on life in southern Utah is Nels Anderson (1942). Gregory (1945) is a summary of settlement to about 1940, with statistics.

17—On his return from Oraibi in 1862, Hamblin escorted three Hopis to Salt Lake where they were entertained by church officials who expressed their wish to send more missionaries to Hopi land, a move preliminary to Young's plan to colonize the Little Colorado. On their return to Oraibi, Hamblin and his Hopi charges paid a visit to the Havasupais in their canyon home. Hamblin's own account of his trips to the Hopi villages in 1862–1863, dictated to James A. Little (1881), is sketchy, though the essential facts are present. See also Smith, comp. (1964), 43–46, and Bailey (1948).

18—The history of commerce on the Colorado and of the Mormon interest in it is covered by Leavitt (1943), Woodward (1955), Arrington (1966), Faulk (1964), and Hunter (1939). When the South-

ern Pacific Railroad reached Yuma in 1877, commerce on the lower Colorado River virtually ceased. Hufford (1965), 177–187, develops the activities of William H. Hardy.

19—Details on the founding of the settlements of the Muddy Mission are found in A. Larson (1961), McClintock (1921), Edwards (1965), Hafner (1967), and Fleming (1967).

7
Powell of the Colorado

1—There is an abundant literature on John Wesley Powell. To commemorate the centennial of the 1869 voyage, the U.S. Geological Survey, which claimed Powell as its director from 1881 to 1894, issued *Professional Paper 669* (1969), "The Colorado River Region and John Wesley Powell," containing papers by Rabbitt, McKee, Hunt, and Leopold. The Survey also issued *Professional Paper 670* (1969), "John Wesley Powell and the Anthropology of the Canyon Country," with papers by Fowler and Fowler, and Euler. The American Geological Institute commemorated Powell in a special issue, *Geotimes*, 14 (May–June, 1969), with papers by W. T. Pecora, Mary Rabbitt, W. C. Darrah, Charles B. Hunt, and Ellis Yochelson.

A handsome special issue of the *Utah Historical Quarterly*, XXXVII (Spring, 1969), was dedicated to Powell, with articles by W. C. Darrah, Don D. Fowler and Catherine S. Fowler, O. Dock Marston, T. G. Alexander, W. L. Rusho, C. Gregory Crampton, P. T. Reilly, and Robert W. Olsen, Jr. *Arizona Highways*, XLV (March, 1969), was a special number devoted to Powell with articles by Jerrold G. Widdison and David Toll, and an abundance of beautiful photographs. More beautiful photographs by Walter Meayers Edwards and an article by Joseph Judge, "Retracing John Wesley Powell's Historic Voyage down the Grand Canyon," appeared in *National Geographic*, 135 (May, 1969).

The river trips are very well documented indeed. For these one should consult Powell, *Exploration* (1875 and 1895), Dellenbaugh (1920), and the diaries of expedition members published in the special issues of the *Utah Historical Quarterly*, XV (1947), edited by Darrah, and XVI–XVII (1948–1949), edited by Morgan and others.

Some of the commemorative articles, noted above, and the books by Stegner (1954) and Darrah (1951) place Powell in the mainstream of American History. The latter lists the main works in Powell's own extensive bibliography. Bartlett (1962) gives perspective to the Powell, King, Hayden, and Wheeler surveys.

2—Anyone who concerns himself with the history of navigation on the Colorado must deal with James White. White's alleged raft trip through the canyons of the Colorado in 1867 has been seized upon by the historians and much has been written of the matter. About the only solid fact we have to work with is that White was taken off a raft at Callville suffering from lack of food and exposure and was more dead than alive. The earliest critical study of White was done by Robert C. Stanton in a work edited by Chalfant (1932). Later studies are by Farquhar, ed. (1950), Lingenfelter (1958), and Bulger (1961). Freeman (1923) discusses White and also Samuel Adams, another 1867 voyager. John Moss, whose account appeared in the San Francisco *Call*, April 9, 1877, claims to have rafted it on a solo trip in 1861 from Lee's Ferry to Fort Mohave in four days! Even if these trips could be proved—and there is some plausibility at least to the White story—a fact with few consequences to history would have been established. See Farquhar's annotated bibliography (1953), Part IV, for additional titles on White and other apocryphal voyages.

3—The diaries kept by the 1869 voyagers through Grand Canyon were edited by Darrah (1947). Powell's remarks on Marble Canyon are in his *Exploration* (1875), 73–77, actually a composite report of the 1869 and 1871–1872 voyages. A preliminary report by Powell of the 1869 expedition was published in Bell (second edition, 1870), 559–564. It has been reprinted in Vol. XV (1947) of the *Utah Historical Quarterly*.

4—I am following Powell's account of the 1869 voyage published in 1875, an elaboration of notes and experiences of both the 1869 and 1871–1872 trips written for popular consumption.

5—Some controversy later developed over the affair at Separation Rapids, generated largely by remarks made long afterward by some of Powell's men who blamed him for the split in the party. More heat than light resulted, and Powell's leadership of the expedition bears little tarnish as a result. There was an outcry when the names of the Howlands and Dunn were not included with the other 1869 voyagers on an elaborate memorial to Powell which was built on Powell Point on the South Rim of the Grand Canyon and dedicated May 20, 1918. For a history of the memorial, see Dellenbaugh (1918). See also Bass (1920) and Chalfant, ed. (1932). On August 28, 1939, seventy years after the event, Julius F. Stone, a business associate of Stanton's and a river traveler, placed a bronze plaque at Separation Rapids commemorating the departure of the Howlands and Dunn and inviting all to read the *Colorado River Controversies* for which he had written a foreword. See Charles Kelly (1945) for the story on the plaque and Stone's bias in the controversy. See Darrah (1951), 141, note 19, for a balanced summary.

6—At high water both Separation and Lava Cliff rapids are inundated by Lake Mead which backs into the lower section of Grand Canyon. Even when not covered by the lake, the rapids are silted up and no longer are menacing. When I ran the canyon in August, 1967, there was only a slight ripple at each of the rapids. Should these places remain uncovered for any length of time the river might remove the silt and restore them to vigor. For a recent study of Grand Canyon rapids, see Leopold (1969).

7—I have followed Powell's account of the 1869 trip published in 1875. See also the journals of Bradley and Sumner, and other documents edited by Darrah (1947). Darrah (1951), Chapter 8, summarizes the 1869 venture. The tenth man, Frank Goodman, left the expedition early in July.

8—Powell's lecture was reported in the Salt Lake City *Deseret News*, September 22, 1869. See his report, *Exploration* (1875), 87–88, for an elaboration of the argument for the defensive character of the canyon ruins. Powell's Methodist bias even suggested to him that the Grand Canyon ruins were of recent origin—built by Indians fleeing from the Catholic Church and the Spanish Crown in New Mexico! It was commonly believed in 1869 that the prehistoric ruins in the Southwest had been left by the Aztecs, or by a folk kindred to them, on their migration to central Mexico; the idea may have derived from Humboldt's *New Spain;* the map accompanying this

work indicates a place between the mouth of the San Juan and Little Colorado rivers where the Aztecs reportedly stayed. Bell (second edition, 1870), whose work carried the first formal report of Powell's 1869 expedition, devotes Part II to the "Native Races of New Mexico," and one chapter to "The Aztec Ruins of New Mexico and Arizona."

9—Some of the pioneer archaeological investigation in Grand Canyon and environs has been done by Euler, "Willow Figurines" (1966; 1967; 1969). Euler (1969) and Fowler and Fowler, "Powell's Fieldwork" and "Ethnography" (1969), highlight Powell's contributions. See also the Fowlers' article, "John Wesley Powell, Anthropologist" (1969). Euler (1963), Lindsay and Ambler (1963), and Schwartz (1966) contain a history of archaeological investigation in the Grand Canyon country and citations to pertinent literature.

10—C. Hart Merriam (1889). Merriam worked out a life-zone classification ranging downward from the "Arctic-Alpine" to the lowest "Lower Sonoran" zones. The classification, with some regional modifications, is still widely used.

11—There is an abundant literature on the prehistory of the Grand Canyon country, most of it technical in nature. An exception is a work by Harold S. Colton, founder of the Museum of Northern Arizona at Flagstaff which has done much to advance the scientific study of the Grand Canyon region. Colton (1960) is a synthesis of knowledge gained by Colton and others associated with the museum for a period of over forty years.

In addition to the sources in note 9, the outlines of Grand Canyon prehistory may be found in the following and in the literature cited by authors: McGregor (1965); see Jennings (1964) for a review of the ancient Desert Culture. On the material culture of the Grand Canyon Indians and of the relationships between ancient and modern cultures consult: McGregor (1951), Schwartz (1956), Whiting (1958), Schroeder (1953), Spier (1928), Euler (1958), Kroeber, ed. (1935), James (1903), Euler (1964; "Southern Paiute," 1966), Isabel Kelly (1964), Steward (1938), Schroeder and others (1955). See Nagata (1967) on Moenkopi and Shutler (1962) on Pueblo Grande de Nevada.

12—On Mormon Indian policy and on Indian–White relations in the Southern Indian Mission, and in Las Vegas, see Hunter (1945), 290–314, 322–333. On the location of the tribes in the Grand Canyon country in 1848, see Katherine Bartlett (1945). See Chapter IX for an extended discussion of Indian–White relations in the South Rim country.

13—The interesting history of Fort Baker's role in the Civil War has been told by Ruhlen (1959). See also Averett (1962), 43, 107.

14—The official report of the 1866 expedition, headed by James Andrus, has been edited by Crampton (1964). For documentation on operations in 1869, see Crampton and Miller, eds. (1961), 148–176. Brooks, "Indian Relations" (1944), and Woodbury (1944) discuss the Indian "war."

15—Cattlemen on the Arizona Strip have long interested themselves in the killing of Powell's men. One of the first to look into the matter was Anthony W. Ivins, a pioneer stockman on The Strip, who in the 1880s acquired water rights on the Shivwits Plateau and established the Oak Grove Ranch near Mt. Dellenbaugh. Ivins became acquainted with the local Indians and from information supplied by them learned that one John To-ab was guilty of the crime, which had been committed on a low juniper-covered ridge less than a mile east of the Parashont Ranch and even closer to Waring's Wildcat Ranch. See Ivins (1924).

16—For references on Powell's explorations of southern Utah and the Arizona Strip in 1870, see note 18 below.

17—War did threaten again in 1873 when some Navajos were killed by whites on the East Fork of the Sevier, but again, Jacob Hamblin came to the rescue. He met the warlike chiefs at Moenkopi in January, 1874, and concluded a lasting peace. This, the treaty-making at Fort Defiance and the visit of Tuba to the Mormons, is reported in detail by Corbett (1952), 298-357.

18—The work of the Powell Survey, 1870-1873, particularly the river trips of 1871 and 1872, is very well documented. In addition to the sources listed in Note 1 above, the following are pertinent. The progress of the survey was followed in the press. F. S. Dellenbaugh, W. C. "Clem" Powell, and E. O. Beaman wrote a series of newspaper articles. E. O. Beaman ran a series published in 1874. Powell's articles in *Scribner's* and *Popular Science* form the substance of his official report, also published in 1875, as well as his *Canyons of the Colorado* (1895).

Powell's official reports before that issued in 1875 are listed in Darrah (1951). For the land survey, one should consult the diaries of the several expedition members published in the special issues of the *Utah Historical Quarterly,* XV-XVII (1947-1949). Dellenbaugh (1908), 244-245, has a particularly full account of the mapping, and he includes reproductions of the preliminary map of the Grand Canyon country completed in 1873. Geologist Gregory has edited the factual diary of Almon Harris Thompson (1939). Olsen (1969) supplies details, and see Crampton, ed. (1969), 214-243.

Watson, comp. and ed. (1954), contains some letters of Professor H. C. DeMotte, who participated in the land survey. Wilkins (1966) has detailed Moran's association with Powell.

Desert Bonanza

1—Durham, ed. (1954), 380.

2—Hafner, comp. (1967), describes pioneer life in the Moapa Valley. A. Larson (1961), 141-149, has a section on the early history of the Muddy Mission. See also Edwards (1965), 25-44, and Jenson, (1941), 520-522, 544-555.

3—The complicated boundary question between Nevada, Arizona, and Utah has been unraveled by Bufkin (1964). See also McClintock (1921), 96-97, 101-104.

4—I have found no satisfactory historical account of the early ferry crossings of the Colorado on that sector of the river from the mouth of Grand Canyon to the Virgin River. Bonelli bought out Stone, who had established an earlier ferry two miles below the mouth of the Virgin; Scanlon was bought out by Tom Gregg, whose name was attached to the crossing. The names of Bonelli, Pearce, Scanlon, and Gregg are all commemorated in local nomenclature. See Averett (1962) for brief facts. Perkins (1947) contains some fuller material on Daniel Bonelli. See also Hafner, comp. (1967), 37-42. All of the old ferry sites are now under the waters of Lake Mead.

5—The settlement of Zion Canyon is treated at length by Woodbury (1944), 150-164. See Reid (1964), 217-218, for a differing version of the naming of Zion Canyon. It was also called "Little Zion." The most recent article on the matter is A. Larson (1969). Taylor (1883), 11-20, contains his remarks on mountains with big feet.

6—Much has been written on the United Order and on the experiment at Orderville. Arrington (1958), 321-341, discusses the entire movement; A. Larson (1961), 290-313, devotes an entire chapter to the "United Order of Enoch" in southern Utah; Ricks (1964), 105-114, has a chapter on Orderville; Carroll, comp. (1960), has two long chapters on Orderville—included are the articles of agreement, rules of order, and much material of lively human interest. Pendleton (1939) and Emma Seegmiller (1939) are important articles.

7— A. Larson (1961), 168-184, contains a good account of the history of Bunkerville and Mesquite. See also Jenson (1941) under the names of the villages.

8—A good history of the Mormon cooperative livestock companies is a much-needed work. Arrington (1958), 293-349, details the history of the cooperative movement at large. A. Larson (1961), 235-248, writes of the business in the basin of the Virgin. Woodbury (1944) has some details on the Arizona Strip. Further information may be found in Dalton (n.d.) and Carroll, comp. (1960). The Winsor Stock Growing Company is discussed by Olsen (1965). See Davies (1951). Davies was a cowboy for the Kanarra Cattle Company in 1874. Haskett (1935) lists the brand owners in Mohave County.

Background articles on the livestock industry in Utah have been written by Walker (1962 and 1964). Palmer (1958) writes of the importance of the mining camp trade in the economy of southern Utah. Far less has been written of sheep raising than of the more glamorous cattle industry. See Wentworth (1948), Chapters 11-12, for historical coverage of Utah, Arizona, and Nevada.

See Nelson (1952) and Spencer (1940) for sketches of this distinctive institution and its relationship to farming and grazing.

9—See A. Larson (1961), Chapter 13, and Woodbury (1944), 189-194, for details of sale and purchase of ranch properties. Price and Darby (1964) detail the operations of Nutter on The Strip from 1893.

10—The expansion of the Mormon frontier eastward from Dixie along the Utah-Arizona boundary may be traced in Gregory (1945). See Jenson (1941), under the name of the several settlements involved, and Carroll, comp. (1960).

11—A. Larson (1961), 248. See Brooks (1949) for a historical sketch with particular reference to grazing.

12—Theorists of the American frontier have had very little to say about the communal frontier movement epitomized by the Mormon experience. For that matter, the Mormons themselves have neglected the subject until recently. A study by Peterson (1967) is a "pioneer" work.

13—Much of the writing on John D. Lee focuses on his involvement in the Mountain Meadows massacre of 1857; much less has been written on Lee's Ferry, or of Lee's experiences elsewhere in Arizona. Cleland and Brooks, eds. (1955), 2 vols., have edited Lee's diaries for the years 1848-1876. Brooks (1962) is a biography largely based on the diaries. Brooks (1957) and Crampton (1960) have details on the founding and subsequent history of Lee's Ferry.

14—The details of the 1873 trek are in Peterson (1967), 26–31. McClintock (1921) is a basic book on the subject.

15—For a full scholarly study see Peterson (1967) and McClintock (1921). The scouts by Jones and Brown are recounted by Jones (1890) and by Brown (1900). The colonization of southeastern Utah, related to the Mormons' push southward, has been told by Miller (1959).

16—Barnes (1934).

17—Nagata (1967) contains a good review of the history of the Moenkopi-Tuba City oasis. An excellent study is by Gregory (1915). Judd (1969) is a short sketch.

18—John D. Lee lived at Lonely Dell for a short time. Soon after ferry service was begun, Lee was arrested and on March 23, 1877, gave up his life to the firing squad after conviction for his participation in the Mountain Meadows massacre. Stalwart Emma Batchelor Lee, one of his most faithful and devoted wives, operated the ferry until 1877, when the property was acquired by the Mormon Church. Warren Johnson, followed by James Emett, ran the ferry until 1910 when it was sold to the Grand Canyon Cattle Company. Lee's involvement in the ferry operation and details of his long imprisonment and execution are recounted in his diary, edited by Cleland and Brooks (1955). See also Brooks (1962 and 1957). See Beadle (1879), Chapters XVII–XIX, for an account of one of the more articulate travelers to cross the ferry in its earliest days.

19—There is a substantial body of geological and technical literature on Silver Reef. Proctor (1953) cites the literature and summarizes the history and economic geology of the unique district. See also Butler and others (1920), 582–594, Brooks, "Silver Reef" (1961), Pendleton (1930), and Reid (1964), 199–211.

20—The beneficial economic effects of Silver Reef to the Saints in Dixie are related by A. Larson (1961), Chapter 18. He discusses the building of the tabernacle, temple, and the Washington County courthouse in Chapter 33.

The history of Dixie has been well told by A. Karl Larson, H. Lorenzo Reid, Hazel Bradshaw, Angus Woodbury, and others; I have not attempted to go much beyond the beginnings of the Cotton Mission.

Opening the South Rim

1—The diarists of the second Powell expedition, few of whom were much interested in prospecting, refer but briefly to Dodds, Riley, and Bonnemort, and the gold rush to Grand Canyon during the first months of 1872. The best account is W. C. Powell's journal edited by Kelly (1948–1949). Powell visited the mouth of Kanab Creek on a photographic trip for the Powell Survey in mid-January before the rush got underway. E. O. Beaman, who had just separated himself from the Powell Survey, also visited the diggings on a photographic tour. See his articles (1872 and 1874), and Dellenbaugh (1926), 144, 174, 185. News of the gold rush was reported over the Deseret Telegraph and carried in the Salt Lake press. The *Des-*

eret News, June 3, 1872, carried a notice that the excitement had nearly died out.

2—Cleland and Brooks, eds., II (1955), 184–201. Lee has much to say about the miners in his midst at the time when he was getting started at Lonely Dell. Kelly (1947) has edited the journal of F. M. Bishop who refers briefly to the rush at Lee's Ferry, Kanab Canyon, and elsewhere. In a letter written in 1872, Bishop (1947), 253, wrote that gold had been discovered at different points in Grand Canyon and that the greatest fever at the time was at the mouth of "Diamond River." W. D. Johnson, Jr., with one of the Powell Survey parties, mentions in an article to the *Deseret News,* May 29, 1872, that members of the group found some gold at the mouth of what was probably Whitmore Wash. In his diary, edited by Gregory (1939), A. H. Thompson, in charge of the Powell land survey, has little to say about the gold discoveries.

3—Marcy (1866), 249–250.

4—The materials are abundant, but the historian of the mining frontier of southern Nevada and northern Arizona has not appeared. The extent of available periodical literature is indicated by Goodman (1969) and by Elliott and Poulton (1963). See Browne (1868) for many details of the separate districts. Schrader (1909) contains some historical data. "Mining Record," B, Mohave County Recorder's Office, contains notices of locations of mines in El Dorado Canyon, and in the San Francisco and Sacramento districts, going back to 1865. The museum of Mohave Society and Art, Kingman, Arizona, possesses the "Mining Laws and Notices of the Colorado District, El Dorado Canyon, 1863–1865," in manuscript. The work by Dunning and Peplow, Jr. (1959) is useful, but it lacks notes and bibliography.

The extent of mining in the region west of the Grand Canyon region is illustrated by Wheeler (1872), who describes seventy-two districts in the area surveyed, of which about a third were located in northwestern Arizona and southern Nevada.

5—These early mining locations are recorded in Mohave County, Arizona, "Mining Record," B, 1865–1882, 280–282. H. C. Kiesel, "Exploring Expedition," Salt Lake *Tribune,* July 30, 1873, reports that Adams, Bentley, and Snow were en route to their copper mine. These may not be the earliest locations, as the actual recording of mining claims was local and somewhat haphazard before the passage of the federal mining law of 1872 which specified location and recording procedures. I have found no record of any placer locations made during the gold rush of 1872. It is quite likely that a number of prospectors penetrated the canyon country in the 1860s during the mining boom in the region west of Grand Canyon. Wheeler in 1871 found the name of O. D. Gass in the lower end of Grand Canyon. Gass was a Las Vegas pioneer who in 1864 had laid claim to the "pre Historic" salt mine on the lower Virgin River. Mohave County, "Mining Record," B, 10. William H. Hardy, of Hardy's Ferry, told of mining in Cataract or Havasu Canyon in 1866. The story was printed in an issue of Phoenix *Graphic* for 1899 and reproduced by Miller, ed. (1962), 290–295. However, the gold discoveries made by the Powell Survey in 1871, and the rush of 1872, seem to have stimulated widespread prospecting on the Colorado Plateau.

The history of mining in the Grand Canyon region at large has not been written. The pattern of prospecting can be determined from county records. Mohave County, "Mining Record," B, 1865–

1882, 280–282, 434, and "Mining Record," D, 1875–1881, 154–156, 232–233, 388–389, 501–504, are mining location notices in the Grand Canyon country on both sides of the river. Some of the north side locations were also recorded in Washington County, Utah. "Deed Record," D, 1869–1874, 235–236, 246–249; "Deed Record," G, 1874–1878, 340–342; "Record," J, 1875–1876, 6–8, 81–84, 103–104, 151–152. A number of locations are recorded in Yavapai, one of the original counties of Arizona, "Record of Mines," 3, 1873–1876, 405–408. The Salt Lake City *Deseret News,* May 22, 1878, reports the smelter in operation at the Grand Gulch mine. The Prescott weekly, *Arizona Miner,* December 14, 1877, reports Spencer's and O'Leary's "silver" discovery near the mouth of the Little Colorado. Both men were pioneers in the South Rim country. A catalog card in the Arizona Pioneers' Historical Society, Tucson, reveals that Spencer was born in England, arrived in Mohave County in 1863, and married an Indian woman. He became a guide, interpreter, mail carrier, and prospector. In November, 1886, he was killed in a quarrel with his partner, Charles Cohen. See Prescott *Journal-Miner,* November 26, December 7, 15, 1886, for details. Born in Ireland, Dan, or Daniel, O'Leary came to Arizona in the 1860s, perhaps earlier, and his colorful life as guide, scout, and prospector somewhat parallels that of Spencer. See Thrapp (1965). Schrader (1909), 142–150, notes that the first mines in the Music Mountain District were located in 1879 or 1880. At the same time the Gold, or Lost, Basin gold mines in the White Hills across Hualapai Wash from the Grand Wash Cliffs were opened and a boom developed. See Lenon, ed. (1867), 256–268. Meanwhile, mining in the Cerbat Range to the south was active. See Long, Jr. (1962).

6   Mining claims on the Arizona Strip, 1880–1883, are found in Mohave County, "Mining Record," D, E, F, which include the years 1875–1883. The Copper Mountain Mining Company, James Andrus, president, relocated the claims on Copper Mountain, *ibid.,* E, 1880–1882, 373–374. A brief history of the Grand Gulch mine and the neighboring "Bronze L" mine is reported by Hill (1915). Hill cites a lengthy bibliography of studies pertaining to copper ores in the "Red Beds." Mining on the Arizona Strip in the early days was mainly in the hands of the Dixie Mormons, but they have not written much about it. See Chapter 18, A. Larson (1961), and pages 205–508 in Miller (1946).

7—The place of Leadville in American mining history is indicated by Paul (1963), 127–132. In 1880 alone Leadville produced over eleven million dollars in metal.

8—The operation of the Beckman-Young prospecting party and the death of Mooney were reported in a long article in the Prescott *Arizona Miner,* April 7, 1880, and this was copied elsewhere in the western press.

9—The scope of prospecting in the Grand Canyon region during the early 1880s can be determined by a review of the locations notices filed in the counties: Mohave County, "Mining Record," D-F, 1875–1883; Yavapai County, "Record of Mines," 1879–1885, 8–21. The Prescott *Arizona Miner,* April 12, 1880, notices the formation of the Little Colorado River Mining District.

10—Seargeant, whose father prospected Havasu Canyon in 1883, has written an informative article on the mining history (1959). Ferris and Busch, mineral examiners, General Land Office, prepared mining reports on the "Bridal Veil" mines in Havasu Canyon (1924). Birdseye saw and described the great ladder (1925).

11—The "Grand Cañon" claim, "about one mile from the Colorado River," was recorded both in Yavapai County, "Record of Mines," 9, 1880, 125–126, and in Mohave County, "Mining Record," D, 1875–1881, 695. The Prescott *Arizona Miner,* July 4, 1884, reports eighty percent copper assays from the "Copper King" mine owned by Ridenour and Spencer. This article alludes to the presumed discovery by John D. Lee. Lee's name has been identified with a number of "lost" mines in Grand Canyon, but there is little evidence to suggest he ever prospected there. See Kelly, ed. (1946). Whiting (1948) discredits the many stories which identify a long residence by Lee in Havasu Canyon, though he admits the possibility of brief visits, 1871–1874. Lee is thought by some to have discovered the mines below the Indian village.

12—I have written of the Glen Canyon gold rush and its background (1964), Chapter 10.

13—Palmer's book (1869), with a number of sections written by Dr. C. C. Parry, is a significant work in the literature of the Grand Canyon country. It is accompanied by a large map on which appear the words "Grand Cañon of the Colorado River," which some writers believe is the first application of the term on a map. See Farquhar (1953), 20, and Wheat, V (1963), 253–254; the map is reproduced by Wheat opposite page 243. C. C. Parry wrote an account of the James White "voyage" through the Grand Canyon in 1867 and thereby introduced one of the more controversial subjects in Colorado River history. Parry concluded as a result of White's raft solo that the Colorado would not become a commercial route. W. A. Bell was with Palmer on the survey (though not on the thirty-fifth parallel route across northern Arizona), and his book (1870) is a lively account; as before noted, he printed Powell's summary of the 1869 voyage.

14—Consensus is wanting on the history of Flagstaff's naming. Colton (1942) assembled the conflicting data. See also Hochderfer (1965), 68–69. Cozzens (1876) is a rambling account. He has little to say in the book of the Grand Canyon country or the valley of the Little Colorado, but evidently his lectures on the promise of the latter area were convincing. See McClintock (1921), 149–151; the author obtained information from some survivors of the Boston party.

15—The complicated Gilded Age dealings by which the Atchison, Topeka and Santa Fe extended its system across the Southwest are revealed, together with some details of construction, by Waters (1950) and by Myrick (1963), 762–793. The popular account by Marshall (1945) contains statistical details on construction, trains, nomenclature, and chronological development. See also Greever (1954). Winther gives an overview of western railroad building (1964).

16—Marshall (1945), 351–357, gives the origin of Santa Fe town names; pages 396–449 carry details of the chronological development of the system.

17—There is a scattered literature on the history of the Arizona range industry. Greever (1954) is a detailed review of the A&P's relationship with adventurous entrepreneurs. Morrisey (1950), 151–156, and Haskett (1935) provide useful outlines; the latter lists pioneer cattlemen by counties. Wentworth (1948) sets the Arizona industry in national perspective. Haskett (1936) is a detailed survey containing lists by counties of pioneer sheepmen.

Roger Kelly (1964) has written of J. W. Young's Fort Moroni, later called Fort Rickerson. For local developments in and about

Flagstaff, see Hochderfer (1965), Sykes (1944), Forrest (1924 and 1964). The struggle for the range in the 1880s reached savage proportions in the Tonto Basin south of the Mogollon Rim. The Graham-Tewksbury feud, or the Pleasant Valley War, and its relationship to the outfits along the A&P has been examined in detail by Forrest (1950). See also Tinker, ed. (1969), of a work first issued in 1887, and Fuchs (1953) for a study of Williams.

18—The development of the lumbering industry is described by Greever (1954) and Fuchs (1953). The business records of the Arizona Lumber and Timber Company from 1882 are in Special Collections of the Library, Northern Arizona University, Flagstaff. A portrait of Edward Everett Ayer was written by Lockwood (1968), 89–105.

19—The mining records on file in the recorders' offices of Yavapai and Mohave counties reflect that the number of mining locations in the Grand Canyon area greatly increased after the coming of the railroad in 1883.

20—See two articles by Stewart (1967 and 1969). Brandes (1960), 56–58, gives a brief sketch of the founding and subsequent history of Fort Mojave, now usually spelled Mohave. Wright (1946) has edited the John Udell journal first published in 1859. Udell was a member of the wagon train attacked by the Mohaves in 1858, and his is one of the primary accounts of the event. Woodward (1953) is a brief biography of Irataba.

21—Dobyns and Euler (1960) write mainly of the western Pai, or Hualapai. Three posts, Camp Beale's Springs, Camp Willow Grove, or Willow Springs, and Camp Hualapai, or Toll Gate, were established during the Hualapai war. The latter two were on the main line of travel between Beale's Springs and Fort Whipple and Prescott: Brandes (1960); Skinner (1968); Edmonds and Vivian, eds. (1968). Primary documents relating to the Hualapai relations with the United States to the 1930s are found in U.S. 74th Congress, 2nd Session, Senate Document 273, *Walapai Papers* (1936). Anthropologists seem to prefer the "Walapai" spelling, but the tribe itself spells it 'Hualapai.''

22—Some of the background documentation, including an extract of the report by Lieutenant Colonel W. R. Price, is found in the U.S. 74th Congress, 2nd Session, Senate Document 273, *Walapai Papers*. The full, printed report by Price, dated July 1, 1881, together with other related documents, printed and manuscript, are found in U.S. National Archives, Record Group 74, Special Case No. 1.

The original Haulapai reservation conforms approximately to the present boundaries. However, the prior railroad land grant of odd-numbered sections, together with a dispute over the ownership of Peach Springs, was productive of enduring controversy. See Greever (1954) for a review of the earlier aspects of the struggle.

23—The proposed visit of General O. B. Willcox is reprinted in the Prescott *Arizona Miner*, April 10, 1880. The background documents on the establishment of the Havasupai reservation have not been published. The *Report* submitted by Lieutenant Colonel W. R. Price, July 1, 1881 (see note 22), includes the results of a reconnaissance made of the Havasupais in June. At that time the bounds of the reservation were fixed by Lieutenant C. F. Palfrey.

24—Underhill (1956), 148–149, graphically illustrates the growth of the Navajo reservation. As the reserve grew, the Mormons were frozen out of their holdings at Moenkopi and Tuba, but the Hopis retained theirs. See Nagata (1967), Chapter V.

25—The report by Powell and Ingalls (1874) on their study of the Paiutes and other Indians of the plateau and Great Basin country is an important ethnological document by concerned and dedicated men. The Moapa Indian reservation was created early in 1873 by presidential order before the Powell-Ingalls survey began. The commissioners recommended a reservation that would have incorporated a large corner of southeastern Nevada, but upon insistence of the Nevada congressional delegation, the reservation was reduced to one thousand acres in 1875. See Sadovich (1968). Euler (1966) contains the outlines of Southern Paiute history but much remains to be done, particularly with the Nevada Indians. The Shivwits and Kaibab reservations were established in 1891 and 1907, respectively. Ella Seegmiller (1939) has a short piece on the Shivwits Reservation. Much credit for achievement under difficult conditions must be given to Dr. E. A. Farrow (1930), who was agent at Shivwits and Kaibab for a number of years. He wrote a short article, "The Kaibab Indians," *Utah Historical Quarterly*, III (1930), 57–59. Palmer (1946) is a sympathetic rendering of tales and legends.

26—See Wallace, ed. (1965), for an abridged edition of the great work on the Ghost Dance by James Mooney, first published in 1896. Dobyns and Euler (1967) is a scholarly ethnohistorical study. Although accepted by the Southern Paiutes, the Wovoka doctrine was much more zealously embraced by the Hualapais; the Havasupais tried it briefly in 1891. Bailey (1957) is a popular account of the movement. See Iliff (1954) for an account of the effects of Christian teaching in Indian schools.

Grand Ensemble

1—Wheeler (1870) is a very rare pamphlet of twenty-three pages. An abstract appears in Wheeler (1889), 22–30.

2—Wheeler (1872) summarizes the 1871 reconnaissance, but little is said of the Grand Canyon exploration. In his final report, Wheeler (1889), 147–171, summarizes the upriver trip. He includes a chronology of Colorado River exploration and a detailed itinerary of his own trip together with a detailed map of the river and adjacent country from Camp (Fort) Mohave to Diamond Creek.

See Bartlett (1962), Chapters 17–18, for a summary of the Wheeler Survey, 1869–1879. Freeman (1923) devotes Chapter XI to Wheeler's push-pull trip up the Grand Canyon.

3—The topographic work of the Powell Survey in the Grand Canyon region resulted in a number of maps. The preliminary maps, completed in 1873, were published by Dellenbaugh (1926). The map of Utah Territory published in Powell (1878; second edition, 1879) in large part is based on the topographic work of the Powell Survey but some data were supplied by the King, Wheeler, and Hayden surveys. G. K. Gilbert, C. E. Dutton, A. H. Thompson, and Willis Drummond, Jr., contributed to the work. The atlases accompanying Powell's work on the Uinta Mountains and Dutton's studies on the High Plateaus and the Grand Canyon were products of the survey. The early topographic reconnaissance quadrangle maps issued by the U.S. Geological Survey were mainly drawn from the data accumulated by the Powell Survey. The following sheets, still in use in the 1940s, nearly covered the Grand Canyon country: St. George, Kanab, Escalante, St. Thomas, Mt. Trumbull, Echo Cliffs. These have been replaced in part by the accurate large-scale topographic quadrangles now being issued by the Geological Survey.

The Powell Survey published eight quarto volumes, *Contributions to North American Geology, 1877-1893,* but the subject matter of none of them touched the Grand Canyon region. See Schmeckebier (1904).

Wheeler (1889) contains a detailed map of the western part of the Grand Canyon below Diamond Creek including the Colorado River down to Fort Mohave. The separate topographic maps (Nos. 59, 66, 67, 75, 76) issued by the Wheeler Survey blanketed the Grand Canyon region. The mapping of Wheeler and Powell is discussed by Wheat, V (1963).

4—The descriptive passages quoted are from Dutton (1880), 208-209, 253-255. See Chapter XIII for an equally moving description of the "Aquarius Plateau," outside the bounds of this work, but see Crampton (1964), 149.

5—The descriptive passages cited here are a sampling from Dutton (1882), Chapter II, 37, and Chapter III.

6—The passages cited here are taken from Dutton (1882). Chapters III, V, VII, and VIII are written in a "popular" and at times "effusive" style, as he put it. Dutton's fieldwork in the region of the High Plateaus and the Grand Canyon was undertaken during the warm seasons of 1875, 1876, 1877, and 1880. Stegner (1936 and 1954), 158-174, has given us an appraisal of Dutton.

7—Hillers' photographs have been published since the 1870s, though not widely. The Indian photos, especially those of the Southern Paiutes, have been used as ethnological source material. See Fowler and Fowler, "Powell's Anthropological Fieldwork" (1969); Steward (1939), 1-23; Euler, "Paiute Ethnohistory" (1966), appendix, 1-33, reproduces a number of the photos with notes made by Frederick S. Dellenbaugh. Dellenbaugh (1908) published a number of photos by Hillers and E. O. Beaman and this revived considerable interest in Powell's photographers. Taft (1938) has some material on Hillers and other photographers of the great western surveys.

8—Thomas Moran, I would say, is the most neglected of our western landscapists. The first full-length biography was done by Wilkins (1966). A biographical sketch with some articles by others was prepared by Fryxell (1958). Moran did not write, he painted, and there is precious little autobiographical material. Letters written by Moran to his wife, Mary Nimmo Moran, 1860-1892, have been gathered by Bassford and Fryxell (1967).

Even though late in life Moran was called the "Dean of American Painters," his art has been ignored, or but politely mentioned, by the critics and historians. Robert Taft, for example, in his otherwise thorough study (1953) treats of him only in the notes. Incredibly, very few of the books on Grand Canyon even mention Moran, yet he has been called the "Father of the National Parks." Powell wrote little about him and Powell's men on the survey said even less. Stegner (1954) gives him his due, 174-185.

9—W. H. Holmes does not appear in the art histories at all; a biography of the man, whose achievements in geology, art, archaeology—and scientific illustration—were great, is overdue. The raw materials are to be found in his own "Random Records of a Lifetime," a fifteen-volume collection in the Smithsonian Institution. See Stegner (1954), Chapter II, for the achievements of Moran and Holmes in revealing the lands explored by the Powell Survey. As a frontispiece Stegner reproduces on a reduced scale the marvelous Holmes panoramas of the view from Point Sublime. Some of the panoramas are also reproduced by Goetzmann (1966) and by Widdison (1968). Taft (1953) has a few words on Holmes and on John Weyss of the Wheeler Survey; Taft (1938) touches on the work of William Bell and T. H. O'Sullivan. Horan (1966) has provided a full-length biography of one of the best survey photographers, Timothy O'Sullivan.

10—The formation of the U.S. Geological Survey and Powell's subsequent career in government science are covered by Stegner (1954) and Darrah (1951). The exploration by Dutton and Holmes in 1880 actually came under the supervision of the new survey, Clarence King, Director, and Dutton's Grand Canyon work (1882) was the second volume in the *Monograph* series of the survey. The geological studies, initiated by Dutton in the Grand Canyon district, were carried on by Charles D. Wolcott, whose scientific papers are listed by R. T. Moore and E. D. Wilson (1965). H. E. Gregory (1945) has summarized government explorations in southern Utah.

11
The Pullman Frontier

1—The essential facts of the railroad survey are from Stanton's own pen as edited by D. L. Smith (1965); see also his detailed summary, based on Stanton's field notes (1960). When Brown and Stanton reached the mouth of Green River, they tied in with the survey which had been brought down from Grand Junction by Frank C. Kendrick. See Stiles, ed. (1964).

2—The primary documentation of the railroad survey consists of Stanton's own work summarized by Smith (1965 and 1960). In the first work, 226, Stanton classifies the construction required for the railroad line through the canyons from Grand Junction to the gulf, a distance of 1037.69 miles! The field notes of the entire survey, and other pertinent documents, have been edited by D. L. Smith and C. Gregory Crampton, and are scheduled for early publication. Stanton's article, "Availability of the Cañons" (1892), was the first detailed presentation to be given to the public. The survey, particularly the disasters in Marble Canyon, was covered by the contemporary press, and many of these are referred to in the first two titles in this note.

Stanton (1890 and 1893) wrote two popular articles about the survey; Nims (1890 and 1892) wrote two; Smith (1967) has edited an unpublished diary by Nims. Freeman, (1923) devotes a long chapter to the railroad survey, as does Dellenbaugh (1904).

3—Stanton's own account of the gold-mining venture has been edited by Crampton and Smith (1961).

4—The full title of Robert B. Stanton's history reads, "The River and the Canyon, the Colorado River of the West, and the Exploration, Navigation, and Survey of its Canyons, from the Standpoint of an Engineer." Stanton researched, carried on an extensive correspondence with river men, and interviewed others. He became, possibly, the best authority on river history of his own day. Most of the work was written during the years 1906–1909; he kept revising and adding new material until the work grew too large for any publisher to handle. Stanton's account of his survey of the river, 1889–1890, takes up eleven chapters and this has been edited by Smith (1965). Another portion, dealing with the James White voyage and separation of the Howlands and Dunn from Powell's 1869 trip, was edited by Chalfant (1932). The large bulk of Stanton's Colorado River papers is deposited in the New York Public Library. A large album of the railroad survey photographs, presented to the American Society of Civil Engineers in 1892, is deposited in the Engineering Societies Library, New York City.

5—The quotations here are from Smith, ed. (1965).

6—The quotations in the last three paragraphs are from the last pages of Stanton's "The River and the Canyon." Stanton probably refers to Thomas Telford, 1757–1834, a Scottish civil engineer.

7—The Yavapai County "General Index to Mines," 1889–1890, and the Coconino County, "Record of Mines," 1891–1901, are filled with notices of location made throughout the eastern section of the Grand Canyon country, which in 1891 came within the boundaries of the newly formed Coconino County. Several mining districts are referred to in these records. Most of the locations were made in the Grand Canyon Mining District, but Cataract, or Havasu, Canyon, the Pine Spring District (Prospect Valley and vicinity), Lee's Ferry, and Buckskin Mountain (Kaibab) were heavily prospected through the 1890s. There was a flurry of activity in National Canyon in 1891, and in Mohaw, Moho, or Mohawk Canyon in 1898.

8—The testimony taken in 1929 in the "River Bed Case" (U.S. vs. Utah, Supreme Court, Number 14, 1929) is a mine of information about the navigation and use of the Colorado River within the state of Utah. The suit was brought to determine ownership of the bed of the river. Harry McDonald, Elmer Kane, and W. H. Edwards, who had been with Stanton and Best, testified fully in the case. A typescript of the thirty-two volumes of testimony is in the Utah State Historical Society, Salt Lake City. One of the two boats was wrecked and lost at the head of Cataract Canyon. The Salt Lake Herald, November 22, 1891, carried a lengthy story of the Best expedition, based on an interview of John Hislop and J. A. McCormick, expedition members. Hislop and McCormick were pretty quiet about their prospecting, not so much because they had found something, but because they hadn't. Most of the article is taken up with descriptions of canyon country scenery with much space devoted to the splendid wilderness of Bright Angel Creek and its canyon. Stories on the company's activities were run in the Flagstaff Coconino Sun, June 13, October 8, 1891. R. B. Stanton (1920), 739–743, summarized the venture of the Denver, Colorado Canyon Mining and Improvement Company. A check of the "Record of Mines," Recorder's Office, Flagstaff, reflects that the company, or its members, filed notices of location of mining claims in the Grand Canyon area as late as April, 1893.

9—It is quite likely that the copper deposits on the Kaibab, which are to be seen on the surface along or near the western crest of the plateau for forty miles, were discovered in the 1870s. However, the boom in copper on the Kaibab began about 1890 and continued intermittently past the turn of the century. In the first three volumes of the "Record of Mines," Coconino County, filed in the Recorder's Office, Flagstaff, there are literally hundreds of claims recorded in the "Buckskin Mountains," 1891–1901. See Chapter IX for the earlier mining history of the Arizona Strip.

The origin of copper ore in sedimentary rocks was as puzzling to geologists as the silver at Silver Reef. Jennings (1903) reported on the matter. An article of broader scope is Emmons (1905). In the White Mesa District, at Coppermine, about fifty miles east of Jacob Lake, copper in sandstone had been mined since 1882. See Crampton Standing Up Country (1964), 144.

Few prospects or mines were found on or about the bases of Utah's High Plateaus; Silver Reef, of course, being the important exception.

10—Along with many others, of course, noted in the Yavapai County, "General Index to Mines," 2–3, 1884–1894, in the Recorder's Office, Prescott, Arizona, and in the Coconino County, "General Index to Mines," 1891–1901, 1–3, in the Recorder's Office, Flagstaff, Arizona.

11—The brief "Rules and Regulations of the Grand Canyon Mining District," were filed in the Recorder's Office, Falgstaff, "Record of Mines," I, 225–227. Ashurst was chairman of the meeting; P. D. Berry was elected permanent secretary. The county mining records constitute an excellent indicator of the intensity of the rush. In Coconino County only a few locations were made between February, 1893, and mid-1897, when the rush began again. The same pattern is observable in the records of Mohave County.

12—The South Rim mining boom of the 1890s is well known. Verkamp (1940) touched on it. The best and most detailed synthesis is Chapter VI of Hughes (1967).

The acknowledged authority on trails in Grand Canyon is Professor J. H. Butchart of Flagstaff. He has walked thousands of trail miles and has rediscovered many forgotten historic routes. See his titles in the bibliography. Filed in the Recorder's Office, Yavapai County, Prescott, is a record book "Toll Records," 1871–1901, containing claims to toll roads and ferries, some in Grand Canyon, 1890–1891. The Bright Angel Trail, claimed by P. D. Berry, is elaborately plotted.

The following give details on specific mines: Waesche (1933 and 1934), Lauzon (1934), Noble (1914), 93–96. Smalley (1897–1898) wrote a number of informative articles on Grand Canyon mines, including the O'Neill prospects, for the Phoenix Republican. Keithley (1949) has written a popular biography of Buckey O'Neill, a dashing Arizona figure who lost his life in Cuba in 1898 when Roosevelt's Rough Riders charged up San Juan Hill. Rose Lombard, the wife of Thomas Russell Lombard, of Lombard, Goode and Company, wrote an account (1949) about O'Neill's Grand Canyon mining and included matter touching on his relations with the engineering firm. The Papers of Ralph Cameron, touching his activities in the Grand Canyon and elsewhere from 1890, are in Special Collections, University of Arizona Library, Tucson.

The Orphan Mine, just west of Maricopa Point, was revived during the uranium boom of the 1950s. Hogan had found uranium ore in the 1890s, but that was before the atomic bomb.

13—Cushing's (1882) article has been reprinted by Euler, ed. (1965). Euler attests to the validity and ethnological significance of Cushing's piece. However, well over half of the article is taken up with adventures along the way—"the journey thither."

14—See Casanova, ed. (1968), for the diary and detailed editorial notes. Aside from contemporary news stories in the regional press, Crook's "tour" received small public notice.

15—The properties of the "Grand Canyon Stage Line" were put up for sale in 1895 by Mrs. Celia Farlee. See letter in the Martin Buggeln Papers. I have quoted an early traveler, "A. G." (1885), who wrote of his experiences in reaching the canyon by this route. See Hughes (1967), 69.

16—The Flagstaff *Coconino Sun,* which began publication in 1882 as the *Arizona Champion,* contains the raw material for a history of the South Rim country from the coming of the railroad. For the opening of the stage line to Grand Canyon, see issues of May 5, 12, 19, 26, June 2, 9, 16, 1892.

17—The article by Lummis (1893), reporting the opening of the canyon to all sightseers, is only one of several articles on a favorite subject; writing of the canyon in 1892, he called it the "grandest gorge," and in 1895, "The Greatest thing in the world." Lemmon's (1888) article, a bird's-eye view from Mt. Agassiz, is one of the best of the few done from that lofty viewpoint. Virginia Dox (1891) was possibly the first non-Indian woman to visit the Havasupais. Warner's long piece (1891) describes a tour through California and the Southwest. Grove Karl Gilbert also accompanied the party of the International Geological Congress, reported in the *Coconino Sun,* September 26, 1891. A list of the members is given. See also Darrah (1951), 332.

18—Hughes (1967), Chapter VI, has summarized the history of tourism on the South Rim. Hance, the story-teller, received a better press than Bass. He is mentioned in numerous travel accounts and other pieces including Lockwood (1940) and Garrison (1949). A register of visitors maintained by John Hance was compiled by Woods (1899). Bass found a strong advocate in James (1900). Bill Bass was interested in Grand Canyon history, but he soon developed a strong anti-Powell bias which was evident in a pamphlet (1920) he issued on the James White trip and the separation of Powell's men on the 1869 voyage. The Bass papers, including examples of his poetry, material on Grand Canyon, and Bass' tourist activities, are in the Arizona Collection of the Library, Arizona State University, Tempe. See Murbarger (1958).

19—Lummis (1893), 10-18. Harriet Monroe's (1899) article is not altogether snobbish in tone; it is a period piece but good reading.

20—It is instructive to note the trend in Grand Canyon periodical literature. This may be done easily by consulting Goodman's (1969) bibliography. About half the articles on Grand Canyon were published between 1890 and 1900. C. A. Higgins for the Passenger Department of the Santa Fe system produced a notable brochure (1893), a new edition of a similar work issued in 1892. The 1893 edition was the basis for several later pamphlets culminating in a superior work issued in 1902. Promotional material issued by the other stage lines was less pretentious; they did, of course, benefit from the Santa Fe's publicity up to the time when the branch line to the canyon put them out of business. Henry G. Peabody's album (1900) was reissued many times. Individual photographs by Peabody appeared in a number of publications including James' work noted above. An earlier photographer of note, Ben Wittick, took a notable series of pictures in 1883 during construction along the Atlantic and Pacific. He visited Havasu Canyon and Diamond Creek but not the South Rim east of those places. He sold some photographs, but few were published. See Van Valkenburg (1942) and Ellis (1958). See Stoddard (1898) and Holmes (1901) for articles on Grand Canyon by two of the most popular lecturers of the time.

21—Hughes (1967), Chapters VI-VII. On Fred Harvey, see Waters (1950), Chapter VIII; Henderson (1966), revised in 1969.

12
The Insistent Earth

1—Woodbury (1944), 190-191, wrote of the Kaibab venture and reproduced a photograph of Buffalo Bill and company on MacKinnon Point. In 1958, Ranger Frank J. Winess found a tin can containing two notebook pages of autographs left by the party; the document is in the reference collection, Grand Canyon National Park Visitors' Center. The Flagstaff *Coconino Sun,* November 10, 1892, listed the names of the "distinguished party."

2—Hughes (1967), 121-123, cites newspaper references to the annexation moves by Utah.

3—Hughes (1967) has provided details of the first government reservations. See also Verkamp (1940). The history of the national park idea and Theodore Roosevelt's role in furthering it is fully discussed by Huth (1957) and by Nash (1967).

4—Miller (1901), Muir (1902), White (1905), Prudden (1906), Hall (1906 and 1907), Burroughs (1911). This, of course, is only a sample. See "Comments by Noted Americans" in Higgins (1913), 27-31, a promotional booklet for the Santa Fe, and James (1910).

5—Easton and Brown (1961); Barnes (1927). The buffalo still roam in House Rock Valley; the herd was acquired by Arizona and is managed and controlled by the state's Game and Fish Department. Zane Grey (1908) in large part deals with the cattalo experiment and lion-hunting on the Kaibab; see also Grey's (1922) autobiographical account of his outdoor experiences on the Colorado Plateau. Etulian (1970) is a recent appraisal of Grey, the writer. See also Roosevelt (1913).

6—Marston (1960) has data on the canyon runs, few of which were much publicized. Stone's account was not published until 1932. In May, 1913, Ellsworth Kolb finished the river run from Needles to tidewater; his book (1914; new edition, 1915), deservedly popular, has been reprinted a number of times. Included as an appendix is a list of those who preceded the Kolbs on the river. See Corle (1946), 137-151.

7—See Wilkins (1966) for the later work of the "Dean of American Painters." The other, later artists of the Grand Canyon have received little attention. The one exception is the beautiful book on Gunnar Widforss by the Belknaps (1969). Artist W. R. Leigh (1911) wrote his impressions of Grand Canyon. The guidebook, N. H. Darton and others (1915), was one of several issued by the U.S. Geological Survey covering the transcontinental railroads. The Santa Fe issued a number of notable pamphlets from 1892 up to 1915. The series was initiated by C. A. Higgins. See Farquhar (1953), 40-42. The best of the Santa Fe publications (1906) contained articles by Powell, Stanton, Lummis, Moran, Higgins, and a number of others.

8—See Hughes (1967), 128–129, for details. Louis Cramton, a strong supporter in Congress of the national parks, made the statement on the floor of the House, March 3, 1924, in connection with a dispute over private ownership of the Bright Angel Trail, *Congressional Record* (1924), 3489–3500.

9—Full details on the building of the Salt Lake Route are given by Myrick (1963), 622–683. On the development of southern Nevada and Las Vegas and the formation of Clark County and subsequent history see the work by Las Vegas pioneers Squires and Squires (1955). See also Davis, ed. (1913), Scrugham (1935), and Hulse (1965).

10—The "See America First" movement appears to have been conceived by Fisher S. Harris, secretary of the Salt Lake Commercial Club, an organization which did much to promote the scenic attractions of Utah. The Utah State Historical Society has two volumes of the Fisher S. Harris "Scrapbook, See America First. Correspondence and Clippings, October, 1905–January, 1906." I have found little to indicate that the "See America First League" functioned long after its formation. In 1912, the Great Northern Railway adopted the slogan, and after World War I the idea was mouthed by many. Lummis' American boosterism is fully demonstrated in Chapter I of his 1892 work and his quote on Grand Canyon appears in an 1898 article. The magazine *Land of Sunshine* (later called *Out West*), ran many articles during Lummis' editorship on the Grand Canyon and its history. See the biography by Bingham (1955).

11—The opening of the Grand Canyon to auto traffic is discussed by Hughes (1967), 107–109, and by Woodbury (1944), 193–194. Winfield C. Hogaboom, Los Angeles newspaperman, wrote an account of the 1902 trip to the South Rim published in the Flagstaff *Coconino Sun*, February 8, 1902. Rust (1910) is a brief account of the pioneer motor trip to the North Rim. An account by Lynch (1911) indicates that commercial tourist traffic in 1911 was in operation between Flagstaff and Grand Canyon. Kitt (1970) is an account of motoring to the canyon in 1914. On the "automobile revolution" in the West, see Pomeroy (1957).

12—On the work of Mather, see Shankland (1951), and for the development of the national parks idea, see James (1939). The portfolio prepared by Yard (1921) was largely an assembly of striking black and white photographs; in the preface Mather said it was "the first really representative presentation of American scenery of grandeur ever published, perhaps ever made." An article by James Bryce (1922), containing an abundance of photographs, gave some emphasis to the Painted Desert, the Grand Canyon, and to "the secret of the charms of desert scenery."

13—Dellenbaugh (1904). Woodbury (1944) has full details of the emergence of Zion National Park; see also Reid (1964). Some of Dellenbaugh's paintings were exhibited in 1904 at the Louisiana Purchase Exposition at St. Louis. Dellenbaugh aroused interest, but the Utah citizenry pushed the parks idea through to completion with substantial help from officials of the Union Pacific. See Swain (1970). Actually the name of the monument had been changed to Zion in 1918. See U.S. National Park Service (1970) for the legislative history of the parks and monuments.

Articles by Mitchell (1917) and Jeffers (1918) are good examples of publicity given Zion and Bryce, respectively, before they achieved national park status. An interesting account of the adventure of travel by automobile from Salt Lake City to Bryce Canyon and the North Rim is Willy (1919).

14—Harding spent part of the day of June 27, 1923, in Zion National Park. The Salt Lake *Tribune*, June 26–28, covered the trip. *Speeches and Addresses* made by Harding on his western trip between June 20 and August 2 (when he died in San Francisco) were compiled by Murphy (1923).

15—Details about the dedication of the Union Pacific's spur line to Cedar City were published (1923) under the head "Golden Rail Laying, Cedar City, Utah." Woodbury (1944) contains many details of tourist development up to 1930. The James and Murphy books were beautifully designed with pictorial covers and illustrated with photographs and color plates. The James volumes were devoted to a number of subjects besides travel, but the Murphy book was altogether for the enlightenment of tourists bound to the "civilized wildernesses" of the national parks. Alter (1927), with chapters on Bryce, Cedar Breaks, Zion, and the North Rim, was a revision of articles originally published in the Salt Lake *Tribune*. An important article on the North Rim and Zion was written by Emerson Hough (1922). Hough advocated that the Kaibab forest be set aside as a wilderness preserve. Steele (1926) reports an extensive tour of the north country parks and monuments. Representative Louis C. Cramton of Michigan, strong supporter in Congress of the national parks, on April 17, 1924, upon an invitation of the American Automobile Association, broadcast a radio speech on Bryce Canyon and other Utah parks; it was printed in the *Congressional Record*, LXV, Part 7 (April 18, 1924), 6651–6652.

James, *Utah* (1922). Chapter XX, discusses Utah artists who have painted the canyon country. He singles out for particular mention H. L. A. Culmer, who was influential in attracting national attention to the sandstone landscape of southeastern Utah. See Crampton, *Standing Up Country* (1964), for details.

The available facilities and accommodations and tours in 1929 are all described in the *Circular of General Information Regarding Grand Canyon National Park, Arizona,* issued by the U.S. National Parks Service in that year. Although there were other tour operations, the Utah Parks Company enjoyed the largest share of the business.

16—The raw materials for the history of the post-World War I revolution brought on by the automobile are to be seen in the popular magazines of the 1920s. See the *Literary Digest,* May 26, 1923, "Four Great Highways from Sea to Sea," and a map of the nation with fourteen "organized" highways indicated. An article, with map attached, "Motor Routes from the Mississippi to the Rockies and the Pacific Coast," *Sunset,* 50 (June, 1923), shows that not a single mile of those highways peripheral to the Grand Canyon region was paved. The opening and development of roads and highways within the Grand Canyon country is covered by Woodbury and Hughes, both frequently cited herein.

The history of the route that became U.S. Highway 89 is dramatic throughout. A bridge was put over the Little Colorado at Cameron in 1911 and this eliminated the sandy ford at Tanner's Crossing, but Lee's Ferry and the left bank approach over Lee's Backbone was a hazardous bottleneck. See Hanna's adventurous account (1928). The building of Grand Canyon Bridge (as it was called in the dedicatory program, but later changed to Navajo Bridge) greatly facilitated travel over the only direct route between central Utah and Arizona, and the wider significance of the event was celebrated June 14–15, 1929, when the bridge was dedicated.

McClintock (1928) reviewed the history of the Colorado crossing from 1776. The *Official Program of the Dedication at Grand Bridge, Arizona, June 14, 15, 1929* (1929) carried details of construction, a history of Lee's Ferry, as well as the program which included addresses by the governors of the four adjacent states and a pageant summarizing the Mormon settlement of Arizona. Plummer (1929) reflects some of the symbolism with which the event was endowed. A special issue of *Arizona Highways*, V (May, 1929), was devoted to the "Grand Canyon Bridge." Rusho (1968) is a capsule history of the Colorado crossing. See McGaffey (1929) for an account of a circle tour through Arizona, Utah, and Nevada.

17—Murphy (1925), preface, used the term "civilized wildernesses" to describe the national parks. Woodbury and Hughes review modern developments in the Grand Canyon country parks to 1930, and 1966, respectively. Travelers to the parks decreased for a few years early in the Great Depression, but by 1935 new records had been set, at least in Grand Canyon. Two rather general books to guide motorists were issued by Tillotson and Taylor (1929, and reprinted as late as 1949), and by Scoyen and Taylor (1931). The guide books of Utah, Arizona, and Nevada, all published in 1940, prepared under the auspices of the Work Projects Administration, are still useful. Fuchs (1953) lists statistics of travel to the South Rim, 1919-1951. See Hegemann (1963).

As travel to the Grand Canyon country increased in the twenties and thirties the stream of writing about it increased in volume. As in earlier decades the South Rim received most of the attention. Indeed, a bibliography of the descriptive literature of Grand Canyon alone would make a good-sized book. Here are some samples: Priestley (1935 and 1937), Wolfe (1951), and a book in Swedish by Sven Hedin (1925).

18—After the pioneer period, population growth in the Grand Canyon country was slow, and most of the increase was recorded in the villages and towns. For instance, in 1914 A. M. McOmie (1915) made a state reconnaissance of the Arizona Strip and in the entire area he found only 335 residents, of which 250 were living in Fredonia and Littlefield. The recent history of this vast open country is touched upon by Brooks (1949), Lauritzen (1951), Whipple (1952). See also Wilson (1941). See Culmsee (1967) for a discussion of "post frontier" activity in Utah and the West and some of its results.

19—Reclamation and dam building on the Colorado has produced an abundant literature. LaRue (1916) is but one of the many government publications on the subject. Golzé (1952) is a background book. Kleinsorge (1941) details the history of Hoover Dam. See Waters (1946) for the project set in broad perspective, and Stegner (1954) for the contributions made by J. W. Powell to the reclamation movement. Mann (1963) brings together the elements of science, economics, aesthetics, and emotion that have governed water policies in a water-short state.

20—The official publication resulting from the 1923 survey was prepared by LaRue (1925). *The Plan and Profile of Colorado River from Lees Ferry, Arizona, to Black Canyon, Arizona–Nevada, and Virgin River, Nevada*, issued by the U.S. Geological Survey (1924), in twenty-one sheets still serves voyagers on the Colorado as the most trustworthy charts. Freeman, one of the members of the party, wrote a lengthy article on the survey (1924). Freeman's two books (1923 and 1924) also emerged from the survey. Birdseye and Moore (1924) summarized the geographical results. Birdseye (1938) is a summary of river trips from 1869. Eddy (1929) is the entertaining chronicle of his 1927 trip. Marston (1960) gives details of even the most obscure voyages. Before his death in 1949, Norman Nevills was the best known of the commercial river men, and numbers of his trippers wrote important articles. One example: Goldwater (1941), an extended chronicle of which was issued in 1970.

There is, of course, much more to Las Vegas than resort hotels, gambling, and lavish shows, but its rise as a desert tourist attraction is surely unique in the American experience. Modern Las Vegas and southern Nevada have found appreciative historians in Charles P. Squires and Delphine A. Squires, whose unpublished work (1955) indicates that the county east within 150 miles of Las Vegas is still a land of mystery. Johnston (1931) made a reconnaissance of the area before it was covered by Lake Mead and predicted it would become a celebrated playground.

Hulse (1965) gives some emphasis to the recent years. See Elliott and Poulton (1963) for a listing of more serious works on Boulder Dam and Las Vegas. Oddly enough, there is very little material on the Hoover Dam in an elaborate work on recreation issued by the National Park Service (1950). An interpretation of southern Nevada as it was before World War II is found in Lillard (1942).

21—Much of this section grows out of my own experience and reflection. I have referred specifically to Prudden (1906), 61; Prudden (1927) contains a number of significant reflections on the canyon country; Ferde Grofé (1938) tells the story of "Grand Canyon Suite"; Priestley (1937), 285. Further I wish to acknowledge Clough (1964), Austin (1924), Mills (1917), Lauritzen (1947), and Cobb (1914).

Bibliography

A. G.: "How to Reach the Grand Cañon." *Science*, V (June 26, 1885), 516–517.

Adams, Eleanor B., and Angelico Chavez, trans. and eds.: *The Missions of New Mexico, 1776, a Description by Fray Francisco Atanasio Domínguez with Other Contemporary Documents.* Albuquerque: University of New Mexico Press, 1956.

Albright, George Leslie: *Official Explorations for Pacific Railroads, 1853–1855.* Berkeley: University of California Press, 1921.

Alter, J. Cecil: *Through the Heart of the Scenic West.* Salt Lake City: Shepard Book Company, 1927.

———: *Utah the Storied Domain.* Chicago and New York: American Historical Society, 1932. 3 vols.

Anderson, Nels: *Desert Saints, the Mormon Frontier in Utah.* Chicago: University of Chicago Press, 1942.

Angel, Myron, ed.: *History of Nevada, with Illustrations and Biographical Sketches of Its Prominent Men and Pioneers.* Oakland, Cal.: Thompson and West, 1881.

Arrington, Leonard J.: *Great Basin Kingdom, an Economic History of the Latter-day Saints, 1830–1900.* Cambridge, Mass.: Harvard University Press, 1958.

———: "Inland to Zion, Mormon Trade on the Colorado River, 1864–1867." *Arizona and the West,* 8 (Autumn, 1966), 239–250.

Ashliman, D. L.: "The Image of Utah and the Mormons in Nineteenth-Century Germany." *Utah Historical Quarterly,* XXXV (Summer, 1967), 209–227.

Atwood, Wallace W.: *The Physiographic Provinces of North America.* Boston: Ginn and Company, 1940.

Auerbach, Herbert S., ed.: "Father Escalante's Journal, 1776–77, Newly Translated with Related Documents and Original Maps." *Utah Historical Quarterly,* XI (1943).

Auerbach, Herbert S., and J. Cecil Alter, eds.: *Life in the Rocky Mountains, 1830–1835,* by Warren Angus Ferris. Salt Lake City: Rocky Mountain Book Shop, 1940.

Austin, Mary: *The Land of Journeys' Ending.* New York and London: Century Company, 1924.

Averett, Walter R.: *Directory of Southern Nevada Place Names.* Las Vegas: Walter R. Averett, 1962.

Ayer, Edward C.: "Reminiscences, 1860–1918." MS, Arizona Pioneers' Historical Society, Tucson, n.d.

Baedeker, Karl, ed.: *The United States, with an Excursion into Mexico: Handbook for Travelers.* Second revised edition. Leipsic: Karl Baedeker; and New York: Charles Scribner's Sons, 1899.

Bailey, L. R.: *Indian Slave Trade in the Southwest.* Los Angeles: Westernlore Press, 1966.

———: "Lt. Sylvester Mowry's Report on His March in 1855 from Salt Lake City to Fort Tejon." *Arizona and the West,* 7 (Winter, 1965), 329–346.

Bailey, Paul: *The Claws of the Hawk, the Incredible Life of Wahker, the Ute.* Los Angeles: Westernlore, 1966.

———: *Jacob Hamblin, Buckskin Apostle.* Los Angeles: Westernlore Press, 1948.

———: *Walkara, Hawk of the Mountains.* Los Angeles: Westernlore Press, 1954.

———: *Wovoka, the Indian Messiah.* Los Angeles: Westernlore Press, 1957.

...ong-stemmed sego lilies on the Arizona Strip.

Bancroft, Hubert Howe: *History of Arizona and New Mexico, 1530-1888.* San Francisco: The History Company, 1889.

———: *History of Utah, 1540-1886.* San Francisco: The History Company, 1889.

Barnes, Will C.: "Arizona Place Names." University of Arizona *Bulletin,* VI: 2, *General Bulletin No. 2* (1935).

———: "The Bison of House Rock Valley." *Nature Magazine,* X (October, 1927), 218-220.

———: "The Honeymoon Trail to Utah." *Arizona Highways,* X (December, 1934), 6-7, 17.

Bartlett, Katherine: "The Distribution of the Indians in Arizona in 1848." *Plateau,* 17 (January, 1945), 41-45.

———: "How Don Pedro de Tovar Discovered the Hopi and Don Garcia Lopez de Cardenas Saw the Grand Canyon, with Notes upon Their Probable Route." *Plateau,* 12 (January, 1940), 37-45.

Bartlett, Richard A.: *Great Surveys of the American West.* Norman: University of Oklahoma Press, 1962.

Bass, William Wallace: *Adventures in the Canyons of the Colorado by Two of Its Earliest Explorers, James White and W. W. Hawkins, with an Introduction and Notes.* Grand Canyon, Ariz.: the authors, 1920.

———: Papers. MSS, Arizona Collection, Hayden Library, Arizona State University, Tempe.

Bassford, Amy O., and Fritiof Fryxell, eds.: *Home-Thoughts from Afar, Letters of Thomas Moran to Mary Nimmo Moran.* East Hampton, N.Y.: East Hampton Free Library, 1967.

Beadle, J. H.: *Western Wilds, and the Men Who Redeem Them: an Authentic Narrative, Embracing an Account of Seven Years Travel and Adventure in the Far West; Wild Life in Arizona; Perils of the Plains; Life in Cañon and Death on the Desert; Adventures Among the Red and White Savages of the West; the Mountain Meadow Massacre; the Custer Defeat; Life and Death of Brigham Young.* Cincinnati and Chicago: Jones Brothers and Company, 1879.

Beal, Merrill D.: *Grand Canyon, the Story Behind the Scenery.* Flagstaff, Ariz.: KC Publications, 1967.

Beale, E. F.: "Wagon Road—Fort Smith to Colorado River." U.S. 36th Cong., 1st Sess., House Ex. Doc. 42. Washington, D.C.: Thomas H. Ford, 1860.

———: "Wagon Road from Fort Defiance to the Colorado River." U.S. 35th Cong., 1st Sess., House Ex. Doc. 124. Washington, D.C.: James B. Steedman, 1858.

Beaman, E. O.: "The Cañon of the Colorado, and the Moquis Pueblos: a Wild Ride through the Cañons and Rapids; a Visit to the Seven Cities of the Desert; Glimpses of Mormon Life." *Appleton's Journal,* XV (April 18–May 30, 1874).

———: "Notes of the Powell Expedition and the Moquis Pueblos." Salt Lake *Tribune,* October 28, 1872.

Beckwith, E. G.: "Report of Explorations for a Route for the Pacific Railroad, by Capt. J. W. Gunnison, Topographical Engineers, near the 38th and 39th Parallels of North Latitude, from the Mouth of the Kansas River, Mo., to the Sevier Lake, in the Great Basin," in *Reports of Explorations and Surveys to Ascertain the Most Practicable and Economical Route for Railroad from the Mississippi to the Pacific Ocean,* II. Washington, D.C.: Beverley Tucker, 1855. Pp. 9-114.

Belknap, Bill, and Frances Spencer Belknap: *Gunnar Widforss, Painter of Grand Canyon.* Flagstaff, Ariz.: Museum of Northern Arizona by the Northland Press, 1969.

Belknap, Buzz: *Powell Centennial Grand Canyon River Guide.* Salt Lake City: Canyonlands Press, 1969.

Bell, William A.: *New Tracks in North America, a Journal of Travel and Adventure Whilst Engaged in a Survey for a Southern Railroad to the Pacific Ocean, 1867-68.* Second edition. London: Chapman and Hall, 1870.

Bender, A. B.: "Government Explorations in the Territory of New Mexico, 1846-1859." *New Mexico Historical Review,* IX (January, 1934), 1-32.

———: *The March of Empire, Frontier Defense in the Southwest, 1848-1860.* Lawrence: University of Kansas Press, 1952.

Bentley, Harold W.: *A Dictionary of Spanish Terms in English, with Special Reference to the American Southwest.* New York: Columbia University Press, 1932.

Bieber, Ralph P., ed., with Averam B. Bender: *Exploring Southwestern Trails, 1846-1854, by Philip St. George Cooke, William Henry Chase Whiting, François Xavier Aubry.* Glendale, Cal.: Arthur H. Clark, 1938.

Bingham, Edwin R.: *Charles F. Lummis, Editor of the Southwest.* San Marino, Cal.: The Huntington Library, 1955.

Birdseye, C. H.: "Exploration in the Grand Canyon." *Reclamation Era,* 28 (August, 1938), 170-171.

Birdseye, Claude H., and Raymond C. Moore: "A Boat Voyage Through the Grand Canyon of the Colorado." *Geographical Review,* XIV (April, 1924), 177-196.

Birdseye, R. W.: "Greatest Ladder in the World Built on the Cliff of Havasu Canyon." *Travel,* 46 (December, 1925), 33.

Bishop, F. M.: "Letters to the Bloomington, Illinois, Daily *Pantagraph,* June 17–February, 1872." *Utah Historical Quarterly,* XV (1947), 239-253.

Bleak, James G.: "Annals of the Southern Utah Mission, Book A to 1869." MS, L.D.S. Church Historian's Office Library, abridged copy, Utah State Historical Society, Salt Lake City.

Bolton, Herbert E.: *Coronado, Knight of Pueblos and Plains.* Albuquerque: University of New Mexico Press, 1949.

———: "Escalante in Dixie and the Arizona Strip." *New Mexico Historical Review,* III (January, 1928), 41-72.

———, ed.: *Font's Complete Diary, a Chronicle of the Founding of San Francisco, Translated from the Original Spanish Manuscript.* Berkeley: University of California Press, 1931.

———: *Outpost of Empire, the Story of the Founding of San Francisco.* New York: Alfred A. Knopf, 1939.

———: *Pageant in the Wilderness, the Story of the Escalante Expedition to the Interior Basin, 1776, Including the Diary and Itinerary of Father Escalante, Translated and Annotated.* Salt Lake City: Utah State Historical Society, 1950.

———: *Spanish Exploration in the Southwest, 1542-1706.* New York: Charles Scribner's Sons, 1916.

Bradshaw, Hazel, ed.: *Under Dixie Sun, a History of Washington*

County by Those Who Loved Their Forebears. Panguitch, Utah: Washington County Chapter, Daughters of the Utah Pioneers, 1950.

Brandes, Ray: *Frontier Military Posts in Arizona.* Globe, Ariz.: Dale S. King, 1960.

Brooks, Juanita: "The Arizona Strip." *Pacific Spectator,* 3 (Winter, 1949), 290–301.

———: "Indian Relations on the Mormon Frontier." *Utah Historical Quarterly,* XII (January–April, 1944), 1–68.

———: "Jacob Hamblin, Apostle to the Indians." *Arizona Highways,* XIX (April, 1943), 31–35.

———: *John Doyle Lee, Zealot-Pioneer-Scapegoat.* Glendale, Cal.: Arthur H. Clark, 1962.

———, ed.: "Journal of Thales H. Haskell." *Utah Historical Quarterly,* XII (January–April, 1944), 69–98.

———: "Lee's Ferry at Lonely Dell." *Utah Historical Quarterly,* XXV (October, 1957), 283–295.

———: *The Mountain Meadows Massacre.* Stanford, Cal.: Stanford University Press, 1950. Second edition, Norman: University of Oklahoma Press, 1963.

———: "Silver Reef." *Utah Historical Quarterly,* XXIX (July, 1961), 281–287.

———: "Utah's Dixie, the Cotton Mission." *Utah Historical Quarterly,* XXIX (July, 1961).

Browne, J. Ross: *Report on the Mineral Resources of the States and Territories West of the Rocky Mountains.* Washington, D.C.: Government Printing Office, 1868.

Brown, James S.: *Life of a Pioneer, Autobiography of James S. Brown.* Salt Lake City: George Q. Cannon and Sons, 1900.

Bryant, William Cullen, ed.: *Picturesque America; or, the Land We Live in: a Delineation by Pen and Pencil.* New York: D. Appleton, 1872–1874. 2 vols.

Bryce, James: "The Scenery of North America." *National Geographic Magazine,* XLI (April, 1922), 339–389.

Bufkin, Donald: "The Lost County of Pah-Ute," *Journal of Arizona History,* V (Summer, 1964), 1–11.

Buggeln, Martin: Papers, 1895–1938. MSS, Northern Arizona University Library, Flagstaff, Ariz.; 3 file boxes.

Bulger, Harold A.: "First Man Through the Grand Canyon." *Bulletin of the Missouri Historical Society,* XVII (July, 1961), 321–331.

Burroughs, John: "The Grand Cañon of the Colorado." *Century Magazine,* LXXXI (January, 1911), 425–438.

Butchart, J. Harvey: "Backpacking Grand Canyon Trails." *Summit,* 10 (June, 1964), 12–15, 18.

———: "Backpacking on the Colorado." *Appalachia,* n.s., XXVI (December, 1960), 176–182.

———: "Grand Canyon's Remote Upper Corner." *Summit,* 14 (March, 1968), 23–28.

———: "The Grandview Trail." *Plateau,* 31 (October, 1958), 37–40.

———: "The Lower Gorge of the Little Colorado." *Arizona Highways,* XLI (September, 1965), 34–42.

———: "Old Trails in Grand Canyon." *Appalachia,* n.s., XXVIII (June, 1962), 45–64.

———: "Wotan's Throne." *Summit,* 11 (September, 1965), 8–11.

Butler, B. S., G. F. Loughlin, V. C. Heikes, and others: "The Ore deposits of Utah." U.S. Geological Survey *Professional Paper,* 111. Washington, D.C.: Government Printing Office, 1920.

C

Cameron, Ralph Henry: Papers, 1890–1915. MSS, Special Collections, University of Arizona Library, Tucson; 5 boxes and 1 vol.

Camp, Charles L., ed.: *George C. Young and His Chronicles of the West, Comprising Extracts from His "Memoirs" and from the Orange Clark "Narrative."* Denver: Old West Publishing Company, 1966.

Carroll, Elsie Chamberlain, comp.: *History of Kane County.* Salt Lake City: Utah Printing Company, 1960.

Casanova, Frank E., ed.: "General Crook Visits the Supais, as Reported by John G. Bourke." *Arizona and the West,* 10 (Autumn, 1968), 253–276.

———: "Trails to Supai in Cataract Canyon." *Plateau,* 39 (Winter, 1967), 124–130.

Chalfant, James M., ed.: *Colorado River Controversies,* by Robert Brewster Stanton. Foreword by Julius F. Stone. New York: Dodd, Mead and Company, 1932.

Chittenden, Hiram M.: *The American Fur Trade of the Far West.* New York: F. P. Harper, 1902. 3 vols.

Cleland, Robert Glass: *This Reckless Breed of Men, the Trappers and Fur Traders of the Southwest.* New York: Alfred A. Knopf, 1952.

Cleland, Robert Glass, and Juanita Brooks, eds.: *A Mormon Chronicle, the Diaries of John D. Lee, 1848–1876.* San Marino, Cal.: Huntington Library, 1955. 2 vols.

Cline, Gloria Griffen: *Exploring the Great Basin.* Norman: University of Oklahoma Press, 1963.

Clough, Wilson O.: *The Necessary Earth, Nature and Solitude in American Literature.* Austin: University of Texas Press, 1964.

Cobb, Irvin S.: *Roughing It Deluxe.* Illustrated by John T. McCutcheon. New York: George H. Doran, 1914.

Coconino County, Arizona: "General Index to Mines," 1–3, 1891–1901. MSS, Recorder's Office, Flagstaff, Ariz.

———: "Record of Mines," 1–3, 1891–1900. MSS, County Recorder's Office, Flagstaff, Ariz.

Colorado District, El Dorado Canyon, Nevada: "Mining Laws and Notices of Location, 1863–1865." MS, Mohave Society of History and Art, Kingman, Ariz.

Colton, Harold S.: *The Basaltic Cinder Cones and Lava Flows of the San Francisco Mountain Volcanic Field.* Revised edition. Flagstaff, Ariz.: Museum of Northern Arizona, 1967.

———: *Black Sand, Prehistory in Northern Arizona.* Albuquerque: University of New Mexico Press, 1960.

———: "How Flagstaff Was Named." *Plateau,* 15 (October, 1942), 17–21.

Colton, Harold S., and Frank C. Baxter: *Days in the Painted Desert and the San Francisco Mountains, a Guide.* Flagstaff, Ariz.: Museum of Northern Arizona, 1932.

Conrad, David E.: "The Whipple Expedition in Arizona, 1853–1854." *Arizona and the West*, 11 (Summer, 1969), 147–178.

Cooley, M. E., comp.: *Arizona Highway Geologic Map.* Tucson: Arizona Geological Society, 1967.

———: "Hydrogeologic Reconnaissance of the Surficial Deposits in Grand Canyon, Marble Canyon, and Little Colorado River Gorge, Arizona. Preliminary Report, Subject to Revision." Typescript, Tucson, U.S. Geological Survey, 1967.

Cooley, M. E., J. W. Harshbarger, J. P. Akers, and W. F. Hardt: "Regional Hydrogeology of the Navajo and Hopi Indian Reservations, Arizona, New Mexico, and Utah." U.S. Geological Survey *Professional Paper*, 521-A. Washington, D.C.: Government Printing Office, 1969.

Corbett, Pearson H.: *Jacob Hamblin, the Peacemaker.* Salt Lake City: Deseret News Press, 1952.

Corle, Edwin: *Listen, Bright Angel.* New York: Duel, Sloan and Pearce, 1946.

Corominas, J.: *Diccionario Crítico Etimológico de la Lengua Castellana.* Madrid: Editorial Gredos, 1954. 4 vols.

Cozzens, Samuel Woodworth: *The Ancient Cibola, The Marvelous Country; or, Three Years in Arizona and New Mexico.* Boston: Lee and Shepard, 1876.

Coues, Elliott, ed.: *On the Trail of a Spanish Pioneer, the Diary and Itinerary of Francisco Garcés in His Travels through Sonora, Arizona, and California, 1775–1776, Translated from an Official Contemporaneous Copy of the Original Spanish Manuscript, and Edited, with Copious Critical Notes.* New York: Francis P. Harper, 1900. 2 vols.

Crampton, C. Gregory: "The Discovery of the Green River." *Utah Historical Quarterly*, XX (October, 1952), 299–312.

———, ed.: "F. S. Dellenbaugh of the Colorado: Some Letters Pertaining to the Powell Voyages and the History of the Colorado River." *Utah Historical Quarterly*, XXXVII (Spring, 1969), 214–243.

———: "Historical Sites in Glen Canyon, Mouth of San Juan River to Lee's Ferry." University of Utah *Anthropological Papers*, 46, *Glen Canyon Series*, 12 (June, 1960).

———: "Humboldt's Utah, 1811." *Utah Historical Review*, XXVI (July, 1958), 268–281.

———, ed.: "Military Reconnaissance in Southern Utah, 1866." *Utah Historical Quarterly*, XXXII (Spring, 1964), 145–161.

———: *Standing Up Country, the Canyon Lands of Utah and Arizona.* New York and Salt Lake City: Alfred A. Knopf and the University of Utah Press in Association with the Amon Carter Museum of Western Art, 1964.

Crampton C. Gregory, and Gloria G. Griffen: "The San Buenaventura, Mythical River of the West." *Pacific Historical Review*, XXV (May, 1956), 163–171.

Crampton, C. Gregory, and David E. Miller, eds.: "Journal of Two Campaigns by Utah Territorial Militia Against the Navajo Indians, 1869." *Utah Historical Quarterly*, XXIX (April, 1961), 148–176.

Crampton, C. Gregory, and Dwight L. Smith, eds.: "The Hoskaninni Papers: Mining in Glen Canyon, 1897–1902, by Robert B. Stanton." University of Utah *Anthropological Papers*, 54, *Glen Canyon Series*, 15 (November, 1961).

Cramton, Louis C.: "Bryce Canyon and Scenic Southern Utah." *Congressional Record*, LXV, Part 7 (April 18, 1924), 6651–6652.

———: "Remarks." *Congressional Record*, LXV, Part 4 (March 3, 1924), 3489–3500.

Creer, L. H.: "The Activities of Jacob Hamblin in the Region of the Colorado." University of Utah *Anthropological Papers*, 33, *Glen Canyon Series*, 4 (May, 1958).

———, ed.: *History of Utah 1847 to 1869*, by Andrew Love Neff. Salt Lake City: Deseret News Press, 1940.

———: "Spanish-American Slave Trade in the Great Basin, 1800–1853." *New Mexico Historical Review*, XXIV (July, 1949), 171–183.

Culmsee, Carlton: "The Frontier: Hardy Perennial." *Utah Historical Quarterly*, XXXV (Summer, 1967), 228–235.

Cushing, Frank Hamilton: "The Nation of Willows." *Atlantic Monthly*, L (September–October, 1882), 362–374, 541–559.

———: *The Nation of Willows.* Foreword by Robert C. Euler. Flagstaff, Ariz.: Northland Press, 1965.

Cutter, Donald C., ed.: *The Coronado Expedition, 1540–1542*, by George Parker Winship. Chicago: Rio Grande Press, 1964. Reprint of the work issued by Winship in 1896.

D

Dale, Harrison Clifford: *The Ashley-Smith Explorations and the Discovery of a Central Route to the Pacific, 1822–1829, with the Original Journals.* Revised edition. Glendale, Cal.: Arthur H. Clark, 1941.

Dalton, Luella Adams: *History of the Iron County Mission and Parowan the Mother Town.* N.p., n.d.

Darrah, William Culp, ed.: "The Exploration of the Colorado in 1869" (includes the journals of G. Y. Bradley, J. C. Sumner, and J. W. Powell, together with other original documents and newspaper reports, with biographical sketches). *Utah Historical Quarterly*, XV (1947), 1–153.

———: *Powell of the Colorado.* Princeton: Princeton University Press, 1951.

Darton, N. H.: "A Reconnaissance of Parts of Northwestern New Mexico and Northern Arizona." U.S. Geological Survey *Bulletin*, 435. Washington, D.C.: Government Printing Office, 1910.

———: *Story of the Grand Canyon of Arizona, a Popular Illustrated Account of Its Rocks and Origin.* Kansas City: Fred Harvey, 1917, and later editions.

Darton, N. H., and others: "Guidebook of the Western United States: Part C., the Santa Fe Route with a Side Trip to the Grand Canyon of the Colorado." U.S. Geological Survey *Bulletin*, 613. Washington, D.C.: Government Printing Office, 1915.

Davies, John H.: "From the Journal of John H. Davies." *Heart*

Throbs of the West, 12 (Salt Lake City, 1951), 308–319.

Davis, Daniel E.: *A Résumé of the Scientific Values and Interpretive Potential of the Lower Portion of the Canyon of the Little Colorado River and Its Environs*. Grand Canyon National Park: National Park Service, 1959.

Davis, Sam P., ed.: *The History of Nevada*. Reno and Los Angeles: Elms Publishing Company, 1913. 2 vols.

Davis, W. M.: "An Excursion to the Grand Canyon of the Colorado." *Bulletin of the Museum of Comparative Zoology at Harvard College*, XXXVIII, *Geological Series*, V (May, 1901), 105–201.

Day, A. Grove: *Coronado's Quest, the Discovery of the Southwestern State*. Berkeley and Los Angeles: University of California Press, 1940.

Dellenbaugh, Frederick S.: *A Canyon Voyage: The Narrative of the Second Powell Expedition down the Green–Colorado River from Wyoming, and the Explorations on Land in the Years 1871 and 1872*. Second edition, New Haven: Yale University Press, 1926; first edition, New York and London: G. P. Putnam's Sons, 1908.

———: *Frémont and '49: the Story of a Remarkable Career and Its Relation to the Exploration and Development of Our Western Territory, Especially of California*. New York and London: G. P. Putnam's Sons, 1914.

———: "Memorial to John Wesley Powell." *American Anthropologist*, n.s., 20 (October–December, 1918), 432–436.

———: "A New Valley of Wonders." *Scribner's Magazine*, XXXV (January, 1904), 1–18.

———: *The Romance of the Colorado River: the Story of Its Discovery in 1540, with an Account of the Latter Explorations, and with Special Reference to the Voyages of Powell Through the Line of Great Canyons*. New York and London: G. P. Putnam's Sons, 1902.

Dobyns, Henry F., and Robert C. Euler: "A Brief History of the Northeastern Pai." *Plateau*, 32 (January, 1960), 49–57.

Dobyns, Henry F., and Robert C. Euler: *The Ghost Dance of 1889 Among the Pai Indians of Northwestern Arizona*. Prescott, Ariz.: Prescott College Press, 1967.

Dox, Virginia: "The Grand Canyon." Florence, Ariz., *Enterprise*, September 19, 1891, from the Albuquerque *Citizen*.

Dumke, Glenn S.: "Mission Station to Mining Town: Early Las Vegas." *Pacific Historical Review*, XXII (August, 1953), 257–270.

Dunning, Charles H., with Edward H. Peplow, Jr.: *Rock to Riches: the Story of American Mining Past, Present and Future, as Reflected in the Colorful History of Mining in Arizona, the Nation's Greatest Bonanza*. Phoenix: Southwest Publishing Company, 1959.

Durham, G. Homer, ed.: *The Gospel Kingdom: Selections from the Writings and Discourses of John Taylor, Third President of the Church of Jesus Christ of Latter-day Saints*. Salt Lake City: Bookcraft, 1943.

Dutton, C. E.: *Report on the Geology of the High Plateaus of Utah, with Atlas*. U.S. Geographical and Geological Survey of the Rocky Mountain Region. Washington, D.C.: Government Printing Office, 1880.

———: "Tertiary History of the Grand Cañon District with Atlas." U.S. Geological Survey Monographs, II. Washington, D.C.: Government Printing Office, 1882.

E

Easton, Robert, and Mackenzie Brown: *Lord of Beasts, the Saga of Buffalo Jones*. Foreword by Jack Schaefer. Tucson: University of Arizona Press, 1961.

Eddy, Clyde: *Down the World's Most Dangerous River*. New York: Frederick A. Stokes Company, 1929.

Edmonds, Kermit M., and R. Gwinn Vivian, eds.: "Report of Inspection of Camp Willow Springs, April, 1968." *Plateau*, 41 (Summer, 1968), 14–26.

Edwards, Elbert: "Early Mormon Settlements in Southern Nevada." *Nevada Historical Society Quarterly*, VIII (Spring, 1965), 25–44.

Egan, William M., ed.: *Pioneering the West, 1846 to 1878: Major Howard Egan's Diary, Also Thrilling Experiences of Prefrontier Life Among Indians . . .* Richmond, Utah: Howard R. Egan Estate, 1917.

Eiseman, Jr., Fred B.: "The Hopi Salt Trail." *Plateau*, 32 (October, 1959), 25–32.

Elliott, Russell R., and Helen J. Poulton: *Writings on Nevada, a Selected Bibliography*. Reno: University of Nevada Press, 1963.

Elliott, Wallace W., pub.: *History of Arizona Territory, Showing Its Resources and Advantages, with Illustrations Descriptive of Its Scenery, Residences, Farms, Mines, Mills, Hotels, Business Houses, Schools, Churches, etc.* San Francisco: Wallace W. Elliott, 1884.

Ellis, Bruce T., ed.: "A Ben Wittick Item, 1883; a Letter from Tom Wittick." *El Palacio*, 65 (June, 1958), 95–103.

Emmons, S. F.: "Copper in the Red Beds of the Colorado Plateau Region." U.S. Geological Survey *Bulletin*, 260. Washington, D.C.: Government Printing Office, 1905. Pp. 221–232.

Etulain, Richard W.: "A Dedication to the Memory of Zane Grey, 1872–1939." *Arizona and the West*, 12 (Autumn, 1970), 217–220.

Euler, Robert C.: "Archeological Problems in Western and Northwestern Arizona, 1962." *Plateau*, 35 (Winter, 1963), 78–85.

———: "The Archeology of the Canyon Country," in Don D. Fowler, Robert C. Euler, and Catherine S. Fowler, "John Wesley Powell and the Anthropology of the Canyon Country." U.S. Geological Survey *Professional Paper*, 670. Washington, D.C.: Government Printing Office, 1969. Pp. 8–20.

———: "The Canyon Dwellers." *The American West*, IV (May, 1967), 22–27, 67–71.

———: "Southern Paiute Archaeology." *American Antiquity*, 29 (January, 1964), 379–381.

———: "Southern Paiute Ethnohistory." University of Utah *Anthropological Papers, 78, Glen Canyon Series,* 28 (April, 1966).

———: "Walapai Culture History." Ph.D. dissertation in anthropology, University of New Mexico, 1958.

———: "Willow Figurines from Arizona." *Natural History,* 75 (March, 1966), 62–67.

Farquhar, Francis P.: *The Books of the Colorado River & the Grand Canyon, a Selective Bibliography.* Los Angeles: Glen Dawson, 1953.

———, ed.: *The Colorado River,* by J. B. Kipp. Los Angeles: Muir Dawson, 1950.

Farish, Thomas Edwin: *History of Arizona.* Phoenix: Filmer Brothers Electrotype Company, 1915–1918. 8 vols.

Farrow, E. A.: "The Kaïbab Indians." *Utah Historical Quarterly,* III (1930), 57–59.

Faulk, Odie B.: "The Steamboat War That Opened Arizona." *Arizoniana, the Journal of Arizona History,* V (Winter, 1964), 1–9.

Fenneman, Nevin M.: *Physiography of Western United States.* New York and London: McGraw-Hill, 1931.

Ferris, H. A., and J. E. Busch: "Bridal Falls Mines in Cataract Canyon." *Arizona Mining Journal,* VIII (September, 1924), 9–10, 23–24.

Flagstaff, Ariz., *Coconino Sun,* June 13, September 26, October 8, 1891; May 5, 12, 19, 26, June 2, 9, 16, November 10, 1892; and February 8, 1902.

Fleming, L. A.: "The Settlements on the Muddy, 1865–1871, 'a God Forsaken Place.'" *Utah Historical Quarterly,* XXXV (Spring, 1967), 147–172.

Fletcher, Colin: *The Man Who Walked Through Time.* New York: Alfred A. Knopf, 1967.

Foreman, Grant, ed.: *A Pathfinder in the Southwest: the Itinerary of Lieutenant A. W. Whipple During His Exploration for a Railway Route from Fort Smith to Los Angeles in the Years 1853 and 1854.* Norman: University of Oklahoma Press, 1941.

Forrest, Earle R.: *Arizona's Dark and Bloody Ground.* Introduction by William Macleod Raine. Revised edition. Caldwell, Idaho: Caxton Printers, 1950.

———: "A Cattle Town of the Old West." *Travel,* 43 (June, 1924), 14–17, 44.

———: "Riding for the Old C O Bar." *Arizoniana, the Journal of Arizona History,* V (Spring, 1964), 1–19.

"Four Great Highways from Sea to Sea." *Literary Digest,* LXXVII (May 26, 1923), 59–65.

Fowler, Don D., and Catherine S. Fowler: "The Ethnography of the Canyon Country," in Don D. Fowler, Robert C. Euler, and Catherine S. Fowler: "John Wesley Powell and the Anthropology of the Canyon Country." U.S. Geological Survey *Professional Paper,* 670. Washington, D.C.: Government Printing Office, 1969. Pp. 20–28.

———: "John Wesley Powell, Anthropologist." *Utah Historical Quarterly,* XXXVII (Spring, 1969), 152–172.

———: "John Wesley Powell's Anthropological Fieldwork," in Don D. Fowler, Robert C. Euler, and Catherine S. Fowler: "John Wesley Powell and the Anthropology of the Canyon Country." U.S. Geological Survey *Professional Paper,* 670. Washington, D.C.: Government Printing Office, 1969. Pp. 2–7.

———: "John Wesley Powell's Journal: Colorado River Exploration, 1871–1872." *The Smithsonian Journal of History,* 3 (Summer, 1968), 1–44.

Fowler, Don D., Robert C. Euler, and Catherine S. Fowler: "John Wesley Powell and the Anthropology of the Canyon Country." U.S. Geological Survey *Professional Paper,* 670. Washington, D.C.: Government Printing Office, 1969.

Freeman, Lewis R.: *The Colorado River: Yesterday, Today and Tomorrow.* New York: Dodd, Mead, 1923.

———: *Down the Grand Canyon.* London: William Heineman, 1924.

———: "Surveying the Grand Canyon of the Colorado." *National Geographic Magazine,* XLV (May, 1924), 471–548.

Frémont, John Charles: *Geographical Memoir upon Upper California in Illustration of His Map of Oregon and California, Addressed to the Senate of the United States.* U.S. 30th Congress, 1st Sess., Sen. Misc. Doc. 148. Washington, D.C.: Wendell and Van Benthuysen, 1848.

———: *Report of the Exploring Expedition to the Rocky Mountains in the Year 1842, and to Oregon and North California in the Years 1843–44.* U.S. 28th Congress, 2nd Sess., House Ex. Doc. 166. Washington, D.C.: Blair and Rives, 1845.

Fryxell, Fritiof, ed.: *Thomas Moran, Explorer in Search of Beauty.* East Hampton, N.Y.: East Hampton Free Library, 1958.

Fuchs, James R.: "A History of Williams, Arizona, 1876–1951." University of Arizona *Bulletin,* XXIV, No. 5, *Social Science Bulletin,* 23 (November, 1953).

Furniss, Norman F.: *The Mormon Conflict, 1850–1859.* New Haven, Conn.: Yale University Press, 1960.

Galvin, John, ed.: *A Record of Travels in Arizona and California, 1775–1776, Fr. Francisco Garcés, a New Translation.* San Francisco: John Howell, 1965.

Garrison, Lon: "John Hance, Guide, Trail Builder, Miner, and Windjammer of the Grand Canyon." *Arizona Highways,* XXV (June, 1946), 4–11.

Gilbert, E. W.: *The Exploration of Western America, 1800–1850, an Historical Geography.* Cambridge, Mass.: The University Press, 1933.

Gilbert, G. K.: "Report on the Geology of Portions of Nevada, Utah, California, and Arizona, Examined in the Years 1871 and 1872," in U.S. Geographical and Geological Explorations and Surveys West of the Hundredth Meridian, *Report upon Geographical and Geological Explorations and Surveys West of the Hun-*

dredth Meridian, III: *Geology.* Washington, D.C.: Government Printing Office, 1875. Pp. 17–187.

———: *Report on the Geology of the Henry Mountains.* U.S. Geographical and Geological Survey of the Rocky Mountain Region. Washington, D.C.: Government Printing Office, 1877.

Goetzmann, William H.: *Army Explorations in the American West, 1803–1863.* New Haven, Conn.: Yale University Press, 1959.

———: *Exploration and Empire, the Explorer and the Scientist in the Winning of the American West.* New York: Alfred A. Knopf, 1966.

———: *The Personal Narrative of James O. Pattie, the 1831 Edition Unabridged.* Philadelphia: J. B. Lippincott, 1962.

"Golden Rail Laying, Cedar City, Utah." *Union Pacific Magazine* (October, 1923), 15.

Goldman, Rosalie: "The Wrinkled Pink Walls of Kanab Canyon." *Arizona Highways,* XL (July, 1964), 16–35.

Goldwater, Barry M.: *Delightful Journey down the Green and Colorado Rivers.* Tempe, Ariz.: Arizona Historical Foundation, 1970.

———: "An Odyssey of the Green and Colorado." *Arizona Highways,* XVII (January, 1941), 6–13, 30–37.

Golzé, Alfred R.: *Reclamation in the United States.* New York: McGraw-Hill, 1952.

Goodman, David M.: *Arizona Odyssey, Bibliographic Adventures in Nineteenth-century Magazines.* Tempe, Ariz.: Arizona Historical Foundation, 1969.

"Grand Canyon Bridge." *Arizona Highways,* V (May, 1929).

Granger, Byrd H.: *Will C. Barnes' Arizona Place Names, Revised and Enlarged.* Tucson: University of Arizona Press, 1960.

Greever, William S.: *Arid Domain, the Santa Fe Railway and Its Western Land Grant.* Stanford, Cal.: Stanford University Press, 1954.

Gregory, Herbert E., ed.: "Diary of Almon Harris Thompson, Geographer, Explorations of the Colorado River of the West and Its Tributaries, 1871–1875." *Utah Historical Quarterly,* VII (January–July, 1939), 3–138.

———: "The Geology and Geography of the Paunsaugunt Region, Utah: a Survey of Parts of Garfield and Kane Counties." U.S. Geological Survey *Professional Paper,* 276. Washington, D.C.: Government Printing Office, 1951.

———: "Geology and Geography of the Zion Park Region, Utah and Arizona: a Comprehensive Report on a Scenic and Historic Region of the Southwest." U.S. Geological Survey *Professional Paper,* 220. Washington, D.C.: Government Printing Office, 1950.

———: "Geology of Eastern Iron Country." Utah Geological and Mineralogical Survey *Bulletin,* No. 37 (February, 1950).

———: "Geology of the Navajo Country: a Reconnaissance of Parts of Arizona, New Mexico, and Utah." U.S. Geological Survey *Professional Paper,* 93. Washington, D.C.: Government Printing Office, 1917.

———: "The Navajo Country, a Geographic and Hydrographic Reconnaissance of Parts of Arizona, New Mexico, and Utah."

U.S. Geological Survey *Water-Supply Paper,* 380. Washington, D.C.: Government Printing Office, 1961.

———: "Oasis of Tuba City, Arizona." *Annals of the Association of American Geographers,* 5 (1915), 110–119.

———: "Population of Southern Utah." *Economic Geography,* 21 (January, 1945), 29–57.

———: "Scientific Explorations in Southern Utah." *American Journal of Science,* 243 (October, 1945), 527–549.

Gregory, H. E., and Raymond C. Moore: "The Kaiparowits Region, a Geographic and Geologic Reconnaissance of Parts of Utah and Arizona." U.S. Geological Survey *Professional Paper,* 164. Washington, D.C.: Government Printing Office, 1931.

Grey, Zane: *The Last of the Plainsmen.* New York: Outing Publishing Company, 1908.

———: *Tales of Lonely Trails.* New York and London: Harper and Brothers, 1922.

Grofé, Ferde: "Story of the Grand Canyon Suite." *Arizona Highways,* XIV (December, 1938), 6–9.

Hafen, LeRoy R., and Ann W. Hafen, eds.: *Central Route to the Pacific by Gwinn Harris Heap, with Related Material on Railroad Explorations and Indian Affairs by Edward F. Beale, Thomas H. Benton, Kit Carson, and Col. E. A. Hitchcock, and in Other Documents, 1853–54.* Glendale, Cal.: Arthur H. Clark, 1957.

———: *Journals of Forty-Niners, Salt Lake to Los Angeles, with Diaries and Contemporary Records of Sheldon Young, James S. Brown, Jacob Y. Stover, Charles C. Rich, Addison Pratt, Howard Egan, Henry W. Bigler, and Others, Edited with Historical Comment.* Glendale, Cal.: Arthur H. Clark, 1954.

———: *Old Spanish Trail, Santa Fe to Los Angeles, with Extracts from Contemporary Records and Including Diaries of Antonio Armijo and Orville Pratt.* Glendale, Cal.: Arthur H. Clark, 1954.

———: *The Utah Expedition, 1857–1858: a Documentary Account of the United States Military Movement Under Colonel Albert Sidney Johnston, and the Resistance of Brigham Young and the Mormon Nauvoo Legion.* Glendale, Cal.: Arthur H. Clark, 1958.

Hafner, Arabell Lee, comp.: *100 Years on the Muddy.* Springville, Utah: Art City Publishing Company, 1967.

Hall, Sharlot M.: "Beautiful Havasu, the Great Arm of Grand Canyon." *Out West,* XXIII (October, 1905), 305–317.

———: "A Christmas at Grand Canyon." *Out West,* XXVI (January, 1907), 3–14.

Hamblin, W. Kenneth, and J. Keith Rigby: "Guidebook to the Colorado River. Part 1: Lee's Ferry to Phantom Ranch in Grand Canyon National Park. Part 2: Phantom Ranch in Grand Canyon National Park to Lake Mead, Arizona–Nevada." Brigham Young University *Geology Studies,* 15, Parts 2, 5, *Studies for Students,* 4–5 (1968–1969).

Hamblin, W. Kenneth, and Joseph R. Murphy: *Grand Canyon Perspectives, a Guide to the Canyon Scenery by Means of Interpretive Panoramas.* Illustrations by William L. Chesser. Provo, Utah: Brigham Young University, 1969.

Hammond, George P.: "The Search for the Fabulous in the Settlement of the Southwest." *Utah Historical Quarterly,* XXIV (January, 1956), 1–19.

Hammond, George P., and Agapito Rey, eds.: *Don Juan de Oñate, Colonizer of New Mexico, 1595–1628.* Albuquerque: University of New Mexico Press, 1953. 2 vols.

———: *Narratives of the Coronado Expedition, 1540–1542.* Albuquerque: University of New Mexico Press, 1940.

Hanna, Phil Townsend: "Behind the Beyond." *Progressive Arizona,* VII (October, 1928), 12–15, 25–26, 31–32.

Harris, Fisher S.: "Scrapbook, See America First. Correspondence and Clippings, October, 1905–January, 1906." Salt Lake City: Utah State Historical Society. 2 vols.

Harris, W. R.: *The Catholic Church in Utah, Including an Exposition of Catholic Faith by Bishop Scanlan; a Review of Spanish and Missionary Exploration; Tribal Divisions: Names and Regional Habits of Pre-European Tribes; the Journal of the Franciscan Explorers and Discoverers of Utah Lake; the Trailing of the Priests from Santa Fe. With a Map of the Route, Illustrations and Delimitations of the Great Basin.* Salt Lake City: Intermountain Catholic Press, 1909.

Haskett, Bert: "Early History of the Cattle Industry in Arizona." *Arizona Historical Review,* VI (October, 1935), 3–42.

———: "History of the Sheep Industry in Arizona." *Arizona Historical Review,* VII (July, 1936), 3–49.

Hayden, F. V.: *The Yellowstone National Park and the Mountain Regions of Portions of Idaho, Nevada, Colorado and Utah, Illustrated by Chromolithographic Reproductions of Watercolors by Thomas Moran, Artist to the Expedition of 1871.* Boston: L. Prang and Company, 1876.

Hedin, Sven: *Grand Canyon.* Stockholm: Albert Boniers Förlag, 1925.

Hegemann, Elizabeth Compton: *Navaho Trading Days.* Albuquerque: University of New Mexico Press, 1963.

Henderson, James D.: "Meals by Fred Harvey." *Arizona and the West,* 8 (Winter, 1966), 305–322.

———: *"Meals by Fred Harvey," a Phenomenon of the American West.* Fort Worth: Texas Christian University Press, 1969.

Hewett, D. F.: "Geology and Ore Deposits of the Goodsprings Quadrangle, Nevada." U.S. Geological Survey *Professional Paper,* 162. Washington, D.C.: Government Printing Office, 1931.

Higgins, C. A.: *Grand Cañon of the Colorado River, Arizona, with Original Illustrations by Thomas Moran, H. F. Farny, and F. H. Lungren.* Chicago: Passenger Department, Santa Fe Route, 1893.

———: *Titan of Chasms, the Grand Canyon of Arizona.* Chicago: Rand McNally, 1913.

Hill, James M.: "The Grand Gulch Mining Region, Mohave County, Arizona." U.S. Geological Survey *Bulletin,* 580. Washington, D.C.: Government Printing Office, 1915. Pp. 39–58.

Hine, Robert V.: *Edward Kern and American Expansion.* New Haven, Conn.: Yale University Press, 1962.

Hochderfer, George: *Flagstaff Whoa! The Autobiography of a Western Pioneer.* Flagstaff: Museum of Northern Arizona, 1965.

Hodge, Frederick Webb: *History of Hawikuh, New Mexico, One of the So-Called Cities of Cíbola.* Los Angeles: Southwest Museum, 1937.

———, ed.: *Spanish Explorers in the Southern United States, 1528–1543 . . . The Narrative of the Expedition of Coronado by Pedro de Castañeda.* New York: Charles Scribner's Sons, 1907.

Holmes, Burton: *Travelogues,* 6. New York: McClure, 1901.

Holmes, William Henry: "Random Records of a Lifetime Devoted to Science and Art, 1846–1932." MS, National Collection of Fine Arts, Smithsonian Institution, Washington, D.C. 15 vols.

Horan, James D.: *Timothy O'Sullivan, America's Forgotten Photographer.* New York: Bonanza Books, 1966.

Hough, Emerson: "The President's Forest." *Saturday Evening Post,* 194 (January 21, 1922), 23, 57–58, 60, 63.

Hufford, Kenneth: "William H. Hardy: Merchant of the Upper Colorado, by John L. Riggs." *Journal of Arizona History,* VI (Winter, 1965), 177–187.

Hughes, J. Donald: *The Story of Man at Grand Canyon.* Grand Canyon: Grand Canyon Natural History Association, 1967.

Hulse, James W.; *The Nevada Adventure, a History.* Reno: University of Nevada Press, 1965.

Humboldt, Alexander von: *Political Essay on the Kingdom of New Spain. Containing Researches Relative to the Geography of Mexico, the Extent of Its Surface and Its Political Division into Intendancies, the Physical Aspect of the Country, the Population, the State of Agriculture and Manufacturing and Commercial Industry, the Canals Projected Between the South Sea and the Atlantic Ocean, the Crown Revenues, the Quantity of Precious Metals Which Have Flowed from Mexico into Europe and Asia Since the Discovery of the New Continent, and the Military Defense of New Spain. With Physical Sections and Maps, Founded on Astronomical Observations, and Trigonometrical and Barometrical Measurements.* Translated from the original French by John Black. London: Longman, Hurst, Rees, Orme and Brown, 1811. 4 vols. and atlas.

Hunt, Charles B.: "Cenozoic Geology of the Colorado Plateau." U.S. Geological Survey *Professional Paper,* 279. Washington, D.C.: Government Printing Office, 1956.

———: "Geologic History of the Colorado River." U.S. Geological Survey *Professional Paper,* 669. Washington, D.C.: Government Printing Office, 1969. Pp. 59–130.

———: *Physiography of the United States.* San Francisco and London: W. H. Freeman, 1967.

Hunter, Milton R.: *Brigham Young the Colonizer.* Independence, Mo.: Zion's Printing and Publishing Company, 1945.

———: "The Mormons and the Colorado River." *American Historical Review,* XLIV (April, 1939), 549–555.

Huth, Hans: *Nature and the American: Three Centuries of Changing Attitudes.* Berkeley and Los Angeles: University of California Press, 1957.

I

Iliff, Flora Gregg: *People of the Blue Water: My Adventures Among the Walapai and Havasupai Indians.* New York: Harper and Brothers, 1954.

Ives, Joseph C.: *Report upon the Colorado River of the West, Explored in 1857 and 1858.* U.S. 36th Congress, 1st Sess., House Ex. Doc. 90. Washington, D.C.: Government Printing Office, 1861.

Ives, Ronald L.: "Reconnaissance of the Zion Hinterland." *Geographical Review,* XXXVII (1947), 618–638.

Ivins, Anthony W.: "Traveling Forgotten Trails, a Mystery of Grand Canyon Solved." *Improvement Era,* XXVII (September, 1924), 1017–1025.

J

Jackson, W. Turrentine: *Wagon Roads West: a Study of Federal Road Surveys and Construction in the Trans-Mississippi West, 1846–1869.* Berkeley and Los Angeles: University of California Press, 1952.

James, George Wharton: *Arizona the Wonderland.* Boston: Page Company, 1917.

———: *The Grand Canyon of Arizona, How to See It.* Boston: Little, Brown, 1910.

———: *In and Around the Grand Canyon: the Grand Canyon of the Colorado River in Arizona.* Boston: Little, Brown, 1900.

———: *Indians of the Painted Desert Region: Hopis, Navahoes, Wallapais, Havasupais.* Boston: Little, Brown. 1903.

———: *Utah, the Land of Blossoming Valley.* Boston: Page Company, 1922.

James, Harlean: *Romance of the National Parks.* New York: Macmillan Company, 1939.

Jeffers, LeRoy: "Temple of the Gods in Utah." *Scientific American,* CXIX (October 5, 1918), 1.

Jennings, E. P.: "The Copper-deposits of the Kaibab Plateau, Arizona." *Transactions of the American Institute of Mining Engineers,* XXXIV (1903), 839–841.

Jennings, Jesse D.: "The Desert West," in Jesse D. Jennings and Edward Norbeck, eds.: *Prehistoric Man in the New World.* Chicago: University of Chicago Press for William Marsh Rice University, 1964. Pp. 149–174.

Jenson, Andrew: *Encyclopedic History of the Church of Jesus Christ of Latter-day Saints.* Salt Lake City: Deseret News Publishing Company, 1941.

———: "History of the Las Vegas Mission." *Nevada State Historical Society Papers,* V (1925–1926), 117–284.

Jett, Stephen C.: *Navajo Wildlands: "As Long as the Rivers Shall Run."* With Selections from Willa Cather, Oliver La Farge, and others, and from the Navajo Creation Myth and Navajo Chants. Edited by Kenneth Brower, foreword by David Brower, photographs by Philip Hyde. San Francisco: Sierra Club, 1967.

Johnson, W. D., Jr.: "The Powell Expedition." Salt Lake City *Deseret News,* May 29, 1872.

Johnston, Philip: "A National Park in the Desert." *Touring Topics,* 23 (January, 1931), 12–21, 55.

Jones, Daniel W.: *Forty Years Among the Indians.* Salt Lake City: Juvenile Instructor's Office, 1890.

Judd, B. Ira: "Tuba City, Mormon Settlement." *Journal of Arizona History,* 10 (Spring, 1969), 37–42.

Judge, Joseph: "Retracing John Wesley Powell's Historic Voyage down the Grand Canyon." *National Geographic,* 135 (May, 1969), 668–713.

K

Keithley, Ralph: *Buckey O'Neill.* Caldwell, Idaho: Caxton Printers, 1949.

Kelly, Charles, ed.: "Captain Francis Marion Bishop's Journal, August 15, 1870–June 3, 1872." *Utah Historical Quarterly,* XV (1947), 159–238.

———: "John D. Lee's Lost Gold Mine." *Desert Magazine,* IX (August, 1946), 9–11.

———. "Journal of W. C. Powell, April 21, 1071–December 7, 1072." *Utah Historical Quarterly,* XVI–XVII (1948–1949), 253–478.

———: "The Three Who Lost." *Desert Magazine,* 8 (April, 1945), 4–6.

Kelly, Isabel T.: "Southern Paiute Bands." *American Anthropologist,* n.s., 36 (1934), 548–560.

———: "Southern Paiute Ethnography." University of Utah *Anthropological Papers,* 69, Glen Canyon Series, 21 (May, 1964).

Kelly, Roger E.: "Flagstaff's Frontier Fort: 1881–1920." *Plateau,* 36 (Spring, 1964), 101–106.

Kiesel, H. C.: "Exploring Expedition." Salt Lake *Tribune,* July 30, 1873.

Kitt, Edith: "Motoring in Arizona in 1914." *Journal of Arizona History,* 11 (Spring, 1970), 32–65.

Kleinsorge, Paul L.: *The Boulder Canyon Project, Historical and Economic Aspects.* Foreword by Eliot Jones. Stanford, Cal.: Stanford University Press, 1941.

Kolb, Ellsworth L.: *Through the Grand Canyon from Wyoming to Mexico.* Foreword by Owen Wister. New York: Macmillan Company, 1914.

Kolb, Ellsworth L., and Emery C. Kolb: "Experiences in the Grand Canyon." *National Geographic Magazine,* XXVI (August, 1914), 99–184.

Koons, E. Donaldson: "Geology of the Unikaret Plateau, Northern Arizona." *Bulletin of the Geological Society of America,* 14 (February, 1945), 151–180.

Korn, Bertram Wallace, ed.: . . . *Incidents of Travel and Adventure in the Far West, by Solomon Nunes Carvalho.* Philadelphia: Jewish Publication Society, 1954.

Kroeber, A. L., ed.: "Walapai Ethnography," by Fred Kniffen, Gordon MacGregor, Robert McKennan, Scudder McKeel, and Maurice Mook, *Memoirs of the American Anthropological Association, 42, Contributions from the Laboratory of Anthropology,* I (1935).

Kroeber, Clifton B., ed.: "The Route of James O. Pattie on the Colorado in 1826, a Reappraisal by A. L. Kroeber with Comments by R. C. Euler and A. H. Schroeder." *Arizona and the West,* 6 (Summer, 1964), 119–136.

Krutch, Joseph Wood: *Grand Canyon, Today and All Its Yesterdays.* New York: William Sloane Associates, 1958. New edition as *Grand Canyon.* New York: Doubleday and the American Museum of Natural History, 1962.

L

Larson, Andrew Karl: *"I Was Called to Dixie": The Virgin River Basin, Unique Experiences in Mormon Pioneering.* Salt Lake City: Deseret News Press, 1961.

———: *The Red Hills of November, a Pioneer Biography of Utah's Cotton Town.* Salt Lake City: Deseret News Press, 1957.

———: "Zion National Park, with Some Reminiscences Fifty Years Later." *Utah Historical Quarterly,* XXXVII (Fall, 1969), 408–425.

Larson, Gustive O.: *Iron County Centennial, 1851–1951.* Cedar City, Utah: n.p., 1951.

LaRue, E. C.: "Colorado River and Its Utilization." U.S. Geological Survey *Water-supply Paper,* 395. Washington, D.C.: Government Printing Office, 1916.

———: "Water Power and Flood Control of the Colorado River Below Green River, Utah." U.S. Geological Survey *Water-supply Paper,* 556. Washington, D.C.: Government Printing Office, 1925.

Lauritzen, Jonreed: "Arizona Strip, the Lonesome Country." *Arizona Highways,* 27 (June, 1951), 16–25.

———: "Walls of Fair Color." *Arizona Highways,* 23 (April, 1947), 10–25.

Lauzon, H. R.: "Is There Gold in the Canyon?" *Grand Canyon Nature Notes,* 8 (January, 1934), 233–234.

Leavitt, Francis Hale: "Steam Navigation on the Colorado River." *California Historical Quarterly,* XXII (March–June, 1943), 1–25, 151–174.

Lee, Weston, and Jeanne Lee: *Torrent in the Desert.* Flagstaff, Ariz.: Northland Press, 1962.

Lee, Willis T.: "Geologic Reconnaissance of a Part of Western Arizona, with Notes on the Igneous Rocks by Albert Johannsen." U.S. Geological Survey *Bulletin,* 352. Washington, D.C.: Government Printing Office, 1908.

Leigh, Rufus Wood: *Five Hundred Utah Place Names, Their Origin and Significance.* Salt Lake City: Deseret News Press, 1961.

Leigh, W. R.: "Impressions of an Artist While Camping in the Grand Canyon of the Colorado." *Out West,* 2, n.s. (June, 1911), 15–27.

Lemmon, J. G.: "Grand Cañon of the Colorado." *Overland Monthly,* n.s., XII (September, 1888), 244–256.

Lenon, Robert, ed.: "Documents of Arizona History: the Mines of Gold Basin, a Report of 1883." *Journal of Arizona History,* 8 (Winter, 1967), 256–268.

Leopold, Luna B.: "The Rapids and the Pools—Grand Canyon." U.S. Geological Survey *Professional Paper,* 669. Washington, D.C.: Government Printing Office, 1969. Pp. 131–145.

Leydet, François: *Time and the River Flowing, Grand Canyon.* Edited by David Brower. San Francisco: Sierra Club, 1964.

Lillard, Richard G.: *Desert Challenge, an Interpretation.* New York: Alfred A. Knopf, 1942.

Lindsay, Alexander, Jr., and J. Richard Ambler: "Recent Contributions and Research Problems in Kayenta Anasazi Prehistory." *Plateau,* 35 (Winter, 1963), 86–92.

Lingenfelter, R. E.: *First Through the Grand Canyon.* Foreword by Otis Marston. Los Angeles: Glen Dawson, 1958.

Little, James A.: *Jacob Hamblin: a Narrative of His Personal Experience as a Frontiersman, Missionary to the Indians and Explorer, Disclosing Interpositions of Providence, Severe Privations, Perilous Situations and Remarkable Escapes* . . . Salt Lake City: Juvenile Instructor Office, 1881.

Lockwood, Frank C.: "Captain John Hance." *Desert Magazine,* 3 (July, 1940), 15–18.

———: *Pioneer Portraits, Selected Vignettes.* Introduction by John Bret Harte. Tucson: University of Arizona Press, 1968.

Lombard, Rose: "The Grand Canyon and Bucky O'Neill." MS, Library, Northern Arizona University, Flagstaff.

Long, Paul, Jr.: "Mineral Park: Mohave County Seat, 1877–1887." *Arizoniana, the Journal of Arizona History,* 3 (Summer, 1962), 1–8.

Longwell, Chester R.: "Geology of the Muddy Mountains, Nevada, with a Section through the Virgin Range to the Grand Wash Cliffs, Arizona." U.S. Geological Survey *Bulletin,* 798. Washington, D.C.: Government Printing Office, 1928.

Lummis, Charles F.: "The Grand Canon of the Colorado." *Californian,* IV (June, 1893), 10–22.

———: "The Greatest Thing in the World." *Land of Sunshine,* III (September, 1895), 195–198.

———: "Into the Grand Canyon." *Land of Sunshine,* 9 (August, 1898), 145–149.

———: *Some Strange Corners of Our Country, the Wonderland of the Southwest.* New York: Century Company, 1892.

Lynch, Fred: "An Automobile Trip to the Grand Canyon of Arizona." *Out West,* n.s., 2 (October, 1911), 243–245.

M

McClintock, James H.: *Arizona, Prehistoric, Aboriginal, Pioneer,*

Modern. Chicago: S. J. Clarke Publishing Company, 1916. 3 vols.

———: "Crossing the Mighty Colorado." *Arizona Highways,* IV (October, 1928), 9–10, 19.

———: *Mormon Settlement in Arizona, a Record of Peaceful Conquest of the Desert.* Phoenix: Manufacturing Stationers, 1921.

McGaffey, Ernest: "Inside the Magic Circle." *Arizona Highways,* V (August, 1929), 5–8, 16.

McGregor, John C.: *The Cohonina Culture of Northwestern Arizona.* Urbana: University of Illinois Press, 1951.

———: *Southwestern Archaeology.* Second edition. Urbana: University of Illinois Press, 1965.

McKee, Edwin D.: *Ancient Landscapes of the Grand Canyon Region: the Geology of Grand Canyon, Zion, Bryce, Petrified Forest, and Painted Desert.* Atchison, Kan.: Edwin D. McKee, 1931, and later editions.

———: "Kanab Canyon: The Trail of Scientists." *Plateau,* 18 (January, 1946), 33–42.

McKee, Edwin D., Richard F. Wilson, William J. Breed, and Carol S. Breed: *Evolution of the Colorado River in Arizona, an Hypothesis Developed at the Symposium on Cenozoic Geology of the Colorado Plateau in Arizona, August, 1964.* Flagstaff, Ariz.: Museum of Northern Arizona, 1967.

McNitt, Frank, ed.: *Navaho Expedition: Journal of a Military Reconnaissance from Santa Fe, New Mexico, to the Navaho Country Made in 1849 by Lieutenant James H. Simpson.* Norman: University of Oklahoma Press, 1964.

McOmie, A. M., C. C. Jacobs, and O. C. Bartlett: *The Arizona Strip, Report of a Reconnaissance of the Country North of the Grand Canyon.* Phoenix: Board of Control, 1915.

Macomb, J. N.: *Report of the Exploring Expedition from Santa Fe, New Mexico, to the Junction of the Grand and Green Rivers of the Great Colorado of the West, in 1859, Under the Command of J. N. Macomb, with a Geological Report by Prof. J. S. Newberry.* Washington, D.C.: Government Printing Office, 1876.

Malmquist, Allen J.: "Exploring the Western Grand Canyon." *Sierra Club Bulletin,* 53 (March, 1968), 6–11.

Mann, Dean E.: *The Politics of Water in Arizona.* Tucson: University of Arizona Press, 1963.

Marcy, R. B.: "Application for Command of an Expedition [sic] upon the Colorado River. New York City, June 30, 1853." MS, Washington, D.C., National Archives, Record Group 77.

———: *Thirty Years of Army Life on the Border.* New York: Harper and Brothers, 1866.

Marshall, James: *Santa Fe, the Railroad that Built an Empire.* New York: Random House, 1945.

Marston, Otis R.: "River Runners: Fast Water Navigation." *Utah Historical Quarterly,* XXVIII (July, 1960), 291–308.

Mathews, Mitford M., ed.: *A Dictionary of Americanisms on Historical Principles.* Chicago: University of Chicago Press, 1951.

Matthes, François E.: "Grand Canyon Data—Discovery." MS, File, Grand Canyon National Park Reference Library, 1902–1936.

———: "Place Names in Grand Canyon." MS, File, Grand Canyon National Park Reference Library, 1902–1936.

Matthes, François E., and Richard T. Evans: "Map of Grand Canyon National Park." *Military Engineer,* XVIII (May–June, 1926), 188–201.

Maxson, John H.: *Grand Canyon, Origin and Scenery.* Flagstaff, Ariz.: Grand Canyon Natural History Association, 1962.

Merriam, C. Hart: "Results of a Biological Survey of the San Francisco Mountain Region and the Desert of the Little Colorado." U.S. Department of Agriculture, Bureau of Biological Survey, *Fauna,* 3. Washington, D.C.: Government Printing Office, 1889.

Miller, Albert E.: *The Immortal Pioneers, Founders of St. George, Utah.* N.p.: Albert E. Miller, 1946.

Miller, David E.: "Discovery of Glen Canyon." *Utah Historical Quarterly,* XXVI (July, 1958), 220–237.

———: *Hole-in-the-Rock: an Epic in the Colonization of the Great American West.* Salt Lake City: University of Utah Press, 1959.

Miller, David H.: "The Impact of the Gunnison Massacre on Mormon-Federal Relations: Colonel Edward Jenner Steptoe's Command in Utah Territory, 1854–1855." M.S. thesis, University of Utah, 1968.

Miller, Joaquin: "A New Wonder of the World." *Overland Monthly,* XXXVII (March, 1901), 786–790.

Miller, Joseph, ed.: *Arizona Cavalcade, the Turbulent Times.* New York: Hastings House, 1962.

Mills, Enos A.: *Your National Parks, with Detailed Information for Tourists by Laurence F. Schmeckebier.* Boston and New York: Houghton Mifflin, 1917.

Mitchell, Guy Elliott: "Mukuntuweap, a Desert Yosemite." *Travel,* XXIX (June, 1917), 7–12.

Mohave County, Ariz.: "Mining Record," B, D–F, 1865–1883. MSS, Recorder's Office, Kingman.

Möllhausen, Baldwin: *Diary of a Journey from the Mississippi to the Coasts of the Pacific with a United States Government Expedition.* Introduction by Alexander von Humboldt. Translated by Mrs. Percy Sinnett. London: Longman, Brown, Green, Longmans, and Roberts, 1858. 2 vols.

———: *Reisen in die Felsengebirge Nord-Amerikas bis zum Hoch-Plateau von New-Mexico, Unternommen als Mitglied der im Auftrage der Regierung der Vereinigten Staaten Ausgesandten Colorado-Expedition.* Leipzig: H. Costenoble, 1861. 2 vols.

Monroe, Harriet: "The Grand Cañon of the Colorado." *Atlantic Monthly,* LXXXIV (December, 1899), 816–821.

Mooney, James: "The Ghost-dance Religion and the Sioux Outbreak of 1890." Bureau of American Ethnology, Fourteenth *Annual Report.* Washington, D.C.: Government Printing Office, 1896. Part 2.

Moore, Raymond C.: "Geologic Report on the Inner Gorge of the Grand Canyon of the Colorado River," in E. C. LaRue: "Water Power and Flood Control of the Colorado River Below Green River, Utah." U.S. Geological Survey *Water-Supply Paper,* 556. Washington, D.C.: Government Printing Office, 1925. Pp. 125–171.

Moore, Richard T., and Eldred D. Wilson: "Bibliography of the Geology and Mineral Resources of Arizona, 1848–1964." Arizona Bureau of Mines *Bulletin,* 173. Tucson: University of Arizona Press, 1965.

Morgan, Dale L.: "Introduction. The Exploration of the Colorado River in 1869." *Utah Historical Quarterly*, XV (1947), 1–8.

———: *Jedediah Smith and the Opening of the West*. Indianapolis and New York: Bobbs-Merrill, 1953.

Morgan, Dale L., and others, eds.: "The Exploration of the Colorado River and the High Plateaus of Utah in 1871–72." *Utah Historical Quarterly*, XVI–XVII (1948–1949).

Morrisey, Richard J.: "The Early Range Cattle Industry in Arizona." *Agricultural History*, 24 (July, 1950), 151–156.

"Motor Routes from the Mississippi to the Rockies and the Pacific Coast." *Sunset*, 50 (June, 1923), 36–37.

Muir, John: "The Grand Cañon of the Colorado." *Century Magazine*, LXV (November, 1902), 107–116.

Muir, Leo J.: *A Century of Mormon Activities in California*, I: *Historical*. Salt Lake City: Deseret News Press, n.d.

Murbarger, Nell: "Trail-blazer of Grand Canyon." *Desert Magazine*, 21 (October, 1958), 5–9.

Murphy, James W., comp.: *Speeches and Addresses of Warren G. Harding, President of the United States, Delivered During the Course of His Tour from Washington, D.C., to Alaska and Return to San Francisco, June 20 to August 2, 1923*. Washington, D.C.: privately printed, 1923.

Murphy, Thomas D.: *Seven Wonderlands of the American West*. Boston: L. C. Page Company, 1925.

Myrick, David F.: *Railroads of Nevada and Eastern California*, II: *The Southern Roads*. Berkeley, Cal.: Howell-North Books, 1963.

Nagata, Shuichi: "Modern Transformations of Moenkopi Pueblo." Ph.D. dissertation, Anthropology, University of Illinois, Urbana, 1967.

Nash, Roderick: *Wilderness and the American Mind*. New Haven, Conn., and London: Yale University Press, 1967.

Nelson, Lowery: *The Mormon Village, a Pattern and Technique of Land Settlement*. Salt Lake City: University of Utah Press, 1952.

Nevins, Allan: *Fremont, Pathmarker of the West*. New York: Longmans, Green, 1955.

Nevins, Allan, and Dale L. Morgan, eds.: *Geographical Memoir upon Upper California in Illustration of His Map of Oregon and California by John Charles Fremont, Newly Reprinted from the Edition of 1848 with Introductions*. San Francisco: Book Club of California, 1964.

Nims, F. A.: "Through the Colorado River." *Commonwealth*, III (Denver, August, 1890), 257–272.

———: "Through the Mysterious Cañons of the Colorado." *Overland Monthly*, Second Series, XIX (March, 1892), 253–270.

Noble, Levi F.: "The Shinumo Quadrangle." U.S. Geological Survey *Bulletin*, 549. Washington, D.C.: Government Printing Office, 1914.

Official Program of the Dedication at Grand Canyon Bridge, Arizona, June 14, 15, 1929. Flagstaff, Ariz.: Coconino Sun, 1929.

O'Kane, Walter Collins: *Sun in the Sky*. Norman: University of Oklahoma Press, 1950.

Olsen, Robert W., Jr.: "Pipe Spring, Arizona, and Thereabouts." *Journal of Arizona History*, VI (Spring, 1965), 11–20.

———: "The Powell Survey Kanab Base Line." *Utah Historical Quarterly*, 37 (Spring, 1969), 261–268.

Palmer, William J.: *Report of Surveys Across the Continent in 1867–68, on the Thirty-fifth and Thirty-second Parallels for a Route Extending the Kansas Pacific Railway to the Pacific Ocean at San Francisco and San Diego, December 1st, 1868*. Philadelphia: W. B. Selheimer, 1869.

Palmer, William R.: "Early Day Trading with Nevada Mining Camps." *Utah Historical Quarterly*, XXVI (October, 1958), 353–368.

———: "Indian Names in Utah Geography." *Utah Historical Quarterly*, I (January, 1928), 5–26.

———: "Paiute Indian Homelands." *Utah Historical Quarterly*, VI (July, 1933), 88–102.

———: *Paiute Indian Legends*. Salt Lake City: Deseret Book Company, 1946.

Parkhill, Forbes: *The Blazed Trail of Antoine Leroux*. Los Angeles: Westernlore Press, 1965.

Paul, Rodman Wilson: *Mining Frontiers of the Far West, 1848–1880*. New York: Holt, Rinehart and Winston, 1963.

Peabody, Henry G.: *Glimpses of the Grand Canyon of Arizona*. Kansas City, Mo.: Fred Harvey, 1900.

Peattie, Roderick, ed., and Weldon F. Heald, Edwin D. McKee, and Harold S. Colton: *The Inverted Mountains, Canyons of the West*. New York: Vanguard Press, 1948.

Pendleton, Mark A.: "Memories of Silver Reef." *Utah Historical Quarterly*, III (October, 1930), 98–118.

———: "The Orderville United Order of Zion." *Utah Historical Quarterly*, VII (October, 1939), 141–159.

Peplow, Edward H., Jr.: *History of Arizona*. New York: Lewis Historical Publishing Company, 1958. 3 vols.

Perkins, George E.: *Pioneers of the Western Desert: Romance and Tragedy Along the Old Spanish or Mormon Trail and Historical Events of the Great West*. Los Angeles: Wetzel Publishing Company, 1947.

Peterson, Charles Sharon: "Settlement on the Little Colorado, 1873–1900: a Study of the Processes and Institutions of Mormon Expansion." Ph.D. dissertation, University of Utah, 1967.

Péwé, Troy L.: *Colorado River Guidebook, a Geologic and Geographic Guide from Lee's Ferry to Phantom Ranch, Arizona.* Second edition. Tempe, Ariz.: the author, 1969.

Phillips, Paul C., ed.: *Life in the Rocky Mountains: a Diary of Wanderings on the Sources of the Rivers Missouri, Columbia, and Colorado from February, 1830, to November, 1835, by W. A. Ferris . . . And Supplementary Writings by Ferris with a Detailed Map of the Fur Country Drawn by Ferris in 1836, Edited, and with a Life of Ferris, and a History of Exploration and Fur Trade.* Denver: Old West Publishing Company, 1940.

Plummer, Charles Griffin: "Cutting the Gordian Knot of Inaccessibility." *Improvement Era,* XXXII (August, 1929), 794-803.

Pomeroy, Earl: *In Search of the Golden West, the Tourist in Western America.* New York: Alfred A. Knopf, 1957.

Porter, Eliot, and Don D. Fowler, eds.: *Down the Colorado: John Wesley Powell, Diary of the First Trip Through the Grand Canyon, 1869; Photographs and Epilogue (1969).* New York: E. P. Dutton, 1969.

Powell, John W.: "The Ancient Province of Tusayán." *Scribner's Monthly,* XI (December, 1875), 193-213.

————: "The Cañons of the Colorado." *Scribner's Monthly,* IX (January-March, 1875).

————: *Canyons of the Colorado.* Meadville, Pa.: Flood and Vincent, 1895.

————: *Exploration of the Colorado River of the West and Its Tributaries. Explored in 1869, 1870, 1871, and 1872, Under the Direction of the Secretary of the Smithsonian Institution.* Washington, D.C.: Government Printing Office, 1875.

————: "Physical Feature of the Colorado Valley." *Popular Science,* 7 (August-October, 1875).

————: "An Overland Trip to the Grand Cañon." *Scribner's Monthly,* X (October, 1875), 659-678.

————: *Report on the Geology of the Eastern Portion of the Uinta Mountains and a Region of Country Adjacent Thereto, with Atlas.* U.S. Geological and Geographical Survey of the Territories. Washington, D.C.: Government Printing Office, 1876.

Powell, J. W., and G. W. Ingalls: "Report, Washington, D.C., December 18, 1873," in *Annual Report of the Commissioner of Indian Affairs, 1873.* Washington, D.C.: Government Printing Office, 1874. Pp. 41-74.

Powell, J. W., and others: *Report on the Arid Lands of the United States, with a More Detailed Account of the Lands of Utah* (1878). Second edition. Washington, D.C.: Government Printing Office, 1879.

Prescott *Arizona Miner,* December 14, 1877; January 22, April 7, 10, 12, 1880; July 4, 1884; and November 26, December 7, 15, 1886.

Price, Virginia N., and John T. Darby: "Preston Nutter: Utah Cattleman, 1886-1936." *Utah Historical Quarterly,* XXXII (Summer, 1964), 232-251.

Price, William Redwood: [*Report*] Whipple Barracks, A. T., July 1, 1881. U.S. National Archives, Record Group 75, with other related papers in Special Case No. 1.

Priestley, J. B.: "Grand Canyon, Notes on an American Journey." *Harper's Magazine,* 170 (February-March, 1935), 269-276, 399-406.

————: *Midnight on the Desert, Being an Excursion into Autobiography During a Winter in America, 1935-36.* New York and London: Harper & Brothers, 1937.

Proctor, Paul Dean: "Geology of the Silver Reef Mining District, Washington County, Utah." Utah Geological and Mineralogical Survey *Bulletin,* 44 (April, 1953).

Prudden, T. Mitchell: *Biographical Sketches and Letters.* New Haven, Conn.: Yale University Press, 1927.

————: *On the Great American Plateau: Wanderings Among Canyons and Buttes in the Land of the Cliff-Dweller, and the Indian of Today.* New York and London: G. P. Putnam's Sons, 1906.

R

Rabbitt, Mary C.: "John Wesley Powell: Pioneer Statesman of Federal Science." U.S. Geological Survey *Professional Paper,* 669. Washington, D.C.: Government Printing Office, 1969. Pp. 1-21.

Rabbitt, Mary C., Edwin D. McKee, Charles B. Hunt, and Luna B. Leopold: "The Colorado River Region and John Wesley Powell. A. John Wesley Powell: Pioneer Statesman of Federal Science. B. Stratified Rocks of the Grand Canyon. C. Geologic History of the Colorado River. D. The Rapids and the Pools—Grand Canyon." U.S. Geological Survey *Professional Paper,* 669. Washington, D.C.: Government Printing Office, 1969.

Reeder, Ray M.: "The Mormon Trail: a History of Salt Lake to Los Angeles Route to 1869." Ph.D. dissertation, Brigham Young University, 1966.

Reid, H. Lorenzo: *Brigham Young's Dixie of the Desert, Exploration and Settlement.* Zion National Park, Utah: Zion Natural History Association, 1964.

Ricks, Joel Edward: "Forms and Methods of Early Mormon Settlement in Utah and the Surrounding Region, 1847 to 1877." Utah State University *Monograph Series,* XI (January, 1964).

Robinson, Henry Hollister: "The San Franciscan Volcanic Field, Arizona." U.S. Geological Survey *Professional Paper,* 76. Washington, D.C.: Government Printing Office, 1913.

Roosevelt, Theodore: "Cougar Hunt on the Rim of Grand Canyon." *Outlook,* 105 (October 4, 1913), 259-266.

Ruhlen, George: "Carleton's Empty Fort." *Nevada Historical Society Quarterly,* 2 (April-June, 1959), 68-75.

Rusho, W. L.: "Living History at Lee's Ferry." *Journal of the West,* VII (January, 1968), 64-75.

Rust, D. D.: "From Salt Lake to the Grand Canyon." *Improvement Era,* XIII (March, 1910), 408-412.

Sadovich, Maryellen Vallier: "The Paiutes of Moapa." *Golden West,* 4 (January, 1968), 23-25, 56-58.

Salt Lake City *Deseret News*, August 7, 1852; June 2, 9, July 28, 1858; September 22, 1869; June 3, 1872; and May 22, 1878.

Salt Lake City *Herald*, November 22, 1891.

Salt Lake City *Tribune*, June 26–28, 1923.

San Francisco *Call*, April 9, 1877.

Santa Fe Railway: *The Grand Canyon of Arizona, Being a Book of Words from Many Pens About the Grand Canyon of the Colorado River in Arizona*. Chicago: Santa Fe Railway, 1906.

Schellbach, Louis: "Grand Canyon: Nature's Story of Creation." *National Geographic Magazine*, CVII (May, 1955), 589–629.

Schmeckebier, L. F.: "Catalogue and Index of the Publications of the Hayden, King, Powell, and Wheeler Surveys." U.S. Geological Survey *Bulletin*, 222. Washington, D.C.: Government Printing Office, 1904.

Schrader, F. C.: "Mineral Deposits of the Cerbat Range, Black Mountains and Grand Wash Cliffs, Mohave County, Arizona." U.S. Geological Survey *Bulletin*, 397. Washington, D.C.: Government Printing Office, 1909.

Schroeder, Albert H.: "A Brief History of the Havasupai." *Plateau*, 25 (January, 1953), 45–52.

Schroeder, Albert H., and others: "Archeology of Zion Park." University of Utah *Anthropological Papers*, 22 (June, 1955).

Schwartz, Douglas W.: "The Havasupai, 600 A.D.–1955 A.D.: a Short Culture History." *Plateau*, 28 (April, 1956), 77–85.

———: "A Historical Analysis and Synthesis of Grand Canyon Archaeology." *American Antiquity*, 31 (April, 1966), 469–484.

Scoyen, Eivind T., and Frank J. Taylor: *The Rainbow Canyons*. Stanford, Cal.: Stanford University Press, 1931.

Scrugham, James G.: *Nevada, a Narrative of the Conquest of a Frontier Land Comprising the Story of Her People from the Dawn of History to the Present Time*. Chicago and New York: American Historical Society, 1935. 3 vols.

Seargeant, Helen Humphrey: "Mooney Falls." *Arizona Highways*, XXXV (August, 1959), 18–28.

Seegmiller, Ella J.: "Shebit Indian Reservation." *Heart Throbs of the West*, I (1939), 132–134.

Seegmiller, Emma Carroll: "Personal Memories of the United Order of Orderville, Utah." *Utah Historical Quarterly*, VII (October, 1939), 160–200.

Shankland, Robert: *Steve Mather of the National Parks*. New York: Alfred A. Knopf, 1951.

Shelton, John S.: *Geology Illustrated*. San Francisco and London: W. H. Freeman, 1966.

Shutler, Richard, Jr.: "Lost City, Pueblo Grande de Nevada." Nevada State *Museum Anthropological Papers*, No. 5. Carson City: State Printing Office, 1962.

Simmons, George C., and David L. Gaskill: *River Runners' Guide to the Canyons of the Green and Colorado Rivers, with Emphasis on Geologic Features*, III: *Marble Gorge and Grand Canyon*. Flagstaff, Ariz.: Northland Press in Cooperation with Powell Society, 1969.

Simmons, Leo W., ed.: *Sun Chief, the Autobiography of a Hopi Indian*. New Haven, Conn.: Yale University Press, 1942.

Simpson, J. H.: *Journal of a Military Reconnaissance from Santa Fe, New Mexico, to the Navajo Country, Made with Troops Under the Command of Brevet Lieutenant Colonel John M. Washington, Chief of the 9th Military Department, and Governor of New Mexico, in 1849*. U.S. 31st Congress, 1st Sess., Sen. Ex. Doc. 64. Washington, D.C.: Union Office, 1850.

———: *Report of Explorations Across the Great Basin of the Territory of Utah for a Direct Wagon-route from Camp Floyd to Genoa, in Carson Valley, in 1859*. Washington, D.C.: Government Printing Office, 1876.

Sitgreaves, L.: *Report of an Expedition down the Zuni and Colorado Rivers*. U.S. 32nd Congress, 1st Sess., Sen. Ex. Doc. 59. Washington, D.C.: Robert Armstrong, 1853.

Skinner, S. Alan: "Camp Willow Grove, Arizona Territory." *Plateau*, 41 (Summer, 1968), 1–13.

Slater, John M.: *El Morro, Inscription Rock, New Mexico: the Rock Itself, the Inscriptions Thereon, and the Travelers Who Made Them*. Los Angeles: Plantin Press, 1861.

Smalley, George N.: Scrap Book, 1896–'97–'98, II. Tucson: Arizona Pioneers Historical Society.

Smith, Albert E., comp.: *Thales Haskell, Pioneer—Scout—Explorer—Indian Missionary, 1847–1909*. Salt Lake City: Albert E. Smith, 1964.

Smith, Dwight L., ed.: *Down the Colorado* [by] *Robert Brewster Stanton*. With an introduction. Norman: University of Oklahoma Press, 1965.

———: "The Engineer and the Canyon." *Utah Historical Quarterly*, XXVIII (July, 1960), 262–273.

———: *The Photographer and the River, 1889–1890: the Colorado Cañon Diary of Franklin A. Nims with the Brown–Stanton Railroad Survey Expedition*. Santa Fe: Stagecoach Press, 1967.

Smith, Jesse N.: Jesse N. Smith to Pres. G. A. Smith, Parowan, September 22, October 6, 1858. MS, L.D.S. Church Historian's Office Library, Salt Lake City.

———: *Journal of Jesse Nathaniel Smith, the Life Story of a Mormon Pioneer, 1834–1906*. Salt Lake City: Jesse N. Smith Family Association, 1953.

Smith, Melvin T.: "Colorado River Exploration and the Mormon War." *Utah Historical Quarterly*, XXXVIII (Summer, 1970), 207–223.

Smith, Pauline V.: *Captain Jefferson Hunt of the Mormon Battalion*. Salt Lake City: Nicholas G. Morgan, Sr., Foundation, 1958.

Snow, William J.: "Utah Indians and Spanish Slave Trade." *Utah Historical Quarterly*, II (July, 1929), 67–73.

Sonne, Conway B.: *World of Wakara*. San Antonio, Texas: Naylor Company, 1962.

Spencer, Joseph E.: "The Development of Agricultural Villages in Southern Utah." *Agricultural History*, 14 (October, 1940), 181–189.

Spencer, Robert F., Jesse D. Jennings, and others: *The Native Americans*. New York: Harper and Row, 1965.

Spicer, Edward H.: *Cycles of Conquest: the Impact of Spain, Mexico and the United States on the Indians of the Southwest, 1533–1960*. Tucson: University of Arizona Press, 1962.

Spier, Leslie: "Havasupai Ethnography." *Anthropological Papers of the American Museum of Natural History* (New York), XXIX, Part III (1928).

Squires, Charles P., and Delphine A. Squires: "Las Vegas, Nevada, Its History and Romance." MS, University of Nevada at Las Vegas, Library, 1955. 2 vols.

Stanton, Robert B.: "Availability of the Cañons of the Colorado River of the West for Railway Purposes." American Society of Civil Engineers *Transactions*, XXVI (April, 1892), 283–361.

———: *The Cañons of the Colorado River of the West. Photographs Presented to the American Society of Civil Engineers by Robert Brewster Stanton, M. AM. Soc. C.E., 1892* . . . Album of about 700 photographs, Engineering Societies Library, New York City.

———: "Engineering with a Camera in the Cañons of the Colorado." *Cosmopolitan Magazine*, XV (July, 1893) 292–303.

———: "The River and the Canyon: the Colorado River of the West, and the Exploration, Navigation, and Survey of Its Canyons, from the Standpoint of an Engineer." MS, New York Public Library, 1920.

———: "Through the Grand Cañon of the Colorado." *Scribner's Magazine*, VIII (November, 1890), 591–613.

Steele, Rufus: "The Celestial Circuit." *Sunset*, 56 (May, 1926), 24–26, 92–94.

Stegner, Wallace: *Beyond the Hundredth Meridian, John Wesley Powell and the Second Opening of the West*. Introduction by Bernard DeVoto. Cambridge, Mass.: Houghton Mifflin, 1954.

———: *Clarence Edward Dutton, an Appraisal*. Salt Lake City: University of Utah Press, 1936.

———: "Powell and the Names on the Plateau." *Western Humanities Review*, VII (Spring, 1953), 105–110.

Steward, Julian: "Basin-Plateau Aboriginal Sociopolitical Groups." Bureau of American Ethnology *Bulletin*, 120. Washington, D.C.: Government Printing Office, 1938.

———: "Notes on Hillers' Photographs of the Paiute and Ute Indians Taken on the Powell Expedition of 1873." Smithsonian Institution *Miscellaneous Collections*, 98. Washington, D.C.: Government Printing Office, 1939. Pp. 1–23.

Stewart, Kenneth M.: "A Brief History of the Mohave Indians Since 1850." *Kiva*, 34 (April, 1969), 219–236.

———: "Chemehuevi Culture Changes." *Plateau*, 40 (Summer, 1967), 14–21.

———: "The Mohave Indians and the Fur Trappers." *Plateau*, 39 (Fall, 1966), 73–79.

Stiles, Helen J., ed.: "Down the Colorado in 1889." *Colorado Magazine*, XLI (Summer, 1964), 225–246.

Stoddard, John L.: *Lectures*, X. Boston: Balch Brothers, 1898.

Stokes, William Lee, and Lehi F. Hintze, comps.: *Geologic Map of Utah*. Salt Lake City: College of Mines and Mineral Industries, University of Utah, and Utah State Land Board, 1961–1963. Published in four sections.

Stone, Julius F.: *Canyon Country, the Romance of a Drop of Water and a Grain of Sand*. Foreword by Henry Fairfield Osborn and geological explanation of photographs by W. T. Lee. New York and London: G. P. Putnam's Sons, 1932.

Strahler, Arthur N.: "A Guide to the East Kaibab Monocline in the Grand Canyon Region." *Plateau*, 17 (July, 1944), 1–13.

———: "Landscape Features of the Kaibab and Coconino Plateaus." *Plateau*, 18 (July, 1945), 1–6.

Sullivan, Maurice S.: *The Travels of Jedediah Smith, a Documentary Outline Including the Journal of the Great American Pathfinder*. Santa Ana, Cal.: Fine Arts Press, 1934.

Swain, Donald C.: *Wilderness Defender, Horace M. Albright and Conservation*. Chicago and London: University of Chicago Press, 1970.

Sykes, Godfrey: *The Colorado Delta*. Washington and New York: Carnegie Institution of Washington and the American Geographical Society of New York, 1937.

———: *A Westerly Trend, Being a Veracious Chronicle of More Than Sixty Years of Joyous Wanderings, Mainly in Search of Space and Sunshine*. Tucson: Arizona Pioneers Historical Society, 1944.

Taft, Robert: *Artists and Illustrators of the Old West, 1850–1900*. New York: Charles Scribner's Sons, 1953.

———: *Photography and the American Scene, a Social History, 1839–1889*. New York: Macmillan, 1938.

Taylor, John: "Discourse by President John Taylor, Delivered in the St. George Tabernacle, Nov. 9th, 1881." *Journal of Discourses*, XXIII (Liverpool, John Henry Smith, 1883), 11–20.

Tenney, Ammon M.: "Biographical and Autobiographical Material, 1853–1923." MS, L.D.S. Church Historian's Office Library, Salt Lake City.

Thrapp, Dan L.: "Dan O'Leary, Arizona Scout: a Vignette." *Arizona and the West*, 7 (Winter, 1965), 287–298.

Tillotson, M. R., and Frank J. Taylor: *Grand Canyon Country*. Stanford, Cal.: Stanford University Press, 1929.

Tinker, Ben H., ed.: *Northern Arizona and Flagstaff in 1887, the People and Resources*, by George H. Tinker. Revised edition. Glendale, Cal.: Arthur H. Clark, 1969.

Titiev, Mischa: "A Hopi Salt Expedition." *American Anthropologist*, n.s., 39 (April–June, 1937), 244–258.

Toll, David W.: "The Violent Mountains of Arizona." *Arizona Highways*, XLVI (January, 1970).

Twenter, F. R.: "Geology and Promising Areas for Ground Water Development in the Hualapai Indian Reservation, Arizona." *Water Supply of Indian Reservations*. U.S. Geological Survey *Water-Supply Paper*, 1576-A. Washington, D.C.: Government Printing Office, 1962.

Tyler, S. Lyman: "The Myth of the Lake of Copala and the Land of Teguayo." *Utah Historical Quarterly*, XX (October, 1952), 313–329.

U

Underhill, Ruth: *The Navajos*. Norman: University of Oklahoma Press, 1956.

United States vs. Utah (Supreme Court of the United States, Number 14, October Term, 1929): "Testimony Before Charles Warren, Special Master, September–December, 1929, at Washington, D.C., Denver, Los Angeles, and Salt Lake City." Typescript, Utah State Historical Society, Salt Lake City. 32 vols.

U.S. 74th Congress, 2nd Sess., Sen. Doc. 273: *Walapai Papers, Historical Reports, Documents, and Extracts from Publications Relating to the Walapai Indians of Arizona*. Washington, D.C.: Government Printing Office, 1936.

U.S. Geographical and Geological Surveys West of the Hundredth Meridian: *Report upon Geographical and Geological Explorations and Surveys West of the Hundredth Meridian*, III: *Geology*. Washington, D.C.: Government Printing Office, 1875.

U.S. Geological Survey: *Plan and Profile of Colorado River from Lees Ferry, Arizona, to Black Canyon, Arizona-Nevada, and Virgin River, Nevada*. Washington, D.C.: Government Printing Office, 1924. 21 sheets.

U.S. National Park Service: *Areas Administered by the National Park Service*, January 1, 1961. Washington, D.C.: Government Printing Office, 1961.

———: *Circular of Information Regarding Grand Canyon National Park, Arizona*. Washington, D.C.: Government Printing Office, 1929.

———: *A Survey of the Recreational Resources of the Colorado River Basin, Compiled in June, 1946*. Washington, D.C.: Government Printing Office, 1950.

U.S. War Department: *Reports of Explorations and Surveys to Ascertain the Most Practicable and Economical Route for a Railroad from the Mississippi River to the Pacific Ocean, Made Under the Direction of the Secretary of War . . .* Washington, D.C.: A. O. P. Nicholson, and others, 1855–1861. 12 vols. in 13.

U.S. Work Projects Administration: *Arizona, a State Guide*. New York: Hastings House, 1940.

———: *Nevada, a Guide to the Silver State*. Portland, Ore.: Binsford and Mort, 1940.

———: *Origins of Utah Place Names*. Third edition. Salt Lake City: State Department of Public Instruction, 1941.

———: *Utah, a Guide to the State*. New York: Hastings House, 1940.

V

Van Dyke, John C.: *The Grand Canyon of the Colorado, Recurrent Studies in Impressions and Appearances*. New York: Charles Scribner's Sons, 1920.

Van Valkenburg, Richard: "Ben Wittick, Pioneer Photographer of the Southwest." *Arizona Highways*, XVIII (August, 1942), 36–39.

Verkamp, Margaret M.: "History of Grand Canyon National Park." M.A. thesis, University of Arizona, Tucson, 1940.

Vinton, Stallo, ed.: *Overland with Kit Carson, a Narrative of the Old Spanish Trail in '48*, by George Douglas Brewerton. New York: Coward-McCann, 1930.

W

Waesche, H. H.: "The Anita Copper Mine." *Grand Canyon Nature Notes*, 7 (February, 1933), 108–112.

———: "The Grand View Copper Project." *Grand Canyon Nature Notes*, 8 (March. 1934), 250–258.

Wagner, Henry R.: *The Cartography of the Northwest Coast of America to the Year 1800*. Amsterdam: N. Israel, 1968. Reprint of the edition issued at Berkeley, 1937.

Walker, Don D.: "The Cattle Industry of Utah, 1850–1900, an Historical Profile." *Utah Historical Quarterly*, XXXII (Summer, 1964), 182–197.

———: "Longhorns Come to Utah." *Utah Historical Quarterly*, XXX (Spring, 1962), 135–147.

Wallace, Anthony F. C., ed.: *The Ghost-dance Religion and the Sioux Outbreak of 1890*, by James Mooney. Chicago: University of Chicago Press, 1965.

Wallace, Edward S.: *The Great Reconnaissance: Soldiers, Artists and Scientists on the Frontier, 1848–1861*. Boston: Little, Brown and Company, 1955.

Warner, Charles Dudley: "The Heart of the Desert." *Harper's Monthly*, LXXXII (February, 1891), 392–412.

Warren, Gouverneur K.: ". . . Memoir to Accompany the Map of the Territory of the United States from the Mississippi River to the Pacific Ocean, Giving a Brief Account of Each of the Exploring Expeditions Since A.D. 1800, with a Detailed Description of the Methods Adopted in Compiling the General Map . . . 1859," in *Reports of Explorations and Surveys to Ascertain the Most Practicable and Economical Route for a Railroad from the Mississippi River to the Pacific Ocean, Made Under the Direction of the Secretary of War, in 1853–56*, XI. Washington, D.C.: George W. Bowman, 1861. Pp. 7–115.

Washington County, Utah: "Deed Record," D, 1869–1874, G, 1874–1878; "Record," J, 1875–1876. MSS, Recorder's Office, St. George.

Waters, Frank: *Book of the Hopi; Drawings and Source Material Recorded by Oswald White Bear Fredericks*. New York: Viking Press, 1963.

———: *The Colorado*. New York and Toronto: Rinehart and Company, 1946.

Waters, L. L.: *Steel Trails to Santa Fe*. Lawrence: University of Kansas Press, 1950.

Watson, Elmo Scott, comp. and ed.: *The Professor Goes West: Illinois Wesleyan University Reports of Major John Wesley

Powell's Explorations, 1867–1874. Bloomington: Illinois Wesleyan University Press, 1954.

Weber, David Joseph: "The Taos Trappers, the Fur Trade from New Mexico, 1540–1846." Unpublished Ph.D. dissertation, University of New Mexico, 1967.

Wentworth, Edward Norris: America's Sheep Trails, History, Personalities. Ames, Iowa: Iowa State College Press, 1948.

Wheat, Carl I.: 1540–1861: Mapping the Transmississippi West. I (1957): The Spanish Entrada to the Louisiana Purchase, 1540–1804; II (1958): From Lewis and Clark to Frémont, 1804–1845; III (1959): From the Mexican War to the Boundary Surveys, 1846–1854; IV (1960): From the Pacific Railroad Surveys to the Onset of the Civil War, 1855–1860; V (1963): From the Civil War to the Geological Survey. San Francisco: Institute of Historical Cartography, 1957–1963. 5 vols., vol. V in two parts.

Wheeler, George M.: Preliminary Report Concerning Explorations and Surveys Principally in Nevada and Arizona, 1871. Washington, D. C.: Government Printing Office, 1872.

————: Preliminary Report of the General Features of the Military Reconnaissance Through Southern Nevada Conducted Under the Direction of Lieutenant George M. Wheeler, Assisted by Lieutenant D. W. Lockwood, 1869. San Francisco: Military Department of California, 1870.

————: Report upon United States Geographical Surveys West of the One Hundredth Meridian . . . I: Geographical Report. Washington, D.C.: Government Printing Office, 1889.

Whipple, A. W.: "Report of Explorations for a Railway Route, Near the 35th Parallel of North Latitude, from the Mississippi River to the Pacific Ocean," in U.S. War Department: Reports of Explorations and Surveys to Ascertain the Most Practicable and Economical Route for a Railroad from the Mississippi River to the Pacific Ocean, Made Under the Direction of the Secretary of War, in 1853–1856, III (1856). Washington, D.C.: A. O. P. Nicholson, 1856, 1–136.

Whipple, Maurine: "Arizona Strip—'America's Tibet.'" Colliers, 129 (May 24, 1952), 24–25, 64–67.

————: This Is the Place: Utah. New York: Alfred A. Knopf, 1945.

White, William Allen: "On Bright Angel Trail." McClure's Magazine, XXV (September, 1905), 502–515.

Whiting, Alfred F.: "Havasupai Characteristics in the Cohonina." Plateau, 30 (January, 1958), 55–60.

————: "John D. Lee and the Havasupai." Plateau, 21 (July, 1948), 12–16.

Whiting, Lilian: The Land of Enchantment from Pike's Peak to the Pacific. Boston: Little, Brown and Company, 1906.

Whitney, Orson F.: History of Utah Comprising Preliminary Chapters on the Previous History of Her Founders, Accounts of Early Spanish and American Explorations in the Rocky Mountain Region. The Advent of the Mormon Pioneers, the Establishment and Dissolution of the Provisional Government of the State of Deseret, and the Subsequent Creation and Development of the Territory. Salt Lake City: George Q. Cannon and Sons, 1892–1904. 4 vols.

Widdison, Jerold G.: "Premier Artist of the Grand Canyon." Arizona Highways, XLIV (June, 1968), 4–9.

Wilkins, Thurman: Thomas Moran, Artist of the Mountains.

Norman: University of Oklahoma Press, 1966.

Willy, John: "A Journey to North Rim of Grand Canyon." Hotel Monthly, (October, 1919), 45–62.

Wilmarth, N. Grace: "Lexicon of Geologic Names of the United States (Including Alaska) . . ." U.S. Geological Survey Bulletin, 896. Washington, D.C.: Government Printing Office, 1938. 2 parts.

Wilson, Allie K.: "History of the Arizona Strip to 1913." M.A. thesis, Arizona State Teacher's College, Flagstaff, Ariz., 1941.

Wilson, Iris Higbie: William Wolfskill, 1798–1866: Frontier Trapper to California Ranchero. Glendale, Cal.: Arthur H. Clark, 1965.

Winship, George Parker: "The Coronado Expedition, 1540–1542." Bureau of Ethnology, Fourteenth Annual Report, Part I. Washington, D.C.: Government Printing Office, 1896. Pp. 329–613.

————: "Finding the Colorado River." Land of Sunshine, 12 (April, 1900) 268–280.

Winther, Oscar Osburn: The Transportation Frontier: Trans-Mississippi West, 1865–1890. New York: Holt, Rinehart and Winston, 1964.

Wolfe, Thomas: A Western Journal, a Daily Log of the Great Parks Trip, June 20–July 2, 1938. Pittsburgh: University of Pittsburgh Press, 1951.

Woodbury, Angus M.: "A History of Southern Utah and Its National Parks." Utah Historical Quarterly, XII (July–October, 1944), 110–223. Revised edition printed separately by the Utah State Historical Society, 1950.

Woods, G. K., comp.: Personal Impressions of the Grand Cañon of the Colorado River near Flagstaff, Arizona, as Seen Through Nearly Two Thousand Eyes, and Written in the Private Visitor's Book of the World-famous Guide Capt. John Hance, Guide, Story-teller, and Pathfinder. San Francisco: Whitaker and Ray, 1899.

Woodward, Arthur: Feud on the Colorado. Los Angeles: Westernlore Press, 1955.

————: "Irataba, Chief of the Mohaves." Plateau, 25 (January, 1953), 53–68.

Wright, Lyle H., ed.: John Udell Journal Kept During a Trip Across the Plains Containing an Account of the Massacre of a Portion of His Party by the Mojave Indians in 1859. Los Angeles: N. S. Kovach, 1946.

Wyllys, Rufus Kay: Arizona, the History of a Pioneer State. Phoenix: Hobson and Herr, 1950.

Wyman, Walker D.: "F. X. Aubry: Santa Fe Freighter, Pathfinder and Explorer." New Mexico Historical Review, VII (January, 1932), 1–31.

Yard, Robert Sterling: The National Parks Portfolio. Third edition. Washington, D.C.: Government Printing Office, 1921.

Yavapai County, Ariz.: "General Index to Mines," 2–3, 1884–1894. MS, Recorder's Office, Prescott.

————: "Record of Mines," 3–21, 1873–1885. MSS, Recorder's Office, Prescott.

————: "Toll Roads," 1871–1891. MS, Recorder's Office, Prescott.

Index

III

The walls of Grand Canyon and the upper end of Lake Mead at high water. Arizona

VI

Quartermaster Canyon, one of the many canyons draining into Grand Canyon from the Hualapai Plateau. Arizona.

VII

Notes About the Book

The Author

C. Gregory Crampton is Duke Research Professor at the University of Utah, where since 1945 he has taught courses on the history of the American West and Latin America. A Berkeley Ph.D., he has taught occasional terms at a number of universities in the United States, Europe, and Latin America and is well known for his studies in historical archaeology in the Glen Canyon region of the Colorado River. Since 1967 he has been coordinating the nation-wide Duke Program in Indian Oral History. Editor, author, photographer, explorer, "river rat," he is altogether at home and very much in love with the great canyon country of the Colorado of Arizona, Utah, and Nevada. His prize-winning *Standing Up Country*, published by Alfred A. Knopf in 1964, was one issue of this love affair. *Land of Living Rock*, a regional biography—prehistory, geology, ecology, history, and man and the wilderness—is the first complete portrayal of one of the most beautiful places in the world.

The Type

The title face of this book is Profile, designed by Eugen and Max Lenz. The text was set in Medallion, the film version of Melior, a typeface designed by Hermann Zapf and issued in 1952. Born in Nürnberg, Germany, in 1918, Zapf is one of today's leading calligraphers and type designers. Typical of Zapf's designs, Melior exhibits a strong calligraphic influence. However, while the squareness of the ovals in Melior suggests the Venetian and Old Style Romans, the vertical stress of the heavy strokes is more akin to the Modern Roman type family.

The Craftsmen

The book was designed and illustrated by Keith Eddington & Associates, Salt Lake City, Utah; composed by York Graphic Services, York, Pennsylvania, and Twin Typographers, Salt Lake City, Utah; printed by Judd and Detweiler, Washington, D.C.; and bound by Kingsport Press, Inc., Kingsport, Tennessee.